Kino-Eye

The Writings of Dziga Vertov

EDITED AND WITH AN INTRODUCTION BY

Annette Michelson

TRANSLATED BY

Kevin O'Brien

University of California Press • Berkeley • Los Angeles • London

University of California Press
Berkeley and Los Angeles, California

University of California Press, Ltd.
London, England

Library of Congress Cataloging in Publication Data

Vertov, Dziga, 1896–1954.
Kino-Eye : the writings of Dziga Vertov.

Filmography: p. 330
Includes index.
1. Moving-pictures, Documentary—Soviet Union—History—Sources. I. Michelson, Annette. II. Title.
PN1995.9 D6V44 1983 791.43′53′0947 82-11189
ISBN 0-520-05630-2 (alk. paper)

Printed in the United States of America

08 07 06 05 04 03 02
12 11 10 9 8 7 6 5

Illustrations from the collection of Annette Michelson

The paper used in this publication meets the minimum requirements of ANSI/NISO Z39.48-1992 (R 1997) (*Permanence of Paper*). ♾

To Elizaveta Svilova and Mikhail Kaufman
In Memoriam

Contents

Some Creative Projects, Proposals

Translator's Acknowledgments

I would like to thank Tim Bow for his support and friendship, Simon Karlinsky for his kindness and patience in explicating troublesome passages within the Russian text, and especially Annette Michelson, who went far beyond the duties of a normal editor in committing her time and lending her expertise in order to enhance the legibility of this translation.

Kevin O'Brien

Preface

The texts assembled in this volume, selected by the Soviet historian of documentary film, Sergei Drobashenko, were published in 1960 by the Iskusstvo Press in Moscow. It is my hope—and not mine alone—that the full range of unpublished items in the Vertov Archive, including correspondence, reports, verse, shooting logs, scripts, and notes for unrealized projects, will, at a date not too far distant, be made available for publication.

Through early conversations with P. Adams Sitney I was led to focus my somewhat general interest in the theory and practice of Soviet film on Vertov. The warmth of Mr. Sitney's support together with the encouragement of Jonas Mekas, co-founder and director of the Anthology Film Archive, gave to this project a tone of especial ease and pleasure. To them and to the students with whom I have studied the work of Vertov go my first expressions of gratitude.

I have been aided by colleagues and friends in the study and preparation of the present material. The Anthology Film Archive and the Museum of Modern Art in New York, both of whose holdings in Soviet film form an indispensable resource for scholars in this country, have over the past several years facilitated the necessary viewings and re-viewings of Vertov's mature work. At both institutions, my students and I have found a friendly welcome as we considered Vertov's work and its historical context.

To Jay Leyda, our premier Eisensteinian, I owe much more than can be accounted for on this single occasion. From him, I, like so many others, gained a first intimacy with the film theory and practice of the postrevolutionary era. He has, with characteristic modesty and authority, offered a multitude of concrete suggestions for research in the period and sustained a benevolent interest in this belated presentation of the positions of Eisenstein's old antagonist.

To Noël Carroll, I am indebted for the unfailing generosity, promptness, and rigor of response to my developing view of this project, and for much else.

In 1974 a grant from the Media Program of the National Endowment for the Arts enabled me to travel for the first time to the Soviet Union, where the open-handed and vivacious response to my research gave added impetus to this project. I had the good fortune, during that first journey and on subsequent ones, to be warmly welcomed by the surviving quorum of the Council of Three; both Mikhail Kaufman and Elizaveta Svilova generously opened their store of documents and memories to me. Their gifts included many of the stills and portraits and all of the production shots included in this volume.

I have had as well the consistent aid of the Association of Filmmakers of the USSR, under the direction of Lev Kulijanov and the deputy chairmanship of Alexander Karaganov. Aided by Mss. Volchenko and Epstein, they have on every possible occasion facilitated the screening of material not available in this country, extending invitations to conferences and festivals that have increased my contacts with other scholars in this field.

Among these, two in particular must be saluted. Victor Listov's exceptionally meticulous investigations of the years immediately after the Revolution have enriched my understanding of the Moscow landscape of that time. To Naum Kleiman, the Director of the Eisenstein Museum in Moscow, whose enthusiasm, intelligence, and exceptionally discriminating taste have transformed a shrine into a live and important center of discourse on a spectrum of cultural practices far wider than cinema, my debt will never be quite discharged. But that is the pleasant burden I now share with innumerable students of the Culture of Revolution.

From Matvej Sliwowski, Ellen Trost, Pat Keeton, and Scott Bukatman, I have had expert assistance in the preparation of materials for publication. And to Professors Thomas A. Beyer, Jr., and Alexandra Baker of Middlebury College I owe the strenuous delights of swift progress in the mastery of Russian grammar.

Annette Michelson
New York—Moscow—Paris—New York
1983

The supersession of private property is, therefore, the complete emancipation of all the human qualities and senses. It is such an emancipation because these qualities and senses have become human, from the subjective as well as the objective point of view. The eye has become a human eye when its object has become a human, social object, created by man and destined for him. The senses therefore become directly theoretical in practice.

Karl Marx, *Third Manuscript of 1844*

Introduction

I

We are in Moscow in January 1935. A dozen men, suspending for a moment the contradictions and rivalries which involve them in cross-fire polemic and tactical maneuvering, are poised in the uneasy amity of a command performance. They are the Class of 1925: assuming attitudes of official concord for the still photographer, they sit surrounded by their juniors for a portrait of the All-Union Creative Conference of Workers in Soviet Cinematography.[1]

The photograph will instruct us in the contours of a heroic era, projecting the topography of a culture that engendered a new grammar of cinema. The position of these men, their attitudes, the trajectories of glances exchanged and deflected, disclose an interplay of character and sensibility that articulates a grand collective aspiration. This picture is a historic text; it demands close reading.

In the first row are four elder masters: Pudovkin, Eisenstein, Tissé, and Dovzhenko, prime animators of revolutionary cinema's

1. Eisenstein emerged from this conference, at which he delivered a major address (reprinted as "Film Form: New Problems," in *Film Form: Essays in Film Theory*, ed. and trans. Jay Leyda [New York, 1949], pp. 122–49), with a humiliating fourth-class award. An account of the conference, called in celebration of the fifteenth anniversary of the Soviet film industry, is presented in Marie Seton's *Eisenstein: A Biography* (New York, n.d.), pp. 330–50.

The All-Union Creative Conference of Workers in Soviet Cinematography, 1935

first dozen or so years. Yury Raizman, Mikhail Romm, Mark Donskoy, Sergei Yutkevich, Amo Bek-Nazarov, Mikhail Chiavreli and Yefim Dzigan form a second rank. The man peering at top left over the heads of his colleagues, just coming into view and smiling—as well he might—is Georgy Vasiliev, co-director of *Chapayev,* the film whose easy narrative flow and psychological invocation of a revolutionary hagiography has taken that year's honors, and with them the most general official assent. Its success, and his, hover premonitorily in the air of this assembly, thickening it with ironies and ambiguities.

In the center of the first row, Eisenstein, the session's embattled chairman, sits in the authority of his achievement and international reputation and the dignity of his thirty-seven years. "The old man" clutches a briefcase containing, one surmises, elaborate notes and bibliography for his opening address, whose brilliance, irony, and controlled intellectual pathos will bring his listeners to a pitch of fury, will draw from these talented and pressured men a massive and concerted attack. At this moment, however, Eisenstein is alive with a characteristic smile of generous delight in his colleague's success, attending wholly to Pudovkin, who is standing at the left and half-turned from us in an attitude of graceful vivacity. Pudovkin is at work charming and diverting the assembly like the gifted and disciplined actor that from a wide range of film roles we know him to be.

The lean and elegant creature on Eisenstein's other side, bending toward us, poised and concentrated, is Tissé, the great cameraman and Eisenstein's lifelong friend and co-worker. His gaze slants to the right, beyond the scene of action, past the camera, through rather than toward things. Then, almost at a right angle to that gaze, looking far to the left, apparently at nothing in particular, another glance travels. It is Dovzhenko's. As in all his pictures, he is beautiful; he rests slightly slouched, abandoned in meditation, his person half-encircled by the sweep of Tissé's arm. Tissé's pure, focused gaze and Dovzhenko's stare would seem—if this were possible—to cross but nowhere to meet. Tissé's eyes, looking out upon the world, embrace another scene somewhere between our space and his. Dovzhenko's look seems collected back into itself. He smiles slightly—again as if to himself.

The juniors are involved in a general contraposto of body and focus of interest, a tangle that must drive a viewer to distraction—or to pedantry. Eisenstein's eyes, fixed upon the moving object, must see Pudovkin, his old adversary, who has been addressing himself just slightly past Eisenstein to the tangle of the assembled filmmakers.

Two men, however, are missing from this icon of dialectics, and their absence is significant. Kuleshov, the pioneer of montage and once the teenage teacher of these men, is nowhere to be seen. We know that he later spoke from the floor in a splendidly candid and courageous defense of Eisenstein.[2] The arena of public honor and debate, contracting in the Stalinist climate, was precipitating sudden conflicts and realignments; pressures falsified positions. We must suppose that by this time Kuleshov was somewhat removed from the public scene, and with him that one artist most problematic in his radicalism for even the greatest of his peers: Dziga Vertov. As we shall see, Vertov could have had no place in this picture.

We do, of course, have other pictures of him: the really speaking likeness arrests him in midair, leaping or pirouetting, delivering him to us as a body in violent movement, immobilized in the stilled presence of motion that suggests a "frame." The likeness projects a preoccu-

2. Seton, *Eisenstein,* p. 339.

pation spelled out by his abandonment of the name Denis Kaufman: Dziga Vertov, adopted at the very threshold of his working life, is derived from the verb which means to spin or rotate; the onomatopoeia of the first name, as Vertov intimated, reproduces the repetitive sound of a camera crank turning (dziga, dziga, dziga . . .).

> I remember my debut in cinema. It was quite odd. It involved not my filming but my jumping one-and-a-half stories from a summer house beside a grotto at no. 7 Malyi Gnezdnikovsky Lane.
>
> The cameraman was ordered to record my jump in such a way that my entire fall, my facial expression, all my thoughts, etc., would be seen. I went up to the grotto's edge, jumped off, gestured as with a veil, and went on. The result on film was the following:
>
> A man approaches the edge of a grotto; fear and indecision appear on his face; he's thinking: "I won't jump." Then he decides: "No, it's embarrassing, they're watching." Once again he approaches the edge, once again his face shows indecision. Then one sees his determination growing, he's saying to himself, "I must," and he leaves the grotto edge. He flies through the air, flies off-balance; he's thinking that he must position himself to land on his feet. He straightens out, approaches the ground; once more his face shows indecision, fear. Finally his feet touch ground. His immediate thought is that he fell, then that he's got to keep his balance. Next he thinks that he jumped nicely but should not let on that he has, and, like an acrobat who's performed a difficult maneuver on the trapeze, he pretends that it was awfully easy. And with that expression the man slowly "floats off."
>
> From the viewpoint of the ordinary eye you see untruth. From the viewpoint of the cinematic eye (aided by special cinematic means, in this case, accelerated shooting) you see the truth. If it's a question of reading someone's thoughts at a distance (and often what matters to us is not to hear a person's words but to read his

> thoughts), then you have that opportunity right here. It has been revealed by the kino-eye.[3]

Epistemological inquiry and the project of a revolutionary cinema converge in that world of truth seen by the cinematic eye. And Vertov is that world's great discoverer. His work is paradoxically concrete, the original and paradigmatic instance of "an attempt to film, in slow motion, that which has been, owing to the manner in which it is perceived in natural speed, not absolutely unseen but missed by sight, subject to oversight. An attempt to approach slowly and calmly that original intensity which is not given in appearance, but from which things and processes have nonetheless in turn derived."[4]

The evolution of his work renders insistently concrete, as in a series of kinetic icons, that philosophic phantasm of the reflexive consciousness: the eye seeing, apprehending itself as it constitutes the world's visibility: the eye transformed by the revolutionary project into an agent of critical production.

Vertov's is a very special case: a forty-year history of the most distrustful and hostile reception and of systematic critical neglect. The distrust and hostility are not, of course, unique; but the sustained neglect, the shared distrust and bewilderment on the part of generally perceptive and qualified spectators, the evasive and inadequate literature on Vertov's film work give us pause. The history of Soviet film is one of the most elaborately documented and consecrated areas of the medium. It is true, of course, that much research into Soviet film history remains to be done and redone, to be rescued from the damaging mold of piety, but the absence of close and serious attention until very recent times makes Vertov's case singular indeed. Shoved hastily and distractedly into the ash can of film history, his major works were left to tick away, through four decades, like time bombs.

Here is one contemporary judgment of *The Man with a Movie Camera,* published in the December 1931 issue of *Close-Up,* two years after the film's initial release in the Soviet Union. Offered by Jay Leyda in *Kino* as a sample of reactions to the film, it is an excellent index of Vertov's general reception.

3. Dziga Vertov, "*Three Songs of Lenin* and Kino-Eye," p. 123 below.
4. For development see Gérard Granel, *Le Sens du temps et de la perception chez Husserl* (Paris, 1968), p. 108 (translation mine).

> Theorists mostly love their theories more than a father loves an only child. . . . Vertov also has waged fierce, vehement and desperate battles with his materials and his instruments (reality and the film camera) to give practical proofs of his ideas. In this he has failed. He had failed already in the era of the silent film by showing hundreds of examples of most cunning artistry in turning: acrobatic masterpieces of poetic jigsaw, brilliant *conjuring* of filmic association—but never a rounded work, never a clear, proceeding line. His great efforts of strength in relation to detail did not leave him breath for the whole. His arabesques totally covered the ground plan, his fugues destroyed every melody.[5]

The judgment echoes that of Eisenstein most significantly, inducing reflection on a very interesting and knotty issue in Soviet film history and aesthetics: the relationship between the perspectives of Eisenstein and Vertov. For Eisenstein, *The Man with a Movie Camera* is a compendium of "formalist jackstraws and unmotivated camera mischief," and its use of slow motion is unfavorably compared with Jean Epstein's in *La chute de la Maison d'Usher [The Fall of the House of Usher]* and on secondhand evidence at that. Attempting to account for the naked and disingenuous belligerency of those remarks, one recalls Eisenstein's late strictures on his own first mature work.[6] His film closest in style and tone to Vertov's is *Strike,* a work he professed to see, from the vantage point of

5. Jay Leyda, *Kino: A History of the Russian and Soviet Film* (New York, 1960), p. 251. The italics in this quotation are my own and are intended to suggest author A. Kraszna-Krausz's references (writing in *Close-up,* December 1931) to Vertov's association of the themes of magic and prestidigitation in this film. The association of these themes is discussed in detail in my essay *"The Man with a Movie Camera:* From Magician to Epistemologist," *Artforum* (February 1971), which offers a number of the themes of the present Introduction in a somewhat different form.

6. The remarks occur in Eisenstein's important theoretical essay "The Cinematographic Principle and the Ideogram," written in 1929. Discussing the style of the Kabuki theater and its "unprecedented slowing down of all movement," he goes on to say,

> Here we see disintegration of the process of movement, viz., slow motion. I have heard of only one example of a thorough application of this method, using the technical possibilities of the film with a compositionally reasoned plan. It is usually employed with some purely pictorial aim, such as the "submarine kingdom" in *The Thief of Bagdad,* or to represent a dream, as in

maturity, as infected with "the childhood disease of leftism," a metaphor for aesthetic formalism borrowed from Leninist polemics.

But here is a third view, that of Leyda himself, the senior and in every way exemplary scholar of the period, advanced with a characteristic scrupulousness:

> My memory of *The Man with the Movie Camera* is not reliable; I have not seen it since it happened to be, in 1930, the first Soviet film I saw. It was such a dazzling experience that it took two or three other Soviet films with normal "stories" to convince me that all Soviet films were not compounded of such intricate camera pyrotechnics. But I hope to be forgiven for not bringing away any very clear critical idea as I reeled out of the Eighth Street Playhouse—I was even too stunned to sit through it again. The apparent purpose of the film was to show the breadth and precision of the camera's recording ability. But Vertov and his cameraman-brother, Mikhail Kaufman, were not content to show any simple vocabulary of film practice; the cameraman is made an heroic participant in the currents of Soviet life. He and his methods are treated by Vertov in his most fluid montage style, establishing large patterns of sequences: the structure resembles that of *Kino-Eye,* with a succession of "themes"—the audience, the working day, marriage, birth, death, recreation—each with a whirling galloping climax; but the execution of the

---

Zvenigora [Dovzhenko's first film]. Or, more often, it is used simply for formalist jackstraws and unmotivated camera mischief as in Vertov's *The Man with a Movie Camera.* The more commendable example appears to be in Jean Epstein's *La Chute de la Maison d'Usher*—at least according to the press reports. In this film, normally acted emotions filmed with a speeded-up camera are said to give unusual emotional pressure by their unrealistic slowness on the screen. If it be borne in mind that the effect of an actor's performance on the audience is based on its identification by each spectator, it will be easy to relate both examples (the Kabuki play and the Epstein film) to an identical causal explanation. The intensity of perception increases as the didactic process of identification proceeds more easily along a disintegrated action.

Even instruction in handling a rifle can be hammered into the tightest motor-mentality among a group of raw recruits if the instructor uses a "break down" method. (Reprinted in *Film Form: Essays in Film Theory,* ed. and trans. Jay Leyda [New York, 1949], pp. 43–44)

> two films, separated by less than five years, are worlds apart. The camera observation in *Kino-Eye* was alert, surprising, but never eccentric. Things and actions were "caught" but less for the catching's sake than for the close observation of the things themselves. In *The Man with the Movie Camera* all the stunts that can be performed by a cameraman armed with Debrie or hand-camera and by a film-cutter armed with the boldness of Vertov and Svilova can be found in this full-to-bursting film, recognized abroad for what it really is, an avant-garde film, though produced by VUFKU, a state trust.[7]

And Leyda's later viewing at the Paris Cinémathèque confirmed his initial impressions of brilliance.

Now all these texts deserve a closer reading than I shall give them here: they raise problems, directly or implicitly, that are historiographic, stylistic, aesthetic, political. Leyda's estimation of the nature of Vertov's development from *Kinoglaz* ("Kino-Eye" or "Cinema-Eye") on and the precise similarities and differences of style between earlier and later films demand revision, but the films themselves demand a more detailed and analytical consideration than was possible at that time. *The Man with a Movie Camera* was simply unavailable for concentrated study within the Soviet Union, and until 1970 it was equally unavailable, for all practical, critical purposes, in the West. The film was made, as Vertov expressly tells us, for the workers and peasants of the Soviet Union: the unavailability in both East and West informs us that its author indeed has no place in the picture; it is an index of the strangeness of his text.

One is thus led to scrutinize the circumstances of this repression and elision, and to inquire, in particular, whether Vertov's work constitutes an unwelcome redefinition of that "intellectual cinema" which had so haunted Eisenstein, Vertov's work producing the shadow text of Eisenstein's unrealized projects, the planned film versions of *Das Kapital* and of Joyce's *Ulysses.* One might, in fact, see the trajectory between the two men's work as a shift from the articulation of a comprehensive and dialectical critique of political economy to the reflexive exploration of the dynamics of consciousness. I will

7. Leyda, *Kino,* pp. 251–52. Quite understandably, Leyda has exaggerated the film's reputation abroad at that time.

suggest that it is Vertov who poses, in *The Man with a Movie Camera,* the conditions of such a transformation within cinema, sustaining as he does so the method and energies of both constructivism and Marxism. If this argument is sound, we can easily suppose that it was a shock of recognition, a shudder of remembrance and perhaps of reawakened aspiration long repressed, that elicited the bitter triviality of Eisenstein's attack—Eisenstein, the intellectually powerful and generous man we have seen beaming so disarmingly at Pudovkin, his old antagonist.

Vertov, born Denis Arkadyevich Kaufman in 1896, was the son of Jewish intellectuals of Bialystok, then Russian territory. His younger brothers, Mikhail and Boris, were later to work in the cinema. Mikhail was Denis's cameraman and later worked independently as a director. Boris, also a cameraman, emigrated to New York in 1940 by way of France, where he had shot *A Propos de Nice* (1929), *Taris* (1931), *Zéro de Conduite* (1933), and *L'Atalante* (1933) for Jean Vigo. Denis Kaufman studied music at the Bialystok Conservatory, interrupting his studies when obliged to flee with his parents from the invading German army. The family settled in Moscow. There, as a very young man, he began to write verse and science fiction. During this period of youthful literary activity between 1914 and 1916, he was impressed and influenced, like many of the artists and intellectuals of his generation, by futurism, and it was then that he adopted the pseudonym Dziga Vertov. In 1916 and 1917 he studied medicine in St. Petersburg. While pursuing his medical studies, Vertov began experiments with sound recording and assemblage, producing verbal montage structures.

In 1918 Vertov joined the Film Committee of the People's Commissariat of Public Education in Gnezdnikovsky Street in Moscow, becoming editor of the first newsreel programs produced by the Soviet Government: *Kinonedelia* ("Film-week"). It was here that he met his future wife and close collaborator, Elizaveta Svilova, at that time employed in cleaning and preserving film. In 1919 he worked as a war correspondent on the front near Tsaritsyn, reporting on the fighting against the counterrevolutionary White armies. In 1920, together with President Kalinin, he toured the battlefronts of southwest Russia on a propaganda train known as "The October Revolution," returning with a series of documentary films.

Vertov's *Kinopravda* ("Film-truth") films, named in honor of

Pravda, the Soviet daily newspaper founded by Lenin, constituted a newsreel magazine. Issued irregularly, they offered reportage on an extremely wide variety of subjects and acted as a laboratory for the development of a film vocabulary. Georges Sadoul gives 1922 as the date of the constitution of the Council of Three by Vertov, Elizaveta Svilova, and Mikhail Kaufman, who had been recently demobilized and had worked first as a cameraman in newsreel and later in documentary film. With the production of *Kinopravda* no. 6, Kaufman became Vertov's principal cameraman. In December of that year, the Council of Three issued an appeal to Soviet film-makers, published the following year under the title *Appeal for a Beginning* in the magazine LEF, edited by the poet Vladimir Mayakovsky and two friends within the futurist milieu, the poet Nikolai Aseyev and the literary critic Osip Brik. In December of that year, Vertov completed the theoretical manifesto that was published in LEF in June 1923 under the title of *Kinoks: A Revolution.*

The use of the candid camera was adopted by the kinoks (the Council of Three and followers) in 1923 or 1924, possibly in large part as a result of Mikhail Kaufman's filming experience, since Vertov was primarily an editor, not a cameraman. Vertov's *Kinoglaz* was made in 1924, and the majority of his work from that period on was commissioned directly by state agencies and addressed specific issues and problems confronting the young Soviet regime in its period of rapid industrialization. In 1926 Mikhail Kaufman made the documentary film *Moscow,* whose structure, relating a day in the life of a great industrial city, seems to have influenced both Walter Ruttmann's *Berlin: Symphony of a Great City* (1927) and Vertov's *The Man with a Movie Camera* (1929).

Vertov's break with Goskino production studio, due largely to his dissatisfaction with working conditions and the limited distribution of his films, was by mutual agreement and was followed by his departure for the Ukraine with Mikhail Kaufman to work with VUFKU, the Pan-Ukrainian film production unit. Here, in relative freedom, in an atmosphere which encouraged experimentation, he produced three of his most significant films: *The Eleventh Year* (1928), *The Man with a Movie Camera* (1929), and *Enthusiasm,* or *Symphony of the Donbas* (1930), his first sound film. From this time until his death, Vertov worked under circumstances, described in his journal, which were the inexorable result of the growing constraints and contradictions of the Soviet film industry during the massive bureaucratization of the

Stalinist regime. The last decade of his life was therefore one of increasingly intermittent assignments, and these were principally the making of newsreels. He died in Moscow in 1954.

Vertov began his career in 1919 by pronouncing a death verdict on the existing corpus of motion pictures. He categorically redefined cinema's vocation as the capturing of "the feel of the world" through the substitution of the camera, that "perfectible eye," for the human eye, that "imperfect one." For Vertov, the distinction between what we know as the "art film" and the other kinds of cinema then being made was totally without meaning. He relocated the artistic frontier between representation and "the feel of the world," recalling to us Shklovsky's command: "We must recover the world; we live as if coated with rubber." In the preparation of *Enthusiasm,* his first sound film, he shifted the focus of research from exploring the interaction of synchronous and asynchronous sound to distinguishing the fictive from the evidential, the composed from the concrete, entirely redefining the problems and possibilities created by the new compositional parameters of cinema.

Vertov's disdain of the mimetic, his concern with technique and process, their extensions and disclosure, stamp him as a member of the constructivist generation. He shares with them an ideological concern with the role of art as an agent of human perfectibility, a belief in social transformation as the means for producing a transformation of consciousness and a certainty of accession to a "world of naked truth," paradoxically grounding his creed in the acceptance and affirmation of the radically synthetic film technique of montage.

> Kino-Eye means the conquest of space, the visual linkage of people throughout the entire world based on the continuous exchange of visible fact, of film-documents as opposed to the exchange of cinematic or theatrical presentations.
>
> Kino-Eye means conquest of time (the visual linkage of phenomena separated in time). Kino-Eye is the possibility of seeing life processes in any temporal order or at any speed, inaccessible to the human eye.
>
> Kino-Eye makes use of every possible kind of shooting technique: acceleration, microscopy, reverse action, animation, camera movement, the use of the most un-

> expected foreshortenings—all these we consider to be not trick effects, but normal methods to be fully used.
>
> Kino-Eye uses every possible means in montage, comparing and linking all points of the universe in any temporal order, breaking, when necessary, all the laws and conventions of film construction.
>
> Kino-Eye plunges into the seeming chaos of life to find in life itself the response to an assigned theme. To find the resultant force amongst the million phenomena related to the given theme. To edit; to wrest, through the camera, whatever is most typical, most useful, from life; to organize the film pieces wrested from life into a meaningful rhythmic visual order, a meaningful visual phrase, an essence of "I see." ("From Kino-Eye to Radio-Eye")

Vertov's montage, presented as antithetical to that of Eisenstein, nonetheless was like Eisenstein's exceptional in the intensity of its refinement and systematization and in the extension of its compositional procedures to all cinematic parameters. For Vertov, as for Eisenstein, the implications of a film production conceived as a directing force in the revolutionary process were clear.

We may read certain moments in the history of film theory as a series of attempts to constitute filmic ontologies grounded in the discourse of philosophical investigation. André Bazin was later to hypostatize his theory of film into an ontology of existential freedom, rejecting as he did so the "tricks of montage" and asserting the spatiotemporal integrity of deep focus and the long take as the field of the spectator's perceptual and cognitive choice. For the principal theorists of Soviet cinema, montage thinking became "inseparable from dialectical thinking as a whole." The process of intellection elicited in the experience of the montage unit, composed of oppositionally organized shots, is thus hypostatized into the triadic rehearsal of Dialectic.[8]

This process of intellection generating a critique of cinematic representation is united with cinematic production within the construction of a socialist economy by one film-text, which epitomizes

8. This aspect of Eisenstein's attempt to constitute a filmic ontology is discussed in my "Camera Lucida / Camera Obscura," *Artforum,* January 1973.

and sums up the resources and development of cinematic theory and practice until 1929. That film-text, *The Man with a Movie Camera,* could disturb; it could, as well, become the key film-text for the generation of filmmakers who called into question the grounds and claims of cinematic representation through the political uprisings of 1968. It follows that we must turn to this central text in undertaking any consideration of Vertov's theoretical and practical work, reading it through other, related texts of constructivism and Marxism.

The first of these related texts is by Vladimir Mayakovsky (Vertov speaks of him in his journal as someone particularly close to his own project). Here, excerpted from *How are Verses Made?*, are Mayakovsky's directives for a constructivist poetics of revolution:

> As I see it, the fine poetical work would be one written to the social command of the Comintern, taking for its purpose the victory of the proletariat, making its points in a new vocabulary, striking and comprehensible to all, fashioned on a table that is N.O.T. equipment [supplied by the Scientific Organization of Labor] and sent to the publisher "by plane," since the engagement of poetry with contemporary life is one of the most important factors in our production. . . . I want to show . . . that the essence of modern literary work doesn't lie in the evaluation of this or that ready-made thing from the standpoint of literary taste, but in a correct approach to the study of the productive process itself.
>
> Far from being unconcerned with the evaluation of accepted images or devices, this article is concerned with an attempt to uncover the very process of poetic production.
>
> How are verses made?
>
> Work begins long before one receives or is aware of a social command.
>
> Preliminary work goes on incessantly.
>
> You can produce good poetic work to order only when you've a large stock of preliminaries behind you.
>
> . . . Let's drop all this gibberish about unfurling "the epic canvas" during a period of war on the barricades—your canvas will be torn to shreds on all sides. . . . The value of factual material (and this is why docu-

> mentary reports from the workers, and peasants, journalists are so interesting) must be marked at a higher price—and under no circumstances at a lower one—than so-called "poetical works." Premature "poeticization" only emasculates and mangles the material. All textbooks of poetry . . . are pernicious because they don't deduce the poetry from the material, that is, they don't give us the essence of the facts, they don't compress the facts to produce the essential, concentrated economical formulation, but simply impose an old form on a new fact.[9]

This text offers the very features of Vertov's project as articulated through the many journal entries and manifested in the film under discussion: a rationalized production organized in direct and explicit service of the construction of socialism; the necessary elaboration of a new "vocabulary"; the development and use of standardized equipment; the resolutely contemporary nature of production conditions and techniques; the redefinition of the production process, the implacable and public explication of its nature; and the radical revision of aesthetic canons and priorities. We find, as well, the attack upon the aestheticization of material in terms of established codes (those of the "epic canvas" and of "poetry," as of Vertov's "played" or "art" film). The primacy of the "factual" is to be facilitated by the accumulation of "stocks of preliminaries" (those rolls of footage filed and catalogued in the editing room) upon which the poet/filmmaker will draw in his implementation of the production plan. And finally, the articulation of the theoretical issues in the form of the manifesto.

The next text through which we may read Vertov's work is a poetics of architecture postulated upon the "culture of materials" as elaborated in "Constructivism" by Alexei Gan and embodied in Vladimir Tatlin's celebrated project of a *Monument to the Third International.* Gan's manifesto sets forth constructivism's three fundamental principles—tectonic, factura, and construction:

> *Tectonic* emerges and forms itself based, on the one hand, on the expedient use of industrial materials. The

9. Vladimir Mayakovsky, *How Are Verses Made?,* trans. G. M. Hyde (London, 1970), pp. 31, 34.

> word "tectonic" is taken from geology, where it is used to define eruption from the earth's centre.
>
> . . . The tectonic as a discipline should lead the Constructivist in practice to a synthesis of the new content and the new form. He must be a Marxist-educated man who has once and for all outlived art and really advanced on industrial material.
>
> *Faktura* is the whole process of the working of material. The working of material as a whole and not the working of one side.
>
> Here the material is understood in its raw state. . . .
>
> The material is the body or matter. The transformation of this raw material into one form or another continues to remind us of its primary form and conveys to us the next possibility in its transformation. . . .
>
> *Construction*. Construction must be understood as the co-ordinating function of Constructivism. If the tectonic unites the ideological and formal, and as a result gives a unity of conception, and the factura is the condition of the material, then the construction discovers the actual process of putting together. . . .
>
> Thus we have the third discipline, the discipline of the formation of conception through the use of worked material.
>
> All hail to the Communist expression of material building![10]

Vertov's own proposal of a "culture of materials" insists on the manner in which

> Montage means organizing film fragments (shots) into a film-object. It means "writing" something cinematic with the recorded shots. It does not mean selecting the fragments for "scenes" (the theatrical bias) or for titles (the literary bias).
>
> Every kino-eye production is subject to montage from the moment the theme is chosen until the film's release in its completed form. In other words, it is edited

10. Alexei Gan, "Constructivism" (1922), in Camilla Gray, *The Great Experiment: Russian Art, 1863–1922* (New York, 1962), p. 285.

> during the entire process of film production. ("From Kino-Eye to Radio-Eye")

Vertov, in this second lecture on Kino-eye, next describes the stages of montage production: evaluation of documents "directly or indirectly related to the assigned theme" (manuscripts, various objects, film clippings, photographs, newspaper clippings, books); montage synthesis, or the plan of shots; and general montage, the synthesis of the notations on film by the camera or machine-eye. Discussing composition through organization of "intervals" (the movement between frames and the proportions of these pieces as they relate to one another), Vertov takes into account relations of movements within the frame of each piece, relations of light and shade, and relations of speeds of recording. This "theory of intervals" was launched by the kinoks in their manifesto *WE*, written as early as 1919. In practice, it was most brilliantly illustrated in *The Eleventh Year* and especially in *The Man with a Movie Camera.*

> All who love their art seek the essence of technique to show that which the eye does not see—to show truth, the microscope and telescope of time, the negative of time, the possibility of seeing without frontiers or distances; the tele-eye, sight in spontaneity, a kind of *Communist decoding of reality*. . . . Almost all art film workers were enemies of the kinoks. This was normal; it [kinok views] meant they would have to reconsider their *métier*. . . . *Kinopravda* was made with materials as a house is built with bricks.

A "culture of materials" founds the constructivism of Vertov, as of Tatlin; its roots, in turn, are to be found in the engagement with cubism, which was determinant for the entire generation of revolutionary artists. We therefore would do well to explore briefly the nature and consequences of that engagement.

In 1913, Tatlin returned to Russia from a visit to Paris, and most importantly, from a direct encounter with Picasso's early constructions. He then proceeded, in his *Counter Reliefs* and *Corner Reliefs* of 1914–1917, to work in a mode whose radicalism far transcended that of his previous painting and theater designs. Using a diversity of found materials, such as tin, sheet metal, wire mesh, paper, and wood in *Complex Corner Relief* (1915), he had deployed this ma-

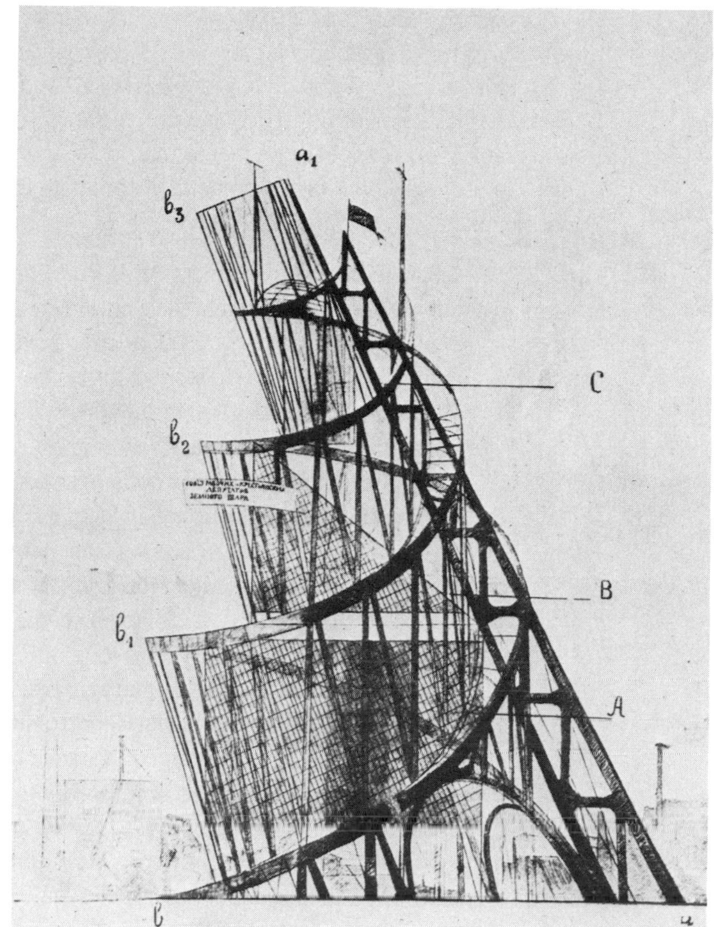

Vladimir Tatlin, ***Elevation of Monument to the Third International,*** **1919–20**

terial as a joining of contiguous wall areas, a bridging of their separateness, signaling the viewer's ambient space as the new scene of sculptural enterprise.

Tatlin's work, exhibiting the dialectic of the "aesthetic" and the "purposive," moves into the space of the functional, while preserving the character of sculpture; it proposes the constitution of "sculptural facts" in the world of functions. The problematic, transgressive nature of this move is nowhere clearer than in the ambiguities and contentions of the debate over the nature and "purpose" of the *Monument to the Third International* (1920).

Commenting upon Tatlin's work after his return from Paris, Kasmir Malevich had described the plain boards now used in his sculpture as taking on a completely new aesthetic texture while preserving their own integrity. He concluded that Tatlin had brought the concept of pure, spatial, pictorial expression to a limit, a terminal point. Malevich saw this limit as the point of departure for a new goal. He notes:

> Cubist features, far from disappearing, remain present but . . . the forming of materials now follows the formula of utilitarian functions. . . . Tatlin passes over the utilitarian significance of his *Monument for the Third International,* stresses that this is nothing other than a construction of the materials, iron and glass. What was important for the author was not so much the combination of the monument's utilitarian functions as the combination of its artistic side with the materials—plus function. The Constructive combination of these functions was based on the Cubist formula, and it is according to this that the work is formed. In such phenomena no utilitarian function ever played a predominant part, but only a painterly one, as such. If we are faced by the fact that life, as utilitarian function, has in it no formula on the basis of which works of new art could be formed, on the contrary [sic], we see that the formulae of the various trends in new art create functions of a utilitarian nature.[11]

The debate on the relation of form to function, of artist to engineer, articulates the ideological tensions of the constructivist enterprise—and, most concretely, those within its central, kinetic ikons. Within the contours of an iron spiral encompassing a great cone, the plan for Tatlin's *Monument,* never to be realized, presented four superimposed halls, each of a different geometrical form, in glass. Each was to move in continuous rotation around its axis at a separate, set speed.

The first story, a cube intended for the legislative assemblies, was to revolve once over a year. The second, a pyramid housing the

11. Kasmir Malevich, *Essays on Art: 1915–1928,* trans. Xenia Glowacki (Copenhagen, 1968), p. 77.

executive bodies, would rotate at the rate of one revolution per month. And the two uppermost structures, cylinder and hemisphere, would turn once daily. The cylinder was reserved for media services: newspaper and telegraph offices to be used for the diffusion of proclamations, pamphlets, and manifestos directed to the international proletariat. Giant screens for film projection were to be placed around the axis of the hemisphere, and radio antennae were to top the structure. The scale of Utopian architecture is always writ large: the structure was to stand four hundred meters high.

The *Complex Corner Relief* had constituted an initial breach of sculptural decorum, an early intrusion into the spectator's "real" or operational space, which was now to be more fully and imperiously occupied by the *Monument,* whose open spiral called into question the closures and categories of sculpture and architecture alike. Nikolai Punin was to see in it "an organic synthesis of the principles of architecture, sculpture, and painting"; Ilya Ehrenburg, an expression of the "dynamic Tomorrow" surrounded by the poverty of the present; Trotsky, an intrusive luxury in the devastated city of the postrevolutionary years. For Eisenstein, it evoked Gogol's vision, as recalled by Andrei Biely, of an architecture of "open cast-iron fundaments," of "transparent cast-iron decorations wrapped around a wondrously beautiful tower, rising into the sky . . . lightness, aesthetic airiness . . ." And, for Victor Shklovsky, it was a monument of "iron, glass and revolution," possessing its own "semantics." [12]

This open and inclusive structure, polyfunctional in design; revolving simultaneously at different speeds (encompassing the full temporal scale of day, month, year with each respective revolution); combining cube, cylinder, and sphere; and uniting the supreme legislative, executive, and cultural agencies proposed thereby the kinetic celebration of the triadic structure of the Dialectic. Receiving and diffusing bulletins and directives, distributing manifestos, projecting film, broadcasting news, inscribing weather forecasts in light upon the heavens, the tower was based upon the cubist formula just as Vertov's master film—multiple, polyvalent, contrapuntal in its structure, celebrating the turning of wheels of industry—was grounded in the technique of montage. Both tower and film propose a hyperbolic intensification of their techniques, insisting upon the materiality of the

12. In Troels Anderson, *Vladimir Tatlin,* Exhibition Catalogue, Moderna Museet (Stockholm, July-September 1968), pp. 56–65.

Tatlin (with pipe) and model of his *Monument to the Third International*

object and its architectonics as determinant. It is for these reasons, and insofar as both structures do in their counterpoint, polyvalence, and circularity *literalize* the notion of Revolution, that they converge in a common movement of transgression upon the definition of a program, the formulation of a semantics of socialist construction.

A reading of one additional text will clarify the depth of Vertov's implication in that program. In the first section of *The German Ideology* Marx and Engels develop the analysis of production as the determinant condition of social formation, setting out, as well, the method of historical materialism.

They declare the production of the means of subsistence to be the way in which men produce the actual material and concretely determinant conditions of their lives. For instance, although the bulk of the population was originally in the countryside, the necessary condition of modern production is the increase of population at the sites of urban industry. The relations or forms of intercourse among nations as well as those obtaining among individuals within a given social formation are also dependent upon production.

The significant index of productive forces is the degree to which the division of labor has developed. The primary effect of that division, which historically originates in and is determined by the system of intrafamilial dependency, is the separation of industrial and commercial labor from that of agriculture, and the consequent separation of town from country. These conflicts and divisions that are familiar to us—between nations, between individuals and groups, between manual and intellectual labor, between branches within a given sector of labor—are to be understood as determined by the primal division.

Moreover, "the various stages of development in the division of labor are just so many different forms of ownership, that is, the existing stage in the division of labor determines also the relations of individuals to one another with reference to the material, instrument and product of labor."[13]

The *division* of labor, grounded in the "natural," intrafamilial dependency system, generates the *distribution* of labor and of its products. That distribution, effected among and across separated, conflicting familial units, is "naturally" unequal. The uneven distribution of property is thus "naturally" grounded in the latent slavery

13. Karl Marx and Friedrich Engels, *The German Ideology,* edited and with an introduction by C. Arthur (New York, 1947), p. 43.

existing within the patriarchal family structure. So, too, are the contradictions that obtain between separate individuals or families and the community. One generalized result is a rigidity of social attribution, a fragmenting and "fixation" that assigns each individual a fixed and inalterable place and function.

It therefore follows that the "real intellectual wealth of the individual depends entirely on the wealth of his real connections." Only through the revolutionary transformation of this mode of production will

> the separate individuals be liberated from the various national and local barriers, be brought into practical connection with the material and intellectual production of the whole world and be put in a position to acquire the capacity to enjoy this all-sided production of the whole earth (the creations of man). *All-round* dependence, this natural form of the world-historical cooperation of individuals, will be transformed by this communist revolution into the control and conscious mastery of these powers, which, born of the action of men on one another, have till now overawed and governed men as powers completely alien to them.
>
> From this it follows that this transformation of history into world history is not indeed a mere abstract act on the part of the "self-consciousness," the world spirit or of any other metaphysical spectre, but a quite material, empirically verifiable act, an act the proof of which every individual furnishes as he comes and goes, eats, drinks and clothes himself.
>
> It is the real process of production, starting out from the material production of life itself, the form of intercourse connected with this and created by this mode of production [which renders this history intelligible].[14]

To reflect upon the theory and practice of Dziga Vertov over the three decades of his career is to realize that they were animated, with a force and specificity that solicit our renewed attention, by the analysis in this early text of Marx and Engels. Developing within

14. Ibid., pp. 55, 58, 59.

and celebrating the forced industrialization of the Soviet Union, Vertov's practice and theory were implicated, however, with a particular and drastic irony, in the contradictions of the accelerating bureaucratization of the postrevolutionary regime.

The Man with a Movie Camera, released in 1929, the year following the final defeat of the Left Opposition and Trotsky's expulsion from the Soviet Union, is, in form and structure, the synthetic articulation of the Marxist project, concretized in every detail of an unprecedented complexity of cinematic design. This film, made in the transitional period immediately preceding the introduction of sound and excluding titles, joins the human life cycle with the cycles of work and leisure of a city from dawn to dusk within the spectrum of industrial production. That production includes filmmaking (itself presented as a range of productive labor processes), mining, steel production, communications, postal service, construction, hydroelectric power installation, and the textile industry in a seamless, organic continuum, whose integrity is continually asserted by the strategies of visual analogy and rhyme, rhythmic patterning, parallel editing, superimposition, accelerated and decelerated motion, camera movement—in short, the use of every optical device and filming strategy then available to film technology. Within the continuum thus established, the fragmentation and contradictions "naturally" generated by the industrial system of production in its urban scene are annulled, as it were, by the rhymes and rhythms that link and propel them all. The rhythm and rhymes are in fact the formal instantiation of a general community, of the common stake in the project that retains both division of labor as indispensable to industrialization and rationalization as indispensable to the construction of socialism, a project that has radically reorganized the property relations subtending industrial production.

Here, in the great city synthesized from Moscow, Kiev, and Odessa on the editing table, live and work a community of productive forces in an "all-around dependence." Here, in fact, "the activities of labor, of coming and going, of eating, drinking, and clothing one's self," of play, are seen as depending upon the material production of "life itself." And, as if to further accentuate and elucidate the manner in which filmmaking as labor is comprehended in the general organization of productive labor processes, Vertov seems to take or reinvent *The German Ideology* as his text, for he situates the production of film in direct and telling juxtaposition to that other particular sector, the textile industry, which has for Marx and Engels a status that is paradigmatic within the history of material production.

In the section of *The German Ideology* devoted to the rise of manufacturing, they consider the immediate consequences of the division of labor between townships as providing the conditions for primitive forms of manufacture—first in Italy and later in Flanders, which was to become a center of foreign commerce. The gradual urban concentration of population (originating, as we have noted, in the countryside) and the concentration of capital in the hands of individuals and of the guilds accompanied the rise of weaving. This was the first industry to "presuppose a machine," and the most susceptible to development. Although originally the work of a home-based peasantry engaged in the fabrication of the family unit's clothing, this was the first industry to benefit by the development of commerce.

> Weaving was the first and remained the principal manufacture. The rising demand for clothing materials, consequent on the growth of population, the growing accumulation and mobilization of natural capital through accelerated circulation, the demand for luxuries called forth by the latter and favoured generally by the gradual extension of commerce gave weaving a quantitative and qualitative stimulus, which wrenched it out of the form of production hitherto existing.[15]

The subsequent growth of the weaving industry provided an occupation requiring relatively little skill and resistant to the constraints of guild structure, facilitating the rise of a merchant class possessing moveable capital. The rise of manufacture in this mode is, therefore, central to the analysis of the history of material production and of its urban sites and to the critique of political economy.

Now it is Vertov's positioning of film-as-production within the cyclical and parallel structure of his cinematic discourse and his insistence on the simultaneous and related revolutions of the wheels of industry and transportation and of the cranks and spindles of the filmmaking apparatus that establishes, through the first two-thirds of

15. Ibid., p. 73.

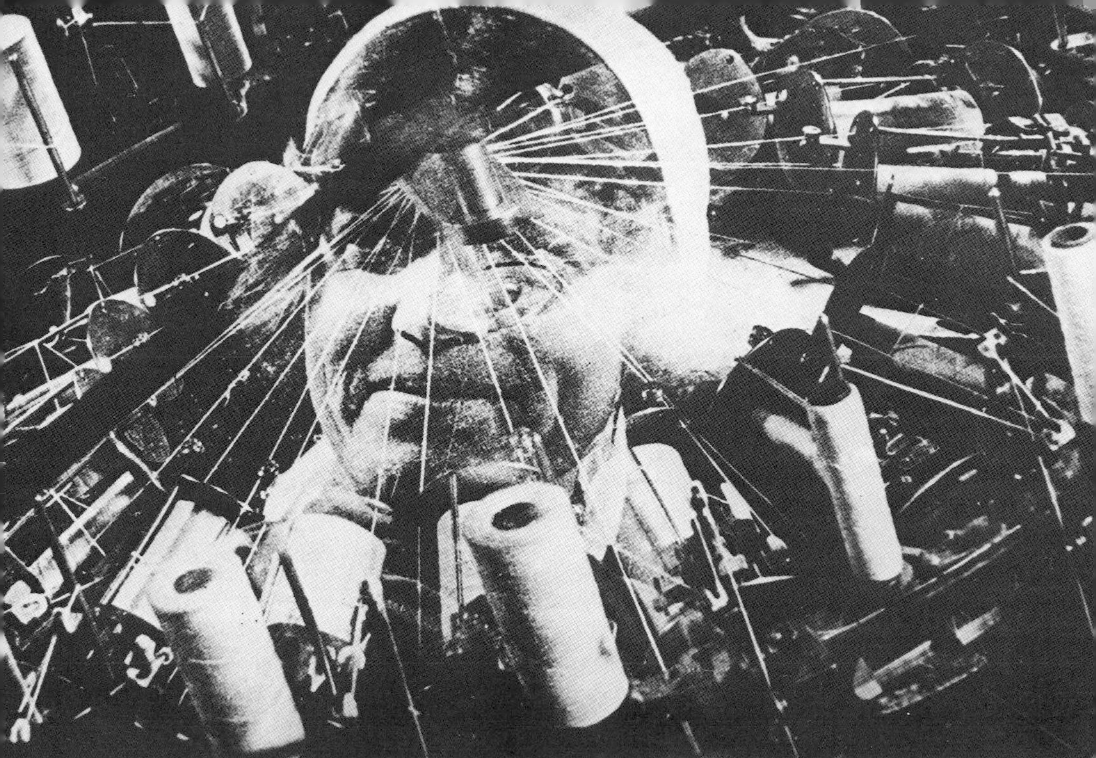

The Man with a Movie Camera

his film-text, the general relation of film production to other sectors of labor. The editing structure has through the first two-thirds of the film established a rhythmic pulsing of energy that binds together the movements of industrial labor (the work of mason, axe grinder, garment manufacturer, miner, switchboard operator, cigarette maker). The editing structure culminates in the identification of film-making (presented throughout the film in the full range of its productive processes: editing, laboratory processing, and exhibition, as well as camera work) as now directly and explicitly related to the paradigmatic form of industry: textile manufacture, itself seen as central in the economy's production.

It is, however, precisely at the film's structural center—at the workday's culmination, upon the threshold of leisure time—that the editing pattern gives us, in mighty *accelerando*, first the rapid and intensified alternation of the image of the spinning bobbins of the cotton factory with the image of the cameraman engaged in shooting both the hydroelectric installation and the mines that provide power for those bobbins in the factory and for the wheels of industry in general.

And this alternation builds to the visual, literal superimposition of the cameraman himself upon the image of the worker tending her textile machine, turning and turned, as in a double vortex, rotated, as it seems, by the general movement of production, recorded by that camera he has cranked, in rapid revolutions, throughout the production of the film we view.

This juxtaposition and subsequent superimposition of filmmaking and textile manufacture are to be read as articulating that unity within which the "natural" inequalities and contradictions formerly generated by a system of division of labor have been suspended. The full range of analogical and metaphorical readings thereby generated signify a general and organic unity, a common implication within the movement of industry, the euphoric and intensified sense of a shared end: the supercession of private property in the young socialist state under construction. If film-work thereby shares in the paradigmatic status of the weaver's labor, it is because for Vertov, with that supercession, the eye has indeed "become a human eye," and "its object a human social object created by man and destined for him." When the senses do thus become "directly theoretical in practice," the eye becomes, indeed, a kino-eye.

II

In Leninskii Gorkii, a town approximately twenty-five miles from Moscow, stands the mansion, originally the property of the Morozov family, in which Lenin spent the last years of his life. Suspended from the ceiling of the long salon hangs a square of fine white cambric and upon a table stands a curious old specimen of a film projector. It was here, the guide informs us, that Lenin liked of an evening to watch films—"almost exclusively documentary"—projected to the piano accompaniment of his sister, Maria Ulyanova, on the instrument that stands in the opposite corner of the room.

Vertov's categorical insistence on the essential vocation of the cinema would seem, then, to have its origin in an implicit directive that "the most important of all the arts" be engaged in the chronicling of the production of the new regime, the life processes of the new socialist nation. One must remember that if Vertov's career begins in newsreel production on the front, during the period of the Civil War, his practice and theory develop towards maturity from 1924, the year of *Kinoglaz;* they are consequently coextensive with the maturity of Leninist practice and theory in general during the decade of its highest intensity in the postrevolutionary period. In the year following Lenin's death, Vertov's "feature-length" production begins, and it covers the decade of transition from the New Economic Policy to the drive towards centrally planned industrialization and collectivization. This is also the period of the formation and elimination of the Left Opposition, the redefinition of the structure and power of the Communist Party, and the bureaucratization that followed the consolidation of Stalin's regime.

Vertov's concern with the truth value of cinema is, in fact, shared and expressed in the intuitions and formulations of the major film theorists of bourgeois Europe at that time. During the period of the swift reorganization and acceleration of the industry following the First World War, unprecedented hopes for both still and motion-picture photography crystallized in an early theoretical literature. Prior to the introduction of sound, converging expectations and achievements intimated that cinema was a uniquely privileged mode of analytic investigation, an epistemological instrument of radically new power. The acceleration of formal and technical development within the intensified rationalization of the film industry and its expanded market is attended by a buoyant expectancy reflected by the speculative rhetoric of that early literature. The sense of cinema as a possible agent of social transformation is general, though nowhere so urgent and concrete as within the Soviet Union. What is particular to the theoretical and critical sensibility of that time is the recognition of a new instrument facilitating critical inquiry with unprecedented immediacy and power, articulated in both theory and practice by René Clair, Jean Epstein, Elie Fauré, Walter Benjamin, Béla Bálasz, Fernand Léger, Laszló Moholy-Nagy, and Vertov.

The texts of Moholy-Nagy and of Epstein offer the closest contemporary parallels to Vertov's claims and aspirations for cinema. Writing in 1925, Moholy-Nagy attacked the notion, which had haunted the aesthetics of the West for more than half a century, of the *Gesamtkunstwerk* as characterizing the specialized and fragmented society, the society, as he saw it, of "yesterday." The destruction of belief in an all-encompassing wholeness of life, the fragmenting of work and of action, had generated, quite naturally, the compensatory reification of the total work of art, exemplified in the ideology of the first period of the Bauhaus and of De Stijl in Holland. Moholy-Nagy calls, then, for a realization of that aspiration which cannot be satisfied with the creation of a mere work of art separate and parallel to the flow of life: he demands "a synthesis of all the vital impulses spontaneously forming itself into the all-embracing *Gesamtwerk* (life) which abolishes all isolation, in which all individual accomplishments proceed from a biological necessity and culminate in a universal necessity."[16]

Moholy-Nagy calls for the just appreciation of the necessity of "the creation of each work in conformity with its own laws and distinctive character." The blurring of forms and categories is to be eliminated; they are to be brought into focus, as it were, so that their discrete natures may be respected within that unity which will comprehend the separate practices.

The camera as "supplement" to the eye and the photographic process as the camera's "complement" are the instruments that will give us access to an "objective vision" freed from the "associative patterns" imposed by pictorial codes. Moholy-Nagy, recalling that camera technology has "already been applied in a few scientific experiments" as in motion studies and in the structure and formation of "zoological, botanical and mineral forms" through the techniques of enlargement and microscopy, remarks that "these experiments have remained isolated phenomena, whose interconnections are not established." Like Vertov, he stresses the fact that the camera has, until now, been used in a way that is "secondary." Insisting upon the clear determination and understanding of photographic means and techniques, he attacks the reproduction of "dramatic action" without the fullest use of the instrument's distinctive capacities and advocates the engagement of the medium in all the sectors of production, including research, education, information, and advertising. And he advocates, to this end, the intensive development and refinement of filmic techniques, the concentration upon "formal tension, penetration, chiaroscuro, relationships, movement, tempo, the use of those objective elements in a conspicuously filmic manner."[17]

The development of optical and filmic specificities for the apparatus will then lead to the realization of its fullest potential. Moholy-Nagy, in a rapid catalogue, proposes the reproduction of the dynamics of movement—the use of "radio-projected film newspapers," and the filming of

16. Laszló Moholy-Nagy, *Painting, Photography, Film,* trans. Janet Seligman (Cambridge, Mass., 1969), p. 17.

17. Ibid., p. 34.

> a man daily from birth to his death in old age. It would be most unnerving even to be able to watch only his face with the slowly changing expression of a long life and his growing beard, etc., all in five minutes; or the statesman, the musician, the poet in conversation and in action; . . . Even with a proper understanding of the material, speed and breadth of thought do not suffice to predict all the obvious potentialities.[18]

This breathless realization of the disquieting range and power of the medium is, however, qualified.

> We have—through a hundred years of photography and two decades of film—been enormously enriched in this respect. We may say that we see the world with entirely different eyes. Nevertheless, the total result to date amounts to little more than a visual encyclopediac achievement. This is not enough. We wish to produce systematically, since it is important for life that we create new relationships.[19]

Jean Epstein was concerned to account for and to preserve the initial sense of wonder elicited by the appearance of the medium, a wonder threatened with extinction by the intensive development of the narrative codes during the twenties. Beginning in 1921 he elaborates a theory of the revelatory power of specifically cinematic techniques and processes in a manner strictly parallel to those of Vertov and Moholy-Nagy. He declares that the modifications of spatial and temporal experience provided by slow, accelerated, or reverse motion will provide fresh access to the true, concealed nature of the phenomenal world. The revisions of perception and judgment impelled by that access would confirm scientific discovery and redirect epistemological inquiry. Like Vertov, Epstein was a member of the generation fascinated by the developments in quantum physics and by the theory of relativity. Theories of physics play a structural role in the formation of his thinking, parallel to the role played by Pavlovian theory in Eisenstein's theory of "attractions," his elaboration of Soviet montage. Like Moholy-Nagy, Epstein recoils before the consequence of revelation.

18. Ibid., p. 36.
19. Ibid., p. 29.

> Little or no attention has been paid until now to the many unique qualities film can give to the representation of things. Hardly anyone has realized that the cinematic image carries a warning of something monstrous, that it bears a subtle venom which could corrupt the entire rational order so painstakingly imagined in the destiny of the universe.[20]

And the subversion of that "rational" order is seen as contained within the development of science itself.

> Discovery always means learning that objects are not as we had believed them to be; to know more, one must first abandon the most evident certainties of established knowledge. Although not certain, it is not inconceivable that what appears to us as a strange perversity, a surprising nonconformity, as a transgression and a defect to the screen's animated images might serve to advance another step into that "terrible underside of things" which was terrifying even to Pasteur's pragmatism. . . . Now, the cinematograph seems to be a mysterious mechanism intended to assess the false accuracy of Zeno's famous argument about the arrow, intended for the analysis of the subtle metamorphosis of stasis into mobility, of emptiness into solid, of continuous into discontinuous, a transformation as stupefying as the generation of life from inanimate elements.[21]

Epstein's wonder—it is a kind of *terreur sacrée et savante*—culminates in the text of 1928, which echoes in a particularly significant way both Vertov's account of his entrance into film and his commitment to a truth value seemingly inflected in the specificity of the cinematic process.

> Slow motion actually brings a new range to dramaturgy. Its power of laying bare the emotions of dramatic enlargements, its infallibility in the designation of the sincere movements of the soul, are such that it obviously outclasses all tragic modes at this time. I am certain

20. Jean Epstein, *Ecrits sur le cinéma* (Paris, 1973), pp. 257-63.
21. Ibid.

> and so are all those who have seen parts of *La Chute de la Maison Usher*, that if a high-speed film of an accused person under interrogation were to be made, then from beyond his words, the truth would appear, writ plain, unique, evident; that there would be no further need of indictment, of lawyers' speeches, nor of any proof other than that provided from the depths of the images.[22]

This notion of the motion picture camera as a truth machine, shared by Benjamin, who saw in it "the psychoanalysis of gesture," is presented by both Epstein and Moholy-Nagy, however, in terms that are wholly innocent of an awareness of social or class determination. Cinema is not seen as a form of production, subject to the material conditions of production.

The ground, then, of theory in the West, as exemplified in these two figures of the European avant-garde, the Bauhaus theorist and the Parisian filmmaker, is to be understood as analogous to the ground of Feuerbach's theory as described by Marx and Engels.

> Feuerbach speaks in particular of the perception of natural science; he mentions secrets which are disclosed only to the eye of the physicist and chemist; but where would natural science be without industry and commerce?[23]

Here, too, is a perception of natural science from which all sense of production and of the "sensuous world as it exists" has been deleted, leaving a science disclosed only to the eye of a scientist in a laboratory, excluding all consideration of the industry and commerce that are the ground of perception.

For Vertov, on the contrary, the systematic development of the specificity of cinematic processes—of slow, accelerated, and reversed motion, of split-screen, and of superimposition, those disjunctions, tensions and movements specific to cinema—were indeed to be harnessed in the services of revelation: but that revelation was a *reading,* a communist *decoding* of the world as social text, inseparable from the identification of class structure and class

22. Jean Epstein, "Une Conversation avec Jean Epstein," *L'Ami du peuple,* May 11, 1928.

23. Marx and Engels, *The German Ideology,* p. 73.

interests. As Moholy-Nagy's general injunction concerning "the creation of new relations" is recast by Vertov in the language of the revolutionary project of films "that will clarify the relations of workers with each other," the epistemological force of the instrument is converted to the uses of socialist construction.

Here is the point of intersection between Vertov's project and that of Eisenstein; here is the site of convergence and of the conflict that has remained until now unexplored. We know that Vertov had been assigned by Goskino in 1923 to direct a short film for insertion in Eisenstein's production of Ostrovsky's *Enough Simplicity in Every Wise Man,* staged the year preceding Eisenstein's entry into film production. Vertov quickly seceded from this project, which involved a somewhat primitive parody of *Kinopravda*. But he notes in late journal entries that Eisenstein had nevertheless shown considerable interest in and respect for his work, attending both screenings and discussions surrounding the release of the the *Kinopravda* series.

Presumably, the Leninist film ratio, promulgated in 1923 and endorsing a predominance of newsreel production over the production of narrative films, lent support to Vertov's militant and repeated attacks. In a time of extreme penury, the preferential allocation of limited existing resources doubtless provided the conditions for the development of an enduring polemical confrontation. And, as Boris Eichenbaum has remarked in another, not unrelated context,

> All compromises had to be cast aside. History demanded from us a genuine revolutionary élan—categorical theses, pitiless irony, a pugnacious refusal to come to terms on any basis whatsoever. In this state of affairs it was vital to counter the subjective aesthetic principles . . . with propaganda for an objective scientific attitude toward facts. That is the source of the new spirit of scientific positivism that characterizes the Formalists, the rejection of philosophical premises, psychological or aesthetic interpretations, and so forth. . . . It was time to turn to the facts and . . . to start from the center—from where the facts of art confront us. Art had to be approached at close range and science had to be made concrete.[24]

24. Boris M. Eichenbaum, "The Theory of the Formal Method," in *Readings in Russian Poetics: Formalist and Structuralist Views,* ed. Ladislav Matejka and Krystyna Pomorska (Cambridge, Mass., 1971), p. 7.

Such were the times and such the setting for the stridency of Vertov's categorical imperatives and the violence of Eisenstein's counterattacks, the latter most strenuously exemplified in the self-serving assault published in 1925 after the release of *Strike* entitled *On the Question of a Materialist Approach to Form,* in which Eisenstein calls, in a gesture of rhetorical escalation, for the replacement of Kino-eye by Kino-fist.[25]

Vertov, suffused with revolutionary optimism and epistemological euphoria, found further confirmation of his views in the theoretical line taken by the constructivist milieu, and more particularly by the editorial committees of *LEF* and *NOVY LEF,* the periodicals that offered to himself and Eisenstein, among others, critical support and an arena for debate. Sergei Tretyakov, the novelist, poet, and playwright, Eisenstein's close collaborator, remarked that *LEF,* which was also publishing photographs, scripts, and film criticism by Alexander Rodchenko, El Lissitsky, and Esfir Shub, was "working nowhere more intensively than in the cinema."[26] Here was a forum for discussing cinematic representation, its modes, and its future evolution within the development of this productivist stage of the constructivist movement.

A general dissatisfaction with the categories and dichotomies that inform the exchange between Vertov and Eisenstein is evident in the exchanges surrounding their debate. For Tretyakov and Shklovsky, in particular, the nature and role of the "factual" and the "fictive," of "played" and "nonplayed," the terminology generated in the efforts toward a militant cinema of class analysis, are highly problematic. For Tretyakov, *The Great Road,* Esfir Shub's compilation film, commissioned, like Vertov's *The Eleventh Year* and Eisenstein's *October,* in celebration of the tenth anniversary of the Revolution, is "played by Esfir Shub."[27] For Shklovsky, subjectivity is necessarily inscribed through camera position in any and all film footage. He stresses, too, the fact that despite the manner in which play inheres within artistic practice, practice must, nevertheless, periodically reorient itself toward the dominance of material. Such, he

25. Sergei M. Eisenstein, "On the Question of a Materialist Approach to Form," in *The Avant-Garde Film: A Reader of Theory and Criticism,* ed. P. Adams Sitney (New York, 1978).

26. S. Tretyakov, in "*LEF* and Film," extracted from "Notes of Discussion in *New LEF,* Nos. 11-12, 1927," *Screen,* vol. 12, no. 4 (Winter 1971-72), p. 74.

27. Ibid., p. 75.

maintains, is the historically justified priority of the day. "Our main tragedy is that we have a Soviet Empire style afflicted with restorationist themes. When a form has been misapplied but persists for a number of decades, it is universalized."[28] Boris Arvatov, however, locates the precise danger point in the establishment of the "unplayed" as paradigm, discovering in the insistence on the "real," on material "as it is," another "ill-concealed aesthetic fetishism"[29] in which the object's material utilitarian aspect is converted into an aesthetic category. And indeed, there was, from Shklovsky among others, a growing insistence on ever more precise identification and authentification of specific film-documents.

We may view that insistence as the transposition, into cinematic terms, of the priority given to found materials already developed by constructivism's theory of *faktura*. For a fuller, more exact understanding of this question and of its implications for the differences and tensions between Eisenstein and Vertov, we must look to Russian pictorial practice in one of its oldest and most powerful instances. This pictorial tradition is explicated in a text, written and published by Vladimir Markov in 1914, in defense of the new sculpture and of Tatlin's work in particular.

> Let us look back to our icons. They were embellished with metal halos in the form of crowns, metal casings on the shoulders, fringes, incrustations. Even paintings were enhanced with precious stones, metals, etc. . . . Through the noise of colors, the sound of materials, the assemblage of *faktura,* the people are called to beauty, to religion, to God. . . . [The icon is] a nonreal image. The real world is introduced into its essence through the assemblage and the incrustation of real tangible objects. One could say that this produces a combat between two worlds.[30]

28. V. Shklovsky, in "*LEF* and Film," extracted from "Notes of Discussion in *New LEF,* Nos. 11-12, 1927," *Screen,* vol. 12, no. 4 (Winter 1971-72), p. 79.

29. B. Arvatov, "Film Platform," *New LEF* no. 3, 1928, translated and reprinted in *Screen,* vol. 12, no. 4 (Winter 1971-72), p. 81.

30. V. Markov (pseudonym of the sculptor, Valdemar Matvejs), *Principles of Creation in the Visual Arts* (St. Petersburg, 1914). Quoted by Margit Rowell, "Vladimir Tatlin: Form/Faktura," *October* no. 7 (Winter 1978), p. 91.

In the production of what we may wish to term "kinetic ikons," the new fetishism of the real is sanctioned by the force of tradition, and the "combat between two worlds" is hypostatized in the polemical discourse within the constructivist milieu. When Eisenstein did come to use newsreel footage for the climactic, penultimate naval sequences of *Potemkin*, he effaced its heterogeneity as best he could, incorporating it unmarked within the diegetic flow. Eisenstein's experience of "the combat of two worlds" had been determinant in his passage from theater to film. That passage has been fully documented.[31] We know that it proceeded through a series of spatial shifts and relocations designed to generate a new intensity and clarity of theatrical effect. As a student of Vsevolod Meyerhold, the most powerful and consistent innovator within the theater of the postrevolutionary era, Eisenstein found himself involved in the thoroughgoing critique of theatrical representation effected through the celebrated series of productions that culminated in the production in 1923 of *The Magnificent Cuckold*. Working as designer on a production of *The Mexican* for the recently created Proletkult theater, he found himself "trespassing," as he puts it, "on the director's job." The climactic boxing match was originally planned as an offstage event eliciting reactions of actors onstage. Eisenstein brought it into view and staged it in the center of the auditorium, surrounded by the audience.

"Thus we dared the concreteness of factual events," he remarks, going on to identify as "the first sign of the cinematic" the presentation of "undistorted events."[32]

Moving in a series of shifts and transgressions that redefined the relation of spectator to spectacle, Eisenstein involved performers and audience in the space of circus and of cabaret. While at work on Tretyakov's *Gas* he "had the marvelous idea of producing the play in a real gas factory," only to find himself in a total impasse; theatrical representation was now overwhelmed by the concrete sensuous force of the decor. The combat of two worlds destroyed his enterprise, or "the cart dropped to pieces and the driver dropped into the cinema."[33] The inexorable logic of this series of

31. See Sergei M. Eisenstein, "Through Theatre to Cinema," reprinted in *Film Form: Essays in Film Theory,* ed. and trans. Jay Leyda (New York, 1949), pp. 3–17.

32. Ibid., p. 7.

33. Ibid., p. 8.

displacements, shifts, transgressions landed him, troupe and all, on location in a factory, through which this proponent of the fixed shot propels us by the vast aerial sweep of a crane shot in an opening sequence of *Strike*. Like Vertov, he describes the working space and inscribes the tools of manufacture on film as the camera rides upon the industrial equipment of the scene.

Vertov's sustained attack upon Eisenstein's project is impelled by a distinct misrecognition of the manner in which Meyerholdian systemics, inflected by Pavlovian reflexology and Taylorist time and motion analysis, represented an eminently strong and consistent general critique of representation effected *through* theater. He could not, did not, acknowledge the force with which it redefined, for an entire culture, the function of text, the position of the spectator, and the nature of authorial voice and presence. Four decades later filmmakers such as Jean-Luc Godard, Jean-Marie Straub, Jean Rouch, and Chris Marker came to propose, in the name of a Vertovian cinema free of the seductive ambiguities and servitudes of dominant production, Brecht's theatrical model as vivifying and determining their assault upon the established codes of cinematic representation.

If we are to understand the import of Vertov's theory and practice, their place within Soviet history, we must now turn to some consideration of the political course of events from 1920 onward. By 1935, as we have remarked, Vertov's situation within the film industry—and within the culture of the postrevolutionary period—was more than problematic; it was one of virtual expulsion. The later diaries are the obstinate and anguished response to that forced and implacable expulsion. What were its causes and conditions, and how is it that Vertov was reduced, in the last two decades of his life, to the position of observer and bitter analyst of the scene of practice?

Vertov's involvement in the construction of the industrial state was threefold: he was a chronicler and celebrant of its development, a worker within the general process, and a force within his own, specific sector of industry. Each new film of the mature period addresses a set of formal problems. And each film, commissioned by a state agency for a given purpose or occasion, addresses a different but specific set of problems within the general project of construction.

Kinoglaz ["Kino-Eye"] (1924) still retains the episodic structure of the newsreel, dealing sequentially with the formation of cooperatives, the distribution of grain and meat, the education of the young and their socialization through the coordinated activities of the Young Pioneers, the providing of public services, and public health care. *Forward, Soviet!* (1926) places present in relation to past so as to derive the shape and meaning of the future. Past and present conditions are contrasted along an axis of the concrete quality of daily living in a celebration of the installation of running water, of heat, and of electrification, which Lenin had declared to be, along with the institution of the Soviets, an integral part of the building of communism. Lenin's appearance in the film signals, in fact, the change "from mutilated plants and factories to a development of industry."

In these two films, as in all the silent work before 1928, Vertov's titles and his manifestos are articulated through a complex mode of address to his reader/viewer, his colleagues and fellow workers. Thus in the manifesto *WE* (1922), Vertov identifies himself as a member of the Council of Three, as well as a worker within the film industry of the Soviet state and a member of the working masses. And in *Kinoks: A Revolution*, another manifesto composed at the beginning of 1922, he addresses, in the second person plural, his readers directly:

> You—the Cinematographers
> You—the patient public
> You—the impatient entrepreneurs
> You wait for what will not happen and what you should not expect.

In *Forward, Soviet!*, the "we" are also the commissioning agency; "the Soviet calls you to a new war. We build dwellings," and for the rest of the work the titles will stress the Soviet's collective effort. But the "we" are also the kinoks in their establishment of a new film practice addressed to a public of workers and peasants. A common "you" is addressed in *One Sixth of the World* (1926), as Vertov confronts the viewer through the articulation of the "*I* see," categorizing and cataloging the resources perceived by the I/Camera throughout the Soviet Union. The "I" of the titles surveys the entire topology of the land in the first reel, conjoining elements over the vast reaches of distance and of time, a socialized kino-eye that instructs each viewer that the riches of the land are "yours."

Yours are the factories
Yours are the plants
Yours the cotton,
Yours the oil

And finally, "We want / to make / Ourselves."

This complex pronominal shifting, then, instructs us in Vertov's sense of his centrality of presence as filmmaker within the early stages of the economy and culture of the postrevolutionary era.

The adoption of the New Economic Policy (NEP) in 1921 provides a setting for the development of these films. The policy is described as

> an attempt to secure an alliance between the peasantry and the working class that would see the Soviet state through the period of enforced isolation until the victorious revolution of the Western proletariat came to its aid. The NEP was a domestic measure of retrenchment that corresponded to the tactics of the Comintern designed to deal with the delay in the world revolution.[34]

The catastrophic losses of war, revolution, and a civil war in which the young Soviet state was obliged to defend itself against a counterrevolution supported by international capital and its expeditionary forces had been followed by enormous demographic shifts and changes that further disrupted the economy. The problem of restimulating the economy was intensified by the lack of domestic capital and the impossibility of securing loans or aid from abroad. The priming of the industrial pump had to depend upon an accumulation of capital within the Soviet Union itself.

The stimulation of manufacture was contingent upon the encouragement of agriculture and the building of a rural market for the manufactured goods produced in the cities. In order to encourage peasants in the production of larger crops, a stimulus was provided by reviving a limited private market at unregulated prices, thus insuring the flow of food into the cities for the industrial proletariat.

In March 1921, the NEP was adopted, somewhat at the expense both of industry and of the industrial proletariat which was the tradi-

34. Leon Trotsky, *The Challenge of the Left Opposition (1923–1924)*, edited with an introduction by Naomi Allen (New York, 1975), p. 21.

tional advance guard of the national and international revolutionary movement. One drastic consequence—and it was to intensify—was the effect on prices known as the "scissors." The simultaneous rise of industrial prices and the fall of agricultural ones produced an industrial crisis. Another disastrous effect was the production of new stratifications: new conflicting and contradictory class relations within the peasantry, as well as the rise of a class of middlemen involved in speculation and profiteering. In this atmosphere the roles of kulak and *Nepman* take on the sinister counterrevolutionary aspect constantly pointed out by Vertov in his sharp attacks on the disorder within the film industry.

Within the Central Committee, a minority led by Trotsky (which came to be known after October 1923 as the Left Opposition) maintained that

> the first successes of the NEP should be consolidated by a comprehensive plan for the industrialization of the country, based on state subsidies to hasten industrial recovery and development. If heavy industry were helped to become rationalized and concentrated, the price of manufactured goods would reflect that improvement by dropping. If it weren't assisted, the boom in light industry (producing consumer goods) would be short-lived and even agriculture would suffer from the lack of equipment and farming tools. Credits directed to heavy industry should be guided by a long-range economic plan rather than the short-range criterion of profitability.[35]

In the context of this early stage of the NEP, the debate over the advisability of a unified, single plan for the nationalized economy originates. It was apparent to the Opposition that the installation of the NEP had acted to divert the party's attention from the "theoretically sound idea of an economic plan that was universally accepted under war communism, to the more immediate problem of reviving the market economy. . . ."[36]

For Trotsky, the integral rationalization of heavy industry was essential to the realization of a workers' state, and competition

35. Ibid., p. 24.
36. Ibid.

between the nationalized and the privately owned sectors of the economy and between units of the nationalized sector left the way open for the restoration of the property relations obtaining under capitalism. Only concerted and immediate planning with a view to the healthy restoration of industry would renew the vitality of the industrial proletariat weakened by war, disheartened by crisis, and unable to carry through its revolutionary function of leadership.

To these strictures, Trotsky was to add his concern for support of the international proletariat—a concern intensified by what he considered to have been the errors of the party in its failure to fully support the aborted revolution in Germany in 1923—and his growing apprehension at the increasing bureaucratization of the party. Its increasing rigidity of structure, due partly to the retention of tsarist-trained cadres and the influx of non-Communists during the period of the NEP, tended to reinforce the process of class stratification begun under the NEP.

In December of 1922 the Central State Photographic and Cinematographic Enterprise (Goskino) was formed for the purpose of centralizing control of all forms of distribution throughout the Russian Republic, "while retaining the right to lease or rent equipment, studios, theaters, etc., to other organizations, both state-owned and private, which would then continue with the production and exhibition of films."[37] This centralized but mixed reorganization was typical of the period's improvisations.

This organization, which shared the difficulties of Soviet industry in general (lack of equipment, of film stock, of capital), was, moreover, still tied to the tradition of prerevolutionary film practice, almost entirely addressed to a bourgeoisie nurtured by the tradition of bourgeois narrative representation and flooded with products imported from abroad. In this period of difficult production, the local distribution units increasingly relied on imports from the capitalist filmmaking centers of the West (Germany and the United States). Goskino was disastrously underfunded and ended by surrendering its distribution monopoly to various local organizations, taking between 50 and 70 percent of their turnover in return. In this way it hoped to finance its own further development. But Goskino's struggles for funds led to the raising of ticket prices, attendance at

37. Richard Taylor, *The Politics of Soviet Cinema, 1917–1929* (Cambridge, 1979), p. 70. I have drawn on Taylor's indispensable study for the brief summary of Goskino's development below.

theaters dropped, and the result was a crisis within the industry. Local distribution units were led to expand outside their own areas. Since Goskino was unable to supply films to its own theaters, an even stronger, private sector emerged, relying largely on foreign films. Not only were imported films of dubious ideological nature, but as Richard Taylor remarks, Soviet film importation remained chaotically unplanned, so that Soviet film organizations again found themselves in mutual competition, prices rose, and the situation remained critically unresolved.

This is the context within which Vertov made his persistent call for a total rethinking of the structure and methods of Soviet film production; his theoretical claims and formulations are grounded in the concrete urgency of that task.

In *WE: Variant of a Manifesto,* Vertov calls for a general purge, insisting first on the specificity of film through the liquidation of a heritage of literary and theatrical representation and the elimination of the psychologism that characterized their narration, and second on the exaltation of the machine, of which the camera is a prime example and whose universal, planned implementation will consummate the construction of socialism. Hence the "wonder of mechanical labor," "the . . . beauty of chemical processes," the "delight . . . in the gestures of searchlights." And hence the stress on meter, tempo, and movement, upon their precise synchronization in relation to the axis and coordinates of a given shot expressing the Movement of Construction. *Kinochestvo* ["filmmaking"], then, is an art of "organization"; "intervals" (the transition from one movement to another) are the material of the art of movement, providing a kinetic resolution.

Vertov proposes the rationalization of cinema as an element of the nationalization of the whole industrial sector: planning the training and organization of cadres and the marshalling of technical resources are its cardinal points of attack. Every line of the manifestos speaks the language of rationalization in the interests of efficiency and the revivification of a damaged film industry. The references to American models should not deceive us, although the entire history of the Soviet cinema in its early period could benefit from some study of that question. The influence of D. W. Griffith upon Vertov's contemporaries has been sufficiently elaborated upon. More important, at this point, would be some study of Soviet integration of American efficiency studies and of time and motion analyses, and of their incorporation within the film theory of Kuleshov, Eisenstein, Vertov, and Pudovkin. Thus Lenin, in an article written shortly before the outbreak of the First World War, had already noted the use of the cinema in capitalist society to improve productivity—and, consequently, also to improve profits—in accordance with the so-called Taylor system for the reduction of labor to its basic mechanical components of movement.

> The cinema is systematically employed for studying the work of the best operatives and increasing its intensity, i.e., "speeding up" the workers. . . . A newly engaged worker is taken to the factory cinema where he is shown a "model" performance of his job; the worker is made to "catch up" with that performance. A week later he is taken to the cinema again and shown pictures of his own performance, which is then compared with the "model."
>
> All these vast improvements are introduced "to the detriment " of the workers, for they lead to their still greater oppression and exploitation.[38]

Interestingly enough, in the period of the Five-Year Plan, Alexander Medvedkin, the author of "Happiness," an ironic farce of peasant life much admired by Eisenstein, toured the Ukraine with his "cinema train." He originated a mobile system of shooting, on-the-spot developing, projection, and discussion of work problems to improve production in the agricultural sector.

Throughout his working life, however, Vertov pressed for the implementation of a plan for the rationalization of film production and the radical reform of the growing bureaucratization of the industry. Hence his penchant for categories, lists, inventories, catalogues. Hence the production of theory in the form of reports, bulletins, memoranda, manifestos. Hence the urgent tone and form of his rhetoric, combining that of administrator, revolutionary, reconnaissance scout, group leader, commissar, and engineer—projecting, as it were, the cast of characters generated by the urgencies of the postrevolutionary situation. Hence the violence of the early manifestos, directed against those abuses whose institutionalization he sensed as a certain, growing danger to the cinematic sector in the

38. S. S. Ginzburg, *Kinematografiia do revoliutsionnoi Rossii,* p. 23, cited in Taylor, *Politics,* p. 29.

period of the NEP: the retention of old models of film practice, inefficient organization of exhibition, a misconceived relation between an administrative bureaucracy and the large, peasant-worker audience, insufficient attention to the rapidly changing nature of the audience addressed.

Vertov's text "On the Organization of a Creative Laboratory" (1936) formulates these problems and their potential solutions in terms that have not changed. It addresses the problem of the audience, whose revolutionary transformation remains "the artist's finest task." And this requires a highly developed technology, the marshalling of all the technical resources cinema can command: a noiseless, flexible, highly mobile, fully accurate system of visual and sound recording; the technology of electrical supply and synchronization; the elimination of possible accident through careful planning; the rational and efficient division of technical tasks; precision of timing and scheduling; *movement and decision that will counter heavy bureaucratic control from above*. Preservation of film will create the stockpiles needed for future production. New personnel and cadres must be formed. All the stages and parameters of film production—shooting, editing, laboratory work, mixing—must be carefully reconsidered and planned. In 1936, Vertov, who had produced *Symphony of the Donbas* (*Enthusiasm*) (1930) and *Three Songs of Lenin* (1934), calls once again with renewed urgency, for this reshaping of production as if for the implementation of stages in a permanent revolution. Why?

The answer lies in the development of the film industry within that of the economy and social formation of the Soviet Union as a whole.

Let us briefly reconsider the role of *Symphony of the Donbas,* Vertov's uniquely innovative response to the challenge of sound.

In an article published in 1931, Karl Radek addressed himself to the evaluation of this film, considered a "model." He begins by defining its purpose and occasion: it was intended as propaganda for the Five-Year Plan, to stimulate enthusiasm for intensified production. Radek continues with a personal expression of his own response of boredom to the film's first sections, then imputes that response to all audiences, insisting that the director has limited himself to "showing" a series of "fatiguing" and dispiriting episodes accompanied by the music of the sound track. He then proposes that "we come to the film's political errors, which amount to what we might term a general 'Hallelujahism.'" (The term undoubtedly refers to the celebratory inflection in the film's analysis of the industrialization process.)

> In what does cinematic propaganda for the struggle for the Five-Year Plan consist? The film should have exposed the conditions under which the masses lived under capitalism, and demonstrated the way which leads to industrialization and to socialist collectivization. It should have shown the difficulties to be surmounted, the levers of command which will help us to win.

Vertov's film, on the contrary, shows none of this and is "merely bluff, and quite useless."

> A film which does not, furthermore, explain how the peasants transform themselves, through the great crucible of the Five-Year Plan, into factory workers and kolkhoz workers; such a film gives us nothing of the *plan's dynamism.*
>
> I know little of the problems of cinematography, but I do realize the difficulty of making a film which expresses the historical process of our times. And yet, our film art has, in a series of works, surmounted these difficulties; it has expressed the social complexity which is ours.
>
> Now, this film, in which real dynamic force is replaced by the mere movement of trains and machines, represents a step backward in Soviet cinematography. Above all, it must be said that no one in the audience was moved by it, despite the perpetual cheering and brandishing of red flags.
>
> It is the very model of how not to make propaganda.[39]

It is, as we shall see, hardly an accident that it is Radek who led the attack upon the masterwork that initiated the sound era. Who, in fact, was Radek, or, more pertinently, what were the place and position from which he was speaking?

Radek had been a prominent member of the Left Opposition. Under Trotsky's leadership he had opposed the extension of the

39. Karl Radek, "Deux Films," in *Mir,* 5 December 1931, cited at length in François Camparnaud, *Révolution et contre-révolution culturelles en U.R.S.S.* (Paris, 1975), pp. 253–57.

NEP and its abuses and pointed to the danger of a weakened industrial proletariat and of insufficient support for the international working class in its revolutionary struggle. He had joined in the sharp warning against the rise of bureaucracy within the party and against all the dangers that this bureaucratization entailed for the construction of a socialist economy. In the summer of 1928, however, under the pressures generated by the consolidation of power in Stalin's hands, Radek broke with Trotsky, composing and circulating, as he did so, "an immensely long memorandum . . . on the theory of proletarian dictatorship . . . devoted to a critical examination of Trotsky's views since 1905." Upon Trotsky's expulsion from the Soviet Union, Radek, together with Yevgeny Preobazhensky and Ivan Smilga, "three outstanding figures of the opposition," recanted:

> [They announced] that they had broken "ideologically and organizationally" with Trotsky and his supporters, withdrew their signatures from all "fractional documents"; they confessed that the Fifteenth Party Congress had been right to reject the opposition platform and that the policy of the party's central committee "was and remains Leninist," and begged to be readmitted to the party. Trotsky, more outraged by this than by any of the earlier defections, published a lengthy article headed "A Wretched Document," in which he called it "a document of political degeneration"; his bitterest comment was reserved for Radek "who began ever since February 1928 to look for motives for 'capitulation.'"[40]

As he moved toward reconciliation with the Stalinist forces, Radek chose to ignore the discourse of analytic montage embodied by Vertov in *Enthusiasm.* Utilizing the invention of mobile sound recording, the play upon sound-image relationships, the asynchrony of that play, and the integration of concrete sounds of industry and labor, Vertov made the first and ultimately the most significant contribution to the Soviet sound film. Radek also chose to ignore the film's precise and concrete references to the debate over rival methods in steel production of the time. The rhetoric of Radek's text has the vulgar prescriptiveness of Zhdanov; it inaugurates the discourse of

40. E. H. Carr, *A History of Soviet Russia: Foundations of a Planned Economy, 1926–1929* (London, 1971), II, 123.

expulsion, from that time on constantly present in Vertov's diary entries. Vertov was faced with increasing isolation, the constant rejection of plans and projects throughout the forties and fifties; his form and methods were criticized as irrelevant.

> I make one proposal after another. While the studio proposes nothing. It's as if I'm on stage, while the management and the script department are in the auditorium.
>
> I run my legs off, proposing one thing, then another.
>
> And the audience watches and listens. And remains silent.
>
> And I feel as if I'm way at the bottom. Facing the first step of a long steep staircase. [. . .]
>
> You want to make a film to a script.
>
> But you're told:
>
> "Well, who can write the script for you?"
>
> You want to make a film without a script.
>
> But you're told:
>
> "This has no plan. A film absolutely must be made according to a script."
>
> You want to make films about real people.
>
> You're told:
>
> "I'm firmly convinced that real people cannot be filmed in documentary fashion; we can't allow that."
>
> [. . .] then you're told:
>
> "We can't have you do that. You have a name and a creative identity. Our studio can't risk it. We've got to keep you the way your reputation in cinema demands."
>
> Where, I ask, is the way out of this impasse? ("From Notebooks, Diaries": 1939, October 24)

There was to be no way out for Vertov. The massive bureaucracy of the Stalinist regime was now entirely reproduced within the Soviet film industry. The ceaseless submission of projects, the haunting of antechambers, and the unending solicitation of official authorization were the only possible responses to the situation. As he very clearly saw, he was now, with a stunning irony, subject to that same fixity of attribution of role and function that the revolutionary project had proposed to abolish. He ends by exclaiming that if Lenin were to appear within the present film industry, he would be dismissed and prohibited from working. We easily sense Vertov's claim, as the revolutionary founder of a cinema that offered the Communist Decoding of the World, to the title of the Lenin of Cinema. Everything—and most of all, his sustained commitment to the construction of socialism within one country—conspired to prevent him from acknowledging that he had instead become cinema's Trotsky.

The Writings of Dziga Vertov

From Articles, Public Addresses

WE: VARIANT OF A MANIFESTO

We call ourselves *kinoks*—as opposed to "cinematographers," a herd of junkmen doing rather well peddling their rags.

We see no connection between true *kinochestvo* and the cunning and calculation of the profiteers.

We consider the psychological Russo-German film-drama—weighed down with apparitions and childhood memories—an absurdity.

Glosses followed by "ed." or "trans." are additions by the present editor or the translator. Glosses which are not so marked are taken from the Moscow edition without substantial alteration.

kinoks. ("cinema-eye men"). A neologism coined by Vertov, involving a play on the words *kino* ("cinema" or "film") and *oko,* the latter an obsolescent and poetic word meaning "eye." The *-ok* ending is the transliteration of a traditional suffix used in Russian to indicate a male, human agent.

Kinoglaz ("Kino-Eye") is the name Vertov gave to the movement and group of which he is the founder and leader. The term was also used to designate their method of work. It is, as well, the title of the feature-length film that, in 1925, initiates the period of his maturity. We have chosen to use the Russian title in all cases involving specific reference to that film, since it is by its Russian title that the film is generally known to scholars and archivists. This work was the culmination of a development begun in 1922 with the production of a series of shorter newsreel films bearing the same title and devoted to aspects and problems of the new Soviet society. When reference is made to the group or movement as such, we have used the name *Kino-Eye,* both in order to distinguish it from the specific productions and to stress the continuity involved in the production, by Vertov and his group, of the *Kinonedelia* ("Kino-week") and *Kinopravda* ("Kino-truth") chronicles, which preceded the appearance of the film *Kinoglaz*—trans. and ed.

kinochestvo. Another of Vertov's neologisms: the suffix *chestvo* indicates an abstract quality, therefore, the quality of the cinema-eye. While its

Vertov and Mark Magridson on location for *Three Songs of Lenin*

To the American adventure film with its showy dynamism and to the dramatizations of the American Pinkertons the kinoks say thanks for the rapid shot changes and the close-ups. Good . . . but disorderly, not based on a precise study of movement. A cut above the psychological drama, but still lacking in foundation. A cliché. A copy of a copy.

---

precise signification is rather vague, it would appear from the context that Vertov is using it, by analogy with *kinok,* in contrast to *cinematography.* In his journal of 1924, he writes, "We almost never used the term *kinochestvo,* as it says nothing and is gratuitous word building." Film theory of the period is characterized, internationally, by a proliferation of terminology, and this particular instance recalls the elaborate speculation surrounding the notion of "photogénie" proposed in France by Vertov's contemporary, Jean Epstein—trans. and ed.

WE proclaim the old films, based on the romance, theatrical films and the like, to be leprous.

—Keep away from them!

—Keep your eyes off them!

—They're mortally dangerous!

—Contagious!

WE affirm the future of cinema art by denying its present.

"Cinematography" must die so that the art of cinema may live. WE *call for its death to be hastened.*

We protest against that mixing of the arts which many call synthesis. The mixture of bad colors, even those ideally selected from the spectrum, produces not white, but mud.

Synthesis should come at the summit of each art's achievement and not before.

WE are cleansing *kinochestvo* of foreign matter—of music, literature, and theater; we seek our own rhythm, one lifted from nowhere else, and we find it in the movements of things.

WE invite you:

—to flee—

the sweet embraces of the romance,

the poison of the psychological novel,

the clutches of the theater of adultery;

to turn your back on music,

—to flee—

out into the open, into four-dimensions (three + time), in search of our own material, our meter and rhythm.

The "psychological" prevents man from being as precise as a stopwatch; it interferes with his desire for kinship with the machine.

In an art of movement we have no reason to devote our particular attention to contemporary man.

The machine makes us ashamed of man's inability to control himself, but what are we to do if electricity's unerring ways are more exciting to us than the disorderly haste of active men and the corrupting inertia of passive ones?

Saws dancing at a sawmill convey to us a joy more intimate and intelligible than that on human dance floors.

For his inability to control his movements, WE temporarily exclude man as a subject for film.

romance. Vertov is referring to a type of sentimental film based on songs ("romances"), popular at that time—trans.

Our path leads through the poetry of machines, from the bungling citizen to the perfect electric man.

In revealing the machine's soul, in causing the worker to love his workbench, the peasant his tractor, the engineer his engine—

we introduce creative joy into all mechanical labor,

we bring people into closer kinship with machines,

we foster new people.

The new man, free of unwieldiness and clumsiness, will have the light, precise movements of machines, and he will be the gratifying subject of our films.

Openly recognizing the rhythm of machines, the delight of mechanical labor, the perception of the beauty of chemical processes, WE sing of earthquakes, we compose film epics of electric power plants and flame, we delight in the movements of comets and meteors and the gestures of searchlights that dazzle the stars.

Everyone who cares for his art seeks the essence of his own technique.

Cinema's unstrung nerves need a rigorous system of precise movement.

The meter, tempo, and type of movement, as well as its precise location with respect to the axes of a shot's coordinates and perhaps to the axes of universal coordinates (the three dimensions + the fourth—time), should be studied and taken into account by each creator in the field of cinema.

Radical necessity, precision, and speed are the three components of movement worth filming and screening.

The geometrical extract of movement through an exciting succession of images is what's required of montage.

Kinochestvo is the art of organizing the necessary movements of objects in space as a rhythmical artistic whole, in harmony with the properties of the material and the internal rhythm of each object.

Intervals (the transitions from one movement to another) are the material, the elements of the art of movement, and by no means the movements themselves. It is they (the intervals) which draw the movement to a kinetic resolution.

montage. In Russian a single word conveys notions that in English are rendered by the two words *montage* and *editing*. In most instances, one English meaning has been chosen according to the context—trans.

material. This term is frequently used by Vertov and others to mean film footage. Its constructivist connotation is significant with respect to Vertov's theory and practice—trans.

The organization of movement is the organization of its elements, or its intervals, into phrases.

In each phrase there is a rise, a high point, and a falling off (expressed in varying degrees) of movement.

A composition is made of phrases, just as a phrase is made of intervals of movement.

A kinok who has conceived a film epic or fragment should be able to jot it down with precision so as to give it life on the screen, should favorable technical conditions be present.

The most complete scenario cannot, of course, replace these notes, just as a libretto does not replace pantomime, just as literary accounts of Scriabin's compositions do not convey any notion of his music.

To represent a dynamic study on a sheet of paper, we need graphic symbols of movement.

WE are in search of the film scale.

WE fall, we rise . . . together with the rhythm of movements—slowed and accelerated,

running from us, past us, toward us,

in a circle, or straight line, or ellipse,

to the right and left, with plus and minus signs;

movements bend, straighten, divide, break apart,

multiply, shooting noiselessly through space.

Cinema is, as well, the *art of inventing movements* of things in space in response to the demands of science; it embodies the inventor's dream—be he scholar, artist, engineer, or carpenter; it is the realization by kinochestvo of that which cannot be realized in life.

Drawings in motion. Blueprints in motion. Plans for the future. The theory of relativity on the screen.

WE greet the ordered fantasy of movement.

Our eyes, spinning like propellers, take off into the future on the wings of hypothesis.

WE believe that the time is at hand when we shall be able to hurl into space the hurricanes of movement, reined in by our tactical lassoes.

Hurrah for *dynamic geometry*, the race of points, lines, planes, volumes.

Hurrah for the poetry of machines, propelled and driving; the poetry of levers, wheels, and wings of steel; the iron cry of movements; the blinding grimaces of red-hot streams.

1922

The Fifth Issue of *Kinopravda*

Because of the framework and the requirements imposed on *Kinopravda*, the screen newspaper, the creative spirit of its newsreel director is bound hand and foot.

With one half confined to political events, it's forced to devote the other half to commercial profit.

Neither political filming nor filming done under economic pressure takes into account the cinematic interest of a subject, and this necessarily results in the recording of static moments together with the dynamic—which is inadmissible in the poetry of movement.

Despite the above-mentioned conditions . . . *Kinopravda* no. 5, like the preceding issues, gradually manages to break the old newsreel routines, controlling the images and rhythms of each separate theme and anxiously seeking out the overall pulse of the *Kinonedelia,* the rhythmic unity of heterogeneous themes.

The link between the separate rhythms introduced into issue no. 5 (a man absorbed in reading *Kinopravda*) is merely a temporary device to soothe the viewer's eye.

The man sees the testimony of witnesses at the trial of the Socialist Revolutionaries; becomes acquainted with a People's Commissariat train in Siberia; is gently transported to health resorts in the Caucasus; and finally, half out of his chair, follows intently the quick, clear pulse of "The Red Derby," with which the issue concludes.

Step by step, deep-rooted methods of shooting and editing are changing in favor of the revelation of pure movement, the celebration of movement on the screen.

Great attention is paid to the design of titles (since titles are unavoidable for the present).

Kinopravda. ("Kino-truth.") A film journal directed by Vertov, named after the newspaper founded by Lenin. Each edition treated two or three subjects. Initiated by Goskino in June 1922, twenty-three irregularly appearing issues were made before its disappearance in 1925. With this journal, Vertov's theoretical position began to become known. The journal served as a laboratory for the development of Vertov's filmic vocabulary and as a stock of footage for use in later feature-length work—ed.

Kinonedelia. ("Kino-week.") A weekly newsreel journal, scripted and directed by Vertov, begun in June 1918 and issued through December 1919. A scarcity of film stock occasioned by an embargo organized by anti-Soviet European film monopolies resulted in irregular production. Fourteen issues were completed—trans. and ed.

The newsreel should feed on reality, and, given the slightest economic freedom, it will immediately open wide its eyes, triumph as well in art (whose creative growth is now stronger than ever before), and be supported by the broad, gesticulating throng of workers, bringing that throng closer to the iron rhythm of advancing—crawling, driven, and flying—machines.

Hundreds of thousands, millions of citizens of the RSFSR [Russian Soviet Federated Socialist Republic]—uneducated or simply hiding from the noisy advance of "today"—will have to sharpen their senses before the shining screen of Cinema.

1922

Kinoks: A Revolution

(From an Appeal at the Beginning of 1922)

You—filmmakers, you directors and artists with nothing to do, all you confused cameramen and writers scattered throughout the world,

You—theater audiences, patient as mules beneath the burden of the emotional experiences offered you,

You—impatient proprietors of theaters not yet bankrupt, greedily snatching at leftovers from the German, or more rarely, the American table—

You—exhausted by memories, await with dreamy sighs the moon of some new six-act production . . . (nervous folk are requested to shut their eyes).

You're waiting for something that will not come; the wait is pointless.

A friendly warning:
Don't hide your heads like ostriches.
Raise your eyes,
Look around you—
There!
It's obvious to me
as to any child
The innards,
the guts of strong sensations

are tumbling out
of cinema's belly,
ripped open on the reef of revolution.
See them dragging along,
leaving a bloody trail on the earth
that quivers with horror and disgust.
It's all over.

(From a Stenographic Record) To the Council of Three—Dziga Vertov

Psychological, detective, satirical, travel film—it doesn't matter what kind—if we cut out all the themes, leaving only the captions, we get the picture's literary skeleton. We can shoot other themes to go with that literary skeleton—realist, symbolist, expressionist—what have you. This situation will not change. The correlation is the same: a literary skeleton plus film-illustrations—such, almost without exception, are all films, ours and those from abroad.

The Council of Three. A policy-making group drawn from the kinoks, Vertov's staff of collaborators. The Council articulated Vertov's projects and imperatives through published statements and manifestos. The group is generally assumed to have been composed of Vertov, Mikhail Kaufman, his chief cameraman and brother, and Elizaveta Svilova, Vertov's editor and wife. Georges Sadoul, in his *Histoire générale du cinéma: L'art muet,* vol. 5 (Paris: Editions Denoël, 1975), lists in addition the painter, Belyaev—ed.

Elizaveta Svilova (1900-1976), Vertov's wife and lifelong collaborator, began her career in film as a photographic printer and editor for Pathé Frères in Moscow, also working for other foreign film companies represented in tsarist Russia. In 1919 she participated in the nationalization of the film industry and in 1921 began work on a long-term project of collecting all available film material on Lenin. From the results of the first year's research she made a compilation film, released in 1922 in celebration of the anniversary of Lenin's birth as a special issue of the Goskino Kalendar series. From 1922 to 1924, she was chief editor for Goskino, the state film production agency. Svilova was a creative collaborator and chief editor for some of Vertov's major work. She acted as co-director on four of Vertov's later films, made during the 1920s. She worked as Assistant Director in the Mezhrabpom Studios at VUFKU, and finally, from 1940 to 1941, acted as the director of Soiuzkinokhronika. In 1944 and 1945 she directed the Central State Studio of Documentary Film. Her filmography lists a great many directorial assignments. She is an outstanding example of the interesting development and realization of careers for women in a cinematic tradition which was grounded in an aesthetically innovative and politically revolutionary era—ed.

(From an Appeal of January 20, 1923)
To Cinematographers—The Council of Three

Five seething years of universal daring have passed through you and gone, leaving no trace. You keep prerevolutionary "artistic" models hanging like ikons within you, and it is to them alone that your inner piety has been directed. Foreign countries support you in your errors, sending to a renewed Russia the imperishable relics of film-drama done up in splendid, technical sauce.

Spring arrives. The film-factories are expected to resume work. The Council of Three observes with unconcealed regret film production workers leafing through literary texts in search of suitable dramatizations. Names of theatrical dramas and epics proposed for adaptation are already in the air. In the Ukraine, and here in Moscow, several pictures with all the signs of impotence are already in production.

A strong technological lag; a loss of active thinking, lost during a period of idleness; an orientation toward the six-act psychodrama—i.e., an orientation toward what's behind you—all these factors doom each attempt [at adaptation] to failure. Cinema's system is poisoned with the terrible toxin of routine. We demand the opportunity to test the antidote we've found upon its dying body. We ask the unbelievers to see for themselves: we agree to test our medicine beforehand on "guinea pigs"—film études . . .

The Resolution of the Council of Three, April 10, 1923

The situation on the film front must be considered inauspicious.

As was to be expected, the first new Russian productions shown recall the old "artistic" models just as Nepmen recall the old bourgeoisie.

"artistic". In Russian, the fictional, narrative film is designated *artistic* in contrast to *documentary*—trans.

Nepmen, NEP. NEP is the acronym of the New Economic Policy instituted in 1921 after the period of War Communism with a view to stimulating the economy of the Soviet Union. The policy's emphasis on market demand and market requirements involved making concessions to private agriculture and reordering many aspects of the country's industrialization. It created, as well, a class of middlemen to organize the exchange between urban and village production and consumption. The "Nepman's" speculative ventures involving quick, high profits are often alluded to by Vertov in his castigation of the effects of a revival of bourgeois norms and practices within the film industry—ed.

The repertoire planned for summer production, both here and in the Ukraine, does not inspire the least confidence.

The proposals for broad experimental work have been passed over.

All efforts, sighs, tears, and expectations, all prayers—are directed toward it—the six-act film-drama.

Therefore the Council of Three without waiting for the kinoks to be assigned work and ignoring the latter's desire to realize their own projects, are temporarily disregarding authorship rights and resolve to immediately publish for general use the common principles and slogans of the future revolution-through-newsreel; for which purpose, first and foremost, kinok Dziga Vertov is directed, in accordance with party discipline, to publish certain excerpts from the pamphlet *Kinoks: A Revolution,* which shall sufficiently clarify the nature of that revolution.

The Council of Three

In fulfillment of the resolution of the Council of Three on April 10 of this year, I am publishing the following excerpts:

1

Upon observing the films that have arrived from America and the West and taking into account available information on work and artistic experimentation at home and abroad, I arrive at the following conclusion:

The death sentence passed in 1919 by the kinoks on all films, with no exceptions, holds for the present as well. The most scrupulous examination does not reveal a single film, a single artistic experiment, properly directed to the emancipation of the camera, which is reduced to a state of pitiable slavery, of subordination to the imperfections and the shortsightedness of the human eye.

We do not object to cinema's undermining of literature and the theater; we wholly approve of the use of cinema in every branch of knowledge, but we define these functions as accessory, as secondary offshoots of cinema.

The main and essential thing is:

The sensory exploration of the world through film.

We therefore take as the point of departure the use of the

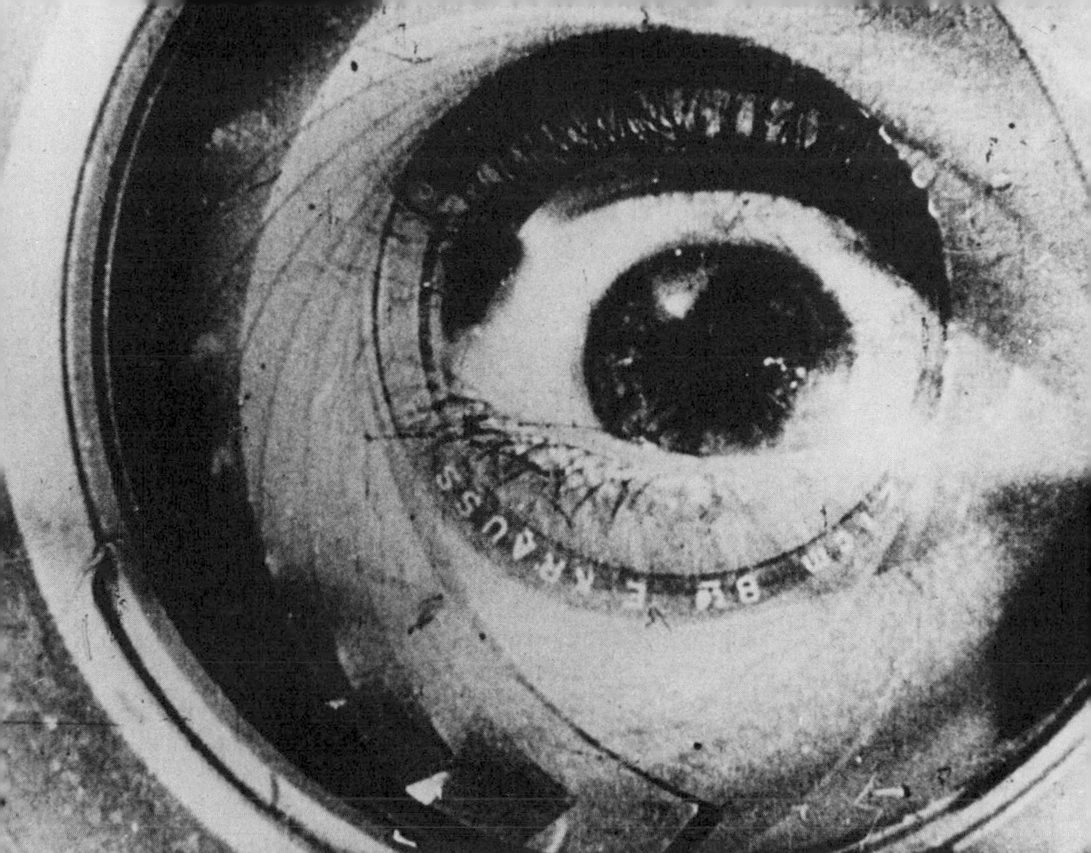

The Man with a Movie Camera

camera as a kino-eye, more perfect than the human eye, for the exploration of the chaos of visual phenomena that fills space.

The kino-eye lives and moves in time and space; it gathers and records impressions in a manner wholly different from that of the human eye. The position of our bodies while observing or our perception of a certain number of features of a visual phenomenon in a given instant are by no means obligatory limitations for the camera which, since it is perfected, perceives more and better.

We cannot improve the making of our eyes, but we can endlessly perfect the camera.

Until now many a cameraman has been criticized for having filmed a running horse moving with unnatural slowness on the screen (rapid cranking of the camera)—or for the opposite, a tractor plowing a field too swiftly (slow cranking of the camera), and the like.

These are chance occurrences, of course, but we are preparing a system, a deliberate system of such occurrences, a system of seeming irregularities to investigate and organize phenomena.

Until now, we have violated the movie camera and forced it to copy the work of our eye. And the better the copy, the better the shooting was thought to be. Starting today we are liberating the camera and making it work in the opposite direction—away from copying.

The weakness of the human eye is manifest. We affirm the kino-eye, discovering within the chaos of movement the result of the kino-eye's own movement; we affirm the kino-eye with its own dimensions of time and space, growing in strength and potential to the point of self-affirmation.

2

I make the viewer see in the manner best suited to my presentation of this or that visual phenomenon. The eye submits to the will of the camera and is directed by it to those successive points of the action that, most succinctly and vividly, bring the film phrase to the height or depth of resolution.

Example: shooting a boxing match, not from the point of view of a spectator present, but shooting the successive movements (the blows) of the contenders.

Example: the filming of a group of dancers, not from the point of view of a spectator sitting in the auditorium with a ballet on the stage before him.

After all, the spectator at a ballet follows, in confusion, now the combined group of dancers, now random individual figures, now someone's legs—a series of scattered perceptions, different for each spectator.

One can't present this to the film viewer. A system of successive movements requires the filming of dancers or boxers in the order of their actions, one after another . . . by forceful transfer of the viewer's eye to the successive details that must be seen.

The camera "carries" the film viewer's eyes from arms to legs, from legs to eyes and so on, in the most advantageous sequence, and organizes the details into an orderly montage study.

3

You're walking down a Chicago street today in 1923, but I make you greet Comrade Volodarsky, walking down a Petrograd street in

1918, and he returns your greeting.

Another example: the coffins of national heroes are lowered into the grave (shot in Astrakhan in 1918); the grave is filled in (Kronstadt, 1921); cannon salute (Petrograd, 1920); memorial service, hats are removed (Moscow, 1922)—such things go together, even with thankless footage not specifically shot for this purpose (cf. *Kinopravda* no. 13). The montage of crowds and of machines greeting Comrade Lenin (*Kinopravda* no. 14), filmed in different places at different times, belongs to this category.

I am kino-eye. I am a builder. I have placed you, whom I've created today, in an extraordinary room which did not exist until just now when I also created it. In this room there are twelve walls shot by me in various parts of the world. In bringing together shots of walls and details, I've managed to arrange them in an order that is pleasing and to construct with intervals, correctly, a film-phrase which is the room.

I am kino-eye, I create a man more perfect than Adam, I create thousands of different people in accordance with preliminary blueprints and diagrams of different kinds.

I am kino-eye.

From one person I take the hands, the strongest and most dexterous; from another I take the legs, the swiftest and most shapely; from a third, the most beautiful and expressive head—and through montage I create a new, perfect man.

I am kino-eye, I am a mechanical eye. I, a machine, show you the world as only I can see it.

Now and forever, I free myself from human immobility, I am in constant motion, I draw near, then away from objects, I crawl under, I climb onto them. I move apace with the muzzle of a galloping horse, I plunge full speed into a crowd, I outstrip running soldiers, I fall on my back, I ascend with an airplane, I plunge and soar together with plunging and soaring bodies. Now I, a camera, fling myself along their resultant, maneuvering in the chaos of movement, recording movement, starting with movements composed of the most complex combinations.

Freed from the rule of sixteen–seventeen frames per second,

Mikhail Kaufman

free of the limits of time and space, I put together any given points in the universe, no matter where I've recorded them.

My path leads to the creation of a fresh perception of the world. I decipher in a new way a world unknown to you.

5

Once more let us agree: the eye and the ear. The ear does not spy, the eye does not eavesdrop.

Separation of functions.

Radio-ear—the montage "I hear!"

Kino-eye—the montage "I see!"

There you have it, citizens, for the first time: instead of music, painting, theater, cinematography, and other castrated outpourings.

Within the chaos of movements, running past, away, running into and colliding—the eye, all by itself, enters life.

A day of visual impressions has passed. How is one to construct the impressions of the day into an effective whole, a visual study? If one films everything the eye has seen, the result, of course, will be a jumble. If one skillfully edits what's been photographed, the result will

Mikhail Kaufman

be clearer. If one scraps bothersome waste, it will be better still. One obtains an organized memo of the ordinary eye's impressions.

The mechanical eye, the camera, rejecting the human eye as crib sheet, gropes its way through the chaos of visual events, letting itself be drawn or repelled by movement, probing, as it goes, the path of its own movement. It experiments, distending time, dissecting movement, or, in contrary fashion, absorbing time within itself, swallowing years, thus schematizing processes of long duration inaccessible to the normal eye.

Aiding the machine-eye is the kinok-pilot, who not only controls the camera's movements, but entrusts himself to it during experiments in space. And at a later time the kinok-engineer, with remote control of cameras.

The result of this concerted action of the liberated and perfected camera and the strategic brain of man directing, observing, and gauging—the presentation of even the most ordinary things will take on an exceptionally fresh and interesting aspect.

How many people, starved for spectacles, are wearing away the seats of their pants in theaters?

They flee from the humdrum, from the "prose" of life. And meanwhile the theater is almost always just a lousy imitation of that same life, plus an idiotic conglomerate of balletic affectation, musical squeaks, tricks of lighting, stage sets (from daubs to constructivism), and occasionally the work of a talented writer distorted by all that nonsense. Certain masters of the theater are destroying the theater from within, shattering old forms, and advancing new slogans for theatrical work; to further their rescue they've enlisted biomechanics (in itself a worthy pursuit), and cinema (honor and glory to it), and writers (not bad in themselves), and constructions (there are some good ones), and automobiles (how can one not admire the automobile?), and gunfire (something dangerous and impressive at the front); and by and large not a damned thing comes of it.

Theater and nothing more.

Not only is this no synthesis; it's not even a legitimate mixture.

And it cannot be otherwise.

We kinoks, as firm opponents of premature synthesis ("For synthesis must come at the summit of achievement!"), understand that it's pointless to mix scraps of achievement: the little ones will immediately perish from overcrowding and disorder. And in general—

The arena's small. Come out, please, into life.

This is where we work—we, the masters of vision, the organizers of visible life, armed with the omnipresent kino-eye. This is where the masters of word and sound, the most skillful editors of audible life, work. And I make bold to slip them the ubiquitous mechanical ear and megaphone—the radiotelephone.

This is:

newsreel,

radio-news.

I promise to drum up a parade of kinoks on Red Square on the day when the futurists release the first issue of a radio-news montage.

Not the newsreels from Pathé or Gaumont (newspaper chronicle), not even *Kinopravda* (political newsreel), but a real kinok newsreel—an impetuous survey of visual events deciphered by the camera, bits of real energy (as opposed to theater) joined through intervals into a tectonic whole by the great craft of montage.

Such structuring of the film-object enables one to develop any given theme, be it comic, tragic, one of special effects, or some other type.

It's entirely a question of the particular juxtaposition of visual details, of intervals.

The unusual flexibility of montage construction enables one to introduce into a film study any given motif—political, economic, or other. And therefore:

- As of now, neither psychological nor detective dramas are needed in cinema,
- As of now, theatrical productions transferred to film are no longer needed,
- As of now, neither Dostoyevsky nor Nat Pinkerton are to be put on the screen.
- Everything is included in the new conception of the newsreel. Into the jumble of life resolutely enter:

1. kino-eye, challenging the human eye's visual representation of the world and offering its own "I see," and
2. the kinok-editor, organizing the minutes of the life-structure seen *this way* for the first time.

1923

On the Organization of a Film Experiment Station

The film office and editorial staff of *Kinopravda* are being eliminated. A small nucleus of workers, united by inner discipline, is being formed—the first film experiment station.

By organized work, the agency aims to break through the front of despair caused by idleness, among other factors, if only on one sector of this front—that of the newsreel and of experimentation. In addition, experimentation is also to be regarded as a kind of ferment that involves interested colleagues in intensive cooperation—a method that is tried and true.

Prospects for the future (a high objective): an institute for continuous invention and perfection, a stake in the worldwide quality of production, the cinema-lighthouse of the USSR.

Let those inclined to smile take note: the higher the objective, the stronger man's incentive to unite in steady work. Here lies the guarantee of ultimate success.

Types of film:

1. *Kinopravda*
2. Flash news bulletins
3. The humorous newsreel
4. Newsreel studies
5. Screen advertising
6. Experiments

Explanation:

The flash news bulletin shows events on the screen the day they occur.

Kinopravda is a periodical of events summarized into an agitational unit.

By screen advertising is meant the filming of commercial concerns advertising their products (special-effects publicity, cartoons, announcements on film).

So-called production orders are divided between scientific (if the film's purpose is scientific demonstration) and advertising (if the film's purpose is only advertisement).

In my opinion there should be no middle category, such as travelogue-style films of industrial enterprises; these should be resorted to only when a client's extreme obtuseness makes it impossible to dissuade him.

All artistic filming is of course transferred to the studio.

The Staff and Administrative Objectives

A director of the film experiment station and two instructors under him: one for organizing the shooting; the other for systematic supervision and inventory and dealings with the provinces and abroad. Two staff cameramen (with the right to engage cameramen from a production center when necessary).

A network of cameramen in the provinces, working under contract . . . similar to the work of provincial correspondents.

A parallel link with the storehouse, laboratory, and editing room.

Here is a list of those who have gathered and grouped around me and who, like myself, are hungry for work:

1. **E. Barantsevich**—electrician, familiar with aviation and sports, quick, quick-witted, given to experimenting.
2. **I. Belyakov**—graduate of the VGIK, draftsman, comic actor, assistant director, familiar with editing, can substitute for the splicer, specialist in subtitles, given to experimenting.
3. **M. Kaufman**—student at the VGIK; works in motion picture and still photography; knows cars; has knowledge of electrical engineering, blacksmithing, and metal work; given to experimentation.
4. **A. Lemberg**—cameraman; has knowledge of laboratory processing; does still photography; the first cameraman to champion, together with myself, new methods of editing and filming; nimble, crafty, and pushy; given to experimentation.
5. **B. Frantzisson**—cameraman, knows animation, eager to work, thirsting for fresh ideas and experiments, inventive.

With favorable conditions we'll have a creative force of great power.

Optimum use of the above-mentioned personnel will depend on the correct distribution of the functions of each worker, on material conditions, on technical factors, and on work slowdowns for reasons that lie outside the experiment station.

Slowdowns and stoppage of projected work represent the most dangerous factor and usually generate disillusionment on the part of a worker and an aversion to hopeless labor.

Belyakov. I. I. Belyakov (1897–), artist and cameraman, was one of Vertov's frequent collaborators during the early 1920s.
graduate of VGIK. VGIK (State Institute of Cinematography) is an institute of higher learning that still prepares cinema cadres.
M. Kaufman. Of the group of exceptionally able and distinguished technicians gathered around Vertov, Mikhail Kaufman (1897–1979), his brother, was his closest and most valued associate. Kaufman's energy, intelligence, and ingenuity played, throughout the seminal period of the 1920s, an essential role in the development of Kino-Eye's innovative practice. After their professional separation in 1929, Kaufman continued to make documentary films of his own, including *Spring* (1930).

Mikhail Kaufman

The elimination of these slowdowns with the help of Goskino, or of even higher authorities, is the pledge of success in our enterprise.

The very best administrative scheme requires a considerable amount of time to overcome unfavorable conditions.

Temporary failures, disappointments are unavoidable. Much will depend on the personnel's cohesiveness and on a similar reorganization of other departments in cinema.

Within six months, we'll have the first evaluation of the results of the work done by the experiment station; the second, in a year.

1923

Goskino. Created in December 1922, Goskino was the production agency of the state cinema. Gosprokat, the state rental agency, was given the monopoly on distribution throughout the USSR and was a branch of Goskino. In February 1923, Goskino's industrial and commercial activities were placed under the control of the State Economic Council, and its cultural activities were retained by the People's Commissariat of Education—ed.

Advertising Films

Types of Advertising Films

1. The most elementary advertisement (30–100 feet)

Example: A fire in the projection room of a theater. No way to put it out. The fire extinguisher has been forgotten. Suddenly it's remembered. The foaming "Bogatyr" fire extinguisher instantly puts out the fire.

2. The newsreel advertisement (35–100 feet)

Example: The unloading of an ocean liner in Petrograd is included in a current newsreel, say *Kinopravda.* "Fordson" tractors are unloaded. A train rushes along. Moscow. The tractors are delivered to Gostorg [the State Import-Export Trade Office], "Techno-import."

3. The special-effects advertisement (35–130 feet)

Example (animation film, model sets): A small boy, an urchin, runs along a street, sprinkling "magic powder" that makes everything grow and swell to unusual proportions. Little dogs grow to be as big as buffaloes; horses, the size of mammoths; people become giants. The little boy is caught, the powder taken from him and put to use. Dough is mixed and bread rises, big as a house. The "magic powder" is yeast made by the Trekhgorny Brewing Company of Mosselprom [the Moscow Association of Establishments for Processing Products of the Agricultural Industry].

4. The cartoon advertisement (165–330 feet)

I cite as an example the film cartoon, *The Dream,* advertising the services of the "Engine" office. Made by B. V. Frantzisson, the cameraman. Animation filming. Twenty-one hundred drawings altogether. Each drawing was filmed separately. The series of successive drawing frames then compose the film.

The office of the president of a trust. There are no customers. Will the trust collapse? The dejected president goes home. That night he dreams of a motor running. Its exhaust forms the letters *e-n-g-i-n-e.*

This dream is followed by another. Interplanetary space. Stars.

The running motor and the globe enter from opposite sides of the screen. The letter *E* is discharged from the motor, heads for the earth's axis, and joins the globe and the motor with a transmission belt. The earth turns by the engine's power. With each revolution the globe hurls the letters *e-n-g-i-n-e,* one after another, onto the screen.

Morning. The president of the trust awakens. The morning paper is on his nightstand. He reads . . . featured: "'Engine' Advertising Agency." He rushes to the address to hand in an ad.

A week later. There's a line of customers at the trust.

5. The Impromptu Advertisement (65–500 feet)

The only impromptu film to appear in the USSR is *The Car,* commissioned by *GUM* [the State Department Store].

It was done in three days, not in a studio.

A plot outline: A father and mother go to Moscow to visit their daughter who is being courted by a Moscow juggler. Immediately upon arriving at the station, they are bombarded by the incomprehensible word GUM. Newsboys run past handing out GUM leaflets. On the stairs of the train station someone in a bowler welcomes them like a close friend, embraces them, and disappears. Upon his departure they discover the GUM trademark in their hands.

The daughter meets the Muscovite in GUM. The latter juggles their purchases.

The daughter returns from her shopping. Her purchases are on the table. Her parents enter with their suitcases, rush toward their daughter, then suddenly fall back. On their daughter's purchases on the table is GUM, GUM, GUM. . . . They look at their suitcases—someone has covered them with GUM emblems as well. A tense standstill. In her armchair the daughter roars with laughter.

At GUM. The magician and wizard of GUM, the head of advertising, a magic wand in his hands, hurls letters onto the screen.

A scene occurs in the street. With a boxer's jab, the girl knocks an impudent pest off his feet. A crowd. The girl apologizes to the public for the deception. "It's only . . . ," she disappears behind the circle of GUM. Then she's gone. And the public's gone. Only the various departments of GUM remain.

The parents are sitting on a bench in the square. They're reading the newspapers. Each of their papers features GUM prominently.

They're tired of it. They put down their papers in irritation. Their hands meet. And as a result, two lap dogs fall from the old woman's hands. She bends over the dogs. They've disappeared. Instead, there's a hatbox on the bench. How did it get there? And GUM is written on the hatbox. The dogs turn up in the hatbox.

The viewers were able to see how a certain suspicious character quickly slipped the dogs into the box.

However, that nuisance of a GUM makes up for its badgering. In the upper rows of shops, the mother wins a samovar in a lottery, and the father, a car.

6. The humorous advertisement (350–600 feet)

Example: A certain citizen, having insured himself with the State Insurance Administration against fire, shipping accidents, and cattle fever, experiences all these calamities. His possessions and property all burn, his shipments by land, sea, and river routes are lost one after the other; he loses all his cattle and horses.

Both the viewer and the State Insurance Company realize that no abuse is involved, that it's a matter of extraordinary coincidence. The company pays for the citizen's losses according to the exchange rate of the gold ruble.

7. The detective advertisement (5,000–6,500 feet)

Example of a theme: advertisement of a lottery loan.

A gang of counterfeiters, connected with White-Guard organizations and using false money, buys up a huge number of lottery loan tickets. The shady business is uncovered. The gang throws the GPU secret police off the track. The president of a trust is wrongly suspected. His daughter and her close friend, "X," make every effort to discover the parties to the crime in order to remove suspicion from her father.

The gang carries out a series of robberies, continually stealing lottery loan tickets.

After many perilous adventures, the three—the daughter, her friend, and the Red Pinkerton—make their way to the gang's "Black Vault" and carry off the stolen lottery tickets.

The issuance of paper money is reduced, the loan strengthens the value of the ruble, the cost of living decreases. White-Guard spies threaten the gang and force it to attack, etc., etc.—as many episodes as are needed, introducing any given political and economic motifs.

8. The satirical detective advertisement (5,000–6,500 feet)

I can point to *Incident in a Department Store,* which I wrote, as the only example of this sort of picture. It's not only a satirical film, but a satire on the detective film as well.

A brief outline: A group of high-school seniors who have seen their fill of detective films and have mastered the methods of American spies and bandits, long to try out what they've learned. They make a number of raids on a Mostorg department store—not with criminal intent, but in sport. Their goal is modest: to get some civilian suits and coats for their high-school graduation without shelling out for it—and only at a department store that's exceptionally well guarded.

Two attempts by the students to get what they need are worked out in the scenario. The first attempt fails immediately because the adventurer-bandits have not provided for all factors and thanks to the excellent functioning of the special security guard, a good alarm system, and the good strong fists of the head of the clothing department.

The second attempt is carefully planned and well executed. A salesgirl in love with one of the students gives them away. She is watched by a jealous cashier who unexpectedly exposes the shady business.

The head of the clothing department, the cashier, the salesgirl and members of the student gang are exaggerated in the extreme: walking circus acts, not people.

The fiancée of the department head (she is from the provinces) arrives from the country in the thick of things, goes wild over the wonderful things in the department store, nurses her fiancé, who's been bruised in one of the melees, and at first appears absurd and comical against the carnivalesque background.

The encounters between characters are arranged so that the viewer is shown most of the departments of the store, the administration, the infirmary, security system, club, and even the military unit maintained by the store.

For want of money the film was not made; it was replaced by the systematic shooting of all floors and sections of the store.

I don't regret the energy spent on working out the scenario, but, to be honest, I was perplexed and upset by such a pointless waste of film at a time of shortage.

Showing Advertising Films

In cities

In movie theaters: Shorter films (35–100 feet) are spliced onto the beginning or end of a current movie program. Advertisements of 350–500 feet (comedies, cartoons, etc.) are shown in addition to the program. Detective advertisement films of five or six reels are shown as a separate program by special arrangement with the appropriate distribution office.

In public squares: Screening of all types of advertisements, using permanent film projection installations or travelling movie theaters. It's advisable to show short, urgent fifteen- to thirty-five-foot trick effects–slogan films—vivid, irritating "dum-dums" in large store windows, on rooftops, on sheets in the street, on sidewalks beneath the viewers' feet.

Along railway lines

Film-cars (specially equipped, modelled after the cars of the agit-trains of the All-Russian Central Executive Committee). Screenings while en route, inside the car; on screens set up at stations during stops. A travelling theater serving settlements within a vicinity of about ten miles. A cameraman and still photographer in the car, ready to serve the local government agencies and private enterprise wishing to advertise. The profitability of such mobile publicity cinemas depends on a correlation between the talents of the film-car's head and the taxes imposed by the state.

Along water routes

Film-steamers, cinema-barges, collapsible cinemas set up on shore, and mobile ones. The installation possibilities are greater than for the railway cinema. Searchlights for attracting the public would be desirable. A film laboratory is possible. Branches on passenger steamers plying rivers are possible.

Film-wagons

travelling from town to town in the countryside, from village to village, also have major significance for advertising and propaganda. In particular, the demonstration (disguised by some engaging subject matter) of the advantages of the agricultural machinery of a particular firm will help to distribute the machines of that firm. If the peasants don't understand everything perfectly, still someone will easily remember the brand of machine that rescued the film characters from their trouble.

The brand name should be singled out and should appear in the plot in large Russian letters.

Automobiles for screening

Swift technical staff, on the model of a fire brigade. Work on call, wherever, whenever needed. A searchlight. A movie camera. A screen. The projector is operated by the car's motor kept idling.

The same car goes out on call, with cameraman on duty and an on-the-spot producer, to shoot an urgent film-advertisement.

A small number of cinematographs of this sort existed in 1920 and 1921 in the Petrograd photography and motion picture department and in the department of instructional agit-trains of the All-Russian Central Executive Committee.

What can be advertised?

Everything—

from lottery loan tickets to hair-growing ointment . . . and back again, from "Sanagri" tooth powder to the Donbas coal industry. Gostorg, syndicates, trusts, cooperative agencies, private individuals—all can advertise their products on the screen, choosing the most suitable form of film advertising.

Traction and oil engines, tractors, safes, furniture, footwear, pianos, textiles, headgear—everything can be broadcast through the special-effects film, can be laughed over through the humorous film, made witty in the film cartoon or exciting in the detective film.

An Example of Bad Advertising

The filming in sequence of all the floors and sections of a Mostorg department store for publicity; at best, a picture of this sort can inventory the state of business on a particular day.

It does not achieve its immediate goal since it elicits yawns from even the most undemanding viewers.

A good advertisement is one that draws the viewer out of his indifference, and only when he's in a state of tension and restlessness, presents to him the product being advertised.

Such are the pictures that make the viewer laugh, that astound him with their trick effects, captivate him with their characters' unusual adventures; such, finally, are pictures whose advertising is latent; they imperceptibly introduce the products advertised into the absorbed viewer's consciousness. Pictures of the opposite kind have very blatant advertising: they alienate the viewer, exposing their own desire to advertise and be advertised, the importunate, vicious pestering of the viewer: me! me! me! I'm a good product! I'm the best product!

How should one proceed?

After choosing a particular type of advertisement, the customer comes to an agreement with the film-advertisement producer. The terms of the agreement will vary with each order, depending on the type of advertisement, the size of the order (the number of prints).

Which type of advertisement does one choose? That depends on the size of the customer's purse. A customer with a great deal of liquid capital will order one or two programs at once.

A program consists of:

Roughly—a detective film in which the advertising is disguised; a humorous one in which the advertised products are not swallowed like medicine but unknowingly by the viewers, during bursts of laughter; and, in addition to the program, a swift-paced, powerful special-effects ad of 35–100 feet, which vividly impresses the product on the subconscious of the viewers who have been prepared by the preceding films.

As though someone were first to notice a single sparkling dot amid a group of glittering dots and raise it high over his head.

Most important:

For five years there was no motion picture production in the Soviet Union. There's none now. There is no money for it. Film advertising is the gateway to work, to production, to prosperity. We must make this "compromise"; we have to.

Small harm to a film if you place the characters precisely in the store that wants advertising, rather than in another that does not.

It makes no difference whether an attack by bandits is set in a Mostorg department store or in another store. It wouldn't be so terrible even if *TsUPVOZ* [Central Directorate of Military Procurement] flashed through the wheel of a moving peasant's cart, or if the title "Raw Materials Section, Central Union of Consumers' Societies" were suddenly to flash on the back of some lady in an astrakhan coat.

This will not harm a film of any genre—socialist, red-detective, or any other.

The money of the advertising client and the abilities of the film production workers, avid for work, should join together.

Therein lies our salvation. Therein lies expansion.

Without it—death throes.

I am pointing out the correct path.

1923

On the Significance of Newsreel

For almost a year now I have not taken part in public discussions either as speaker or opponent.

We *kinoks* have resolved: to replace verbal debate, as a literary phenomenon, with film debate, that is, with the making of film-objects.

We are having some success in carrying this out, fearlessly pitting the newsreels we've released against the best artistic films.

Newsreels, the best examples of which are the issues of *Kino-pravda,* are boycotted by film distributors, by the bourgeois and semibourgeois public. But this state of affairs has not forced us to accommodate ourselves to established, philistine taste. It has only led us to change our audience.

Kinopravda is being shown daily in many workers' clubs in Moscow and the provinces, and with great success. And if the NEP audience prefers "love" or "crime" dramas that doesn't mean that our works are unfit. It means the public is.

Comrades, continue, if you wish, to argue whether the cinema is or is not an art.

Continue to ignore our existence and our work.

I put it to you once more:

Revolutionary cinema's path of development has been found.

It leads past the heads of film actors and beyond the studio roof, into life, into genuine reality, full of its own drama and detective plots.

1923

History of the Civil War

Kinopravda [1923]

Given the swiftness of communication between nations, given the lightning-fast turnover of footage, *Kinogazeta* should be "a survey of the world every few hours."

This is not the case.

We have to make it so.

Kinopravda is an automobile on a leash, an airplane beneath a ceiling, it cannot be a film-daily.

The publication of *Kinopravda* as a film-periodical is a strategical retreat, brought on by economic factors.

Kinopravda lacks and needs: a regular working staff, provincial correspondents, salaries for them, means of transport, sufficient film stock, the practical opportunity for contact with foreign countries.

Kinogazeta. ("Film-newspaper" or "film-daily".) Vertov is simply using this as an alternative phrase for *Kinopravda*. In speaking of "film-magazines" or "film-periodicals," he generally means newsreel series. However, *Kinogazeta* was also the name of a printed newspaper about film—trans. and ed.

The absence of even one of these factors is enough to kill the film-daily.

Kinopravda only exists; it needs to *live.*

The government and the Comintern have not yet understood that in giving serious support to *Kinopravda,* they will find a new megaphone, a visual radio to the world.

Regardless of the changes in the photo-cinema department, it is essential that the world's only revolutionary government should have and maintain a revolutionary film-daily.

1923

On the Film Known as *Kinoglaz*

The world's first attempt to create a film-object without the participation of actors, artists, directors; without using a studio, sets, costumes. All members of the cast continue to do what they usually do in life.

The present film represents an assault on our reality by the cameras and prepares the theme of creative labor against a background of class contradictions and of everyday life. In disclosing the origins of objects and of bread, the camera makes it possible for every worker to acquire, through evidence, the conviction that he, the worker, creates all these things himself, and that consequently they belong to him.

In undressing a flirtatious bourgeoise and a bloated bourgeois, and in returning food and objects to the workers and peasants who've made them, we are giving millions of laborers the opportunity to see the truth and to question the need to dress and feed a caste of parasites.

If this experiment succeeds, the picture, independent (in both its content and formal exploration), will serve as a prologue to the international film, *Workers of the World, Unite!* The spade work for the creation of this film is presently being done under the Council of Three—the supreme organ of the *kinoks.* The Council of Three, basing itself politically on the communist program, is striving to instill cinema with the ideas underlying Leninism and to invest their extremely profound content not in the grimaces of actors, more or less successful as they may be, but in the labor and thoughts of the working class itself.

The experiment is made difficult by our technical backwardness. Unarmed technically, but relying upon the difficult experimentation of nineteen *Kinopravdas,* we nevertheless hope, beginning with this first work, to open the eyes of the masses to the connection (not one of kisses or detectives) between the social and visual phenomena interpreted by the camera.

Proceeding from the material to the film-object (and not from the film-object to the material), the *kinoks* consider it wrong, in beginning work, to present a so-called scenario. In the years to come, the scenario as a product of literary composition will completely disappear.

Allowing, however, for possible reservations on the part of Goskino or Narkompros concerning our ability to construct a film-object correct in ideology and technique without a previously approved scenario, I enclose, with this memorandum, a sketch of the cameras' offensive and an approximate list of characters and places.

1923

On the Significance of Nonacted Cinema

We maintain that despite the comparatively long existence of cinematography as a concept, despite the large number of dramas—psychological, pseudorealistic, pseudohistorical, detective—that have been released . . . despite the infinity of movie theaters that have opened; in its present form, cinema does not exist and its main objectives have not been realized.

Narkompros. The People's Commissariat of Education, created by the Central Committee of the Bolshevik Party in October 1917. It was charged with the enormous task of reorganizing education according to socialist methods and aims. Narkompros also served as mediator between the regime and the nation's intellectuals. Anatole Lunacharsky, the first and most distinguished Commissar of Education, was a man of exceptional culture, intelligence, and gifts. His energetic and understanding administration of this agency are indissociable from the intensity of the Soviet Union's cultural life during the first postrevolutionary decade—ed.

We venture this statement on the basis of information in our possession concerning work and creative exploration at home and abroad.

What is the reason for this?

The reason is that cinema has been and still is on the wrong track. The cinema of yesterday and today is merely a commercial affair. Cinema's path of development has been dictated solely by considerations of profit. And it's hardly surprising that the extensive commerce in motion pictures—illustrations of novels, romances, Pinkerton serials—has dazzled and attracted production workers.

Every motion picture is a mere literary skeleton covered with a film-skin. At best, some film-fat and film-flesh develop beneath that skin (as, for example, in foreign hits). We never see the film-skeleton, however. Our motion picture is merely the well-known "boneless part" impaled on the aspen stake, the goose quill of a writer.

I'll condense what I've said: we have no film-objects. We have the cohabitation of film-illustrations with theater, literature, with music, with whomever and whatever, whenever, at any price.

I want you to understand me correctly. We would wholeheartedly welcome the use of cinema in the service of every branch of human knowledge. These cinematic possibilities, however, we define as secondary, illustrative. Not for a moment do we forget that a chair is made of wood and not of the varnish covering it. We're well aware that a boot is made of leather and not of the wax which makes it shine.

The horror, the irreparable blunder is that you still consider it your aim to polish someone's literary shoes (they have high French heels, if the film's a hit) with cinematic wax.

Recently, I think it was at the showing of the seventeenth *Kino-pravda,* a certain filmmaker declared, "This is a disgrace; these are shoemakers, not filmmakers." Alexei Gan, the constructivist, who

Alexei Gan. Alexei Gan (1889–1942) was a founding member of the First Working Group of Constructivists. During the immediate postrevolutionary years (1918–1920), he directed the Section of Mass Presentations and Spectacles at the Theatre Section of Narkompros. Closely associated with the Institute of Artistic Culture known as Inkhuk, he turned to the design of architectural and typographical projects, posters, and bookplates in the early 1920s. The author of several important constructivist documents and manifestos, an editor of *LEF,* he was later associated with the journal *Sovremennaia arkhitektura* ("Contemporary Architecture").

was nearby, observed with reason, "If we only had more of these shoemakers, everything would be o.k."

Speaking for the author of *Kinopravda,* I have the honor to announce that he is very flattered by such unconditional recognition as the *first shoemaker of Russian cinema.*

That's better than "artist of Russian cinema."

That's better than "artistic film director."

To hell with shoe wax. To hell with boots that are nothing but shine. Give us boots made of leather.

Match yourself against the first Russian film-shoemakers—the kinoks.

We, the shoemakers of cinematography say to you, the shoe shiners, that we do not recognize your seniority in the making of film-objects. And if the claim to seniority has any advantage, then the rightful claim is entirely ours.

However insignificant our practical achievement, nevertheless it's more than your years of *nothing.*

We were the first to make *film-objects* with our bare hands—perhaps clumsy, awkward, lacking shine, perhaps somewhat flawed, but still necessary objects, vital objects, aimed at life and needed in life.

We define the film-object in these words: *the montage "I see."*

The film-object is a finished étude of absolute vision, rendered exact and deepened by all existing optical instruments, principally by the movie camera experimenting in space and time.

The field of vision is life;

the material for montage construction, life;

the sets, life;

the actors, life.

Of course we do not and cannot prohibit artists from drawing pictures, composers from writing for the piano, poets from writing for ladies. Let them have their fun.

But these are toys (though they may be skillfully made), they're not what counts.

One of the chief accusations leveled at us is that we are not intelligible to the masses.

Even if one allows that some of our work is difficult to understand, does that mean we should not undertake serious exploratory work at all?

If the masses need light propaganda pamphlets, does that mean they don't need the serious articles of Engels, Lenin? . . . The LENIN of Russian cinema may appear in your midst today, but you will not allow him to work because the results of his production will seem new and incomprehensible . . .

Our work is not in that situation, however, We have not in fact created a single work more incomprehensible to the masses than any given film-drama. On the contrary, by establishing a clear visual link between subjects, we have significantly weakened the importance of intertitles; in so doing we have brought the movie screen closer to the uneducated viewers, which is particularly important at present.

And as if in mockery of their literary nursemaids, the workers and peasants turn out to be brighter than their self-appointed nursemaids. . . .

Thus, two extremities of viewpoint are present. One—that of the kinoks—has as its goal the organization of *real life;* the other, an orientation toward the propagandistic-artistic drama of emotional experiences and adventures.

All state and private funds, all technical and material resources are mistakenly being poured into the latter end of the scales, into the propagandistic-artistic.

As for us, we're grabbing hold of work as hitherto, with our bare hands, and we confidently await our turn to control production and win our victory.

1923

Kinoglaz

(A NEWSREEL IN SIX PARTS)

The solid front of the film-drama has been broken by *Kinopravda*.

This breach must not be:

plugged up with the NEP stopper,

filled in with the litter of compromise.

The recent appearance of numerous surrogates—motion pictures done in the style of the kinoks (the workers of *Kinopravda*)—compels them to begin, somewhat prematurely, a decisive attack on the reign of bourgeois cinema. The preliminary reconnaissance has been entrusted to the Goskino cell of the kinoks, since they are more experienced. Plans for the cameras' attack have been worked out. The whole film campaign (between ten thousand and thirty thousand feet) will go under the slogan and title *Kino-Eye*. The reconnaissance by the Goskino cell is being carried out with a single camera (we have no more at our disposal) and will probably form the first part or starting point of the battle. A six-part series is projected.

The first of these has taken into account our complete lack of weapons; equipment intended for studio use is unsuited to our work. In this part the camera, having chosen some easily vulnerable point, cautiously enters into life and takes its bearings in its visual surroundings. In subsequent parts, along with an increase in the number of cameras, the area under observation will be extended. Gradually, through comparison of various parts of the globe, various bits of life, the visible world is being explored. Each succeeding part will further clarify the understanding of reality. The eyes of children and adults, the educated as well as the uneducated, are opening, as it were, for the first time. Millions of workers, having recovered their sight, are beginning to doubt the necessity of supporting the bourgeois structure of the world.

We are not employing a single director, actor, or set designer in this mighty film-battle. We renounce the convenience of the studio; we sweep aside sets, makeup, costumes. Just as you cannot describe in advance the battles of a war that's just been declared, you cannot write an advance scenario for our film-campaign. Proceeding from material to film-object, and not from film-object to material, the kinoks are seizing the last (most tenacious) stronghold of artistic cinema in the literary scenario. The scenario, whether in the form of a fascinating short story or a so-called preliminary editing sheet, must disappear forever as an element foreign to cinema.

We cannot foresee the results of the campaign; we do not know if these ten thousand feet will be our cinematic October. The most powerful weapon and the most powerful technology are in the hands of the European and American film-bourgeoisie. Three-fourths of the human race is stupefied by the opium of bourgeois film-dramas.

The battle against the blinding of the masses, the battle for vision can and must begin only in the USSR, where the film-weapon is in the hands of the state.

To see and show the world in the name of the worldwide proletarian revolution—that is the most basic formula of the kinoks.

1924

The Birth of Kino-Eye

It began early in life. With the writing of fantastic novels (*The Iron Hand, Uprising in Mexico*). With short essays ("Whaling," "Fishing"). With long poems (*Masha*). With epigrams and satirical verse ("Purishkevich," "The Girl with Freckles"). It then turned into an enthusiasm for editing shorthand records, gramophone recordings. Into a special interest in the possibility of documentary sound recording. Into experiments in recording, with words and letters, the noise of a waterfall, the sounds of a lumbermill, etc. And one day in the spring of 1918 . . . returning from a train station. There lingered in my ears the sighs and rumble of the departing train . . . someone's swearing . . . a kiss . . . someone's exclamation . . . laughter, a whistle, voices, the ringing of the station bell, the puffing of the locomotive . . . whispers, cries, farewells. . . . And thoughts while walking: I must get a piece of equipment that won't describe, but will record, photograph these sounds. Otherwise it's impossible to organize, edit them. They rush past, like time. But the movie camera perhaps? Record the visible. . . . Organize not the audible, but the visible world. Perhaps that's the way out?

Just then—a meeting with Mikhail Koltsov, who offered me work in cinema. At no. 7 Malyi Gnezdnikovsky Lane I begin work on *Kinonedelia*. But this is initial training. It's far from what I'm after. After

Mikhail Koltsov. A Soviet writer and journalist, Mikhail Koltsov (1898–1942) joined the staff of *Pravda* in 1922, publishing a satirical column for many years in that newspaper. He also served as editor of the journal *Ogonek* and worked in cinema during the first postrevolutionary years. He fought in the Spanish Civil War and published a *Spanish Diary* based on his experiences. Arrested during the purges of the late 1930s, he was executed in prison.

no. 7 Malyi Gnezdnikovsky Lane. The address of the newsreel section of the Cinema Committee of the People's Commissariat of Education. Vertov began work here in the spring of 1918. It was during the move to this location that he made a leap from another building, across roof tops, filmed in slow motion and later projected. In his account of that incident and of its central importance, he says, "Didn't recognize my face on the screen. My all, the eye of the microscope penetrates where the eye of my movie camera cannot. The eye of the telescope reaches distant worlds, inaccessible to my naked eye. What about the camera then? What's its role in my assault on the visible world?

Thoughts about kino-eye. It arises as high-speed eye. Later on, the concept of kino-eye is expanded:

kino-eye as cinema-analysis,

kino-eye as the "theory of intervals,"

kino-eye as the theory of relativity on the screen, etc.

I abolish the usual sixteen frames per second. Together with rapid filming, animation filming and filming with a moving camera, etc. are considered ordinary filming techniques.

Kino-eye is understood as "that which the eye doesn't see,"

as the microscope and telescope of time,

as the negative of time,

as the possibility of seeing without limits and distances,

as the remote control of movie cameras,

as tele-eye,

as X-ray eye,

as "life caught unawares," etc., etc.

All these different formulations were mutually complementary since implied in kino-eye were:

all cinematic means,

all cinematic inventions,

all methods and means that might serve to reveal and show the truth.

Not kino-eye for its own sake, but truth through the means and possibilities of film-eye, i.e., *kinopravda* ["film-truth"].

Not "filming life unawares" for the sake of the "unaware," but in order to show people without masks, without makeup, to catch them through the eye of the camera in a moment when they are not acting, to read their thoughts, laid bare by the camera.

Kino-eye as the possibility of making the invisible visible, the unclear clear, the hidden manifest, the disguised overt, the acted nonacted; making falsehood into truth.

Kino-eye as the union of science with newsreel to further the

---

thoughts were revealed on my face—hesitation, vacillation, firmness (a struggle within myself), and again, the joy of victory. First thought of the kino-eye as a world perceived without a mask, as a world of naked truth (truth cannot be hidden)"—trans. and ed.

battle for the communist decoding of the world, as an attempt to show the truth on the screen—Film-truth.

1924

On *Kinopravda*

Kinopravda is, on the one hand, linked to the old type of newsreel. On the other hand, it is the present-day organ of the kinoks. I shall have to examine both these aspects in my report.

After the October Revolution, the Pathé and Gaumont newsreels and the newsreels of the Skobelev Committee were replaced by *Kinonedelia,* issued by the All-Russian Photo-Cinema Department.

Kinonedelia differed from the newsreels which preceded it perhaps only in that its subtitles were "Soviet." The subject matter remained the same, the same old parades and funerals. These were precisely the years when, still unfamiliar with the techniques of cinema, I began to work in cinema. By that time, despite its youth, cinema had already established unshakeable clichés, outside of which you were not allowed to work. My first experiments in assembling chance film clippings into more or less "harmonious" montage groups belong to this period.

It seemed to me then that one such experiment was a complete success, and for the first time I began to doubt the necessity of a literary connection between individual visual elements spliced together. I had to halt the experiment temporarily to work on a picture for the anniversary of the October Revolution.

This work served as the point of departure for *Kinopravda.* It was precisely during this period of experiment that several of us who had lost faith in the possibilities of "artistic" cinema and had faith in our own strength, sketched the first draft of the manifesto that later caused such commotion and brought our cinema-apostles so many unpleasant moments.

Skobelev Committee. Originally founded as an agency to assist veterans of the Russo-Japanese War, the Skobelev Committee established a Military Film Section in 1914. The Committee survived the Revolution and fell under the control of the Ministry of Education under the provisional government, producing short documentary films and becoming an agent of propaganda for the regime. It was later controlled by the Moscow City Soviet and produced short agitation films—ed.

History of the Civil War

After a long break (at the front) I again wound up in the Photo-Cinema Department and was soon thrown into newsreel. Having learned from bitter experience, I was terribly cautious in the first issues of *Kinopravda.* But as I became convinced that I had the sympathy of, if not all, then at least some viewers, I increased pressure on the material.

Alongside the support received from Alexei Gan, the constructivist, then publishing the journal *Kinofot,* I confronted ever-increasing internal and external opposition.

By the tenth issue of *Kinopravda,* feelings were running high.

The thirteenth issue of *Kinopravda* elicited the unexpected support of the press. The almost unanimous diagnosis—"insane"—after the release of the fourteenth issue, completely puzzled me. That was the most critical point in *Kinopravda*'s existence.

The fourteenth *Kinopravda* not only differed significantly from most newsreels of its time, but bore no resemblance even to the preceding issues of *Kinopravda.* Friends didn't understand and shook their heads. Enemies raged. Cameramen announced that they wouldn't film for *Kinopravda,* and the censors wouldn't pass *Kinopravda* at all (or rather they passed it, but cut exactly half, which was equivalent to destroying it). I myself was perplexed, I must admit. The film's structure seemed simple and clear to me. It took me a while to learn that my critics, brought up on literature, under the force of habit, could not do without a literary connection between the different items.

Later on it proved possible to eliminate the conflict. Young people and workers' clubs gave the film a good reception. There was no need to concern ourselves with the Nepman audience—the sumptuous *Indian Tomb* received them in its embrace.

The crisis passed. But the battle continued.

Kinopravda made heroic attempts to shield the proletariat from the corrupting influence of artistic film-drama. To many, these attempts seemed ridiculous. The paltry number of prints of *Kinopravda* could serve, at most, some thousands of people, not millions. But though *Kinopravda's* role in the creation of an extensive workers' repertoire was small, its propagandistic action in the battle with the commercial movie theater repertoire proved significant.

The charge was soon repudiated. The more farsighted amongst our deprecators clutched their heads and quickly began to imitate us—some of them quite early on. But many remained hostile to our work. A small group of conservative hacks, very obtuse people, tirelessly showered praise on filmed canned goods (mostly imported from abroad). These same people support the fabrication of similar film-surrogates (of far inferior quality, it is true). Thanks to their clumsy efforts every slightly successful revolutionary undertaking is being nipped in the bud.

Shaking off these self-appointed nursemaids is not advisable. In revenge, they'll set about proving it was *their* umbrellas that saved the public from the rain, that is, from the kinoks. And when the rain stops and the artistic drama's sun is shining, they fan the public obligingly. Thanks to these critics, the resplendent image of the

Indian Tomb. *Das Indische Grabmal* (1923), a film directed by Joe May with scenario by Fritz Lang—ed.

American millionaire-hero glows within the stern heart of the Russian proletariat.

Almost all those who work in artistic cinema are either openly or covertly hostile to *Kinopravda* and the kinoks. That is completely logical since, if our viewpoint prevails, they'll either have to learn to work all over again or leave cinema completely.

Neither group represents an immediate danger to the purity of the kinoks' position. Far more dangerous are the newly formed intermediate and, as it were, conciliatory, opportunistic groups. Adopting our methods, they transfer them to the artistic drama, thereby strengthening its position.

In attacking *Kinopravda* our detractors gloatingly point out that it's made from previously shot, and therefore "random" footage. To us this means that the newsreel is organized from bits of life into a theme, and not the reverse. This also means that *Kinopravda* doesn't order life to proceed according to a writer's scenario, but observes and records life *as it is,* and only then draws conclusions from these observations. It turns out that this is our advantage, not our shortcoming. *Kinopravda* is made with footage just as a house is made with bricks. With bricks one can make an oven, a Kremlin wall, and many other things. One can build various film-objects from footage. Just as good bricks are needed for a house, good film footage is needed to organize a film-object.

Hence the serious approach to newsreel—to that factory of film footage in which life, passing through the camera lens, does not vanish forever, leaving no trace, but does, on the contrary, leave a trace, precise and inimitable.

The moment and the manner in which we admit life into the lens and the way in which we fix the trace that remains determine the technical quality; they also determine the social and historical value of the footage and subsequently the quality of the whole object.

The thirteenth *Kinopravda,* released for Lenin's birthday, is constructed from footage demonstrating the relationship between two worlds: the capitalist world and the USSR. The footage is insufficient, but attempts generalization.

It's interesting to note that now, a year after the release of the fourteenth *Kinopravda,* orders are again coming in. As you can see, that newsreel has not grown obsolete and isn't soon likely to do so. And yet it was, in its day, the most berated issue of *Kinopravda.*

Kinopravda fifteen and sixteen concentrate footage shot over several months—one in winter, the other in spring—and both are experimental in character.

The seventeenth *Kinopravda* was released for the opening day of the All-Russian Agricultural Exhibition. It shows not so much the exhibition itself, but rather a "circulation of the blood" effected by the idea of the agricultural exhibition. A big stride from country fields to city. One foot is in rye, among villages; the other is set down in the exhibition area.

The eighteenth *Kinopravda* is the movie camera's marathon run from the Eiffel Tower in Paris via Moscow to the far-off Nadezhdinsk factory. This run through the thick of the revolutionary way of life had a tremendous effect on sincere viewers. Don't think that I'm bragging, comrades, but several people felt compelled to tell me that they regard the day they saw the eighteenth *Kinopravda* as the turning point in their understanding of Soviet reality.

The nineteenth *Kinopravda* you shall see today. The others can't be shown; they're already worn beyond recognition.

I won't attempt to describe in words the content of the latest *Kinopravda*—it's constructed visually. Using many visual threads it connects city with country, south with north, winter with summer, peasant women with urban working women and converges at the end, upon a single family, the amazing family of Vladimir Ilyich Lenin. There we see Lenin alive, and here—dead. Mastering their grief, impelled by their sense of duty, his wife and sister continue working with redoubled energy. The peasant works, and so does the urban woman, and so too, the woman film editor selecting the negative for *Kinopravda* . . .

Simultaneously with the releases of *Kinopravda*, the kinoks took over another area, which would not appear to have any immediate relationship to our goals—that of the cartoon and film-advertisement. Certain reasons impelled us to learn to handle this weapon.

In time it will come in handy.

The next kinok production is an experimental film, which we're making without a scenario, without the preliminary equivalent of a scenario. This effort is a reconnaissance operation of a very difficult and dangerous sort—which should not even be attempted when one's economically and technically unarmed. But we haven't the right to refuse the *impossible possibility* confronting us. We're trying to seize hold of reality with our bare hands.

Comrades, in the near future, perhaps even before the appearance of our next work, you will be seeing on Soviet screens a series of substitutes, motion pictures made in imitation of the kinoks. In some, actors will portray real life in an appropriate setting; in others real people will act out roles according to highly refined scenarios.

These are the work of compromisers—"film Mensheviks." Their work will resemble ours as a counterfeit banknote resembles a real one, or a big mechanical doll resembles a small child.

The international conflagration of "art" is at hand. Sensing destruction, workers in theater, artists, writers, choreographers, and canaries like them are fleeing in panic. Looking for shelter, they're running to cinema. The film studio is the last stronghold of art.

Sooner or later long-haired quacks of all sorts will come running. Artistic cinema will receive a tremendous reinforcement, but it won't escape . . .

We will explode art's tower of Babel.

1924

Artistic Drama and Kino-Eye

Comrades, I am speaking on behalf of the kinok group. As most of you know, our group doesn't connect either its existence or its work with what is called "art."

We engage directly in the study of the phenomena of life that surround us. We hold the ability to show and elucidate life as it is, considerably higher than the occasionally diverting doll games that people call theater, cinema, etc.

The actual theme of today's debate, "Art and Everyday Life," interests us less than the topic, say, of "Everyday Life and the Organization of Everyday Life," since, I repeat, it's precisely in this latter area that we work and consider it proper to do so.

To see and hear life, to note its turns and turning points, to catch the crunch of the old bones of everyday existence beneath the press of the Revolution, to follow the growth of the young Soviet organism, to record and organize the individual characteristics of life's phenomena into a whole, an essence, a conclusion—this is our immediate objective.

It is an objective with tremendous and far from merely experimental significance. It's a general checkup on our entire transitional time and, at the same time, an on-the-spot checkup, among the masses, on each individual decree or resolution.

It's a thermometer or aerometer of our reality, and its significance is unquestionably higher than the inventions of individual authors, individual writers, or directors.

Of course, this objective is beyond the strength of several people, or even several dozen people. It's an objective to be placed on the scale of the entire Soviet state.

A whole group of Soviet and party workers, who at present have turned uncertainly to so-called artistic cinema, ought to be turning their backs on what is essentially child's play. They ought to throw all their strength, their skills, and their experience in the direction of the movie camera's exploration and examination of our reality.

The ever-growing apparatus of worker correspondents and agricultural correspondents testifies to the fact that work of this sort will be real and not imaginary, that observation can be made sufficiently broad and deep, that the camera can reflect in concentrated form the mood and energy of the masses.

With the skillful organization of factual footage, we can create film-objects of *high propagandistic pressure,* without the annoying, suspect affectations of actors and without the romantic-detective fictions of various and sundry "inspired" people.

Artistic drama should occupy the place that newsreel now has in movie theater programs.

The remainder of the program should be filled by kino-eye work in science, education, and everyday life.

Film-drama tickles the nerves. Kino-eye helps one to see.

Kino-drama clouds the eye and the brain with a sweet fog. Kino-eye opens the eyes, clears the vision.

Kino-drama tightens the throat. Kino-eye brings a fresh spring wind to one's face, the free expanse of fields and forests, the breadth of life.

Can it really be that if NEP[1], if shopkeepers—no different from those under the tsar—are only ten proof away from *monopol'ka,* that our motion pictures as well should differ from tsarist and foreign pictures by only 10 percent?

Are we really obliged, in the name of profit, to make drunkards of the proletariat, using cinema-vodka, spiked with the antidote of propagandistic powder?

You can put up with a lot. You can also put up with the *cafés chantants* of NEP, if you know where you're going, if you see even a distant goal ahead.

You can put up with both artistic drama and its creators—the high priests of art—but not for a minute, not for an instant should you make this the chief goal of the Soviet film industry.

1924

The Essence of Kino-Eye

The kino-eye movement, led by us newsreel workers, the kinoks, is an international movement, and its development is keeping stride with the worldwide proletarian revolution.

Our basic, programmatic objective is to aid each oppressed individual and the proletariat as a whole in their effort to understand the phenomena of life around them.

The choice of facts recorded will suggest the necessary decision to the worker or peasant.

In the area of vision: the facts culled by the kinok-observers or cinema worker-correspondents (please do not confuse them with cinema worker-correspondents assigned to reviewing) are organized by film editors according to party instructions, distributed in the maximum possible numbers of prints and shown everywhere.

The method of radio-broadcasting images, just recently invented, can bring us still closer to our cherished basic goal—to unite all the workers scattered over the earth through a single consciousness, a single bond, a single collective will in the battle for communism.

This objective of ours we call kino-eye. The decoding of life as it is. Using facts to influence the workers' consciousness.

What we call radio-ear—that is, the organization of the audible world—does the same thing in the area of sound.

But since this influencing is done through facts, not through acting, dances, or verse, it means we devote very little attention to so-called art.

Yes, comrades, as many of you know, we relegate "art" to the periphery of our consciousness.

And this is wholly understandable. We place life itself at the center of our attention and our work, and by the recording of life we all understand the recording of the historical process; therefore, allow us, the technicians and ideologists of this work, to base our observation on society's economic structure, not screened off from the viewer's eye by a sweet-smelling veil of kisses and hocus-pocus, constructivist or not as the case may be.

Instead of surrogates for life (theatrical performance, film-drama, etc.), we bring to the workers' consciousness facts (large and small), carefully selected, recorded, and organized from both the life of the workers themselves and from that of their class enemies.

The establishing of a class bond that is visual (kino-eye) and auditory (radio-ear) between the proletarians of all nations and all lands, based on the platform of the communist decoding of the world—that is our objective.

1925

To the Kinoks of the South

Dear comrades, I greet you on behalf of the conference of leaders of kino-eye groups.

The letter you've sent, the first since our getting acquainted in Moscow, is a sure step toward establishing a lasting connection with us.

You'll find most of the answers to the topics that interest you in a Proletkult anthology, coming out this month, which includes our long article "Kino-Eye" (I'll send you either the anthology or the article). A book or booklet with the same title, and one that will provide serious support to every kinok, is due to come out sometime in the future. In addition to articles, the program and regulations of the organization will be included in the book.

In the meantime I'll try to briefly answer several of your questions, within the limits of a letter.

The basis of our program is not film production for entertainment or profit (which we leave to artistic drama), but *a film bond between the peoples of the USSR and the entire world based on the platform of the communist decoding of what actually exists.*

We must stubbornly fight the seizure of production by high

priest-directors and resist filling the market with film-junk.

We must wage an extensive campaign in the press; we must not let ourselves get carried away by our successes in the plan for the imitation of foreign junk, we must support *Kinopravda* and other work by the kinoks.

The newsreel offensive is now being waged everywhere in workers' clubs, rural cinemas-on-wheels, village reading rooms and so forth (especially where cinema is being shown for the first time).

The peasant has a particularly developed mistrust of everything artificial, especially fake *muzhiks,* on the screen.

Observations made of peasant viewers during film showings in remote villages showed that the distinction that the peasant makes between the stylized artistic drama and the newsreel is a very deep one.

It can be compared to the difference in the perception of a rag doll and a real child, or the drawing of a horse and the horse itself.

We should make use of this natural and just mistrust of doll-like cinema on the part of the peasant in order to propagandize film-objects with real people and facts, film-objects without actors, sets, and so on. The worker and peasant viewers, having educated their vision on real film-objects (without the moon, love, or detectives) *will dictate their will* to film production, which as yet is completely oriented toward the commercial viewer.

I advise you to make every effort, even in your first newsreel works, to create a slant toward the scientific illumination of reality.

Familiarize yourself with animation films and with other special types of filming. Deepen your observations of life. Compare them with scientific data.

Keep all your achievements, inventions, practical reflections to yourselves, until you are given the opportunity to realize them in earnest.

For the time being, quit filming parades and funerals (too tiresome and boring); stop shooting newsreels of conferences with endless speakers (too untransmittable via the screen).

Organize footage into small film-objects, release, say, a "Russian *Kinopravda*" or something of that sort.

Once you have practiced, start on larger works, on the order of *Kinoglaz.*

1925

Kinopravda & Radiopravda

(BY WAY OF PROPOSAL)

The textile worker ought to see the worker in a factory making a machine essential to the textile worker. The worker at the machine tool plant ought to see the miner who gives his factory its essential fuel, coal. The coal miner ought to see the peasant who produces the bread essential to him.

Workers ought to see one another so that a close, indissoluble bond can be established among them. The workers of the USSR ought to see that in other lands—England, France, Spain—everywhere, there are workers just like themselves, and everywhere the class struggle between the proletariat and the bourgeoisie is being waged. But these workers live far from one another and are therefore unable to see each other.

Workers and peasants have to take the word of some individual (a teacher or propagandist) who describes the situation of workers and peasants living elsewhere. But every teacher, propagandist, priest, writer, etc., describes what's occurring elsewhere in his own words, determined by a whole series of factors: his convictions, education, ability to write or speak, his honesty, integrity, his "mood," and the state of his health at a given moment. How, therefore, can the workers see one another?

Kino-eye pursues precisely this goal of establishing a visual bond between the workers of the whole world. The kino-eye workers, the kinoks, are working in the area of newsreel (*Kinopravda*, *Kinokalendar*, *Kinoglaz*) and in that of scientific film (*Silk Growing*, *Rejuvenation*), or on the scientific part of a given film (*Abortion*, *Radiopravda*, etc).

The kino-eye movement is gradually gaining attention and support. Sympathetic letters from provincial areas, supporting the resolutions of peasant viewers, emerging groups of kinok-observers, the reinforcing of the kinoks by a new shift of Komsomol film production workers, and finally, portions of the state clientele that have turned to kino-eye—all these things are of considerable encouragement to us in our struggle.

Komsomol. The All-Union Lenin Communist Youth League, a mass organization of Soviet youth, founded in 1918 as the Russian Communist Youth League to aid the Communist Party in the education of Soviet youth—ed.

Three Songs of Lenin

In the present instance it's the movie theaters connected with feature-length pictures that are turning out to be the most conservative. It's essential to promote the slogan of "mixed programs":

a. the three-reel newsreel, on the model of *Kinoglaz*, say, *Leninist Kinopravda*;
b. a one-reel cartoon;
c. a one- or two-reel science (or travel) film;
d. a two-reel drama or comedy.

Mixed programs of this sort, to which we must gradually accustom both theaters and the public, are an entry into the commercial movie theaters; through them newsreel and scientific films can begin to pay their way and make a profit, even if they have cost considerable sums.

Enthusiasm

Of course the proportion can be changed in one direction or another. Back in 1922, Comrade Lenin already called for the establishment of a fixed ratio between "entertainment" pictures (made specifically for advertisement and profit) and propagandistic newsreel "from the life of the peoples in every land."

Somewhat later, in a private conversation with Comrade Lunacharsky, Comrade Lenin again mentioned the necessity of establishing a "fixed ratio between entertainment pictures and scientific ones" in movie theater programs, and pointed out that "the production of new films, imbued with communist ideas and reflecting Soviet reality, must begin with the newsreel." Lenin further added: "If you have good newsreels, serious educational films, then it doesn't matter if some useless film, of the more or less usual sort, is shown to attract an audience."

the production of new films. . . . Cf. the collection *Samoe vazhnoe iz vsekh iskusstv* ("The Most Important of the Arts") (Moscow, 1963), p. 123.

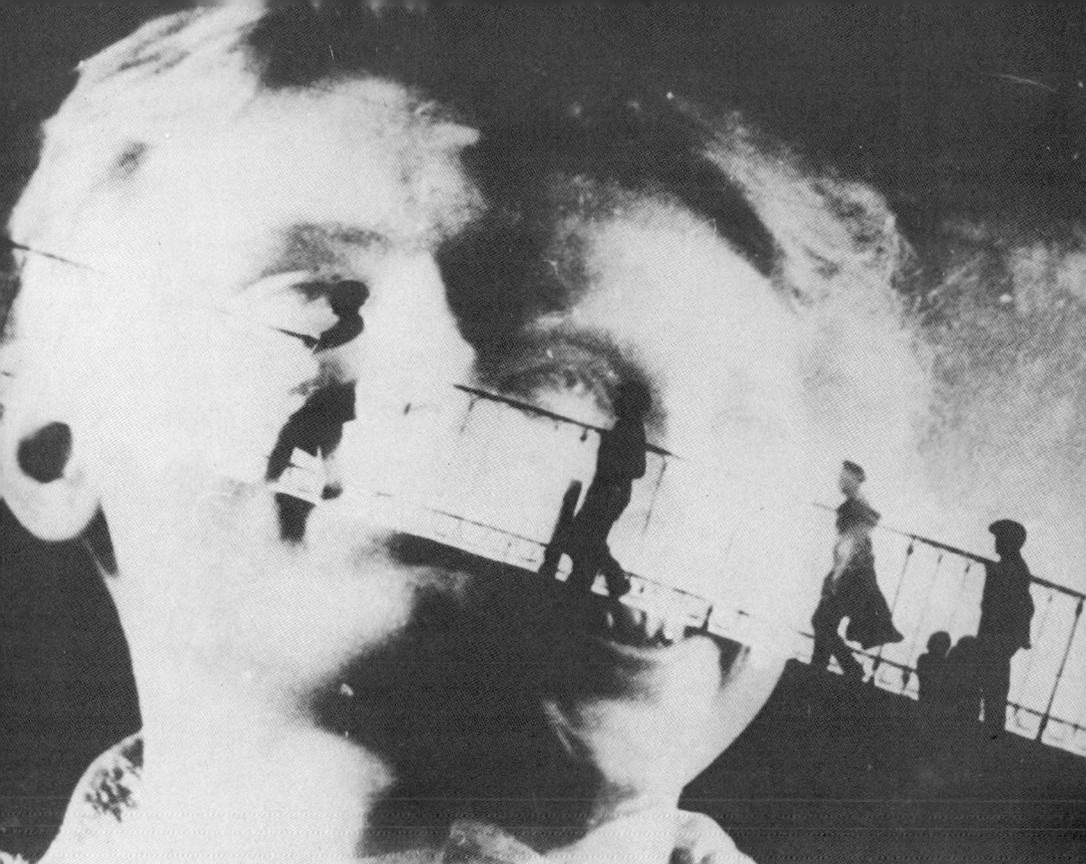

Enthusiasm

It's no secret to anyone that to this day Comrade Lenin's persistent instruction has not begun to be carried out.

The kinok's work in newsreel and scientific film is placed in an extremely disadvantageous and dependent position in relation to artistic cinema, since the latter fills the movie theater program with big capital and all the best tools of production at its disposal.

Against this chart:
Artistic cinema 95%
Scientific, educational films; travelogues 5%

we've got to promote this chart:

Kino-eye (everyday life) 45%
Scientific, educational 30%
Artistic drama 25%

In this way, the question of kino-eye, that is, of organizing the workers' vision, will be solved. The second position of the kinoks has to do with organizing what the workers hear.

We are promoting propaganda using facts, not on the level of vision alone, but on that of hearing too.

How can we establish an audio link right along the front line of the world proletariat?

If, with respect to vision, our kinok-observers have recorded visible life phenomena with cameras, we must now talk about recording audible facts.

We're aware of one recording device; the gramophone. But there are others more perfect; they record every rustle, every whisper, the sound of a waterfall, a public speaker's address, etc.

The broadcast of this record can, after its organization and editing, easily be transmitted by radio, as "Radiopravda."

Here, too, in the broadcasting program of every radio station, a fixed ratio can be established between radio dramas, radio concerts, and radio news "from the life of the peoples in every land."

A "radio-newspaper" minus paper and limits of distance (Lenin), that is radio's basic significance, not the broadcasts of *Carmen, Rigoletto,* songs, and such, with which our radio-broadcasting has begun to develop its work.

Before it's too late, we must save our radio from getting carried away with "artistic broadcasts" (i.e., the domination of artistic cinema).

To artistic cinema we oppose kinopravda and kino-eye; to artistic radio broadcasts we oppose radiopravda and radio-ear.

Technology is moving swiftly ahead. A method for broadcasting images by radio has already been invented. In addition, a method for recording auditory phenomena on film tape has been discovered.

In the near future man will be able to broadcast to the entire world the visual and auditory phenomena recorded by the radio-movie camera.

We must prepare to turn these inventions of the capitalist world to its own destruction.

We will not prepare for the broadcast of operas and dramas. We will prepare wholeheartedly to give the workers of every land the opportunity to see and hear the whole world in an organized form; to see, hear, and understand one another.

1925

The Same Thing from Different Angles

The allegation is false that a fact taken from life, when recorded by the camera loses the right to be called a fact if its name, date, place, and number are not inscribed on the film.

Every instant of life shot unstaged, every individual frame shot *just as it is* in life with a hidden camera, "caught unawares," or by some other analogous technique—represents a fact recorded on film, a *film-fact* as we call it.

A dog running by on the street is a visible fact even if we don't catch up with it to read what's written on its collar.

An Eskimo on the screen remains an Eskimo even if he's not labeled "Nanook."

It would be completely absurd to try to have each individual shot (as a general rule) answer an entire questionnaire: where, when, why, date of birth, family situation, etc.

In a film archive, a storehouse, or museum where footage from current newsreels is kept in numbered chronological order, all the necessary data can be appended to each box of negatives, such as a detailed description of each film-fact, relevant newspaper clippings, biographical and other data.

This is necessary so that a film editor in constructing a film-object on a given theme will not make errors and mix up the facts in time or space.

In those films in which space is overcome by montage (for example, "workers of one country see those of another"), it's all the more essential that the editor take into account all data on the film footage to be organized.

But this does not in any way mean that the editor has to set forth all this data in the picture in the form of an information supplement to each shot or group of shots. This data only represents cover documents, as it were, for the editor, a kind of guide to the correct "editing route."

1926

The Factory of Facts

(BY WAY OF PROPOSAL)

After five years of stubborn prospecting work, the kino-eye method has now won out completely in the area of the *nonacted* film (See *Kino-eye's First Reconnaissance Mission*, *Leninist Kino-pravda*, *Forward, Soviet!*, and *One Sixth of the World* in current release).

Right now—as the experience of the past year shows—the simple adoption of kino-eye's external manner alone by the so-called artistic film (the acted film, the film with actors), suffices to create a big stir *(Strike, Potemkin)* in that area of film as well.

We can see in what divergent ways the kino-eye method is now forcing the "acted," "actor's" film out of cinema. The growing adoption of kino-eye's external manner by the "acted" film *(Strike* and *Potemkin)* is only an isolated incident, a random reflection of the ever-growing kino-eye movement. I won't go into it here. How soon, in what way, at the price of what disillusionments the proletarian viewer will gradually come to realize the impossibility of saving the decrepit and degenerate "actor's" film by even regular injection of certain kino-eye elements—that question belongs to the future.

But the topic for the present, for today, is the issue raised by Comrade Fevralsky in his timely article in *Pravda* (June 15) of a single *center* for the work and workers of kino-eye, the issue of a solid base for kino-eye work.

Comrade Fevralsky is absolutely right to speak of the urgent necessity for immediate centralization of all types of nontheatrical, nonacted film.

The storing of newsreels, the production of Soviet film-magazines, the production of *Kinopravda,* animation rooms, of major kino-eye films, the reediting and correction of foreign "cultural films" finally the production of film hits without actors such as *One Sixth of the World*—all this should be concentrated in a single place and not

Comrade Fevralsky. Alexander V. Fevralsky (1901-), Soviet literary and art critic and author of essays on Meyerhold and Mayakovsky. In 1925 he published an article supporting kino-eye methods and aims and advocating radio and cinema as important and powerful instruments of education and propaganda, of great use in the efforts to reorganize the Soviet economy.

(as currently) splintered throughout all the sections and buildings of Goskino-Sovkino.

All nonacted film in one single place, together with a film laboratory. Together with a vault for nonacted films.

Our point of view is this:

Alongside the unified film-factory of grimaces (the union of every type of theatrical film work, from Sabinsky to Eisenstein) we must form a

FILM-FACTORY OF FACTS

the union of all types of kino-eye work, from current flash-newsreels to scientific films, from thematic *Kinopravda*s to stirring revolutionary film marathon runs.

Once again.

Not FEKS, not Eisenstein's "factory of attractions," not the factory of doves and kisses (directors of this sort have not yet died out), and not the factory of death, either (*The Minaret of Death*, *Death Bay*, *Tripoli Tragedy*, etc.).

Simply:

the FACTORY OF FACTS.

Filming facts. Sorting facts. Disseminating facts. Agitating with facts. Propaganda with facts. Fists made of facts.

- Lightning flashes of facts.
- Mountains of facts.

Sabinsky. Cheslav G. Sabinsky (1885–1941), a set designer and film director, one of the pioneers of prerevolutionary Russian cinema.
FEKS. FEKS is the acronym of the Factory of the Eccentric Actor (Fabrika eksentricheskogo aktera), the name taken by a group of young theater and film artists formed in Leningrad in 1922. According to Grigori Kozintsev, one of its leading exponents, it was "a laboratory in which, through an original alliance between 'left' art [mainly Meyerhold and Mayakovsky] and the filmic practice of Chaplin, Mack Sennett, Stroheim, we formed a system of film acting style. Kabuki, black theatre, circus and a rejection of naturalism composed its basis." (These forms, one might add, also influenced a number of other innovative theatrical styles of that period in the USSR and elsewhere.) Among the films produced by the members of the group was a version of Gogol's *The Cloak* (1926)—ed.
Eisenstein's "factory of attractions". A reference to S. M. Eisenstein's theory of theatrical and cinematographic effect as built upon a series of shock moments or "attractions." The theory is heavily dependent upon Pavlovian reflexology. Eisenstein's article developing these views, "The Montage of Attractions," was published in *LEF* no. 3 (1923)—ed.
The Minaret of Death, Death Bay, Tripoli Tragedy. Third-rate Soviet films of extremely low artistic quality from the mid 1920s.

- Hurricanes of facts.
- And individual little factlets.
- Against film-sorcery.
- Against film-mystification.
- For the genuine cinematification of the worker-peasant USSR.

1926

Kino-Eye

I

A Drawing in the Journal Lapot'

A poster. Showing little flowers. Telegraph poles. Petals. Little birds. A sickle. An operatic, curly-headed peasant with a sheaf of rye is theatrically shaking the hand of a sugary worker, shouldering a hammer and with a roll of calico under his arm. The sun is rising. Beneath is written: "The Union of Town and Country."

It's a poster meant for the countryside. Two peasants stand before it:

"Come and see what union is like, Uncle Ivan. There. But what's it like for us? They've brought two plows, and newspapers . . . and that's it. . . ."

"Be quiet and use your head! Think that's a real union? Those are actors playing in a theater."

This drawing in *Lapot'* reminds me of the peasants' attitude toward the depictions on the painted agit-trains of the All-Russian Central Executive Committee (1919–1921).

Horse-"Actors"

The peasants called not only the drawings of Cossacks daubed on the walls of the train cars "actors" but also the horses depicted there, simply because they were incorrectly shod in the drawing.

The more remote the place, the less the peasants grasped the general, urgent, agitational meaning of the drawings. They'd carefully look over each drawing, each figure individually. They'd answer my questions concerning whether or not they liked the drawings: "We don't know, we're ignorant and uneducated folk."

That did not prevent the peasants from talking and laughing among themselves, however, and laughing unequivocally at the "actor"-horses.

A Film Showing in the Country

1920.

I'm in charge of a cinema-train car. We're showing films at a remote station.

There's a film-drama on the screen. The Whites and the Reds. The Whites drink, dance, kiss half-naked women; during the interludes they shoot Red prisoners. The Reds underground. The Reds at the front. The Reds fighting. The Reds win and put all the drunken Whites and their women in prison.

The content's good, but why should anyone want to show film-dramas based on the same old cliché used five years ago?

The viewers—illiterate and uneducated peasants—don't read the titles. They can't grasp the plot. They examine individual details, like the drawings on the decorated train.

Coolness and distrust.

These still unspoiled viewers don't understand artificial theatricality. A "lady" remains a lady to them, no matter what "peasant clothing" you show her in. These viewers are seeing the film screen for the first or second time; they still don't understand the taste of film-moonshine; and when, after the sugary actors of a film-drama, real peasants appear on the screen, they all perk up and stare at the screen.

A real tractor, which these viewers know of only from hearsay, has plowed over a few acres in a matter of minutes, before their very eyes. Conversations, shouts, questions. There's no question of actors. On the screen are their own kind, real people. There isn't a single false, theatrical movement to unmask the screen, to shake the peasants' confidence.

This sharp division between the perception of film-drama and newsreel has been noted every place where film has been shown for the first, second, or third time—every place where the poison had not yet penetrated, where the addiction to the toxic sweetness of artistic drama and its kisses, sighs, and murders had not yet set in.

"Petrushka" or Life

It was at the time when only the outlines of the kino-eye movement were visible, when we had to decide whether to keep in step with artistic cinematography and with the whole fraternity of directors who produce film-vodka—a legal and profitable business—or declare war on artistic cinema and begin to build cinema anew.

"Is it to be Petrushka or life?" we asked the viewers.

"Petrushka," answered the hopelessly infected. "We already know life—we don't need life. Keep life, boring life, from us."

"Life," answered those viewers who were not hopelessly infected, or free of infection. "We don't know life. We have not seen life. We know our country village and the ten versts around it. Show us life."

At a Kinok Conference

If we really want to understand the effect the motion picture has on the viewer, then we must first settle two things:

1. which viewer?
2. what effect on the viewer are we talking about?

The effect of the usual artistic drama on the steady viewer is that of the customary cigar or cigarette on the smoker. Poisoned by film-nicotine, the viewer sticks like a leech to the screen that tickles his nerves. A film-object made of newsreel footage will do much to sober this viewer, and, if we're speaking of taste, will seem to him *an unpleasant antidote.*

The contrary holds for the untouched viewer who has not yet seen film and consequently has never seen art-dramas. His education, his habits begin with the object that we show him. If, after a number of our *Kinopravda*s, we show him an art-drama, it will taste as bitter to him as a strong cigarette to someone smoking for the first time.

We are well supplied with film-smokes from abroad. Admittedly, there are more butts than cigarettes. The film-cigarettes play first-run houses, while the film-butts are set aside for the countryside, the masses.

Petrushka. The Punch of the Russian puppet theater—trans.

What are our film directors trying to prove when, in imitation of foreign models, they stick red labels on their products? They're not trying to prove anything and they can't. They're working on the poisoned viewer, peddling a poisoned product; and so that it won't remind us of a tsarist product they give it a revolutionary look and scent and pin a red banner on the appropriate spot.

And so the kinoks, wanting no part of this dirty business of pinning banners where they don't belong, have released (following work on nineteen *Kinopravdas*) a major experiment—the first part of *Kino-eye,* which, for all its faults, intended to (and actually did) block the art-drama's path of development and oriented at least part of the audience in the other direction.

II
The Essence of the Artistic Film-Drama

The essence of the artistic drama (like that of the theatrical drama) is to act out before the viewer a romantic, detective, or social "fairy tale" adroitly and convincingly enough to put him in a state of intoxication and to cram some idea, some thought or other, into his subconscious.

> Audience of the faithful with the pope
> (*Prozhektor* ["Spotlight"] no. 3,
> Letter from Sandro Rossetti)
>
> . . . Mournful, monotonous chanting in the nave thronged with the faithful at prayer. Sultriness, the smell of incense, of smoking wicks, of close breathing—all is specially suited, first and foremost, to physically stupefy the poor minds of Christ's flock.

Stupefaction and suggestion—the art-drama's basic means of influence—relate to that of a religion and enable it for a time to maintain a man in an excited unconscious state. We are familiar with examples of direct suggestion (hypnosis), with examples of sexual suggestion, when a woman in exciting her husband or lover can suggest any thoughts or acts to him.

Musical, theatrical, and film-theatrical representations act, above all, on the viewer's or listener's subconscious, completely circumventing his protesting consciousness.

The Man with a Movie Camera

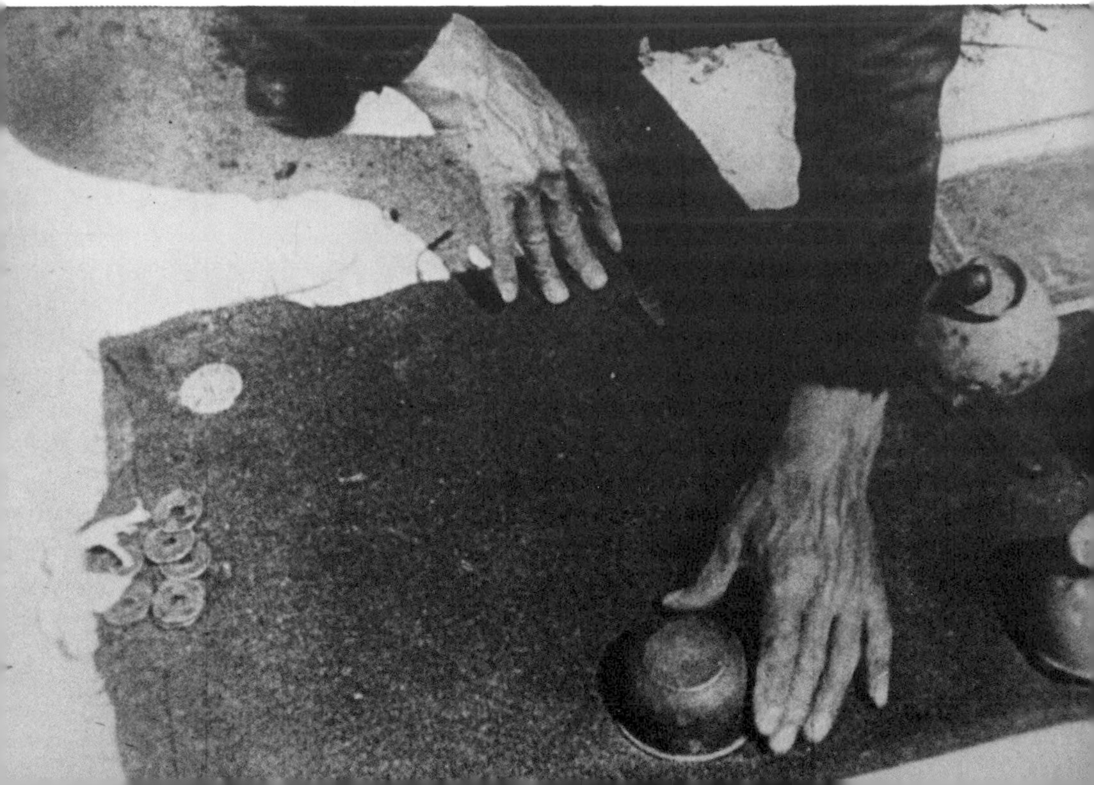

The Man with a Movie Camera

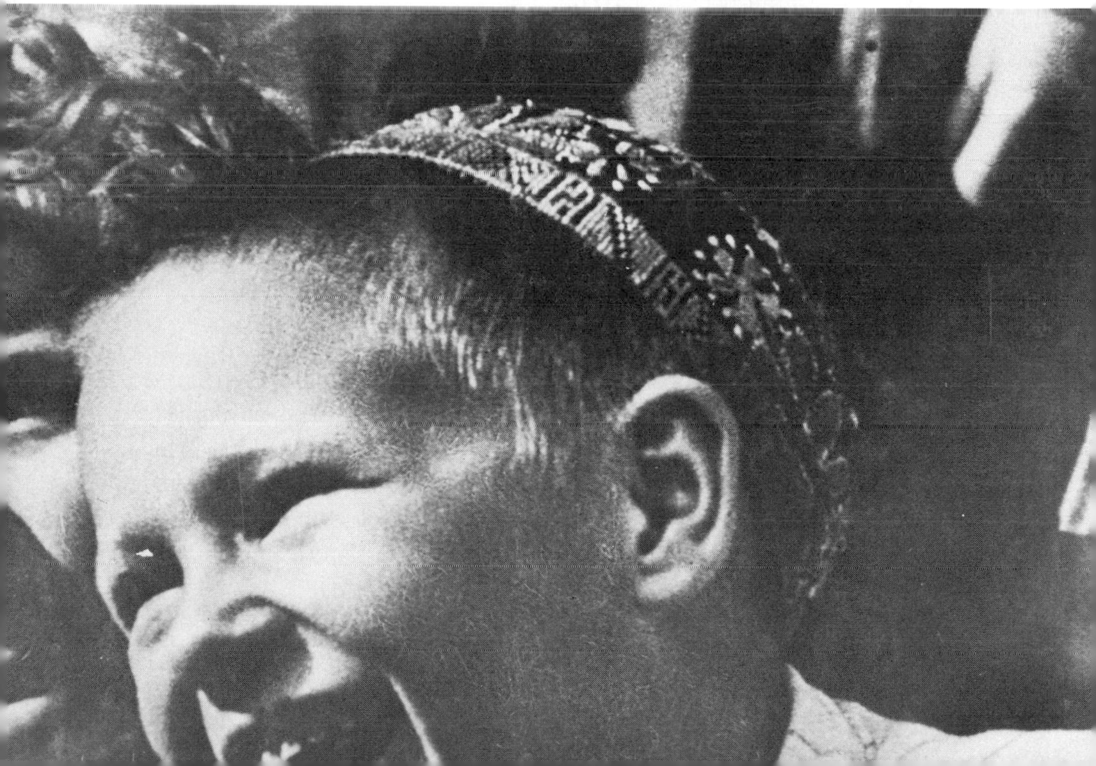

Consciousness or the Subconscious

(From a kinok proclamation)

We oppose the collusion of the "director-as-magician" and a bewitched public.

Only consciousness can fight the sway of magic in all its forms.

Only consciousness can form a man of firm opinion, firm conviction.

We need conscious men, not an unconscious mass submissive to any passing suggestion.

Long live the class consciousness of the healthy with eyes and ears to see and hear with!

Away with the fragrant veil of kisses, murders, doves, and sleight-of-hand!

Long live the class vision!

Long live kino-eye!

III

The Basis of Kino-Eye

The establishment of a visual (kino-eye) and auditory (radio-ear) class bond between the proletariats of all nations and lands on a platform of the communist decoding of world relations.

The decoding of life as it is.

Influence of facts upon workers' consciousness.

Influence of facts, not acting, dance, or verse.

Relegation of so-called art—to the periphery of consciousness.

Placing of society's economic structure at the center of attention.

Instead of surrogates for life (theatrical presentations, film-drama, etc.) carefully selected, recorded, and organized facts (major or minor) from the lives of the workers themselves as well as from those of their class enemies.

From a Talk by a Group Leader

Through this visit we learned how films are made. From production to screening, the fellows followed the making of an artistic drama. They saw for themselves a studio, actors, and directors. They saw the construction of films by kinoks; and as a result, for the seventh anniversary of the October Revolution, the group put up a huge poster on their car: "Down with actors and artistic dramas—

give us a new cinema!" And in brackets, "Friends of the kinoks, eleventh and ninety-third detachments of the Krasnaia Presnia Young Pioneers."

The group has about fifteen active members. Among a number of gifts received on the detachment's anniversary was one from the kinoks: a real still camera with all the accessories. There was no end to our joy.

Right now the fellows are putting out a weekly newspaper of their own, *Photo-eye*, consisting of their own photographs (every photograph, even those that have not turned out, is included). Through this newspaper they can gauge their progress in photography, and, in addition, illuminate all the main events in their lives each week.

The detachment corresponds with the countryside and with pioneers in other cities of the Soviet Union—Rybinsk, Voronezh, Barnaul, etc.—and they feel it's their duty to tell everyone about their group and about *Photo-eye.*

In order to review our work a diary is kept by each in turn. Certain interesting moments in the life of the group are described in it.

Provisional Instructions to Kino-Eye Groups

1. Introduction

Our eye sees very poorly and very little—and so men conceived of the microscope in order to see invisible phenomena; and they discovered the telescope in order to see and explore distant, unknown worlds. The movie camera was invented in order to penetrate deeper into the visible world, to explore and record visual phenomena, so that we do not forget what happens and what the future must take into account.

But the camera experienced a misfortune. It was invented at a time when there was no single country in which capital was not in power. The bourgeoisie's hellish idea consisted of using the new toy to entertain the masses, or rather to divert the workers' attention from their basic aim: the struggle against their masters. Under the

Young Pioneers. The Young Pioneers were established by the fifth Komsomol Congress in 1922 for children between the ages of ten and fourteen. The organization stressed collective action rather than individual incentive and competition. In Vertov's *Kinoglaz* of 1924, members are active in campaigns for price control, the elimination of alcoholism, and in other aspects of public education—ed.

Mikhail Kaufman

electric narcotic of the movie theaters, the more or less starving proletariat, the jobless, unclenched its iron fist and unwittingly submitted to the corrupting influence of the masters' cinema. The theater is expensive and seats are few. And so the masters force the camera to disseminate theatrical productions that show us how the bourgeoisie love, how they suffer, how they "care for" their workers, and how these higher beings, the aristocracy, differ from lower ones (workers, peasants, etc.).

In prerevolutionary Russia the masters' cinema played a precisely similar role. After the October Revolution the cinema was faced with the difficult task of adapting itself to the new life. Actors who had played tsarist civil servants began to play workers; those who had played ladies of the court are now grimacing in Soviet style. Few of us yet realize, however, that all this grimacing remains, in many respects, within the framework of bourgeois technique and theatrical form. We know many enemies of the contemporary theater who are at the same time passionate admirers of cinema in its present form.

Few people see clearly as yet that nontheatrical cinema (with the exception of newsreel and some scientific films) does not exist.

Every theatrical presentation, every motion picture is constructed in exactly the same way: a playwright or scriptwriter, then a director or film director, then actors, rehearsals, sets, and the presentation to the public. The essential thing in theater is acting, and so *every motion picture constructed upon a scenario and acting is a theatrical presentation,* and that is why there are no differences between the productions by directors of different nuances.

All of this, both in whole and in part, applies to theater regardless of its trend and direction, regardless of its relationship to theater as such. *All of this lies outside the genuine purpose of the movie camera—the exploration of the phenomena of life.*

Kinopravda has clearly shown that *it is possible to work outside theater and in step with the revolution. Kino-eye is continuing the work, begun by kinopravda, of creating Red Soviet cinema.*

2. The Work of Kino-Eye

On the basis of reports by film-observers a plan for the orientation and offensive of the movie camera in life's ever-changing environment is being worked out by the Council of Kino-Eye. The work of the movie camera is reminiscent of the work of the agents of the GPU who do not know what lies ahead, but have a definite assignment: to separate out and bring to light a particular issue, a particular affair.

1. The kinok-observer closely watches the environment and the people around him and tries to connect separate, isolated phenomena according to generalized or distinctive characteristics. The kinok-observer is assigned a theme by the leader.

2. The group leader or film [reconnaissance] scout distributes themes to the observers and, in the beginning, helps each observer to summarize his observations. When the leader has collected all the summaries, he in turn classifies them and rearranges the individual data until a sufficiently clear construction of the theme is achieved.

Themes for initial observation can be split into roughly three categories:

a. *Observation of a place* (for example, a village reading room, a cooperative)

b. *Observation of a person or object in motion* (examples: your father, a Young Pioneer, a postman, a streetcar, etc.)

c. *Observation of a theme irrespective of particular persons or places* (examples: water, bread, footwear, fathers and children, city and country, tears, laughter, etc.)

The group leader must teach them to use a camera (later, a movie camera) in order to photograph the more striking moments of observation for a bulletin-board newspaper.

A bulletin-board newspaper is issued monthly or every two weeks and uses photographs to illustrate the life of a factory, plant, or village; it participates in campaigns, reveals surrounding life as fully as possible, agitates, propagandizes, and organizes. The group leader submits his work for approval by the Goskino cell of the Red *kinoks* and is under the immediate supervision of the Council of Kino-Eye.

3. The *Council of Kino-Eye* heads the entire organization. It is made up of one representative from each group of kinok-observers, one representative of the unorganized kinoks, and, provisionally, three representatives of the kinok production workers.

In its practical, everyday work the Council of Kino-Eye relies upon a technical staff—the Goskino cell of Red kinoks.

The Goskino kinoks' cell should be regarded as one of the factories in which the raw material supplied by kinok-observers is made into film-objects.

The Goskino kinoks' cell should also be regarded as an educational, model workshop through which Young Pioneer and Komsomol film groups will be drawn into production work.

Specifically, all groups of kinok-observers will be drawn

into the production of future kino-eye series. They will be the author-creators of all subsequent film-objects.

This departure from authorship by one person or a group of persons to mass authorship will, in our view, accelerate the destruction of bourgeois, artistic cinema and its attributes: the poser-actor, fairy-tale script, those costly toys—sets, and the director–high priest.

3. *Very Simple Slogans*

1. Film-drama is the opium of the people.
2. Down with the immortal kings and queens of the screen! Long live the ordinary mortal, filmed in life at his daily tasks!
3. Down with the bourgeois fairy-tale script! Long live life as it is!
4. Film-drama and religion are deadly weapons in the hands of the capitalists. By showing our revolutionary way of life, we will wrest that weapon from the enemy's hands.
5. The contemporary artistic drama is a vestige of the old world. It is an attempt to pour our revolutionary reality into bourgeois molds.
6. Down with the staging of everyday life! Film us as we are.
7. The scenario is a fairy tale invented for us by a writer. We live our own lives, and we do not submit to anyone's fictions.
8. Each of us does his task in life and does not prevent anyone else from working. The film workers' task is to film us so as not to interfere with our work.
9. Long live the kino-eye of the proletarian revolution!

4. *The Kinoks and Editing*

By editing, artistic cinema usually means the *splicing together of individual filmed scenes* according to a scenario, worked out to a greater or lesser extent by the director.

The kinoks attribute a completely different significance to editing and regard it as the *organization of the visible world.*

The kinoks distinguish among:

1. *Editing during observation*—orienting the unaided eye at any place, any time.
2. *Editing after observation*—mentally organizing what has been seen, according to characteristic features.
3. *Editing during filming*—orienting the aided eye of the movie camera in the place inspected in step 1. Adjusting for the somewhat changed conditions of filming.
4. *Editing after filming*—roughly organizing the footage according to characteristic features. Looking for the montage fragments that are lacking.
5. *Gauging by sight (hunting for montage fragments)*—instantaneous orienting in any visual environment so as to capture the essential link shots. Exceptional attentiveness. A military rule: gauging by sight, speed, attack.
6. *The final editing*—revealing minor, concealed themes together with the major ones. Reorganizing all the footage into the best sequence. Bringing out the core of the film-object. Coordinating similar elements, and finally, numerically calculating the montage groupings.

When filming under conditions which do not permit preliminary observation—as in shadowing with a movie camera or filming unobserved—the first two steps drop away and the third or fifth step comes to the fore.

When filming short moments, or in rush filming, the combining of several steps is possible.

In all other instances, when filming one or several themes, all the steps are carried out and the editing is uninterrupted, *beginning with the initial observation and ending with the finished film-object.*

5. The Kinoks and the Scenario

It is entirely appropriate to mention the script here. Once added to the above-mentioned editing system, a literary scenario immediately cancels its meaning and significance. Because our objects are constructed by editing, by organizing the footage of everyday life, unlike artistic dramas that are constructed by the writer's pen.

Does this mean that we work haphazardly, without thought or plan? Nothing of the kind.

If, however, we compare our *preliminary plan* to the plan of a commission that sets out, let us say, to investigate the living quarters of the unemployed, then we must compare the scenario to a short story of that investigation *written before* the investigation has taken place.

How do artistic cinema and the kinoks each proceed in the present case?

The kinoks organize a film-object on the basis of the factual film-data of the investigation.

After polishing up a scenario, *film directors* will shoot some entertaining film-illustrations to go with it: a couple of kisses, a few tears, a murder, moonlit clouds rushing above, and a dove. At the end they write "Long live. . . . !" and it all ends with "The Internationale."

Such, with minor changes, are all film-art-agitdramas.

When a picture ends with "The Internationale," the censors usually pass it, but the viewers always feel a bit uneasy hearing the proletarian hymn in such a bourgeois context.

A scenario is the invention of an individual or a group of people; it is a short story that these people desire to transfer to the screen.

We do not consider this desire criminal, but presenting this sort of work as cinema's main objective, ousting real film-objects with these little film short stories, and suppressing all the movie camera's remarkable possibilities in worship of the god of art-drama—this we cannot understand and do not, of course, accept.

We have not come to cinema in order to feed fairy tales to the Nepmen and Nepwomen lounging in the loges of our first-class movie theaters.

We are not tearing down artistic cinema in order to soothe and amuse the consciousness of the working masses with new rattles.

We have come to serve a particular class, the workers and peasants not yet caught in the sweet web of art-dramas.

We have come to show the world as it is, and to explain to the worker the bourgeois structure of the world.

We want to bring clarity into the worker's awareness of the phenomena concerning him and surrounding him. To give everyone working behind a plow or a machine the opportunity to see his

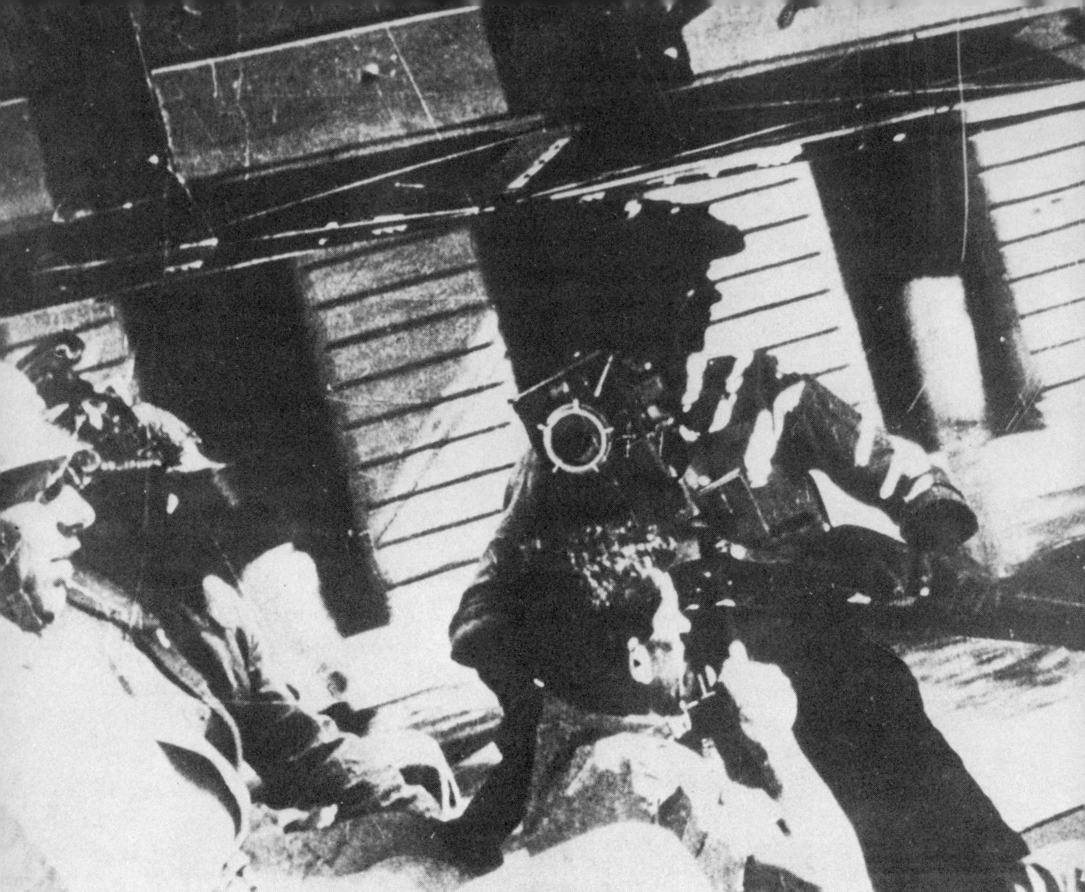

The Man with a Movie Camera

brothers at work with him simultaneously in different parts of the world and to see all his enemies, the exploiters.

We are taking our first steps in cinema, and that is why we are called kinoks. Existing cinema, as a commercial affair, like cinema as a sphere of art, has nothing in common with our work.

Even in technique we only partially overlap with so-called artistic cinema, since the goals we have set for ourselves require a different technical approach.

We have absolutely no need of huge studios or massive sets, just as we have no need for "mighty" film directors, "great" actors, and "amazing," photogenic women.

On the other hand, we must have:

1. quick means of transport,
2. more sensitive film,

3. small, lightweight, hand-held cameras,
4. lighting equipment that is equally lightweight,
5. a staff of lightning-fast film reporters,
6. an army of kinok-observers.

In our organization we distinguish amongst:

1. kinok-observers,
2. kinok-cameramen,
3. kinok-constructors [designers],
4. kinok-editors (women and men),
5. kinok laboratory assistants.

We teach our methods of cinema work only to Komsomols and Young Pioneers; we pass on our skill and our technical experience to the rising generation of young workers in whom we place our trust.

We venture to assure both respectable and not-so-respectable film directors that the cinema revolution is only beginning.

We will hold out without yielding a single position until the iron shift of young people eventually arrives, and then, all together, we will advance, over the head of bourgeois art-cinema, toward the cinematic October of the whole Soviet Union, of the whole world.

6. Kino-Eye on Its First Reconnaissance

Part One of the Film-object *Life Caught Unawares* The editing of *Kinoglaz,* Part One, was done according to the editing scheme set forth in an earlier section of the present article.

In Part One we note the following themes:

1. The "new" and the "old."
2. Children and grown-ups.
3. The cooperative system and the marketplace.
4. City and country.
5. The theme of bread.
6. The theme of meat.
7. A large theme: home-brew—cards—beer—shady business; "Ermakovka"—cocaine—tuberculosis—madness—death. A theme to which I find it difficult to

"Ermakovka." A hostel on Kalanchevsky Street in Moscow—ed.

give a single name, but one which I contrast here with the themes of health and vigor.

It is, if you like, a part of our terrible heritage from the bourgeois system and one that our revolution has not yet had the time or the opportunity to sweep away.

Along with the montage of themes (their coordination) and of each theme individually, we edited individual moments (the attack on the camp, the call for help, etc.).

I can point to the dancing of the drunken peasant women in the first section of *Kinoglaz* as an example of a montage moment not limited by time or space.

They were filmed at different times, in different villages, and edited together into a single whole.

The beer house and the market, actually all the rest . . . were also done through montage.

The raising of the flag on the day the camp opened can serve as a model of a montage instant *limited in time and space.*

Here, for a length of fifty feet, fifty-three moments that have been spliced together go by. Despite the very rapid change of subjects on the screen (one-fourth of a second is the maximum length of time an individual subject is present on the screen), this fragment can be viewed easily and does not tire one's vision (as verified by the worker-viewer).

On Shortcomings of *Kinoglaz,* Part One The film's excessive length should be mentioned as its chief shortcoming.

We must not forget that artistic films were also one- or two-reel in the beginning and that their footage was only gradually increased.

The field of kino-eye is a new one, and the portion being served to the viewer should be increased cautiously to avoid tiring him and shoving him into the arms of the art-drama.

Hoping to break into the big movie theaters, we yielded to the demand to provide a six-act film and . . . made a mistake; this has to be admitted. We must correct this mistake in the future and make small objects of various types that can be shown individually or in a group program as desired.

The overly broad sweep of Part One, the excessive number of themes interconnected at the expense of the deepening of each single one, can also be considered shortcomings.

This kind of approach to the first part is not coincidental; it was dictated partly by our intention to provide a broad exploration and, on the basis of that exploration, to penetrate deeper into life in the subsequent parts. Such an approach was also partly necessary since more time, artificial lighting, and a lot of animation filming were needed in order to develop completely some of the themes of *Kinoglaz.*

The expenditure of time meant a greater expenditure of money. The artificial lighting "limped on both legs," while the animation stand was so busy that we had to content ourselves with a ten-meter cartoon and ten illuminated titles.

I mention only these shortcomings—not that there are no others, but because we need to give first consideration to precisely the above-mentioned defects and mistakes and to draw appropriate conclusions for future work.

What We Lost and What We Gained in Releasing Part One We temporarily lost several organizational and technical positions. We had fewer joint meetings, and several members of the group almost left work and disappeared; the central leadership was weakened and the organizational core of it all somehow lost its focus.

At present all these organizational losses are almost fully recouped.

Of the technical positions that we temporarily ceded, the chief one is animation filming (filming each frame individually). We have done animation filming for a long time, since the first issues of *Kinopravda*, and consider it an important weapon in the struggle against artistic cinema.

For practice we shot various things (some were necessary, some were not) by this method: illuminated titles, maps, bulletins, cartoons, advertisements, and so forth.

We always announced at meetings and in the press that what we were doing in this area was only training, mere preparation for a serious departure into another essential area.

When, under the most trying conditions, the kinoks spent sleepless nights filming various cartoons, humoresques, etc., they had to be reassured that it would not be long now, that we were just about to begin the real animation work that was in the kinoks' plan.

Persistently we prepared the union of newsreel and scientific film in which the animation method was to play a decisive role. "Drawings in motion, blueprints in motion, the theory of relativity on the screen"—such was already the direction of the kinoks' first manifesto, written at the end of 1919, and before the film, *The Einstein Theory of Relativity,* was released abroad.

Because we were distracted by work on the first part of *Kinoglaz,* it turned out that our first scientific picture, *Abortion,* in which the kinok Belyakov had a significant part, was joined not with the factual footage in our plan, but with a bad romantic drama of a low order.

As was to be expected, *the union of science and drama did not occur.*

Dramatic footage looks very cheap and colorless beside scientific film. The scientific verity of such a picture is called into question by this sort of "artistic" proximity.

Clearly, if not for work on *Kinoglaz* we would not have lost this position and would have used this splendid opportunity to create something competent, healthy, and interesting.

We are not, of course, going to give up this position we've won.

We will continue this work, whether through an agreement with the department of scientific film, formed by our technical foundation, or by beginning to build afresh.

Kinopravda and the film-calendars have suffered somewhat, but we have already made good 80 percent of the loss.

The commercial cinema world greeted the first part of *Kinoglaz* with hostility, to the great joy of directors, actors, and the entire cinematic priestly caste. The big movie theaters would not even open their doors to such an "abomination."

The popularity of the slogan "kino-eye" nevertheless grew and continues to grow. A series of articles devoted to Part One cut its way through the entire party, Soviet, theatrical, and cinema press.

Kino-eye, photo-eye groups sprang up, etc.

Every day someone would leave a movie theater after seeing an art-drama, feeling disgust for the first time, and remember kino-eye.

As the slogan "kino-eye" spread, the popularity of the name itself grew.

Worker correspondents for various press organs began to sign themselves "kino-eye" when they described everyday phenomena; a kino-eye movie theater opened in Yaroslavl; the "kino-eye" of a

The Einstein Theory of Relativity. A film made in the United States in 1923 with animation by Max Fleischer—ed.

peacock's tail flashed by on Moscow posters; notes on kino-eye and caricatures of it became daily occurrences. . . .

But if it is possible to forgive a worker correspondent for *Komar* for signing "kino-eye" to the little scenes he's spied upon, one can't forgive a kino-eye theater for opening not with Part One of *Kinoglaz,* but with *The Indian Tomb* or something of that sort.

The filming of Part One of *Kinoglaz,* which interrupted our organizational work and deprived us of several technical positions, enriched our knowledge and experience.

In this work of ours we were testing ourselves, above all. Our most pressing tasks presented themselves more clearly and practically.

We really came to know those difficulties awaiting us, and although we haven't overcome them completely, we are already familiar with them now and understand how to overcome them. We learned a great deal in this struggle, and this lesson will not go to waste.

We have ceased to be merely experimenters; we are already assuming responsibility for the proletarian viewer; and, facing the businessmen and specialists boycotting us, we now close our ranks for a fierce battle.

1926

On *The Eleventh Year*

Comrades, *The Eleventh Year,* just like Part One of *Kinoglaz, Forward, Soviet!,* and *One Sixth of the World,* is one model, one type of nonacted film.

As the author of the film-object shown today, I would like to draw your attention to the following aspects of the film:

First of all, *The Eleventh Year* is written in the purest film-language, the "language of the eye." *The Eleventh Year* presumes visual perception, "visual thinking."

Secondly, *The Eleventh Year* is written by the camera in documentary language, in the language of facts recorded on film.

Thirdly, *The Eleventh Year* is written in socialist language, the language of the communist decoding of the visible world.

The Eleventh Year

Before you begin to discuss the film, I would also like to respond to several of the more interesting questions put to me during the last few days in connection with its screening at the Hermitage Cinema.

The first question: "Don't some of the shots in *The Eleventh Year* rely on symbolism?" No. We do not emphasize symbolism. If it turns out that several shots or montage phrases, when brought to perfection, develop the significance of symbols, we do not panic or feel we must exclude them from the film. We believe that a symbolist film and a series of shots constructed on the principle of expediency but developed to the significance of symbols are two completely different concepts.

The second question: "Why do you make use of complex shots, cinema-photo-montage?" We resort to complex shots either to show simultaneous action, or to separate a detail from the overall

The Eleventh Year

film-image, or to contrast two or more facts. The explanation of this as a trick method does not correspond to reality.

The third question: "Doesn't it seem to you that the first few reels are better edited than the subsequent ones?" Lately this question has been asked especially often. Such an impression is deceptive. The first reel is apparently on a level more easily perceived by the viewer. The fourth and fifth are constructed in a more complex way. There is much more inventive montage in them than in the first two; they look more to the future of cinematography than the second and third reels. I must say that the fourth and fifth reels have the same relationship to the first ones that college does to high school. It is natural that the more complex montage causes the viewer to experience greater tension and requires special attention in order to be perceived.

The fourth question: "Was *The Eleventh Year* made without a script?" Yes, like all kino-eye films, *The Eleventh Year* was made without a script. You know, in exploiting this rejection of the script our numerous opponents have attempted to present things as though we are against planned work altogether. Whereas, contrary to prevailing notions, the kinoks devote far more labor and attention to a preliminary plan than do workers in dramatic cinema. Before setting to work, a given theme is studied with great care in all of its aspects; literature on the issue is studied; in order to gain the clearest possible understanding of the matter every source is used. Before shooting, thematic, itinerary, and calendar plans are drawn up. How do these plans differ from a script? They differ in that all of this is the *plan of action for the movie camera* once the given theme appears in life, but not a *plan for staging* the same theme. How does the filming plan of an actual battle differ from a plan for staging a series of separate battle scenes? The difference between kino-eye's plan and the script in artistic cinematography amounts roughly to this.

The final question concerns titles and has been put by many comrades in this form: "How do you explain the abundance of titles in *One Sixth of the World* and the lack of them in *The Eleventh Year*?" In *One Sixth of the World* we were experimenting by putting titles in parentheses through the creation of a specific series of "word-themes." The word-theme has been abolished in *The Eleventh Year* and the significance of the titles reduced nearly to zero. The picture is constructed through the interweaving of film-phrases, without using titles. Titles have almost no significance in *The Eleventh Year*. Which is better, then? The first experiment or the second? I feel that both experiments—the creation of word-themes and their abolition—are equally important and of very great significance, for kino-eye and for all of Soviet cinema.

1928

The Man with a Movie Camera

Work on *The Man with a Movie Camera* required greater effort than previous works of kino-eye. This can be explained by the greater number of locations under observation as well as by complex organizational and technical operations while filming. The montage experiments demanded exceptional effort. These experiments went on constantly.

The Man with a Movie Camera is straightforward, inventive, and sharply contradicts that distributor's slogan: "The more clichés, the better." That slogan prevents us, the workers on this film, from thinking of rest despite great fatigue. We must make the distributors put aside their slogan with respect to the film. *The Man with a Movie Camera* needs maximal, inventive presentation.

In Kharkov I was asked: "How is it that you're in favor of stirring titles, and suddenly we have *The Man with a Movie Camera*—a film without words or titles?" My response was, "No, I'm not in favor of stirring titles, not in favor of titles at all—that's the invention of certain critics!"

Indeed, the kino-eye group, following its renunciation of the film studio, of actors, sets, and the script, fought for a decisive cleaning up of film-language, for its complete separation from the language of theater and literature. Thus, in *One Sixth of the World* the titles are, as it were, factored out of the picture and isolated into a contrapuntally constructed word-radio-theme.

"Very little room is devoted to titles in *The Eleventh Year* (their modest role is further expressed by the graphic execution of the titles), so that a title can be cut out without in any way disturbing the film's force." (*Kinofront* no. 2, 1928)

And further: "In its specific weight and practical significance the intertitle in a genuine film-object (and *The Eleventh Year* is such) is just like the quotation about gold from *Timon of Athens* in Marx's analysis of money in *Capital*. Incidentally, for the most part these titles are precise quotations, which might stand for the text during the layout of a book." (*Kinofront* no. 2, 1928).

Thus the complete absence of titles in *The Man with a Movie Camera* does not come as something unexpected, but has been prepared for by all the previous kino-eye experiments.

The Man with a Movie Camera represents not only a practical result; it is, as well, a theoretical manifestation on the screen. That is apparently why public debates on it in Kharkov and Kiev assumed the aspect of a fierce battle between representatives of various trends in so-called art. Moreover, the dispute took place on several levels at once. Some said *The Man with a Movie Camera* was an experiment in visual music, a visual concert. Others saw the film in

The Man with a Movie Camera

terms of a higher mathematics of montage. Still others declared that it was not "life as it is," but life the way *they* do not see it, etc.

In fact, the film is only the sum of the facts recorded on film, or, if you like, not merely the sum, but the product, a "higher mathematics" of facts. Each item or each factor is a separate little document. The documents have been joined with one another so that, on the one hand, the film would consist only of those linkages between signifying pieces that coincide with the visual linkages and so that, on the other hand, these linkages would not require intertitles; the final sum of all these linkages represents, therefore, an organic whole.

This complex experiment, whose success is admitted by the majority of those comrades who have expressed any opinion, frees us, in the first place, from the tutelage of literature and the theater and brings us face to face with 100 percent cinematography. Secondly, it sharply opposes "life as it is," seen by the aided eye of the movie camera (kino-eye), to "life as it is," seen by the imperfect human eye.

1928

From Kino-Eye to Radio-Eye

(FROM THE KINOKS' PRIMER*)*

I

The village of Pavlovskoe near Moscow. A screening. The small place is filled with peasant men and women and workers from a nearby factory. *Kinopravda* is being shown, without musical accompaniment. The noise of the projector can be heard. On the screen a train speeds past. A young girl appears, walking straight toward the camera. Suddenly a scream is heard in the hall. A woman runs toward the girl on the screen. She's weeping, with her arms stretched out before her. She calls the girl by name. But the girl disappears. On the screen the train rushes by once more. The lights are turned on in the hall. The woman is carried out, unconscious. "What's going on?" a worker-correspondent asks. One of the viewers answers: "It's kino-eye. They filmed the girl while she was still alive. Not long ago she fell ill and died. The woman running toward the screen was her mother."

A park bench. The assistant director of a trust and a woman typist. He asks permission to embrace her. She looks around and says, "All right." A kiss. They get up from the bench, look into one another's eyes and walk along the path. Disappear. The bench is empty. Behind it there's a lilac bush. The lilac bush parts. A man comes out from the bush, lugging some sort of equipment on a tripod. A gardener, who's witnessed the whole scene, asks his assistant: "What's that all about?" The assistant answers: "That's kino-eye."

A fire. Tenants are hurling their possessions from the burning building. Any second now they expect the fire department to arrive. Police. An anxious crowd. At the end of the street fire engines appear and rapidly approach. At the same time a car rushes from a side street into the square. A man is cranking the handle of a camera. Another man stands next to him and says: "We made it in time. Film the arrival of the fire department." "Kino-eye, kino-eye," runs the murmur through the crowd.

The Hall of Columns in Moscow's Palace of Unions. Lenin's body lies in an open coffin placed on a raised bier. Day and night the workers of Moscow file past. The entire square and adjoining streets are filled. Nearby, in Red Square, the Mausoleum is being built at night under floodlights. A heavy snow is falling. Covered with snow, a man with a camera stands watch all night lest he miss something important or interesting. This, too, is kino-eye.

"Lenin is dead, but his cause lives on," say the workers of the Soviet Union, and they labor to build a socialist country. At a reconstructed cement plant in the city of Novorossiisk two men are in an aerial car suspended above the sea. A supervisor and a cameraman. Both have cameras and are filming. The trolley moves swiftly. The supervisor crawls out onto the side of the car for a better vantage point. A moment later he's knocked on the head by an iron girder. The cameraman turns around and sees his comrade, bloody and unconscious, clutching his equipment, half-dangling into the sea. He turns his camera around, films him, and only then comes to his aid. This, too, is the school of kino-eye.

Moscow, the end of 1919. An unheated room. A small vent-window with a broken pane. Next to the window, a table. On the table, a glass of yesterday's undrunk tea that has turned to ice. Near the glass is a manuscript. We read: "Manifesto on the Disarmament of Theatrical Cinematography." One variant of this manifesto, entitled "We," was later (1922) published in the magazine *Kinofot* (Moscow).

The next major theoretical statement of the kino-eye adherents was the well-known Manifesto on Nonacted Cinema, published in the journal *LEF* (1923) under the title *Kinoks: A Revolution.*

LEF. **A journal whose title stood for "Left Front of the Arts," founded in Moscow in 1923 by Mayakovsky and a group of intellectuals and artists. Mayakovsky described it as follows: "*LEF* is the envelopment of a great social theme by all the weapons of Futurism. This definition does not exhaust the matter, of course—I refer those interested to *LEF* itself. Those who united: Brik, Aseyev, Kushner, Arvatov, Tretyakov, Rodchenko, Lavinsky. . . . One of the slogans, one of the great achievements of *LEF*—the deaestheticization of the arts of production, constructivism. A poetic supplement: agit-art and economic agitation; the advertisement."—ed.**

These two manifestos had been preceded by their author's work, from 1918 on, in the newsreel section where he put out a series of current *Kinonedelias* and some thematic newsreels.

At first, from 1918 through 1922, the kinoks existed in the singular, that is, there was only one kinok. From 1923 through 1925 there were already three or four. From 1925 on kino-eye's ideas became very widely known. As the original group grew, the number of member-popularizers of the movement increased. And it's now possible to speak not only of the group, of the kino-eye's school, not only of a sector of a front, but of an entire front of nonacted documentary cinematography.

II

Kinoglaz or *kinooko.* Hence the *kinoglazovtsy* or kinoks. The kinoks' primer gives a short definition of *kino-eye* with the formula, "kino-eye = the kino-recording of facts."

Kino-eye = kino-seeing (I see through the camera) + kino-writing (I write on film with the camera) + kino-organization (I edit).

The kino-eye method is the scientifically experimental method of exploring the visible world—

a. based on the systematic recording on film of facts from life;
b. based on the systematic organization of the documentary material recorded on film.

Thus, kino-eye is not only the name of a group of film workers. Not only the name of a film (*Kinoglaz* or *Life Caught Unawares*). And not merely some so-called artistic trend (left or right). Kino-eye is an ever-growing movement for influence through facts as opposed to influence through fiction, no matter how strong the imprint of fiction.

Kino-eye is the documentary cinematic decoding of both the visible world and that which is invisible to the naked eye.

Kino-eye means the conquest of space, the visual linkage of people throughout the entire world based on the continuous exchange of visible fact, of film-documents as opposed to the exchange of cinematic or theatrical presentations.

Kino-eye means the conquest of time (the visual linkage of phenomena separated in time). Kino-eye is the possibility of seeing life processes in any temporal order or at any speed inaccessible to the human eye.

Kino-eye makes use of every possible kind of shooting technique: acceleration, microscopy, reverse action, animation, camera movement, the use of the most unexpected foreshortenings—all these we consider to be not trick effects but normal methods to be fully used.

Kino-eye uses every possible means in montage, comparing and linking all points of the universe in any temporal order, breaking, when necessary, all the laws and conventions of film construction.

Kino-eye plunges into the seeming chaos of life to find in life itself the response to an assigned theme. To find the resultant force amongst the million phenomena related to the given theme. To edit; to wrest, through the camera, whatever is most typical, most useful, from life; to organize the film pieces wrested from life into a meaningful rhythmic visual order, a meaningful visual phrase, an essence of "I see."

III

Montage means organizing film fragments (shots) into a film-object. It means "writing" something cinematic with the recorded shots. It does not mean selecting the fragments for "scenes" (the theatrical bias) or for titles (the literary bias).

Every kino-eye production is subject to montage from the moment the theme is chosen until the film's release in its completed form. In other words, it is edited during the entire process of film production.

Within this continuous process of editing we can distinguish three stages:

The Man with a Movie Camera

The first stage. Editing is the inventory of all documentary data directly or indirectly related to the assigned theme (in the form of manuscripts, objects, film clippings, photographs, newspaper clippings, books, etc.). As a result of this montage-inventory, through the selection and grouping of the more valuable data, the plan of the theme crystallizes, becomes clearer, emerges in the editing process.

The second stage. Editing is the human eye's summing up of observations on the assigned theme (the montage of your own observations or of reports by informants and scouts). A shooting plan, as a result of selecting and sorting the human eye's observations. In making this selection, the author takes into account the indications of the thematic plan as well as the special properties of the "machine-eye," of the "kino-eye."

The third stage. The central editing. The summary of observations recorded on film by kino-eye. A numerical calculation of the montage groupings. The combining (addition, subtraction, multiplication, division, and factoring out) of related pieces. Continuous shifting of the pieces until all are placed in a rhythmical order such that all links of meaning coincide with visual linkage. As the final result of all these mixings, shifts, cancellations, we obtain a visual equation, a visual formula, as it were. This formula, this equation, obtained as a result of the general montage of the recorded film-documents *is* a 100 percent film-object, the concentrated essence of "I see"—"I kino-see."

Kino-eye is:

Montage, when I select a theme (choosing one from among thousands of possible themes);

Montage, when I make observations for a theme (choosing what is expedient from thousands of observations on the theme);

Montage, when I establish the viewing order of the footage on the theme (selecting the most expedient from thousands of possible groupings of shots, proceeding from the qualities of the film footage as well as from the requirements of the chosen theme).

The school of kino-eye calls for construction of the film-object upon "intervals," that is, upon the movement between shots, upon the visual correlation of shots with one another, upon transitions from one visual stimulus to another.

Movement between shots, the visual "interval," the visual correlation of shots, is, according to kino-eye, a complex quantity. It consists of the sum of various correlations, of which the chief ones are—

1. the correlation of planes (close-up, long shot, etc.);
2. the correlation of foreshortenings;
3. the correlation of movements within the frame;
4. the correlation of light and shadow;
5. the correlation of recording speeds.

Proceeding from one or another combination of these correlations, the author determines: (1) the sequence of changes, the sequence of pieces one after another, (2) the length of each change (in feet, in frames), that is, the projection time, the viewing time of each individual image. Moreover, besides the movement between shots (the "interval"), one takes into account the visual relation between adjacent shots and of each individual shot to all others engaged in the "montage battle" that is beginning.

To find amid all these mutual reactions, these mutual attractions and repulsions of shots, the most expedient "itinerary" for the eye of the viewer, to reduce this multitude of "intervals" (the movements between shots) to a simple visual equation, a visual formula expressing the basic theme of the film-object in the best way: such is the most important and difficult task of the author-editor.

This theory known as the "theory of intervals" was put forward by the kinoks in a variant of the manifesto "We" written in 1919.

Kino-eye's position on intervals is most clearly illustrated in our work on *The Eleventh Year* and particularly *The Man with a Movie Camera.*

IV. On Radio-Eye

In their first statements concerning the future of the not yet invented sound cinema, the kinoks (now the radioks) defined their course as leading from kino-eye to radio-eye, that is, to an *audible kino-eye, transmitted by radio.*

My article, "Kinopravda and Radiopravda," published several years ago in *Pravda,* speaks of radio-eye as eliminating distance between people, as the opportunity for workers throughout the world not only to see, but also, simultaneously, to hear one another.

In its day, the kinoks' statement on radio-eye was hotly debated in the press. Later, however, attention paid this question diminished, and it was regarded as one for the distant future.

However, kino-eye workers did not restrict themselves to the struggle for nonacted cinema; at the same time they prepared to meet the transition fully armed, anticipating work within the radio-eye plan, the plan for nonacted sound cinema.

In *One Sixth of the World* the titles were already replaced by a word-radio-theme in contrapuntal construction. *The Eleventh Year* was constructed as a film-object of sight and sound, edited to be heard as well as seen.

The Man with a Movie Camera is constructed in the same manner, moving from kino-eye to radio-eye.

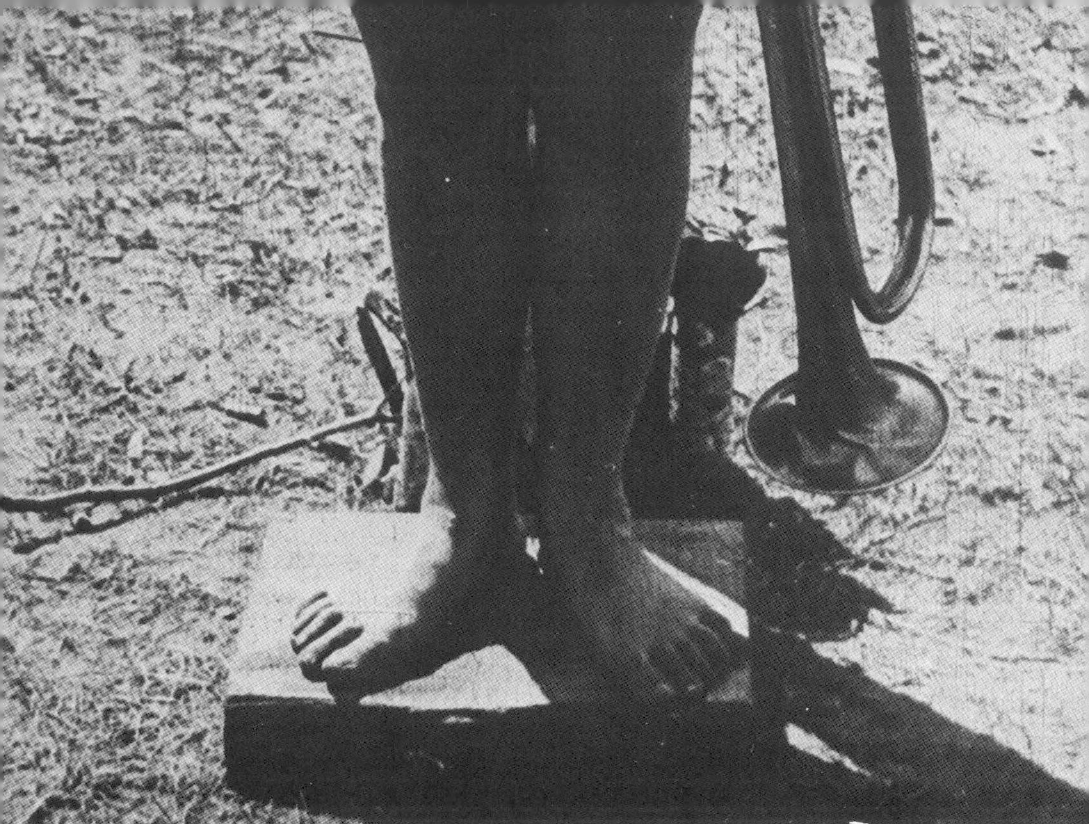

Kinoglaz

The kinoks' theoretical and practical work (in contrast to acted cinematography, caught off guard) was in advance of our technical possibilities; they have long awaited the *overdue* (in relation to kino-eye) technical base for sound film and television.

The latest technical inventions in this field place a most powerful weapon—in the struggle for a nonacted October—in the hands of those who support and work with the sound documentary film.

1929

From the History of the Kinoks

Among the early works of kino-eye, political caricatures and animated films are to be noted. Their shooting involved setting in motion intertitles, drawings, charts, blueprints, etc. It was the

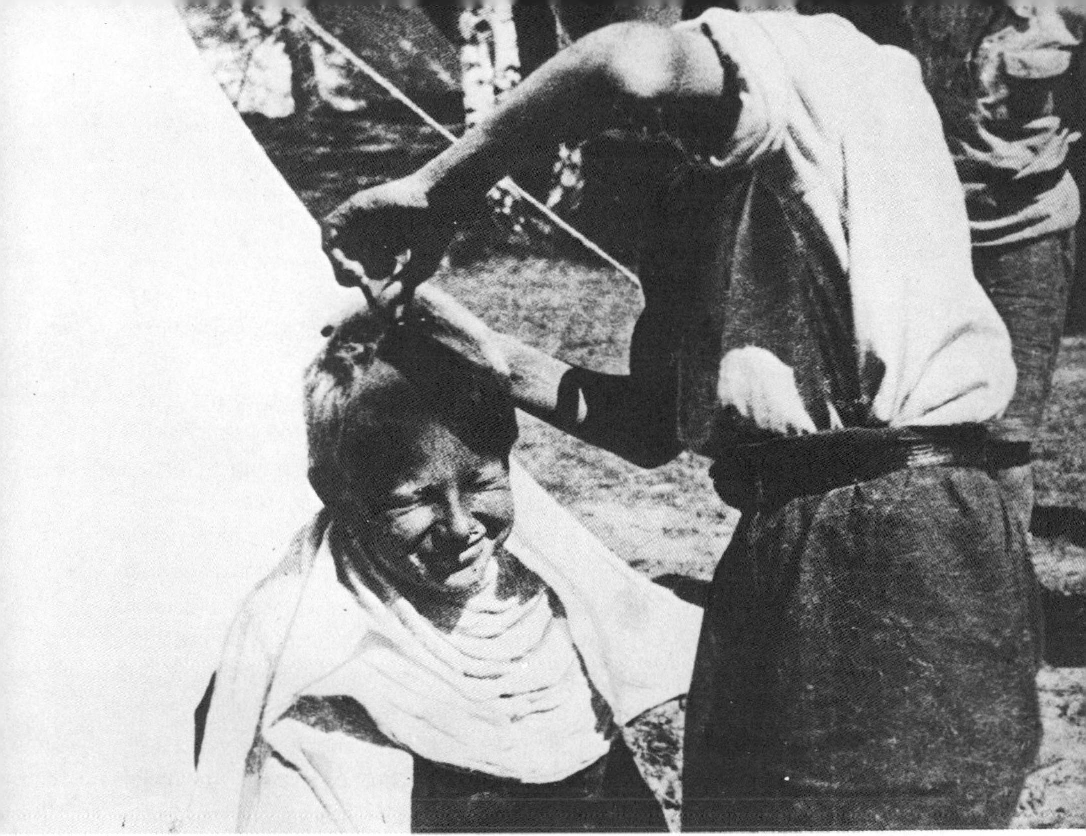

Kinoglaz

dynamic geometry of the shot that interested us. All this was then in a rudimentary state.

The first decisive experimental study was called *The Battle of Tsaritsyn.* It was done with very fast montage and no titles. It was, so to speak, the ancestor of *Kinoglaz* and *The Man with a Movie Camera,* which appeared later. The montage construction of this early study relied on film-language; there were no verbal titles. The montage was already done in frames. Measurement went not according to the metrical system, but by a decimal system of frames: 5, 10, 15, 20 . . . roughly like that. Once the following incident occurred. I told someone to splice the pieces of *The Battle of Tsaritsyn.* As long as the pieces were ten or fifteen feet long, the editing woman spliced them. When, however, she came to short pieces several frames long, she dumped these frames, without thinking, into the wastebasket as odd scraps, waste. Everything had to be redone. Once again I sat at it for about eight days. Once again I put it all back together. This second time I myself looked after the splicing. The pace of the study was extraordinarily rapid for that time. After a while Griffith's *Intolerance* arrived. It then became easier to talk. Nevertheless, the screening of *The Battle of Tsaritsyn* had a negative effect on the chance for further work. Several creative workers really liked the picture. However, the Artistic Council and the government responded negatively. I could not count on repeating experiments like that any more.

After great effort I was finally given the opportunity to shoot *Kinoglaz* (or *Life Caught Unawares*). At first, the idea was to do the six parts of the series simultaneously. We were counting on accumulating footage for the film by working over a considerable length of time and on several themes at once. The lacking parts must not be staged. Following our basic orientation, we wanted to film all shots unobserved. The footage was accumulated as if in vertical columns that we intended to assemble into individual films later on. But something unforeseen occurred . . . when we had shot part of the footage there was a change of administration. We had to stop work. We had to come out with the footage that had been shot for the various parts and assemble them not vertically, but horizontally. At that time I was already sufficiently expert in organizing footage to emerge undefeated. This explains statements by several critics who pointed out that too many themes had been treated while not one had been fully exhausted.

The film *Life Caught Unawares* was presented as "the camera's first reconnaissance" of real life. All the technical processes prescribed in the "nonacted" manifesto, and which we later perfected, were really applied in that film. Proceeding from kino-eye principles I showed life as it is, from the viewpoint of the aided eye, which sees better than the human eye. We felt it was necessary to use all the movie camera's possibilities in a keener presentation of that life which passes by and in a presentation from angles still unknown to us. I must say that the theme of *The Man with a Movie Camera* was already broached then—the only difference being that the camera itself was not shown on the screen. The intertitles, the headings, continually emphasized the fact that something was seen in this way or that, from the kino-eye viewpoint. There were several screenings; several conflicting opinions were expressed. Then the picture

Intolerance. **A film made in 1916 by D. W. Griffith (1874–1948), a major American film director and the producer of many films. [Griffith was admired by the Soviet filmmakers of the revolutionary generation—ed.]**

dropped from view and was not released for distribution.

Our next work was the *Leninist Kinopravda.* It was a newsreel centered on a single figure. That figure was Lenin. It was a full-length, thirty-six-hundred-foot film in which Lenin was shown the entire time, during every part; and the titles themselves were documents, that is, a text from Lenin. It was the first experiment in newsreel with a single character.

For about a year and a half all possibility of work was withheld. The only way to get work was to get a commission, with customer's stipulation that the kino-eye group make the film. That proved to be possible with the Moscow Soviet and Gostorg. That is how *Forward, Soviet!* and *One Sixth of the World* came about. The assignment for the first picture was to follow a primitive plan in filming the institution of the Moscow Soviet. I knew full well that the Moscow Soviet would not be satisfied, but nevertheless I could not let this opportunity slip by, and I expanded the assignment into the theme "Forward, Soviet!"—forward, Soviet land, toward socialism.

I acted in a similar fashion with Gostorg. We were supposed to present a marathon run along the chain of the Gostorg machinery. I turned that into *One Sixth of the World,* contrasted with the capitalist encirclement. The film also managed to cover the broad expanse of our land from Novaia Zemlia to Turkestan.

The center of gravity in these pictures was the combination of different aspects of life, kino-eye's capture of the vastest possible expanses. That, in particular, was how the theme of import-export was expanded and transformed into that of emancipation from dependence on foreign capital.

Once again I was without work for several months, couldn't figure out what to do, and finally decided to go to the Ukraine. When I proposed making *The Man with a Movie Camera* I was told that I must first make an anniversary film, and then I'd be given the opportunity to make that picture as well. So I made *The Eleventh Year.* In terms of film-language I consider that film superior to all the previous kino-eye pictures. Intertitles were of no importance whatsoever in shaping the object. At first the film had no titles, then titles were added, but this in no way affected the cinematic solution.

Finally, our latest picture—*The Man with a Movie Camera.* It's an attempt to present the facts in 100 percent film-language. For this film, we completely rejected the methods of theater and literature.

. . . During the early years the conditions under which we worked

One Sixth of the World

were very difficult. We shot with bad, partially exposed film, with practically no equipment or labs, using condensed-milk cans. Kaufman was crazy about that milk and made double use of the cans. First we drank the milk, then with the can, you could make whatever you pleased—an enlarger light, an American diaphragm. I remember that those cans were good for everything. When we're filming now, it's funny to recall how we made our first cartoons. When *Today* was shot, for example, a map lay on the floor, Belyakov crawled over it and drew, while fastened to the ceiling above him was Kaufman, since you couldn't film at closer range. And so we shot our first animated film continuously for three days and nights. The script was written on the spot, everything was drawn and shot on the spot.

During the Civil War we found ourselves in burning trains, and in bandit-infested areas, and so we just went ahead and shot in that burning train. We had to scatter in a line with grenades, and we once

One Sixth of the World

even fired on our own cavalry who were rushing to our aid. There were many such incidents. An interesting one involved an armored train that was destroyed two hours after we left it.

I mention all this in order to give an idea of our working conditions.

If all our forces had been thrown into the stubborn work of filming the Civil War, then we might not have films as incompetent and similar to one another as we do now. Unfortunately, at that time it was considered too wild, and the work was never properly organized. Each commander felt it essential to have a cameraman by his side to film him in public appearances and speech making somewhere.

. . . Several years ago we raised the issue of radio-ear and radio-eye, anticipating the appearance of sound cinema by quite some time.

This is a big, separate issue, about which much more remains to

History of the Civil War

be said and written; I only mention it now in passing.

In the silent film, *The Eleventh Year,* we already see montage connected with sounds. Recall how the machines thump, how absolute silence is conveyed. At first there's the pounding of axes and hammers, the whining of saws, then it all ceases, followed by dead silence, and in that silence there beats the heart of the machine. Titles were introduced only by way of prompting, so that the film would be perceived correctly. You will recall, as well, that a two-thousand-year-old cliff and the skeleton of a Scythian are shown. The water is absolutely still, there's deserted country all around, and then a "sound" begins to grow, the pounding of hammers starts up, louder and louder, then the blows of a big hammer, and finally when a man appears and hammers on the cliff, a powerful "sound echo" is conveyed. After the transition to radio-eye, all of this will resound impressively from the screen.

Now a word or two about efficiency and montage. The efficient should coincide with the beautiful. Take the racing automobile, for

History of the Civil War

example, meant to go so many miles per hour maximum and made in the shape of a cigar. Here is both beauty and efficiency. We feel that one must not think only of the beauty of this or that shot. First of all, one must proceed from considerations of efficiency. This means that one adapts the angle from which a given object can best be seen. Frequently an efficient angle of this sort represents a new viewpoint for us, one from which we're not yet accustomed to see this or that object. But as soon as it becomes a cliché, repetitious, it ceases to be efficient, that is, effective.

Our montage goes through a whole series of stages. It begins with observations on a definite theme. This theme includes a given number of phenomena in a given place. And this first editing is done with nothing in hand, but your conception, your theme. During reconnaissance you examine your ideas and choose what's most valuable and interesting from everything you've seen. The second stage of editing is when you arrive on location with a movie camera. You now approach your surroundings, not from the viewpoint of the human eye, but from that of the kino-eye, and you make the first adjustment with regard to what you first saw. You make the second adjustment, taking into account all the changes that have occurred at the location you've selected. When all the footage has been shot, you then make a third adjustment, choosing the shots that are most expedient, that best express your theme. After this you reach the fourth stage—the organization of the footage selected. The filmed pieces are combined according to linkage of meaning. You try to make the linkage of meaning coincide with that of images. The rest is eliminated.

Does any kind of editing formula exist?

Attempts in that direction have been made. And it must be said, with some success. Editing tables containing definite calculations, similar to systems of musical notation, as well as studies in rhythm, "intervals," etc., exist. Specifically, I am at present writing a book that will present a series of individual examples and conclusions based on such formulas. But publishing it is very dangerous, for if such methods are indiscriminately applied, the result will be nonsense.

It's not hard to offer a formula. It's hard to specify when and where it should be applied.

On Documentary Shooting Methods: The best method is candid, concealed shooting. There are also the techniques of ordinary newsreel, techniques for work with supersensitive film, etc. When you film a conference or demonstration, that's simple filming, the usual noninterference in the events taking place. Next it's necessary to consider filming in which someone's attention must be diverted. That either occurs naturally, as at a factory, when the worker is engrossed in his labor, in his machine, or through artificial distraction. If someone has focused his attention on the camera, a second camera often helps.

Once in a studio at the moment when the director said to the actor, "Cut!" I started filming. The actress was playing a role, completely immersed in it, completely preoccupied, and precisely at the instant when she hadn't yet come to herself and wasn't paying us the least attention, I filmed her. This moment turned out to be better than anything the director had shot until then, and he asked me to give him those fragments. That's what we mean by distracting attention . . .

In conclusion, I'll dwell briefly on the question of why we are opposed to the acted cinema.

I don't know who's opposed to whom. It's difficult to stand up against the cinema that is acted. It represents 98 percent of world production. We simply feel that the cinema's chief function is the recording of documents, of facts, the recording of life, of historical processes. Acted cinema is a replacement for theater, it is theater restored. A compromise tendency still exists, directed toward the fusion or blending of the two.

We take a stand against all that.

1929

Letter from Berlin

After eleven years of work on the documentary film I arrived in Germany for the first time. I immediately encountered something strange.

A portion of the Berlin press, while noting the cinematic merits of kino-eye, is, at the same time, stressing that in fact kino-eye is, as it were, a more "fanatical" extension of the theory and practice of Ruttmann (*Symphony of a Great City*).

This quasi supposition, quasi assertion is absurd . . .

To take away Soviet Russia's preeminence in kino-eye and in the documentary film generally, one would have to turn back the wheel of history, wipe more than a hundred kino-eye films from the face of the earth, burn the kino-eye manifestos, destroy thousands of reviews and articles, withdraw a number of Russian and French books from circulation.

No one is likely to undertake such a bold operation.

Ruttmann (*Berlin: Symphony of a Great City*). The earliest abstract films of Walter Ruttmann (1887 - 1941) were made under the influence of Viking Eggeling. Ruttmann is, however, best known for his documentary work which, in theme and exploratory stress on editing involving sound and image, impels comparison with that of Vertov. *Berlin: Symphony of a Great City* (1927) is the assertively edited chronicle of a working day in the German capital. Ruttmann was recruited for the production of documentary films during the Second World War and was fatally wounded while serving on the Eastern Front—ed.

Several attempts, which have filtered through into print, to suppress and distort the history of kino-eye appear all the more strange to us. The fact that the Berlin press is not aware of kino-eye's chronological development and its ten-year attack on the stronghold of acted cinema can be explained only by incorrect, false information (or by the complete lack of information) on this issue.

It should be especially emphasized that the majority of kino-eye films were constructed as a symphony of labor, as a symphony of the whole Soviet land, or as a symphony of a particular city. In addition, the action in these films frequently developed from early morning to evening.

Thus in Part One of *Kinoglaz* (awarded a prize at the International Exposition in Paris) a city awakens and comes to life. And in *Forward, Soviet!* a day gradually develops into evening and concludes at midnight.

Kino-eye workers have not the least doubt that their work, both theoretical and practical, though inadequately distributed, is perfectly familiar to the majority of Russian and foreign professionals and without fail spurs them on to separate efforts in this still controversial direction. Ruttmann's recent experiment should therefore be regarded as the result of years of kino-eye's pressure through work and statements, on those working in abstract film. The reverse is wholly untrue, both in terms of fact and chronology.

I ask you to publish this letter, not out of selfish or "patriotic" motives, but only in the interest of restoring historical truth.

1929

Replies to Questions

To the editors of the newspaper Kinofront.

Recently, I've had a lot of work to do, both day and night. I've written this in snatches. My replies to questions should be printed fully and without changes. The fact is that ridiculous attempts to saddle me with formalism are continuing, and I can explain them only by complete *ignorance,* absolute *lack of information* about the question under discussion on the part of the comrades responsible for these texts.

Fraternally yours—D. Vertov.

Question: Do you maintain at present the creative platform published in your 1922 manifesto?

Answer: The question evidently concerns *Kinoks: A Revolution,* the Manifesto on Nonacted Cinema, written in 1922 and published in the journal LEF no. 3 at the beginning of 1923. This manifesto, which announced the newsreel and radio-chronicle offensive, cannot, of course, be viewed merely in its static form, that is, it had not yet been followed by other projects and declarations.

"Provisional Instructions to Kino-Eye Groups," "On the Organization of the First Film Experiment Station," "A Proposal for the Organization of a Documentary Film-Factory," "A Plan for the Reorganization of Soviet Cinema on the Basis of the Leninist Ratio," numerous other articles in *Pravda*, *Kino*, in individual anthologies (of Proletkult et al.) and, simultaneous practical work (about 150 documentary films of all types, sizes, and forms) continually improved, refined, and corrected our project and protected it from errors and obscurities. By 1924–1925 it had expanded into a whole program for an offensive and exerted an extraordinary influence not only on the documentary but on the acted sector of our cinema as well.

We kinoks agreed to define as authentic 100 percent cinema, that which was built on the organization of documentary footage recorded by the camera.

That cinema founded upon the organization of acted footage recorded by the camera we agreed to consider a phenomenon of a *secondary, theatrical* nature.

We admit that in the struggle against the grandiloquent subdivisions of the supporters of acted film (art—nonart, artistic film—nonartistic film) we put these expressions between quotation marks and made fun of "so-called art," the "so-called artistic film."

This was in no way to contradict our respect for individual (actually, very rare) examples of the acted film. We did not, of course, praise these as "altogether a good film." We always qualified them: "a good actor's film, a good acted film."

We admit that in the struggle for the documentary film's right to develop and flourish we did not use the words—widely employed but differently understood—*art* and *artistic* as a cover. At the same time we sharply, persistently underlined the *inventive, stirringly revolutionary* character of the kino-eye documentary films. We described our documentary films as the *pathos of facts,* the *enthusiasm of facts.* To the attacks of critics on this issue, we replied that a kino-eye documentary film is not merely a documentary "keeping of the minutes," but a revolutionary lighthouse set against the background of world film production's theatrical clichés.

We continue to regard the documentary film method as basic to proletarian cinema and the recording of the documents of our socialist offensive, our Five-Year Plan, as the basic objective of Soviet cinema.

This does not in any way mean that the theater or the acted cinema deriving from it are exempted from participation in the battle for socialism. On the contrary, the sooner acted, theatrical cinema abandons the falsification of reality, a feeble imitation of the documentary film, for frankly 100 percent acting, the more honest and powerful its appearance on the socialist front will be.

Question: In your opinion, do films such as *The Man with a Movie Camera* answer the political demands made on revolutionary cinema?

Answer: So far, not a single documentary or acted film has fully answered the political demands made on revolutionary cinema. Released at a time of cinematic crisis (a crisis, not so much of subject matter—there were endless themes—as of means of expression), released as a *film with a particular purpose*—that of bridging the gap within film-language, and the cinefication of "wooden" cinematography, *The Man with a Movie Camera* lays no claim to replacing or ousting our other work. But not even the sum total of these films can hope to have answered (or to answer) fully and opportunely all the political demands the party has made and should make on revolutionary cinema.

It's essential to triple our energy, to reorganize film production and distribution on the basis of the "Leninist ratio," to organize a factory of documentary films, to assign cadres of film production workers along the Five-Year Plan's entire front. The method of socialist competition will help documentary film workers to approach a fuller, better realization of the party's political demands.

The same holds with respect to sound cinema (I'm responding now to the question of documentary sound cinema). In its day, radio-

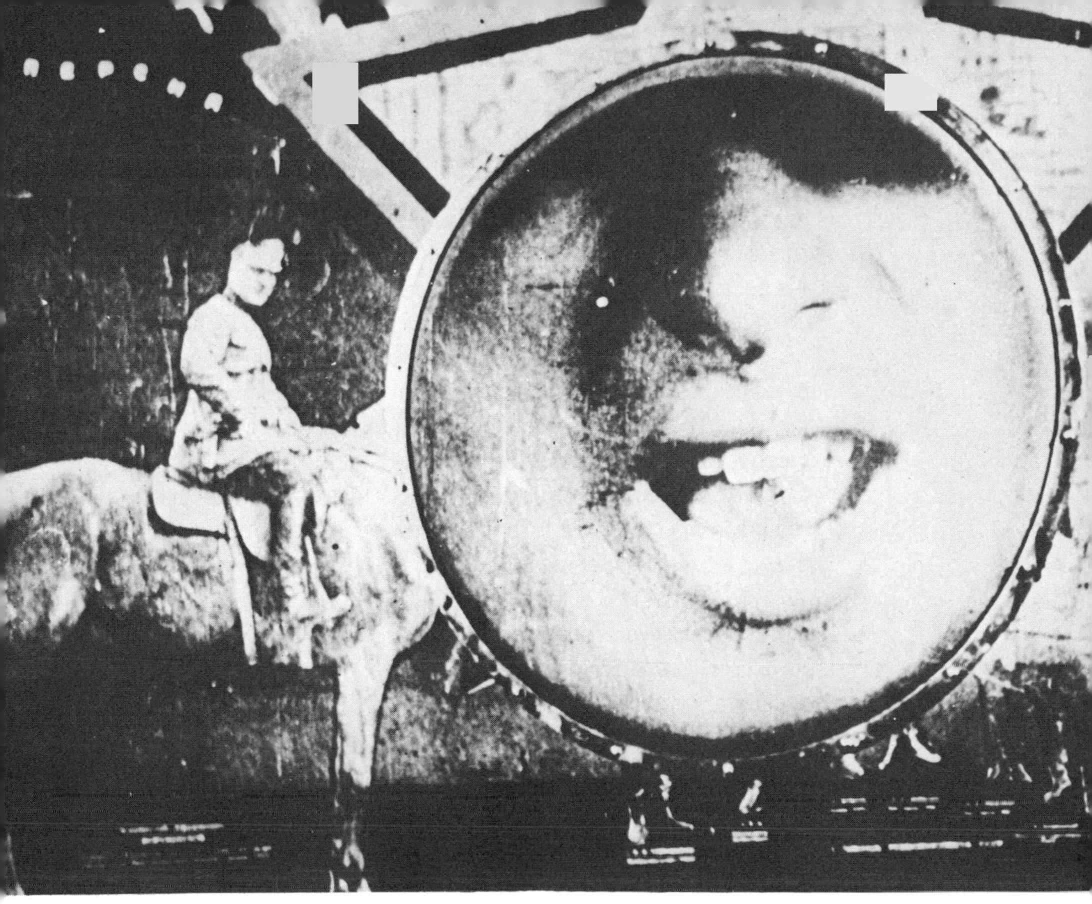

The Man with a Movie Camera

eye already anticipated the "Leninist ratio" for radio-theater programs.

We maintain our previous position on the question of sound in documentary film. We regard radio-eye as a very powerful weapon in the hands of the proletariat, as the opportunity for proletarians of all nations to hear and see one another in an organized manner, as the opportunity—free of the limitations of space—to use facts for purposes of agitation and propaganda, as the opportunity to contrast the radio-cinema documents of our construction of socialism with those of oppression and exploitation, with those of the capitalist world.

Declarations on the necessity for nonsynchronization of the visible and audible, like declarations on the exclusive necessity for sound films or for talking films don't amount to a hill of beans, as the saying goes. In both sound and silent cinema we sharply distinguish between only two types of film: documentary (with real dialogue, sound, etc.) and acted (with dialogue, sound, etc., that are artificial, specially created for the filming).

Neither *synchronization* nor *asynchronization* of the visible with the audible is at all obligatory, either for documentary or for acted films. Sound and silent shots are both edited according to the same principles and can coincide, not coincide, or blend with one another in various, essential combinations. We should also completely reject the absurd confusion involved in dividing films according to the categories of talking, noise, or sound.

Question: Do you intend to alter your method and general position regarding cinema issues, in terms of new objectives generated by the era of socialist reconstruction?

Answer: The method of the documentary film, the method of kino-eye and radio-eye, brought into existence by the October Revolution, shaped on the fronts of the Civil War and the building of socialism, will necessarily come into full bloom in the era of socialist reconstruction, when documentary film-factories will develop with the implementation of the "Leninist ratio" in programming; competing film brigades will increase in number, becoming tempered in an unceasing documentary combat for socialism.

1930

Let's Discuss Ukrainfilm's First Sound Film: *Symphony of the Donbas*

(THE AUTHOR ON HIS FILM)

Some remarks on the special significance of the sound-and-image documentary, *Symphony of the Donbas* (*Enthusiasm*) and on the special obstacles which rose, like a wall, to block this film's production.

To the first group of these special obstacles belong the categorical assertions by sound technicians and film production workers (both here and abroad) that—

- one can and should record sound on film only under the special conditions of a soundproofed, isolated studio;
- one can and should record only artificially produced sounds on film;
- it is impossible to shoot documentary (in particular, outdoor) sound.

These assertions of production workers and sound technicians were refuted not by word, but by deed, in March last year. We overcame this group of obstacles through a series of experiments.

The primary, the particular significance of *Enthusiasm* lies in its decisive resolution of the issue of the possibilities and impossibilities of documentary sound filming on location.

To the second group of special obstacles (let's call it the "group of immobilities") belong—

- the complete immobility of the sound-recording equipment (as though it were immured within the studio walls);
- the immobility of the microphone, which even within the studio's cage was not allowed to budge during shooting.

Not only did we overcome this group of obstacles, not only did we move the "group of immobilities," not only did we move the camera outdoors, where we made both camera and microphone "walk" and "run," but, after completing a series of experiments in sound and image shot by remote control, we seriously approached the question of a radio-recording, sound-and-image station.

The third group of obstacles arose in connection with our firm decision to cast off from the "shore" of the sound-recording station and go to the Donbas. The issue of the rush production of portable sound-recording apparatus was placed on the agenda. Comrades Timartsev, Chibisov, Kharitonov, and Molchanov, working day and night in Professor Shorin's laboratory, put together portable equipment. The first test recordings were made in the middle of April.

Professor Shorin. In 1927, Alexander F. Shorin (1890–1941), scientist and inventor in the fields of communications technology and sound film, developed the first system for cinematic sound recording in the Soviet Union. The "Shorinphone," designed from 1932 to 1934 for sound recording and reproduction, was widely used in the Soviet film industry—ed.

Kinoks on location at the time of *Enthusiasm*

They were followed by the sound filming of May Day, by shooting in the port of Leningrad, and finally, after some rebuilding of the equipment, by the departure to Kharkov to film the Eleventh Ukrainian Party Congress. The equipment was rebuilt once again after the filming of the party congress, and we left for the Donbas.

With the overcoming of this third group of difficulties (the experiments with the portable equipment) the doors—forced open in March—opened wide, leading into the field of sound newsreel and documentary film. Herein lies the special significance of *Enthusiasm* as the *lead icebreaker* in the column of sound newsreels.

The journey to the Donbas represents the fourth group of obstacles. Faced with the deadline of a month, we went to "storm" the sounds of the Donbas. Faced with the complete absence of means of transport, we walked, dragging, as we went, a twenty-seven-hundred-pound load. Crawling on all fours to "the sticks." Completely cut off from a laboratory and reproduction equipment, unable to listen to what had been recorded, to check our work and equipment. Faced with the fact that the group's exceptional nervous

Vertov shooting *Enthusiasm*

tension was accompanied not only by heavy brain work, but by the heavy muscle work of continually lugging our loads from one location to another.

This final, decisive month of our sound shooting took place in a setting of din and clanging, amidst fire and iron, among factory workshops vibrating from the sound. Penetrating into mines deep beneath the earth and shooting from the roofs of speeding trains, we abolished, once and for all, the fixity of sound equipment and *for the first time in history* recorded, in documentary fashion, the basic sounds of an industrial region (the sound of mines, factories, trains, etc.). Herein lies the fourth special significance of the sound documentary, *Enthusiasm.*

In order to set about editing we had first to total up the results of the shooting. To do that we had to confront a new series of difficulties. The Kiev laboratory had to prepare for developing and printing the footage. Things had to be arranged so that errors in printing would not be taken for errors made by the laboratory. So that laboratory errors would not be mistaken for errors in shooting. So

Enthusiasm

that errors made in shooting would not be mistaken for errors in printing. And vice versa.

When we finally conquered this group of difficulties and made our totals, it turned out that part of the footage shot in the Donbas (scenes of public work, of servicing the workers' cultural needs, of the distribution of awards to shock-workers and others) was lost due to technical factors (the strong sound vibrations). These losses called for a certain amount of change in the editing plan. Making adjustments as we went, we set about organizing the recorded documents in sound and image.

We had at our disposal neither a sound-editing table nor any other relatively suitable device for organizing the footage. We worked carefully, persistently, and slowly. Fifty days and nights under the utmost pressure. Nevertheless, we did not follow the line of least resistance; we did not exploit the circumstance in our favor: that we had been working in the Donbas with portable equipment

Enthusiasm

and that therefore we had recorded most of the Donbas sounds on a single track, together with the image. We did not limit ourselves to the simplest concurrence of image with sound, but followed the line of maximum resistance—under existing conditions—that of *complex interaction of sound with image.*

Herein lies the fifth and very singular significance of the film known as *Enthusiasm.*

And finally, the most important observation.

When, in *Enthusiasm,* the industrial sounds of the All-Union Stokehold arrive at the square, filling the streets with their machine music to accompany the gigantic festive parades;

when on the other hand, the sounds of military bands, of parades, the challenge-banners, the red stars, the shouts of greeting, the battle slogans, the orators' speeches, etc., fuse with the sounds of the machines, the sounds of competing factory shops;

when the work of bridging the gap in the Donbas passes before us as an endless "Communist Sabbath," as "the days of industrialization," as a red star, red banner campaign.

we must view this not as a shortcoming, but as a *serious, long-range experiment.*

I shall conclude with some chronological information.

The shooting of *Enthusiasm* was completed more than a half year ago. Released by the factory for the 1930 October celebrations, it's still not been released to the public. It awaits a serious appraisal of its merits and shortcomings. It awaits a strict, but not irrelevant evaluation. Not an evaluation in general terms (outside time and space), but one based on sound cinema's present state of development.

1931

First Steps

A predominance of sound newsreel films characterized the Soviet sound cinema's first year of existence. For an understanding of this, we must take a look backward.

Newsreel film workers spoke long ago of the possibility, not only of radio broadcasting, but of recording and filming sound-and-image documentaries, radio-cinema films from a distance; they discussed the possibility for proletarians of all nations, all countries, to see, hear, and understand one another. It was this preparatory work that enabled filmmakers in newsreel (unlike those in acted cinema who were caught off guard) to embark immediately and confidently on the first experiments in sound newsreel in March 1930.

The start of work on *Enthusiasm* had been preceded by Ippolit

"Communist Sabbath" (*subbotnik*). Literally translated as "little Saturday," *subbotnik* refers to labor volunteered by a collective or group on free time or during overtime—trans.

Ippolit Sokolov's "theory of caterwauling." In an article, "The Possibilities of Sound Cinema," published in *Kino,* no. 45, 1929, the film critic Ippolit Sokolov claimed that nature and life were not "audiogenic," that "sound films in science and for propaganda will not be based in the lap of nature and on the noise of the street, but will be made behind the sound-proofed, double-layered insulating walls of the studio." He added that attempts to record natural sounds would result in cacophony and "caterwauling."

Enthusiasm

Sokolov's "theory of caterwauling" and by the *negation,* on the part of specialists here and abroad, of the very possibility of recording industrial sound. It was preceded by *negation* of the possibility of making the unacted newsreel sound film. The work on *Enthusiasm* and its consequences represented, as it were, *the negation of that negation.*

Enthusiasm not only completely refuted the "theory of caterwauling" and other antinewsreel "theories," it opened the door for the production of sound newsreels, of unacted sound newsreels, and it also cleared the way for future production of sound-and-image documentaries outdoors.

Enthusiasm has its shortcomings. How are we to explain them? To a large extent they can be explained by the split that had occurred at the time of its production between our plans, our preparations for shooting and editing; and the state of sound-cinema technology at the beginning of 1930. Our plans and projects were too far ahead of our technical and administrative possibilities. We had not taken into account all the obstacles in the way of this film's production. It should be stressed that each of the obstacles encountered was in fact enough to disrupt, to stop our work.

We did not give in to obstacles, we surmounted them. We did not follow the line of least resistance either in shooting or in editing. Of course, we also suffered significant losses.

We must, in my view, speak of these shortcomings as those of a film somewhat maimed in battle. Torn apart. Grown hoarse. Covered with wounds. But a film, just the same, that has not retreated in the face of difficulties.

But what were the attitudes of some of our critics?

Either professorial—everything which is not "sharp" or "flat," in a word, everything which does not "doremifasolize" was unconditionally labeled "cacophony." Or we had to deal with the *deaf* critic—only the visual part of the film was critically examined, while the sound content was ignored. Or we had to deal with the *acting-oriented* critic—say, a formalist critic in the guise of an antiformalist, while hunting out and abusing formal qualities of one sort or another in the film. Or we had to deal with an *antinewsreel* critic, *an opponent of the nonacted film,* one of the authors of the "theory of caterwauling," for instance, defensively foaming at the mouth and attempting to prove that *Enthusiasm* is "caterwauling" and that the "theory" is consequently correct, confirmed, etc., etc.

Those who worked on *Enthusiasm* and, I think, all those in newsreel film, are interested in a *many-sided* (and not a one-sided) analysis of this film. Not only of *Enthusiasm*, as a "thing in itself," but of all the work in connection with its production, of all our work in switching rails from the silent to the sound cinema, in this branch of our socialist film industry we call the newsreel, documentary, or nonacted film.

And so we now see rapid growth in the production of newsreel and newsreel films—not only in quantity (*Enthusiasm*, *Olympiade of the Arts*, *The Trial of the Industrialist Party*, *The Country*, etc.) but, despite individual shortcomings, in quality as well. But if individual shortcomings of the nonacted sound film can be explained by the fact that workers in this branch of the film industry have, in their preliminary preparation, outdistanced their technical and administrative facilities, those working in acted or actor-based cinema have, on the contrary, *lagged behind* in their preparation for the technical facilities at their disposal. The arrival of sound cinema caught them off guard. Hence, together with the mastery of the method of dialectical materialism (a necessary condition for both acted and nonacted films),

the former (acted films) must grow bolder and must be more decisive in the transition from the timid postsynchronization of silent films to the production of sound films;

the latter (nonacted films) must tighten up their technique, master it further and use it for the 100 percent realization of their projected plans. To achieve this we need not only a more skillful control of the microphone, not only the perfecting of portable sound equipment, but an orientation toward a *sound-producing* and *sound-recording radio-cinema station* (the filming and broadcasting of sound-images at a distance) such as I have proposed at the First All-Union Sound Film Conference. If, by the end of the Five-Year Plan, we have not only portable sound-cinema equipment, but a powerful radio-recording and radio-transmission station as well, then our goal of "catching up with and surpassing capitalist countries technically and economically" will, in large measure, be realized in the areas of cinema and radio.

1931

How We Made Our Film About Lenin

I've completed work on *Three Songs of Lenin.* This work lasted through almost all of 1933.

In the process of this work we succeeded in discovering ten new film documents concerning Lenin's life. By stubbornly, tirelessly sifting through and studying archival, cinémathèque and various unprocessed footage in Moscow, Tiflis, Kiev, Baku, and other cities, Comrade Svilova, a member of our group, accomplished what we had not been able to accomplish in the nine years following Lenin's death. It should be pointed out that during these nine years only one new film document on Lenin had been discovered. Among our

the mastery of the method of dialectical materialism. Vertov is making a concession to the so-called dialectical method (the direct transference of the philosophical understanding of the world to the sphere of art) forcibly propagated in the 1930s by the cinema section of RAPP (Russian Association of Proletarian Writers).

Krupskaya in *Three Songs of Lenin*

discoveries are: Lenin beside Elizarov's coffin, Lenin on his way to a session of the congress of the Communist International, Lenin in Red Square.

During work on our previous film in Leningrad our group attempted to transfer Lenin's voice to film. Because of the imperfection of the first sound camera, the results obtained were not very satisfactory.

Work in 1933 (done by sound engineer Shtro) turned out more successfully. Lenin's voice came out better on film than on the phonograph record. From Lenin's address to members of the Red Army the following words, clearly audible and easy to make out, went into the film: "Stand firm. . . . Stand united in friendship. . . . Forward, bravely against the enemy. . . . Victory shall be ours. . . . The power of the landowners and capitalists, crushed here in Russia, shall be defeated throughout the entire world!" In this way we found it possible to preserve Lenin's voice on film and to present Vladimir Ilyich speaking from the screen.

In Azerbaijan, Turkmenistan, Uzbekistan our group tape-recorded folk songs about Lenin. The authors are mostly anonymous, but their songs are transmitted by word of mouth, from *yurt* to *yurt,* from *kishlak* to *kishlak.* We included several songs of the Soviet East in the film. Some songs are present on the sound track, some on the image track; still others are reflected in the intertitles. These are songs about the October Revolution, about a woman who has taken off the *yashmak,* about Ilyich's light bulb coming to the desert, about the illiterate who have been educated.

Three Songs of Lenin contains, together with documents of the living Lenin, Lenin's final route from Gorki to Moscow, the funeral procession, scenes from the Civil War.

1934

Without Words

More than ten thousand words of song texts, remarks, monologues, speeches by Lenin and others were recorded on tape. After editing and the final trimming, about thirteen hundred words (1,070 in Russian and the rest in other languages) went into the film. Nevertheless, H. G. Wells declared: "Had not a single word been translated for me I should have understood the entire film from the first shot to the last. The thoughts and nuances of the film all reach me and act upon me without the help of words." When we maintained that the scenes with the strongest meaning and content, such as the address of the Dneprostroi [State Dnepr Construction Project] woman shock-worker or the speech of the woman in charge of a collective farm, were lost on him, Wells objected strenuously that he understood everything, that the sincerity, truthfulness, and *joie de vivre* of

from yurt to yurt, from kishlak to kishlak. A *yurt* is a nomad's tent, usually cone-shaped. A *kishlak* is a village in Turkestan or Central Asia —trans.

Gorki. Leninskii Gorki, a town situated about twenty-five miles from Moscow, is the site of the Morozov estate where Lenin resided during the last few years of his life. The name *Gorki,* meaning "hills," is not to be confused with the pseudonym adopted later by the writer—ed.

those who spoke, their awkward gestures, the sparkle in their eyes, the embarrassment in their faces, and other details enabled him to read their thoughts and he felt not the slightest need for a translation of those words.

Approximately the same thing was said by Japanese, Americans, and English who were invited to a screening. My proposal, after the screening, that all the unintelligible places in the text be read (there were no translators) met with the same objections—that there were no unintelligible places and that the entire film in all its most minute episodes came across without words. It was the same at all the other screenings when it was seen by German, Swedish, and French writers.

Does this mean that all the work on texts, speeches, etc., was for nothing, and that those thirteen hundred words can be discarded from the sound and images? Of course, that is not the point. The point is that the exposition of *Three Songs* develops not through the channel of words, but through other channels, through the interaction of sound and image, through the combination of many channels; it proceeds underground, sometimes casting a dozen words onto the surface. The movement of thought, the movement of ideas, travels along many wires but in a single direction, to a single goal. Thoughts fly out from the screen, entering without verbal translations into the viewer's consciousness. The written and spoken words have their own contrapuntal route within the film. Before us is a huge symphony orchestra of thoughts; an accident to a violin or cello does not put an end to the concert. The flow of thoughts continues even if one of the interconnecting wires is broken.

For that reason no attempt to recount this film in words has really succeeded. It differs so greatly in construction from the ordinary film that the verbal exposition of its contents presents a difficult task, especially if that exposition is not one-sided, but many-sided. The contents of *Three Songs* develop in spiral-fashion, now in the sound, now in the image, now in a voice, now in an intertitle, now through facial expression alone—with no music or words—now through movement within the shot, now in the collision of one group shot with another, now smoothly, now by jolts from dark to light, from slow to fast, from the tired to the vigorous, now through noise, now through silent song, a song without words, through thoughts that fly from screen to viewer without the viewer-listener having to translate thought into words.

This film translates poorly into verbal language, though in its image-language it is easily accessible to any popular audience.

It is, on the one hand, a group of film documents on Lenin's death, on his last forty kilometers, on Lenin's final route from Gorki to Moscow; it is, on the other, Lenin in motion on film, a compendium of the film-documents of Lenin that have been preserved, our film heritage of Lenin.

From still another perspective, it is an interior monologue proceeding from the old to the new, from the past to the present, from slavery to the free and civilized life of the man liberated by the revolution.

1934

I Wish to Share My Experience

In 1918 Mikhail Koltsov invited me to work in cinema. This was not long after the Moscow Soviet's decree on the introduction of control over the film industry during the period preceding its nationalization.

We began to put out *Kinonedelia*—a screen journal. A few months later Comrade Koltsov took up another job and entrusted the management of newsreel to me.

The creative route from *Kinonedelia* (1918 and 1919) to *Three Songs of Lenin* has been long and complex, involving more than 150 experiments in filming and organizing newsreel footage. It's impossible to list all these experiments in a short article. I feel, however, it's essential to recall at least individual examples and types of these films.

So, along with *Kinonedelia* (a serial newsreel) there are experimental studies such as *The Battle of Tsaritsyn.* Together with the "flash newsreel" there are film lead-articles, film-feuilletons, film-poems (the twenty-three issues of *Kinopravda*). In addition to *Kinokalendar* there are large historical pictures such as *A History of the Civil War.* The word-radio-theme *One Sixth of the World* gave rise to an October march (*The Eleventh Year*) and later the "film without words," *The Man with a Movie Camera.* Film diaries (*Pioneer Pravda*), a film epic (*Forward, Soviet!*), film essays (*The Trial of the

S. R.'s), films with a special purpose (*Kinoglaz*), a sound symphony (*Enthusiasm*), and lastly, a film that has its roots in images of folk creation, the "symphony of thoughts" (*Three Songs of Lenin*).

All these newsreel films were committed to a single basic, common goal—showing the truth. Not kino-eye for the sake of kino-eye, but showing *pravda* ["truth"], *kinopravda*. All cinematic means, all cinematic possibilities, all cinematic inventions, techniques and methods in order to make the invisible visible, the unclear clear, the hidden manifest, the disguised overt; in order to tell the truth about our Revolution, about the construction of socialism, the Civil War.

Thus we strive to show people unmasked, not acting; we strive to film people so that they do not notice, to read in faces the thoughts that kino-eye revealed.

In this respect *Three Songs of Lenin* offers examples of "nonacting": the address of the Dneprostroi woman shock-worker, the decorated woman from the kolkhoz [collective farm], and others. Shots of living people reecho in our memory with the wife of the watchman who choked to death in the film *Life Caught Unawares,* the children in *The Man with a Movie Camera,* those at prayer in *Enthusiasm,* etc.

However, it is not enough just to film bits of truth. These bits must be organized in order to produce a truth of the whole. And this task is no less difficult, perhaps even more difficult, than the filming of the individual bits of truth.

Creating kinopravda about Lenin—even within the confines of a theme strictly limited by the assignment—required making use of all previous experience of kino-eye filmings, all acquired knowledge; it meant the registration and careful study of all our previous work on this theme.

Undiscovered and unpublished shots of the living Lenin had to be found. This was done with the greatest patience and persistence by my assistant, Comrade Svilova, who reported ten new film clippings of the living Lenin for the tenth anniversary of his death. For this purpose, Comrade Svilova studied over six hundred kilometers of positive and negative footage located in various cities of the Soviet Union.

A search for documents on the Civil War had to be made, since our film, *A History of the Civil War,* turned out to have been split up and sorted out under different titles in warehouses, and it was impossible to locate it whole anywhere.

We had to try to transfer Lenin's actual voice onto film. Shtro, the

Three Songs of Lenin

sound engineer, succeeded in doing this after a whole series of experiments.

A great deal of work was involved in searching out and recording Turkish, Turkmen, and Uzbek folk songs about Lenin. Along with synchronous sound shooting, it was necessary to shoot a whole series of silent sequences in various parts of the Soviet Union, starting with the Kara-Kum desert and ending with the arrival of the *Cheliuskin* crew in Moscow.

And all of that was done only as work preliminary to the editing, to gather the essential footage.

The footage then was subjected to special laboratory processing in order to improve the quality of the image and sound.

Cheliuskin. The *Cheliuskin* was a Soviet ship that sank in the Chukotsk Sea in February 1934 during a polar expedition. Crew members and scientists, known as *Cheliuskintsy,* were rescued by plane. Several documentary films were made on the subject—trans. and ed.

After all this preliminary work, we started creating a new editing plan (probably the tenth). This should not be surprising since an account of the editing can be foreseen only within those limits permitted by the production of a newsreel film, and of course within limits that permit giving an account of a film's contents, not in screen shots, but in words. A documentary film plan is not something rigid. It's a plan in action. The production of the film follows the preliminary plan. But the definitive editing plan results from the dynamic interaction of this plan of action with newsreel of current events (thus, for example, neither the theme of the *Cheliuskin* crew, nor the content of folk songs that were found later, nor the murder of Comrade Kirov could have been foreseen in the original plan).

In the process of shooting and editing the film, I covered thousands of pieces of paper with my writing, all merely in order to show the truth on the screen.

I had to write poems and short stories, dry reports, travel sketches, dramatic episodes, musical word-collages; I had to make schemata and diagrams—and all this to achieve the graphic, crystalline composition of a given series of shots. It would be incorrect to imagine that all these verbal and engineering compositions go into the final film in the form of a text or as blueprints. They are destroyed as the editing equations are solved, as the sought-for cinematic quality is found.

The elimination of falsity, the achievement of that sincerity and clarity noted by critics in *Three Songs of Lenin* required exceptionally complex editing. In this respect, the experience of *The Man with a Movie Camera*, *One Sixth of the World,* of *Enthusiasm* and *The Eleventh Year* were of great help to our production group. These were, so to speak, "films that beget films."

In deriving the lessons of these films we learned to write full-length documentary films with film-shots and to overcome by invention all the difficulties that barred the way.

the murder of Comrade Kirov. Sergei M. Kirov (1886–1934) became chief of the Communist Party organization in Leningrad in 1926 and entered the Politburo in 1930. He gained added prominence through his opposition to Stalin on the issue of death sentences for dissident Communists. Upheld by a majority in the Politburo, he was elected to the Central Committee in 1934. His mysterious murder, that same year, served as the point of departure for the series of investigations, arrests, and trials that characterized the ruthless purge within the party and the nation in the years immediately preceding the Second World War—ed.

As we approach the fifteenth anniversary of Soviet cinema we should make it our goal to use all previous experience to confer upon our work in film the utmost in simplicity and clarity.

Without lowering the artistic level.

Without loss of quality.

1934

Three Songs of Lenin and Kino-Eye

I'm very touched by your reception of the film, more so than by the results of other screenings. The estrangement that could be sensed between workers in nonacted and those in acted film has always prevented our understanding one another.

From the very beginning our work had to be given some sort of name, and it was called kino-eye. However, the discussions that took place, when people wrote for or against this movement, did not express the essence of our viewpoint. Our ideas and what our opponents or supporters wrote were somehow "out of sync." They always distinguished between kino-eye and kinopravda. Even Lebedev wrote that he was for kinopravda but against kino-eye.

Things continued this way for a long time because the critics didn't understand that there was no kino-eye for the sake of kino-eye, no life caught unawares for the sake of life caught unawares, and no hidden filming for the sake of hidden filming. It wasn't a program; it was a means. Kinopravda, which they accepted, was made possible by means of kino-eye.

How can one explain this? I remember my debut in cinema. It was quite odd. It involved not my filming but my jumping one-and-a-half stories from a summer house beside a grotto at no. 7 Malyi Gnezdnikovsky Lane.

The cameraman was ordered to record my jump in such a way that my entire fall, my facial expression, all my thoughts, etc., would be seen. I went up to the grotto's edge, jumped off, gestured as with a veil, and went on. The result on film was the following:

Lebedev. N. A. Lebedev (1897–), film and art historian, published strongly critical views of Vertov's theory and practice toward the end of the 1920s and at the beginning of the 1930s.

A man approaches the edge of a grotto; fear and indecision appear on his face; he's thinking: "I won't jump." Then he decides: "No, it's embarrassing, they're watching." Once again he approaches the edge, once again his face shows indecision. Then one sees his determination growing, he's saying to himself, "I must," and he leaves the grotto edge. He flies through the air, flies off-balance; he's thinking that he must position himself to land on his feet. He straightens out, approaches the ground; once more his face shows indecision, fear. Finally his feet touch ground. His immediate thought is that he fell, then that he's got to keep his balance. Next he thinks that he jumped nicely but should not let on that he has, and, like an acrobat who's performed a difficult maneuver on the trapeze, he pretends that it was awfully easy. And with that expression the man slowly "floats off."

From the viewpoint of the ordinary eye you see untruth. From the viewpoint of the cinematic eye (aided by special cinematic means, in this case, accelerated shooting) you see the truth. If it's a question of reading someone's thougnts at a distance (and often what matters to us is not to hear a person's words but to read his thoughts), then you have that opportunity right here. It has been revealed by the kino-eye.

It is possible, by means of the kino-eye to remove a man's mask, to obtain a bit of kinopravda. And it was the revelation of just this truth, by all the means available to me, that I designated as my entire future path in cinema.

Speaking symbolically, can't we find a similar "leap" here in *Three Songs of Lenin*? Yes. It's present if only in the woman shock-worker. Why does she have an effect? Because she's good at acting? Nothing of the kind. Because I got from her what I got from myself during the jump: the synchrony of words and thoughts.

If a shock-worker is addressing a congress and speaking words that he has memorized, or if he's thinking about something else at that time, you won't feel that synchrony of word and thought.

I can provide another example from silent cinema. Recall the film *Kinoglaz* (*Life Caught Unawares*). A man—a watchman—dies in the film. How does his wife react? After learning that her husband is dying, you'd suppose she should tear her hair, weep, fall down, etc. Whereas she's motionless. When the doctor makes that famous hopeless gesture, she suddenly raises her hands and fixes her hair.

What was the shooting of *Life Caught Unawares* for us? It was a campaign for those methods that would enable us to reveal kino-pravda, to lay bare the actual emotions, the feelings of that woman, of the homeless child, the conjurer, the children, etc.

But my plans extended much further. I was interested in exposing acting more subtle still. In life, people very often act, and sometimes rather well. I wanted to remove that mask, too.

This was a very difficult task. To solve it, the camera had to penetrate into a room, into the intimate emotional experiences of people. It had to be done so that the camera would penetrate to the level on which a person reveals himself completely.

In previous work I frequently presented my shooting methods outright. I left the construction of those methods open and visible, Meyerhold-style. And this was wrong.

However, whatever I did, I acted as I had that first time when I leaped from the roof.

My latest film is the very same kinopravda, the vast film-truth of life, that has apparently succeeded better than anything else.

I've frequently been criticized because, for example, in showing the Donbas I show it absolutely concretely, with real details, in all its fullness. But if I'm developing, let's say, the theme of industrialization in general, I can take machines, machine tools from various factories and combine them, as though in the palm of my hand.

From the human eye's viewpoint I haven't really the right to "edit in" myself beside those who are seated in this hall, for instance. Yet in kino-eye space, I can edit myself not only sitting here beside you, but in various parts of the globe. It would be absurd to create obstacles such as walls and distance for kino-eye.

In anticipation of television it should be clear that such "vision-at-a-distance" is possible in film-montage.

The idea that truth is only what is seen by the human eye is refuted both by microscopic research and all the data supplied by the technologically aided eye in general.

It is refuted by the *very nature of man's thought.*

Meyerhold-style. Vertov is referring to the critical innovations of Vsevolod E. Meyerhold (1874–1940), the dominant theatrical director of the revolutionary and postrevolutionary periods, who submitted the conventions and codes of theatrical representation to a radical analysis. Meyerhold's work, which profoundly influenced an entire generation of postrevolutionary artists including his student Eisenstein, was entirely consistent with the constructivist aesthetic and thus no longer officially approved at the time Vertov's text was written—ed.

When it was said here that a million grains of sand make a dune, I wanted to remind you that those words, which we once took as our slogan, have now, too, become a great force.

I hope that it's clear after all I've said that those elements in *Three Songs of Lenin* which comrades have liked most and which they considered to be absolutely new represent, in fact, the development of all our previous work.

1934

Kinopravda [1934]

A basement on Tver Boulevard. It's dark and very damp. An earthen floor with holes. You walk and fall into them. Big, hungry rats poke about between your feet. Somewhere above you are a latticed window and the feet of passersby. There's water beneath you—the water pipes are dripping. You hang the ends of the film higher up so the film strips don't get wet. But the rollers become unglued from the dampness; the scissors, rulers, splicers rust. You sit, continually hunched over bits of damp film. It will soon be dawn. It's damp. Cold. Your teeth are chattering. The author-director of *Kinopravda* bundles Comrade Svilova in his short fur coat. It's the last night of work and the next two issues of *Kinopravda* will be ready. Tomorrow the film critics will write that *Kinopravda* is a "stupid nonentity"; that *Kinopravda* workers are "a sore abscess on the body of cinematography"; that it's "cracked cinema"; that it's the "exaggerated flourishes of Dziga Vertov." Tomorrow Anoshchenko, the critic-director, will write that we are "kino-cocci." That we're "another form of the bacteria of futurism" that has struck "the turbid nutrient medium of cinema in revival and begun to ferment in its still fragile organism.". . .

But *Pravda* thinks otherwise. Page one of *Pravda* carries an article by Mikhail Koltsov, in which he says of *Kinopravda*: "They play no music at the showing, but music pours from the screen—in the measured gestures of a playing orchestra, in the smooth rhythm of columns of marching soldiers." And further: "History went by—living, palpitating, tugging at the mind, the heart, the imagination . . . *Kinopravda* is skillfully, deftly, professionally made. The slovenly amateurism of our newsreels is now a thing of the past."

Kinogazeta doesn't want to consider our work seriously. In a jeering feuilleton style it reports a speech by Vertov:

> Dziga Vertov began:
> "I don't know how to speak. And therefore I won't." True to his promise, he went no further, but did something else. "I know what boots are made of. Here I am. Feel me and you'll learn what boots are made of. Down with . . . ! Down with . . . ! Down with . . . !" To make things easier to express, Vertov booed everything in sight.

Pravda doesn't jeer. It treats Vertov differently. It publishes a serious critical article, "The Theory and Practice of Comrade Vertov," which concludes with the following words: " . . . this experimental work, emerging from the process of proletarian revolution, is a big step forward in the direction of the creation of a truly proletarian cinematography."

The nineteenth *Kinopravda* is released. *Kinogazeta* once again jeers:

> The last filmmaker to speak was Dziga Vertov. This kino-cowboy kino-lied about kinopravda for ten minutes, after which the public had to share Vertov's misfortune. The fact is that his movie camera had run away from him, and the completely innocent audience had to watch the camera's entire run—for some unknown reason entitled *Kinopravda* no. 19.

Kinogazeta describes the "content" of the nineteenth *Kinopravda:*

> The mix-up on the screen is beyond belief. One minute the camera rushes toward a naked girl in the Black Sea then jumps on the backs of Vogul deer; a meter later it's in the Moscow House of the Peasant; still another meter and for no earthly reason it's crawling beneath a locomotive . . . and there's no thread of logic to explain all this "camera levity." Apparently it's unclear even to the authors of this latest experiment just what this bacchanal is supposed to prove. It's a "constructivist-aesthetic" mess. . . . Etc., etc.

Pravda reacts differently to the contents of *Kinopravda* no. 19: "*Kinopravda,*" writes *Pravda,*

> is devoted to the woman worker, and the film shows us, filing past, in an associative chain, types of Soviet women—from peasants working in the field to the woman editor selecting the negative for this issue of *Kinopravda.* Comrade Vertov provides many interesting moments. A step forward in simplicity, seriousness, and intelligibility has been made.

Izvestiia writes of the same issue of *Kinopravda:*

> No. 19 is very successful; it graphically demonstrates how the skillful presentation of everyday life can be filled with drama, humor, and gripping, inspired interest. This art has its own drama, painting, and silent film music. Above all, we sorely need such *Kinopravda* throughout the entire Soviet Union, in every corner—whether "backward" or enlightened.

The *Lenin Film-Calendar* and the two *Leninist Kinopravda*s were the first attempts to collect and organize documentary footage on Lenin.

The *Lenin Film-Calendar* is a chronological compendium of film-documents on the living Lenin.

Leninist Kinopravda (no. 21), thirty-five hundred feet of documentary film on the life, illness, and death of Lenin, is organized in three parts, each of which is divided in turn into the following links:

Part I: (1) the wounding of Lenin, (2) Lenin on the dictatorship of the proletariat, (3) Lenin and the Red Army, (4) Lenin on the proletariat and the peasants, (5) Lenin and the Comintern, (6) the masses—for Lenin, (7) the factories—for Lenin, (8) agriculture—for Lenin, (9) the troops—for Lenin, (10) children—for Lenin, (11) the East—for Lenin, (12) Lenin and electrification, (13) the transition from war communism to the NEP.

Part II: (1) Lenin's illness and the children, (2) a bulletin on his illness, (3) death, (4) at Union House, (5) the orphaned Central Committee, (6) Lenin and the masses, (7) the family at the coffin, (8) workers at the coffin, (9) peasants at the coffin, (10) Eastern workers beside the coffin, (11) Red Army soldiers, sailors, young Leninists, (12) "We shall carry out your precepts and your work!"

Lenin's tomb: *Three Songs of Lenin*

Part III: (1) Lenin is no more, but his strength is with us, (2) one hundred thousand join the Russian Communist Party, (3) worker-Leninists, (4) women worker-Leninists, (5) the Leninist party, (6) young Leninists, (7) the Mausoleum, (8) young Leninists—the children of the workers—fight for the cause of Ilyich in the countryside, (9) at a workers' meeting a peasant calls on workers to fulfill Ilyich's precepts regarding the countryside, (10) our most pressing and important task, (11) along the Leninist track.

The following themes are covered in the second *Leninist Kinopravda* ("Lenin Lives in the Hearts of the Peasants"): (1) Lenin, working men and women, (2) Lenin and the peasants, (3) reminiscences of Lenin, (4) Yaroslavsky on Lenin, (5) Lenin and colonial peoples, etc. *Pravda* writes of this *Kinopravda:*

> The picture is made to show those images evoked by the memory of Lenin that live in the hearts of the worker

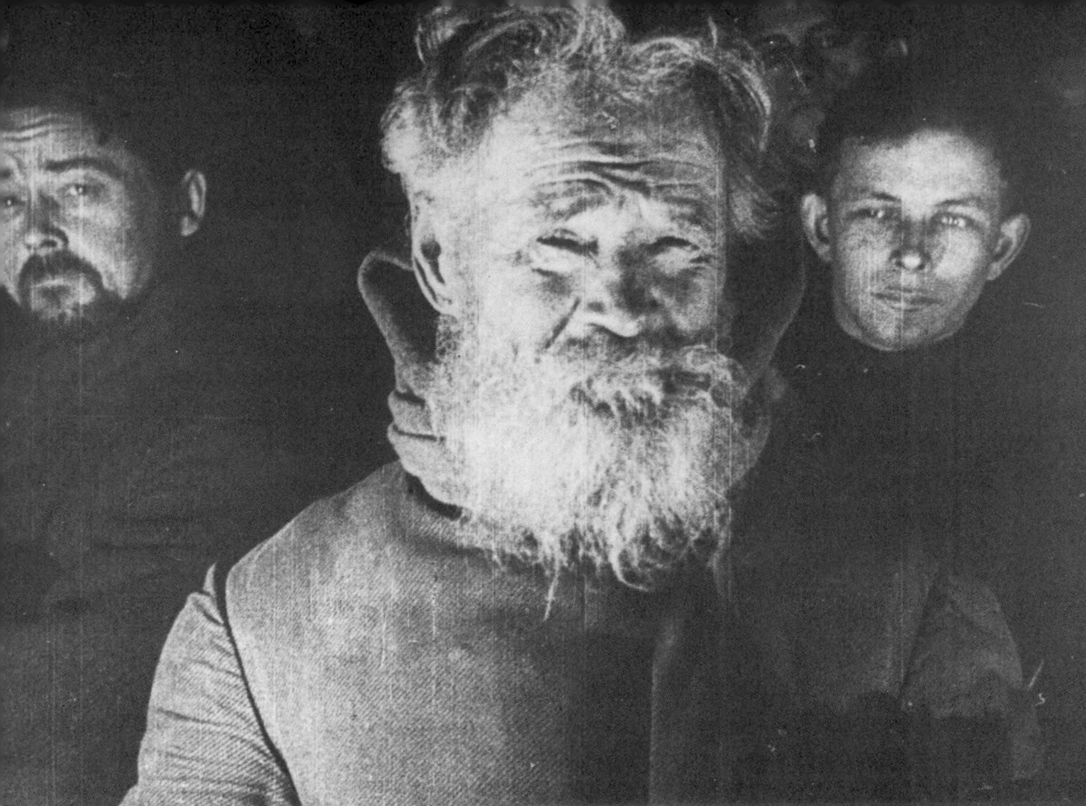

Three Songs of Lenin

> and peasant. A speech at a rally is enlivened through the interesting device of introducing a whole series of episodes that include scenes from the life of colonial and semicolonial peoples. A step further has been taken in the direction of greater simplicity and intelligibility; it should be hailed, since the picture is clearly intended for the mass viewer.

The experience of not only these *Leninist Kinopravda*s but of all twenty-three *Kinopravda*s is put to use in *Three Songs of Lenin.*

The experience of *Kinoglaz* and *The Man with a Movie Camera* is also used. There's nothing terrible in this. Those comrades who say, "We're for kinopravda but against kino-eye" are wrong. *"Three Songs of Lenin,"* they say, "marks Vertov's renunciation of his kino-eye position and his return to kinopravda." Is this so?

Let's examine things.

If we look at history, at old records and diaries, we see that in 1918 (my slow-motion leap from the top of a grotto, then slow-

Clara Zetkin in *Three Songs of Lenin*

motion leapfrog, etc.) kino-eye was understood as a "slow-motion eye." Cranking the camera at maximum speed made it possible to see my thoughts during my leap on the screen. Thus, kino-eye, from the very moment of its conception, was not a matter of trick effects, or of kino-eye for its own sake. Slow-motion filming was understood as the opportunity to make the invisible visible, the unclear clear, the hidden manifest, the disguised overt, the acted nonacted, untruth truth—kinopravda (i.e., *truth* obtained by cinematic means, in this case, by means of the slow-motion eye).

The original notion of kino-eye as a slow-motion eye is eventually expanded. Definitions of kino-eye such as "kino-eye = cinema-analysis, kino-eye = the theory of intervals, kino-eye = the theory of relativity on the screen," etc., emerge. The usual rate of sixteen frames per second is abolished. Along with slow motion, animation, the single frame, microfilming, macrofilming shooting in reverse or with a moving camera, etc., are declared normal film techniques. Kino-eye is defined as "that which the eye does not see," as the microscope and telescope of time (from the animated blooming of a flower to the ultrarapid flight of a bullet), as the "negative of time" (filming in reverse), as the opportunity to see without limits or distance, as the remote control of cameras, as tele-eye, as X-ray eye, as "life caught unawares," etc.

Definitions so diverse did not exclude but mutually complemented one another, since by kino-eye was understood all cinematic means and possibilities, all cinematic inventions, techniques, and methods that might reveal and show the *truth.*

Not kino-eye for its own sake, but the truth through kino-eye, that is, kinopravda. Not filming "unawares" for its own sake, but to show people without masks, without makeup; to catch them with the camera's eye in a moment of nonacting. To read their thoughts, laid bare by kino-eye.

Not "trick" effects, but the *truth*—that's what matters in kino-eye work. Therefore we should understand kinopravda to mean not only the twenty-three issues of *Kinopravda,* the journal, but *Forward, Soviet!,* the films *Kinoglaz*, *One Sixth of the World*, *The Man with a Movie Camera* as well, and, of course, our latest big kinopravda—*Three Songs of Lenin.*

In these days of victory for the great *kinopravda*s, for *Three Songs of Lenin,* I fervently clasp the hands of my comrades in the long struggle.

1934

My Latest Experiment

For fifteen years I studied writing in film. To be able to write with a camera not with a pen. Hindered by the lack of a film-alphabet, I attempted to create that alphabet. I specialized in "factual film writing." I strove to become a newsreel film writer. I learned this at an editing table. And in an armored train at Lugansk. And beside the exhumed relics of Sergius Radonezhsky. And in Comrade Kalinin's train. And at the trial of Mironov, the Cossack colonel. And in Comrade Kozhevnikov's partisan army. I learned by making the *Kinonedelia*s, by making *The Battle of Tsaritsyn,* by assembling *The Anniversary of the Revolution,* by wracking my brains over the thirteen-reel film review entitled *A History of the Civil War.*

Comrade Kalinin. Mikhail Kalinin (1872–1946), of peasant origin, became President of the All-Russian Central Executive Committee in 1919, succeeding Sverdlov in the position that made him titular head of state. His support of Stalin within the Politburo during the critical period in 1928 furthered both the establishment of the industrialization process and Stalin's growing domination of the party organization—ed.

Three Songs of Lenin

I was not mistaken in my course of action. This can be seen, if only from Comrade Lenin's instruction that "the production of new films inspired by Communist ideas and reflecting Soviet reality should begin with newsreel."

The twenty-three *Kinopravdas* formed the next stage in my studies. I learned how to make film-essays. Film-feuilletons. Film-poems. Film "editorials." I tried composing film-epics. Then the bold *Life Caught Unawares* or *Kinoglaz* Part One. And the next stage in my studies. *Leninist Kinopravda.* The epic *Forward, Soviet!.* The radio-cinema film *One Sixth of the World.* The October march, *The Eleventh Year.* The film without words, *The Man with a Movie Camera.* The sound symphony, *Enthusiasm.* These films were, so to speak, "film begetting films" seen in relation to *Three Songs of Lenin,* my latest, many-sided experiment.

the production of new films . . . Cf. the collection *Samoe vazhnoe iz vsekh iskusstv* ("The Most Important of the Arts") (Moscow, 1963), p. 123.

Three Songs of Lenin

Here is a report on my latest experiment. It is, on the one hand, a film-document of Lenin's death. Of his final forty kilometers. Of Lenin's final route from Gorki to Moscow on January 23, 1924.

If, on the one hand, there is the funeral parade, the parting masses and their leader, there is also Lenin in motion on film. The preserved film-documents of the living Lenin, our film heritage of Lenin. Seen from still another perspective, *Three Songs of Lenin* is a film-document on the Civil War.

There is a fourth group of documents—those of the Dnepr, Magnitogorsk, and White Sea construction projects, and other documents of the building of socialism.

And there is a fifth group of documents—those of living people, heroes, builders, a woman cement worker, a woman from a collective farm, an oil shock-worker, Turkish women students, military students at Fergana, etc., ending with the heroes of the *Chelyuskin* and the proletarians of different countries, fighting for the Revolution under the banner of Lenin.

Three Songs of Lenin

And finally, one of the film's most important features: the documents of popular creation, folk songs about Lenin.

The entire film passes before the viewer-listeners in the light of folk images, from Turkish, Turkmen, and Uzbek folk songs.

I covered many hundreds, perhaps thousands of blank pages with writing as we shot and edited film. And all merely to destroy what I'd written the moment a resolution—as clear and as simple as the smile of Belik, the woman cement worker—would arrive. I had to write poems and short stories, dry reports, travel sketches, dramatic episodes, and *zaum* word-combinations; I had to make outlines and diagrams—and all this to achieve the graphic, crystalline combination of a particular sequence of shots.

It seems to me that not everyone yet understands the difference between amorphous and crystalline states of documentary footage, between the inorganic and organic combining of shots. Some are

zaum. Zaum is the name given to the "transrational" language of the verbal experiments characteristic of Russian futurist poetry—trans.

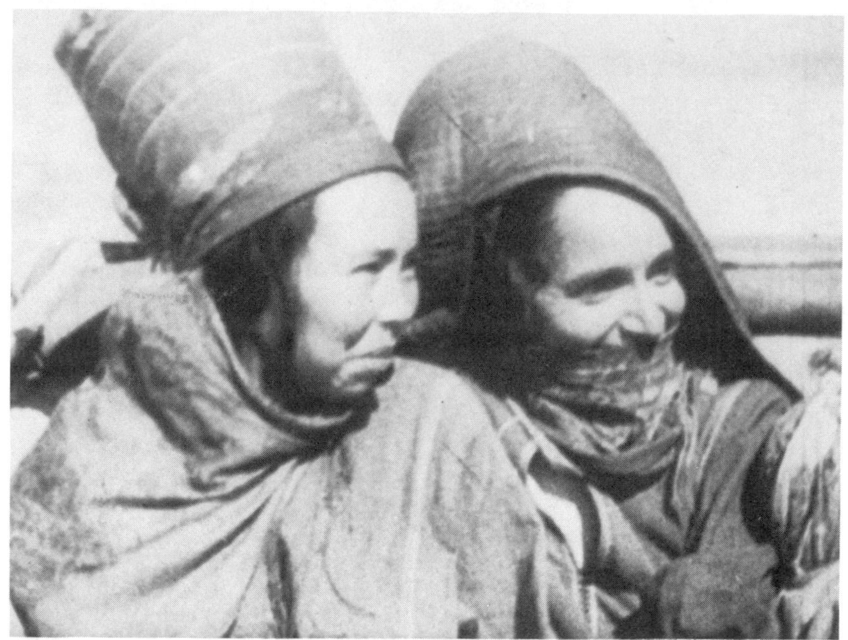

Three Songs of Lenin

Three Songs of Lenin

still unaware of what it means to write a full-length film in film-shots. They still confuse films translated from the theatrical and literary language with film-originals, with work by a film author. And therefore they underestimate the difficulties that block the way of the second path, that of innovation.

The image "Lenin is springtime" passes through the entire film and develops parallel to other themes.

This theme, like the others, is not channeled through words, but takes other routes, through the interaction of sound and image, through the union of many channels . . .

Three Songs of Lenin is a many-sided work. However, it draws its basic strength from its roots in images of popular creation, generated by the emancipated masses. Lenin the giant and the beloved Ilyich, close friend and great leader, and "Lenin has poured into each of us a drop of his blood"—that is how Lenin's image is seen by the emancipated Turkmen and Uzbek; that is how he appears to the doubly, the triply emancipated woman of the Soviet East.

1935

On the Organization of a Creative Laboratory

Man freed from capitalist slavery. Man freed from the condition of the "robot." Man freed from humiliation, from hunger, unemployment, poverty, ruin. Man with his right to creation, with his rich, productive development, with his mastery of technology, science, literature, art.

To show the behavior of these men on the screen. Is there any finer task for the artist? Yet, if we want to fulfill it, we must understand that it is difficult in the extreme, that its realization depends, not on good intentions, but on plain organization, on organizational technique. Its resolution requires not bare enthusiasm, nor bare hands, nor turmoil and exhausting strain.

To perform this task and facilitate our creative group's transition from the production of poetic surveys to films on man's behavior outside the studio and under natural conditions, we must come down to earth. We must leave our ivory tower to do preliminary work for proper organization of this enterprise, for the proper distribution of forces, organization of the location, the proper use of machines.

The proposal on the organization of a creative laboratory was prompted, first of all, by the need to put an end to the waste of our time and energy, by our need to establish rational order in our nonstandardized work processes, to organize correctly our technical base, to introduce rhythm into work, to eliminate all obstacles in the way of realizing the task we have set for ourselves.

The laboratory's goal is to organize our work correctly. Essential for attaining this goal are persistence and firmness of character, which break through any and all barriers.

The first enormous barrier encountered proved to be the impossibility of recording sound and of synchronized shooting in any location where the subject was under observation. The equipment at Mezhrabpomfilm [International Workers' Relief Film Studios] was totally dependent on the presence of a three-phase current on location. We found it impossible, technically, to film people in the country, in fields, under natural conditions, and to observe their behavior. We immediately saw this as our paramount obstacle, and we focused our reports on the construction of portable sound-film equipment such as would permit synchronous shooting anywhere, at any time. However, under the usual, standard conditions of production we could resolve this issue in word only, by promises and resolutions. Concretely, we got nothing except promises, whose fulfillment was postponed till "tomorrow." "Tomorrow" not in the finite but in the infinite sense. A "tomorrow" approaching with the speed of two parallel lines converging.

If given a creative laboratory, we would take it upon ourselves to eliminate this primary obstacle—a difficult but not an insurmountable one.

Filming in our laboratory should satisfy the following technical conditions:

1. The filming should be instantaneous, that is, subject to no delay, simultaneous with the action of the subject under observation.
2. The filming should be noiseless, to avoid attracting the attention of the subject being filmed, and should leave no background noise on the film.
3. Filming should be technically possible anywhere (a peasant hut, a field, an airport, a desert, etc.).

4. Both cameras, silent and sound, should be interconnected so that one camera does not impede the other, so that the filming begins without preparation and signals, so that the whole is in continual readiness, requiring no special guide marks for synchronization.
5. The sound quality should meet standard requirements in effect at the time our best films were completed.
6. The equipment for sync shooting should be compact, without bulky accumulators, and should not depend on the presence of an electrical network on location.
7. The possibility of mishaps should be eliminated since we're filming scenes and actions that cannot be repeated (we are not dealing with people who are acting).
8. The actions of the cameraman and soundman should be maximally coordinated and united, simultaneous—this can be best achieved by combining the sound and silent recordings in a single unified camera with two tracks.
9. While solving the problems related to the sound camera and filming independent of an electric network, etc., we can, at the same time, implement other technical solutions in the laboratory, those that have already been developed but not yet carried out by our group (essential types of film and lenses, shooting indoors, at night, in concealment, from a distance, etc.).
10. To film human behavior competently outside the studio, under natural conditions, it's indispensable to concentrate in a single place all the techniques and methods of filming, as well as the special devices, discovered and invented at various times. This is possible only under the conditions of a creative laboratory.

The second enormous obstacle until now has been the impossibility of properly organizing our editing under standardized conditions.

The inability to preserve, from one film to another, an author's creative stockpile on film. The lack of one's right to make a new creative stockpile. The lack of a permanent place for continual editing.

All this has reduced editing work to individual onslaughts. To having to repeat, two and three times, what one has already discovered and done. One has to begin work anew each time.

The laboratory we have organized solves all these problems by switching from a system of individual editing onslaughts to a continuous editing process. By switching from the unsystematic preservation of individual montage bits to the author's film archive.

The creative laboratory puts an end to the systematic destruction of our preliminary editing work as well as of our shooting.

The third serious obstacle in our work has been the impossibility, thus far, of developing, training, and preserving, under standard conditions, experienced and specially prepared people.

Once a film is finished, people are usually assigned elsewhere, and each time we've had to begin anew the work of preparing special cadres for our particular type of film. Once again, we waste time and energy.

Under laboratory conditions, the cameraman, soundman, director, assistant, information person, production man, and other personnel would improve continuously from film to film. They would continually develop, not retarding, but accelerating, the release of the creative product.

Obstacles of a similar kind have thus far blocked our work in information and all areas of organization. Together they have formed a big, blank wall, resistant to living ideas and upon which all our attempts to break through into films on human behavior have thus far shattered.

In the end, the contradiction between the forms of production organization assigned to us and our creative plans reduced our efforts to naught. No matter how we intensified our efforts under conditions destructive to us, conditions which continue to exist, the result was always the same. As we all know, zero multiplied by any other number remains zero.

The creative laboratory will produce films of a special type, on human behavior, not under hackneyed conditions of organization but under special terms proper to this type of film.

First objective—creative cadres. Not apathetic and indifferent people, but enthusiasts for this new and difficult cause. Not here because they've been assigned, but by calling. Not randomly selected, but chosen by the head of the creative workshop. Not transient, temporary people, but a permanent staff; each developing in his particular area from one film to another, devoting all his talents and strength to this work. Each will receive the opportunity for continuous self-improvement, for the continuous realization of his proposals, both large and small, for the rationalization of the work process.

Second objective—a filming base. Not a random one, but specially adapted to our specific type of work. Not temporary, but permanent. Not dead, but developing. Not stationary, but portable. Not tied to a fixed location, not absolutely dependent on the presence of electrical wiring, but allowing for synchronous shooting on two tracks with no loss of quality, anywhere, any time, under any conditions.

Third objective—an editing base. Not temporary, but permanent. Not random, but carefully adapted. Not anonymous, but bearing the author's signature. Not immobile, but constantly engaged. A film archive of a director's documents on file.

Fourth objective—an information base. Not chance scraps of information (from one call to the next), but a system of continual observation.

Fifth objective—an organizational base. Not organizational rush jobs (from one alarm to the next), but continual readiness for reconnaissance or filming at any moment.

Sixth objective—work at developing not a single, isolated film, but several themes interconnected by creation and organization. No preliminary scenario of the future actions of a subject under observation, but a synthesis of film-observations: the synthetic examination of documents gathered on film. Inconceivable without analysis of the object of synthesis. Unity of analysis and synthesis. The simultaneity of the writing, filming, and editing processes with observation of the actions, behavior, and surroundings of the subject filmed.

Analysis (from the unknown to the known) and synthesis (from the known to the unknown), not in mutual opposition, but indissolubly connected. The synthesis of the behavior of the subject under observation as an inseparable part of the analysis.

Seventh objective—influence on the general level of Soviet film production by the creation of a series of models of different types of cinematic production.

Eighth objective—a gradual quantitative increase (in proportion to the increase of documents accumulated) and a qualitative improvement in the film-models, but without an increase in cost estimates or laboratory staff groups, thanks to continual improvement in that staff's information, organization, shooting, and editing efforts.

Ninth objective—elimination of the director's wastage of film stock thanks to a continuous production process involving a series of themes and to the possibility of using footage not being employed in a particular theme in another theme that's related or is being shot parallel.

Tenth objective—elimination of the usual work stoppages through a continuous production process, by the readiness to film at any given time and the ability to replace immediately shooting cut short for some reason with other work on either the same or a different theme.

N.B.: According to information in my possession, the laboratory could be located at Potylikha, at the Mosfilm studio. They also have an Eclair camera, the type most suited to our work.

1936

The Truth About the Heroic Struggle

The eight issues of the film-magazine released in the past two months and devoted to the events in Spain tell the truth about the Spanish people and its heroic, revolutionary struggle. Documents of great power and persuasiveness are conveyed on the screen. The events in Spain are stirring Soviet citizens.

The filmings in Spain represent an indisputable achievement of Soviet cinematography and reflect the great efforts of Makaseyev and Karmen.

Admittedly, it was difficult at first for the young cameramen who found themselves working under unusual conditions. They had to shoot under battle conditions and yet not get in the way of the fighters on the popular front. At the same time, they had to get into

Makaseyev and Karmen. Boris K. Makaseyev (1907–) was a cameraman and the author of many screenplays and newsreel scenarios. Roman Karmen (1906–1980), cameraman and documentary filmmaker, specialized in the cinematic reportage of current events. During the 1930s and 1940s, he worked on films shot in Spain and China as well as in the USSR. The film to which Vertov refers here is Esfir Shub's *Spain* (1936–37), on which he and Makaseyev worked as cameramen.

the thick of things, to record on film the people's heroic struggle.

In looking over the releases one after another, you can see clearly how, after mastering the material, Makaseyev and Karmen continually improved in their handling of the task before them.

Neither the first journal, nor the next one, fully reflects the extraordinary struggle of the Spanish people.

Makaseyev and Karmen soon realized their basic mistake. Beginning with the journal's fourth issue, a turning point in the cameramen's method of work can be seen. Their lens is now focused on the real, the direct and heroic aspect of the struggle. That struggle elicits a living response, overwhelming the Soviet people. Recall the shots of Huesca under siege by revolutionary forces. How many powerful scenes—a wounded fighter collapsing on an embankment, those who have fallen fighting for the well-being of their homeland carried out on stretchers—anyone can see and feel that this is genuine, totally unembellished, heroic struggle.

What sets comrades Makaseyev and Karmen apart? Their extreme activity and resourcefulness. There are only two of them, after all, but they manage to be in a dozen places at once. Dangerous battles, scenes of peaceful life, the fighting men's leisure moments, the speeches of revolutionary leaders, children's games, the deaths of heroes—none of this escapes the cameramen's attention.

Starting with the fifth issue and continuing, Makaseyev and Karmen show themselves to be sensitive, cultivated film journalists able to orient themselves under any conditions. They are already paying greater attention to the technique of shooting. In this respect, the shots made in the port of Alicante on the cruiser *Jaime I,* among others, are a success.

The sequences are typically becoming shorter in length, but, at the same time, their variety is increasing. The cameramen vary a single theme with different shot sizes. This enables them to edit whole episodes, as, for example, "The Siege of the Alcazar" and "The Destruction of Toledo" (in the latter episode there are interesting touches on the screen that strengthen the picture as a whole, such as the demolished room with an overturned, smashed piano).

The last three issues are joined by a single unbroken thread—only people who have grown up in our country could so film and understand the full significance of the events taking place; everything that occurs on the screen strengthens and supports a single basic idea: "We will not surrender Madrid!" On the screen we see people who've come to seek shelter and refuge in Madrid. They will defend Madrid to the last drop of their blood. They replace today the comrades whom they now accompany in a funeral procession, on their final journey. Their faces are pale and mournful, but filled with resolution.

The other day the newspaper announced, "Insurgents have bombed automobiles carrying children, between Madrid and Getafe. Many children were killed." I remembered a touching and troubling episode shown in the newsreel. Madrid is in danger, and they're taking all the children out of the city, in cars. Dozens, hundreds of sweet little children sadly bid goodbye to their parents. The scene stirs the viewer deeply. Episodes from life, so simple and vivid, should be filmed more often.

The viewer should be shown the people of the revolution, everyone should be familiar with the images and names of the courageous Spanish fighters for freedom. You cannot show all the heroes, of course, but some, at least, must be shown. And in order to convey the full grandeur and meaning of the historic events the Spanish people are now experiencing, authentic sound must be provided together with the visual document. The narrator's reading should be replaced by documentary sound footage. The richness of the Spanish newsreel, its inner power will be increased if Makaseyev and Karmen give us—even if only partially—footage shot in sync. The other day there was a broadcast from Madrid. How powerfully each sound, each rejoinder, shout, laugh came across! How near and dear they were to all those who sat with bated breath, glued to their receivers!

Our cameramen should work with light, portable sound-recording equipment. Unfortunately until now, it has been our custom to shoot only silent film abroad. But after all, even in Madrid one can record the conversation of inhabitants, the sounds of meetings and rallies, the speeches and songs of the fighters, and finally, Spanish folk melodies. This will enable us to put incomparably better releases together.

The first release began with an animated map of Spain showing troop locations and positions at the fronts. After this they stopped including the map. It seems to me that the map is of great interest to every Soviet viewer. In each release, maps of Spain and of the region in which a given event is taking place should be included. This will significantly improve the quality of the releases.

The collective of newsreel workers is aware of the great responsibility incumbent upon them when they release footage depicting the battle days of the Spanish people. The entire nation shows great interest in their work. This should stimulate high quality in each shot, in each detail that reproduces for us the heroic reality, the life and struggle of the Spanish people.

We wish the young Soviet cameramen well as they celebrate the holiday of the great October Revolution among the Spanish freedom fighters so near and dear to us.

1936

In Defense of Newsreel

Comrades, masters of Soviet cinema! I've listened to your speeches, been stirred along with you, and I believe in your deep sincerity.

One thing, however, seems strange and incomprehensible to me. Why is the era of the Civil War missing from your remembrances? It was then, after all, that a very large area of Soviet cinema was born in joyful labor. And from 1918 on, after all, we studied film writing, or how to write with a camera. We were ignorant, and suffered from the absence of a film-alphabet. Back then we attempted to create that alphabet.

At that time I specialized in factual film writing. I tried to become a newsreel film writer, a newsreel poet. I made mistakes, but I learned. I studied persistently. I sank my teeth into this work.

If many of my statements of those years now seem mistaken, my creative practice and basic orientation—filming the Civil War—were correct. That orientation was dictated by reality, by the demands of the time.

At that time Sergei Mikhailovich Eisenstein still held our work in respect. He was present at every screening, every discussion of *Kinopravda.*

We were not grateful to Sergei Mikhailovich, though we respected his mind, his talent. We fought with him. We felt that the creation of an "intermediate" cinema (that expression is not mine, but Eisenstein's) was impeding the development of newsreel. We felt

an "intermediate" cinema . . . See Vertov's article "On *Kinopravda.*"

that the introduction of the techniques of newsreel cinema within the organism of acted cinema was unnatural. From the moment we put forward our slogan, "the Leninist ratio," for movie theater programs, we adopted the following point of view:

> 1. equal rights for newsreel and acted cinema;
> 2. a fixed ratio between acted films, oriented toward the actor; and nonacted films, oriented toward newsreel;
> 3. the renunciation of intermediate, type-based cinema. The struggle against the "acted film in newsreel trousers."

That's why *Chapayev,* which puts acted cinema back on the right track—that of the film with an actor, not a half-actor—does not block but rather opens the way for the development of the newsreel film. *Chapayev* doesn't interfere with the development of newsreel masters, such as Kaufman and Shub, who have produced a whole series of works in that form.

The actor is unnecessary for the development of the newsreel film. A good, talented actor is necessary, essential for the development of the acted film. The newsreel film has its own path of development. The acted film should not have followed that path. Both acted and newsreel films have a right to exist. Both the newsreel's path of development and that of the acted film comprise our Soviet socialist path.

Yesterday I inquired of Comrade Yutkevich and some other com-

Chapayev. Made in 1934 by Serge and George Vassiliev, this film chronicled the exploits of a celebrated partisan leader during the Civil War of 1919. The film's enormous success and prestige helped to reestablish the construction of Soviet film narrative around the development of the individual character—ed.

Shub. Esfir I. Shub (1894–1959) created the form known as the "compilation film," by retrieving and editing existing film and photographic documents, and developed a series of films of major historical and aesthetic interest. *The Fall of the Romanov Dynasty* (1927), *The Great Road* (1928), and *The Russia of Nicholas II and Leo Tolstoy* (1928) were followed by, among other films, *Spain* (1936–37). In her originality and consistency of method, she stands with Vertov as one of the most important and influential figures in the development of the documentary film of the postrevolutionary period.

Comrade Yutkevich. Serge Yutkevich (1904–), a filmmaker of the revolutionary generation, was a member of FEKS, together with Grigori Kozintsev and Ilya Trauberg. Among his best known films are *The Golden Mountains* (1931) and *Counterplan* (1932).

rades why all the speakers were actually avoiding the question of the newsreel film, of Soviet cinema in the period of the Civil War. Did Soviet cinema begin only in 1924–25, after all?

Comrade Yutkevich replied that the speakers were talking only of "artistic" cinema. Does that mean they are not speaking of us because we are not artists, not creative workers? We know full well, however, that the history of Soviet cinema starts with experiments in newsreel film. Pudovkin in particular frequently discussed this at one time.

I repeat once again—*Chapayev* and *Three Songs of Lenin* do not contradict one another. One puts acted cinema on the right track, the other newsreel. If they asked me for films as insistently as they do Comrade Eisenstein, for example, I think I'd turn the world upside down. But no one asks me for anything. That's why it remains so hard for me to speak. Still, I am not laying down arms. I shall try once again to convince my comrades that there is a need for my work.

They say I don't know how to admit my mistakes. That's true.

But I do try to correct my mistakes on the screen by making films that are ever more intelligible to the broad masses.

1939

About Love for the Living Person

"Is the filming of a 'living person,' of his behavior, his emotional experiences possible in a documentary-poetic, unstaged film?"

My opponents have frequently asked this question. I have tried to answer by citing examples, facts. I pointed out episodes from *Life Caught Unawares.* I enumerated many uncompromisingly documentary places in later films.

But my opponents smiled somewhat condescendingly.

"Fortunately," they said, "with the arrival of sound cinema and its complex machinery, you won't have to waste your time any more on

Pudovkin. Vsevolod I. Pudovkin (1893–1953), a well-known film director, was one of the founders of Soviet cinematography and the producer of the films *Mother, The End of St. Petersburg, The Heir to Genghis-Khan* [*Storm Over Asia*], and other works.

Three Songs of Lenin

exhausting experiments. You're powerless, and the 'living person' will remain only within sight of acted, actor-based cinema."

Wanting to reply with facts, I responded to this issue somewhat later. To be exact, the woman cement worker in *Three Songs of Lenin* responded for me. And rather powerfully:

> I was working at span 34, we gave out concrete there with three cranes. We'd made 95 buckets. . . . When we'd poured out a tubful and crushed the concrete, I saw that a shield had fallen . . . I went over and picked it up. I was beginning to turn around when that same shield caught hold of the frame and dragged me in . . . I grabbed hold of the ladder, but my hands were slipping. . . . Everyone was scared. There was a girl there, a tar worker who kept screaming. Someone ran up, grabbed me, pulled me out; I was all covered with concrete (she laughs), wet . . . my whole face was wet, my hands nearly got baked in tar for a while. . . .
>
> They pulled me and the tub up . . . I went to the drier, dried off near the stove—the stove was so tiny there—and went back to the concrete place. And I began

> giving the three crane's worth again. And I was at my spot again, till the next shift, till 12. . . . (pause) And they decorated me for . . . (she smiles in embarrassment, turns away, shy—sincerely and like a child) with the Order of Lenin for fulfilling and over-fulfilling the plan . . . (she turns away shyly).

My opponents can't take their eyes off the screen, but as soon as the lights are turned on, they hide their true feelings. They are already speaking less confidently: "No doubt about it. This experiment has succeeded. But it's an exceptional concurrence of circumstances. A favorable subject for filming. . . . You can't repeat such an experiment."

I then give the floor to the old man from the collective farm in *Three Songs:* "I'm sixty-three . . . I got over sixteen tons of grain. . . . When they brought me the grain, there was a rally—a celebration. . . . When all the collective farmers work the way I did, they'll live prosperously just like me. . . . "

At this point he's interrupted by a collective farm woman, awarded the Order of the Red Banner. She continues:

> Women are a great force on the collective farm, and they can't be kept back. . . . I'm the president of the Lenin collective farm here. . . . We have three women on the administrative board, and two are group leaders. . . . We carry on our merciless work, despite the fact that we have no men. (Pause) . . . And I feel "where've we come to!" . . . and what our leaders are saying. They're speaking words of gold. You should write them down and put them in your head, and when you've come home, you've got to tell them . . . you want to get things organized on the collective farm. . . . The Bolsheviks allow no turning back; forget you've gone through difficulties and march ahead. . . . Well, you all get that into your head, and the tears will start all by themselves.

(And indeed, real, nonacted tears start to appear in the woman's eyes, while her face is smiling; and we think of a rainbow. The absolute, genuine sincerity, the 100 percent synchronization of thoughts, words, image is astounding. It's as if we are seeing the invisible—seeing thoughts on the screen.)

Three Songs of Lenin

My opponent is silent for a while, then he gets up, starts pacing back and forth, then stops and says: "Yes, sir! Stanislavsky should have seen and heard that. What might have happened to him. That's where you've got the genuine truth now, not the appearance of truth!"

I explain to my opponent that Stanislavsky sought the natural behavior of man on stage (and apparently on screen) in a completely different way. It is one thing when an actor is supposed to enter the role of another person. It's another when a person is supposed to show us himself naturally. Both are very difficult. But in the two cases the difficulties are different.

My opponent and I conversed for a long time. I told of my experiments in filming the "living person," of projects, scenarios that were not accepted in their day, of the outlook for this little-explored field. We decided to write a book about this. So these experiments

Stanislavsky. Konstantin Sergeyevich Stanislavsky (1863–1938) founded the Moscow Art Theatre in 1898, together with Nemirovich-Danchenko—ed.

will not be lost for our posterity in film. So they may continue this beginning.

"I'm a poor opponent," said my partner, when leaving at dawn. "It turns out that kino-eye was not your final goal at all!"

How could I answer him? He was still not free of the confusion once created by my adversaries in representing the means as my goal. And I patiently formulated, probably for the thousandth time, the answer to that question:

"The goal was truth, the means kino-eye."

The following day I again met my opponent.

"I was thinking about our conversation," he said. "If I remember correctly you said yesterday that your goal was *truth*, while kino-eye was the means. Isn't this where *Kinopravda* comes from—that is, truth made manifest through film?"

"That's partly correct," I answered. "But not only the journal *Kinopravda*. When I spoke of kinopravda as truth expressed through the whole spectrum of cinematic possibilities, I also had in mind such films as *One Sixth of the World*, *Three Songs of Lenin*, *Lullaby*, and other films of that sort."

"But, after all, it was with the journal *Kinopravda* that you began your activity in cinema?"

"No, I began with *Kinonedelia* in 1918. On the first anniversary of the October Revolution I passed my first production exam with a full-length film. And a few months later I decided to do a series of studies that were experimental and innovative for their time."

"And then?"

"Then there were trips to the front with the cameraman Yermolov. The results were two short experimental films and documentary film footage for a future work, *A History of the Civil War*."

"And after that you began to produce *Kinopravda*?"

"No, the next step was my work on the agit-trains of the All-Russian Central Executive Committee. Comrade Lenin attached great significance to the use of film in the work of the agitational trains and steamers. And so on January 6, 1920, I leave with Comrade Kalinin for the southeast front. I take films with me. Including *The Anniversary of the Revolution*. We study the new viewer. We screen that film at all the train stops and carry it to urban movie

Yermolov. Pyotr V. Yermolov (1887–1953) was a cameraman and a long-time figure in Soviet cinema.

theaters. At the same time, we shoot. The result is a film about the journey of the all-Russian senior leader, Kalinin. This period of my work concludes with the big film *A History of the Civil War.*"

"And when was *Kinopravda* finally begun?"

"Shortly after that. At the very beginning of 1922."

"How do you explain the special prominence that *Kinopravda* enjoyed? It seems to have been simply a film-journal, isn't that so?"

"Nominally that's so, but in reality it was not simply the usual film-journal. If you'll allow me, I can dwell on *Kinopravda* in more detail . . .

"This journal was special, you see, since it was in constant motion, constantly changing from one issue to the next. Each successive *Kinopravda* differed from the preceding one. The method of montage exposition changed. The approach to the filming process changed. The character of the intertitles and their use changed. *Kinopravda* strove to speak the truth through cinematically expressive means. Slowly and persistently within this distinctive laboratory, an alphabet of the cinematic language began to take shape. In their attempt to fully exploit a theme, several *Kinopravda*s already took on the proportions of full-length films. Debate already began then, and supporters and opponents appeared. Discussions followed one after another. But *Kinopravda*'s influence continued to spread. Especially after it appeared on the screens of Europe and America. In Berlin, as announced by the press at the time, there were even plans for a laboratory to produce as many prints of *Kinopravda* as necessary. Individual followers appeared in various countries. As *Kinopravda* developed, its crew grew. Svilova mastered the new alphabet. Kaufman developed into a first-rate cameraman. Belyakov became absorbed in the problem of expressive intertitles. Frantzisson, the cameraman, showed a strong tendency toward bold experimentation. Every day something new had to be invented. There was no one to teach it; we were on an untrodden path. Inventing and experimenting, we wrote—in film shots—editorials, feuilletons, film-essays, and film-poems. We attempted in every way to justify Comrade Lenin's faith in the newsreel: "The production of new films, imbued with communist ideas and reflecting Soviet reality, must begin with newsreel."

"The production of new films . . . " Cf. the collection *Samoe vazhnoe iz vsekh iskusstv* ("The Most Important of the Arts") (Moscow, 1963), p. 123.

"So your 'laboratory,' as you call it, was primarily involved in producing *Kinopravda* at that time?"

"One should not forget *Kinokalendar* which we issued in parallel fashion, and the 'flash news,' the special releases for various campaigns and celebrations. This was also a pretty good 'school.' We also paid particular attention to the development of animation. As the director of Goskino, Comrade Goldobin announced in print Vladimir Ilyich [Lenin] took an interest in our first (and chronologically, the very first Soviet) film-caricature, *Today.*"

"Among the *Kinokalendar*s weren't there issues devoted to Lenin?"

"Yes. One of the calendars was called just that—*Lenin Film-Calendar.* It was the first complete compendium of film-documents on the living Lenin. The major role in that work was that of E. I. Svilova, and she later continued this work. Recall the *Leninist Kinopravda*, *Lenin Lives in the Heart of the Peasant*, and finally *Three Songs of Lenin.* In each instance the brunt of the work involved in exploring gigantic amounts of archive footage fell on Svilova's shoulders. For the tenth anniversary of Lenin's death she particularly distinguished herself, when, through a painstaking examination of hundreds of thousands of feet of film in various archives and storehouses, she not only located shots essential for *Three Songs of Lenin* but reported finding, in addition, ten original negatives that render the living Ilyich on film. They are now in the Lenin Institute."

"What do you have to say about *Life Caught Unawares*, *Forward, Soviet!*, and *One Sixth of the World*?"

"These films are all very different. The work of a single author. But films, nevertheless, different in nature, of different construction. Different solutions. And they all aim at the truth. Film-truth."

"Well, and *The Man with a Movie Camera*?"

"You're trying to say that if my goal was truth, and the means kino-eye, then in this film the means had the upper hand?"

"But what do you yourself think?"

"It all depends on the viewpoint from which we consider this film. When *The Man with a Movie Camera* was made, we looked upon the project in this way: in our Michurin garden we raise different kinds

Michurin garden. The work of Ivan Vladimirovich Michurin (1855-1935), a scientist of the prerevolutionary era, served as the basis for the system of genetics developed by the biologist Lysenko and, until recently, officially promulgated in the Soviet Union—ed.

Mikhail Kaufman in *The Man with a Movie Camera*

of fruit, different kinds of film; why don't we make a film on film-language, the first film without words, which does not require translation into another language, an international film? And why, on the other hand, don't we try, using that language, to speak of the behavior of the "living person," the actions, in various situations, of a man with a movie camera? We felt that in so doing we would kill two birds with one stone: we would raise the film-alphabet to the level of an international film-language and also show a person, an ordinary person, not just in snatches, but keep him on the screen throughout the entire film.

"We did not film Emil Jannings or Charlie Chaplin but our cameraman, Mikhail Kaufman. And I don't reproach him because he didn't move spectators like Jannings or cause bursts of laughter like Chaplin. An experiment's an experiment. There are all kinds of flowers. And each new breed of flower, each newly produced fruit, is the result of a series of complex experiments.

"We felt that we had an obligation not just to make films for wide consumption but, from time to time, films that beget films as well. Films of this sort do not pass without leaving a trace, for one's self, or for others. They are as essential as a pledge of future victories.

"And if *Three Songs of Lenin* brought its authors and directors a universally acclaimed victory, then *The Man with a Movie Camera* (strange though it seems) played a by no means minor role as a school. And though it may seem paradoxical, the woman cement worker in *Three Songs* and the woman parachutist in *Lullaby* were brought about through the results of experiments in that same wordless film. When Red Army units marched through Moscow with banners that said: 'We're going to *Three Songs of Lenin*,' no one remembered or would have even dared remember a certain experiment, a youthful error of the same author.

"If, in *The Man with a Movie Camera* it's not the goal but the means that stand out, that is obviously because one of the film's objectives was to acquaint people with those means and not to hide them, as was usually considered mandatory in other films. If one of the film's goals was to acquaint people with the grammar of cinematic means, then to hide that grammar would have been strange. Whether or not this film should have been made at all is another matter. That is a different question; let others answer."

"And you, what do you think? Was that experiment essential?"

"It was absolutely essential for that time. In point of fact, it was a brave, and even a bold attempt to grasp all approaches to the filming of the 'living person' as he behaves, free of any scenario. . . ."

"Allow me to take you at your word. You said, 'free of any scenario.' That means it's true, what they say about you. . . ?"

"What do they say?"

"They say that you've always been on principle an opponent of the scenario. Is this so?"

"Not altogether so. Or rather not so at all. I was for an almost 'iron-clad' scenario where the acted film was concerned. And I was at the same time against a 'scenario' for the nonacted, that is, the nonstaged film. I felt that a 'scenario for the unstaged film' was an absurdity. An absurdity not just in terminology.

"I proposed a superior sort of plan. An administrative and creative plan of action to ensure the continued interaction of plan with reality, not as dogma, but rather as a mere 'guide to action.' An administrative and creative plan that would ensure the unity of analysis and synthesis in film-observation. Analysis (from the unknown to the known) and synthesis (from the known to the unknown) were, in this case, not opposed but indissolubly connected to one another. We understood synthesis to be an inseparable part of analysis. We strove for the simultaneity of the writing, filming, and editing processes with continuous and uninterrupted observation. And we adhered to Engels's instruction that 'without analysis there is no synthesis.'"

"And that was called 'planlessness'?"

"Not everyone said that. After all there are two kinds of opponents. There are those who talk confidently about things of which they have not the faintest idea. And there are others, people who are very demanding of themselves, who speak without assurance of things of which they are in actual fact deeply confident. The first group self-confidently shouted about planlessness. The second modestly and shyly objected that a new plan, more perfect and more realistic, was being proposed. That the self-confident know-nothings sometimes stifle the humble truth with their shouting means nothing. Sooner or later the truth of our attitude toward plans and planlessness will become clear to everyone."

"In concluding our conversation, I'd like to have you confirm a thought that just occurred to me. Don't *Three Songs*, *Lullaby*, etc., represent a continuation of your experiments in penetrating the thoughts of the 'living person'? Remember your first experiment—the thoughts you had while leaping. I read about that in your article, 'Kinopravda,' in the journal *Soviet Cinema*. . . ."

"You've touched upon a rather complex question, one that requires another special conversation. As a matter of fact, everything I have done in cinema was connected, directly or indirectly, with my persistent effort to reveal the thinking of the 'living person.' Sometimes that person was the film's author-director, not shown on the screen. Sometimes this image of the 'living person' included traits not of a single concrete person, but of several and even many people who had been chosen accordingly.

"As the action develops in *Lullaby*, the mother rocking her child—and in whose name the exposition of the action seems to proceed—turns into a Spanish mother, now a Ukrainian, now a Russian, now an Uzbek. Still, it's as though there were one mother in the film. The image of the mother is divided among several people. The image of the young girl in the film is also formed from the images of several people. We have before us not a mother, but the Mother, not a girl, but the Girl. As you can see, it's rather hard to explain. You can come to understand it only directly from the screen. Not a man, but Man!

"But I repeat, the question you've touched on is a topic for a separate conversation.

"As you can see, to reach the great common goal, every artist takes his own path. The socialist Motherland assures each artist of the chance to develop his individuality and helps him to be bold, to open new paths, to serve the people by his own creative innovation."

1958

From Notebooks, Diaries

1924

Our movement is called kino-eye. We who fight for the kino-eye idea call ourselves kinoks. We hardly ever use the term *kinochestvo,* since it is a meaningless and gratuitous derivation. For some reason our opponents use it readily.

And we have many opponents. It could not be otherwise. It hinders the realization of our ideas of course, but it does, on the other hand, temper us in battle and sharpen our thinking.

We take a stand against the artistic cinema, and it pays us back a hundredfold. We construct our small film-objects from the crumbs remaining from the resources of the artistic cinema and sometimes with no resources at all.

Kinopravda has been kept out of the theaters, but it couldn't be concealed from public opinion or from that of the independent press. *Kinopravda* has been unequivocally recognized as a turning point in Russian cinema.

The success or failure of any of our film-objects has a merely commercial significance, with no effect upon our strength of purpose or our ideas. For us, all our film-objects—whether successful or not—are of equal value since they further the idea of kino-eye and since every 100–200 meters of unsuccessful footage serve as a lesson for the next that are successful.

One kinok has quite aptly called the *Kinoglaz* series, Part One, "kino-eye groping about." It is the cautious reconnaissance mission of a single camera whose main task is to avoid getting entangled in life's chaos and to get its bearings in any surroundings it happens to come upon.

◀ *Dziga Vertov, ca. 1920*

The succeeding parts of the series attempt to expand our reconnaissance as far as possible, while improving technically, to continually deepen our observation.

Everyone has something of the poet, artist, musician.

Or else there are no poets, artists, or musicians.

The millionth part of each man's inventiveness in his everyday work contains an element of art, if one must use that term.

We would, of course, prefer the dry newsreel to the scenario's interference in the daily lives and work of living people. We interfere with no one's life. We film facts, organize them, and introduce them through the screen into the consciousness of workers. Our main task, as we see it, is elucidating the world as it is.

Kino-eye has managed to find its way in the struggle with bourgeois cinema, and we seriously doubt that the latter (despite its present international dominance) can long withstand our revolutionary onslaught.

There is another, greater danger—the distortion of our ideas. Substitutes and intermediary trends which swell like soap bubbles, until, like bubbles, they burst: these are more dangerous.

All workers must attentively watch the struggle that is beginning and must distinguish between the real and the false, between saccharine substitutes and copies and the rigorous originals.

From the Kinoks' Field Manual

General instruction for all techniques: the invisible camera.

1. Filming unawares—an old military rule: gauging, speed, attack.
2. Filming from an open observation point set up by kinok-observers. Self-control, calm, and, at the right moment—lightning attack.
3. Filming from a hidden observation point. Patience and complete attention.
4. Filming when the attention of the subjects is diverted naturally.
5 . Filming when the attention of the subjects is artificially diverted.

Substitutes and intermediary trends . . . See Vertov's article "On *Kinopravda.*"

6. Filming at a distance.
7. Filming in motion.
8. Filming from above.

1926

April 12

Saw *Paris qui Dort* at the Ars movie theater. It pained me.

Two years ago I drew up a plan whose technical design coincides exactly with this picture. I tried continually to find a chance to implement it. I was never given the opportunity. And now—they've done it abroad.

Kino-eye has lost one of its attack positions. Too long a time between idea, conception, and realization. If we are not allowed to implement our innovations promptly, we may be in danger of continually inventing and never realizing our inventions in practice.

The construction of the USSR is the main, the constant theme of my present work and that of the immediate future. The *Leninist Kinopravda, Forward, Soviet!*, and *One Sixth of the World*—all these are, as it were, the individual components of a single huge assignment.

If in *Forward, Soviet!* the viewer's attention is focused on the capital, on the center of the USSR, then *One Sixth of the World* (as if in continuation of the first film) acquaints us with the vast expanses of the USSR, the peoples of the USSR, the role of state trade in drawing even the most backward peoples into the construction of socialism (here, in the last two reels, we deliberately bring together the goals of state trade and those of the cooperatives, aiming towards the gradual replacement of the former by the cooperative system). At the same time we pour all the picture's streamlets into the channel of our country's industrialization; and while strongly emphasizing the theme "machines that produce machines," we

Paris qui Dort. *Paris qui Dort* (1924) was the first feature-length film by René Clair. This comedy explores the interlacing themes of city life, temporality, work, and, by implication, film production by deploying many of the cinematic processes and optical techniques later to be more fully exploited in Vertov's *The Man with a Movie Camera* (1929)—ed.

One Sixth of the World

attack along the lines of "our economic independence" and "we ourselves will produce the machines essential to us."

From there, by "uniting our industry with our peasant agriculture" (the cooperative system), by drawing millions of peasant farms (the cooperative system) into the building of socialism, we arrive at the conclusion: "We are becoming the center of attraction for all other countries that are gradually breaking away from international capital and are flowing into the channel of our socialist economy."

Soviet cinema is currently experiencing an unforgettable turning point.

The work of kino-eye, which generated so many trends, movements, and groups in Soviet and, to some extent, in foreign cinema, has managed to conquer all obstacles, crawl out of its prison cellar and through the barbed-wire entanglements of high-level or ordinary administration and distribution; it has burst through the ranks of theater management onto the screen.

Everything was against its success.

New Year's Eve. A frost of thirteen degrees below zero. A 100 percent frost of mistrust from the army of distributors. A 100 percent frost from those at the top of the administrative ladder.

And those who drowned *Kinoglaz* in their mistrust, those who smothered the *Leninist Kinopravda* with their slow-witted indifference, those who let *Forward, Soviet!* rot, are now faced with the "sold out" notices at the Malaia Dmitrovka Cinema for *One Sixth of the World* during these days that are so inconvenient and inopportune [because of the extremely low temperatures].

Whether or not we get full houses in the future, we already have thirteen screening days behind us. Considering the failure of a whole series of the latest "artistic" pictures, it is something to be proud of.

This is our first major victory, because, on the one hand, we have made our way to the screen, and on the other, because we have not failed commercially.

Our second victory consists of stopping the exodus of workers from the field of the nonacted film into that of the "artistic film." As a matter of fact, we're now witnessing a reverse flow from the studio to newsreel and the scientific film. This phenomenon must be seen as indicating the solidity of our position and the correctness of our course.

It must nevertheless be admitted that a great number of deserters from the field of the acted film constitute a dangerous obstruction on our front of the nonacted film.

It's difficult to ward off this danger. We will fight against it. We will decipher and expose all the semistaged works, and stand guard, as before, over the 100 percent fact film.

And finally, our victory (and this is most important for us) lies in the growing sympathy toward our work throughout the Soviet Union, in the formation of ever more photo-eye and kino-eye groups, in the transition to independent work of those promoted in those groups, in the comments that appear everywhere on our work, and in the reviews and letters received from various cities and rural villages in our country.

They're beginning to understand us—that's the main thing. *They want to help us* in our difficult task—that is what encourages, strengthens, and spurs us on to further struggle.

1927

March 6

Is it worth proving to my hypocrite that every fact from life recorded by the camera represents a film-document even if it's not wearing a medal or dog collar . . .

March 15

Reply to A. R.

The relentless exposure of present shortcomings and the drawing of vigorous revolutionary conclusions for the future—this is not "the posture of tragedy" but genuine revolutionary optimism.

Maintaining the policy of the ostrich, shutting one's eyes to surrounding disgrace, smiling blissfully or politely when one is mocked, grateful bootlicking, bowing and scraping, while receiving a sop by way of the production or editing of a picture—that's neither optimism, nor "posture of tragedy," it's *toadyism.*

No matter how high they climb, bootlickers of this sort cannot become revolutionaries either in life or in cinema.

Their pseudo-optimism, that of temporary well-being, must be exposed just like their playacting as revolutionaries.

The decoding of mystification, both in life and on the screen, is obligatory for the kinok. The stubborn exposure of the hidden plagues of film production (kinoks follow the same firm line in their lives as in their screen work) in the process of one's current work. No concealment of the shortcomings, injustices, crimes, obstacles encountered in work, no fear of showing, speaking of them, and so forth—so as to overcome and eliminate them—that is a truly revolutionary objective, that's a springboard for vigor, for optimism, for the will to fight.

Our invariable victories over so-called tragic situations, over every difficulty lead you to think that we apparently exaggerate our difficulties.

No. We do not exaggerate. Herein lies our strength. Here is the difference between feigned and real optimism: making our way through the most difficult obstacles put in our path, not by hiding behind a veil of prosperity, but rather in full view; and—no matter how hopeless the situation—emerging victorious into the arena of a

The Man with a Movie Camera

new struggle. Against imaginary optimism, the stupid mask of invariable prosperity, we offer the genuine optimism of revolutionary struggle.

March 20

We leave the film studio for life, for that whirlpool of colliding visible phenomena, where everything is real, where people, tramways, motorcycles, and trains meet and part, where each bus follows its route, where cars scurry about their business, where smiles, tears, deaths, and taxes do not obey the director's megaphone.

With your camera you enter the whirlpool of life, and life goes on.

The race does not stop. No one obeys you. You must adapt yourself so that your investigation will not interfere with others.

Your first failures. People stare at you, urchins surround you, your subjects peer into the camera. You gain experience. You use all sorts of techniques to remain unnoticed, to do your work without preventing others from doing theirs.

Every attempt to film people who are walking, dining, working invariably ends in failure. Girls begin to primp; men make "Fairbanks" or "Conrad Veidt" faces.

They all smile affably for the camera. Sometimes traffic stops.

Curiosity-seekers crowd around the camera and block the filming location.

It's even worse in the evening when the lights attract throngs of curious onlookers. Life does not wait, people move about. Each goes about his business.

The cameraman has to be very inventive in his work.

He must abandon the camera's immobility and develop maximum mobility and resourcefulness.

June 22, *Zaporozh'e*

We are completing our filming of the Dzherzhinsky plant. Covered with red dust, coated with slivers of cast iron, tired and soaked to the skin, we grow close to the blast furnaces, the Bessemers converters, the molten metal, to the rivers of fire, the red-hot, flowing rails, the fiery spinning wheels, the glowing wire that, as if alive, rises, bends, swings, slices through the air like lightning, and in a final spiral, winds itself into neat stacks.

Our shoes are charred, our throats parched, our eyes strained, but we can't tear ourselves away from the blast engines; we just have to wait for still another smelting of cast iron.

The clock shows four. Up there above ground, dawn must be breaking. We feel the effects of almost twenty-four hours spent beneath the earth. We're very tired, chilled. Some are feverish. In the mine shaft shooting proceeds under a continuous cold shower. We

make "Fairbanks" or "Conrad Veidt" faces. Douglas Fairbanks and Conrad Veidt, well-known actors of the twenties.

can turn our cameras on only during those moments when the water pumps stop. We spend hours waiting for those moments, shifting from one leg to the other, hunched against the cold. Kaufman sleeps standing up. Barantsevich warms himself by hugging a rheostat which has not yet cooled. Kagarlitsky sits on another rheostat, thinking of Moscow, steam heat, and expresses a strong desire for a sandwich.

The sun stands high above the horizon. We've just come up to the surface, and we rejoice in each and every ray of sunlight.

I hesitate to talk of "love" when speaking of my feelings toward this plant. And yet I do really feel as though I want to embrace and caress those gigantic smokestacks and black gas tanks . . .

The Eleventh Year

(Fragment from a shooting log)

A trumpet sounds the signal. There is a pause. The workers disperse. Horsemen patrol the area of the explosions. A bell rings. A pause. Bells call slowly to each other. Tiny little men (seen from a distance) prepare to light the fuses. A fast ringing of bells. The men light the fuses and run to dugout shelters. An explosion. Another follows. A series of explosions, one after another. A fountain of rocks and sand. Fragments fly into the distance . . . over the rails, over rail-lorries, over a crane. They drum on the lorry beneath which we've taken shelter. They fly as far as an opened grave where a Scythian has lain asleep for the last two thousand years. Beside his skeleton lie a spear and bronze arrowheads, pierced to hold poison. A cracked earthenware cup. At the head of the grave are some sheep's bones and the skeleton of a war horse. The Scythian stares from his eye sockets, through the black holes of his skull. As though he's listening to the explosions. Over him are sky and clouds. Rails run right beside the grave. Along the rails, freight trains pass, and forty-ton cranes roll. Behind the rails are the scaffolding of a pump house under construction, quarries, rail-lorries, and thousands of men armed with hammers and picks. The Scythian in his grave— and the din of the new offensive.

The Scythian in his grave–and cameraman Kaufman focusing in amazement on a silence of two thousand years.

1931

November 10

Arrived in London from Berlin, via Holland today. The sea is restless. I'm spending the night at an architect's. It's cold. Gas fireplace. Headache. Very tired.

November 11

Still have a headache, but shaving helped as always. Drew up a plan of action. Except for the lady of the house, no one understands German or French or Russian. I go about with a dictionary, pointing.

Drafty window. Fingers numb with cold. Fog and clouds drift past the window.

November 12

Can't understand a single word. No interpreter. Saw a nightmarish film about a sinking submarine: hackwork. Theater decorated with blue sky, twinkling stars, and other such sentimentalities.

A theater with a variety program was better. Mickey Mouse, newsreel, etc.

November 15

Showing of *Enthusiasm.* Interesting sound control. Using dials in the auditorium, not signals, but direct control. Introductory remarks by Montagu.

November 17

A meeting with Charlie Chaplin. He jumps up during the showing. Exclaims something. Says a lot about the film. Sends a note through Montagu: his response to *Enthusiasm:*

> Never had I known that these mechanical sounds could be arranged to sound so beautiful. I regard it as one of the most exhilarating symphonies I have heard. Mr. Dziga Vertov is a musician. The professors should learn from him, not quarrel with him. Congratulations.
>
> Charles Chaplin

Three Songs of Lenin

1933

June 13, Tashkent

Lenin is when an Uzbek woman on a tractor starts spring with plowing.

Lenin is when the melancholy songs of slavery grow gay and lively.

Lenin is a power station on the Dnepr. Ukrainian girls awarded medals, an Uzbek farmhand as head of administration, a Turkmenian woman who has thrown off the *yashmak,* an orchestra of Uzbek Pioneers (former waifs) playing in a tearoom, the newspaper *Leninskii put'* [''Leninist Way''], a nursery school in a collective farm.

Lenin is honesty, uprightness, selflessness, enthusiasm, and straightforwardness.

Three Songs of Lenin

July 15, Moscow

Most important: concentrate. I'm constantly distracted from work on the film. One minute there's no camera, or the stock's no good, then the lab won't return the footage, there are no shelves, no light. . . . Deadlines and promises are never kept. . . . They call me in and ask: "Why? Why?" They hound, hound, hound me. They're trying to take away Shtro, the sound man, the only enthusiastic one, for another film. Svilova works by day at the Lenin Institute, by night at the Mezhrabpom editing room. She's tireless. If all the others were equally committed, victory would be assured.

1934

Once, in school, a classmate copied my composition. I got an F (for copying); he got the highest grade. He was a lively, cheerful boy.

He didn't like to be serious about anything and lived, as they say nowadays, "through connections." Everything was easy for him, and he was quite pleased with the composition he'd copied from me.

In Germany the last reel of my film *The Eleventh Year* was shown under a different title and with a different author credited. When I showed *The Eleventh Year* in Germany a year later I was nearly accused of plagiarism. I barely managed to restore the truth.

April 8

Some say "I" and think "we"; others say "we" and think "I."

Some speak uncertainly about matters of which they're confident; others, on the contrary, speak confidently of things of which they're uncertain.

April 10

I'm always doing something, but never what's required. In school, for example, when a lesson was assigned, I'd read the whole book, skipping the assignment. When I forced myself to read the assignment, I couldn't understand a thing.

Two "I"s. One observes the other. One's a critic, the other a poet. And it's as if there were a third "I" observing both.

First "I": You've been told to study the lesson. Second "I": Why have I been told? Who's ordered me to? I don't want orders "from . . . up to . . ." I want to write poetry, to play the violin, to solve a math problem . . .

The third "I" joins in the argument: Enough discussion! I, the conqueror of nature, the conqueror of desires, of chaos, throw the switch: heart, beat more evenly, brain cells, dress ranks! Forward, to work, in a united front! Quickstep!

The main thing is to concentrate on the important, the decisive point.

Give up smoking. Eat less. Get up earlier. Do, not what you want, but what needs to be done. You must want what is needed. A plan for each day and a long-range one for the next five years.

Laziness is wanting to do what you want, not what is necessary. Fight laziness.

April 16

My attitude toward my previous films is that of an inventor toward his inventions. Much has become outdated and seems comic today, like Buster Keaton's train. But in their day these now funny experiments evoked not laughter but a storm of controversy, ideas, plans, outlooks.

These were not films for "general consumption" so much as "films that beget films." And not just films. A fair number of years have passed from the first part of our *Kinoglaz* series to the kino-eye of Dos Passos (*The Forty-Second Parallel*). But the structural scheme and even the terminology of both are the same.

Ilya Ehrenburg, apparently under the influence of *Kinoglaz,* Part One, once wrote:

> Vertov's work . . . is a laboratory analysis of the world—complex and agonizing. . . .
>
> The kinoks take reality and transform it into primary elements, perhaps an alphabet of film, . . . "
>
> (*The Materialization of the Fantastic.*)

Everyone now understands that those who worked on *Kino-pravda* and *Kinoglaz* created an alphabet of film, not for its own sake, but in order to show the truth.

We were not content to make invisible shots visible, masked shots overt, staged shots unstaged. We wanted to do more than show isolated bits, individual shots of the truth. We set ourselves a broader task: editing, organizing, combining together the separate shots to completely avoid falseness, to make each montage phrase, and our works as a whole, show us the truth.

I am accused of corrupting Dos Passos by having infected him with kino-eye. Otherwise he might have become a good writer, some say. Others object and say that if it were not for kino-eye, we wouldn't have heard of Dos Passos.

Dos Passos' work involves a translation from film-vision into literary language. The terminology and construction are those of kino-eye.

Buster Keaton's train. The reference is to the train figuring in Buster Keaton's film *The General* (1927)—ed.

May 17

About four months have already passed since *Three Songs of Lenin* was completed.

The torture of waiting. My body is like a drawn bow. Anxiety day and night. I can't release the wound-up springs. Better standard forms of torture—needles inserted under fingernails or burning at the stake. I used to think I'd always be tireless. Not so. They've exhausted me. My brain's so tired that a breeze knocks me over. I now walk like the hobbling Eastern woman in the first Song of Lenin.

May 18

Rode about on a bicycle. Even at intersections I was thinking not about the traffic signals but about the film. Thinking in a muddle. With indifferent despair. Compared with this latest ordeal, what's an exam in school? A few hours of anxiety. Neither rest nor work. Hours, days, weeks, months of life are canceled out. Who needs this? What am I doing? Waiting, hanging over an abyss, with one hand clutching the branch of life. "To live means to die." You're robbing me of my final hours, you don't allow me to act decisively, you order me to wait patiently. But after all, "victory never comes of itself," it must be organized. Politics? But the soundest politics, after all, are those of principle. As Lenin said. And our film is about Lenin. One must be especially principled in this case.

May 19

I myself no longer know whether I am a living person or a diagram invented by critics. I've forgotten how to talk with people, how to speak in public, forgotten how to write ever since I noticed that words do not express my thoughts at all. I speak, listen to, and check myself. The words do not convey the thoughts. I should stop writing right now because I'm not writing what I'm thinking at all.

I'll stop.

[My] thoughts are most easily conveyed in film, through montage; but I am asked not for a film of thoughts but for a film of incident, event, adventure, and so on.

I could think on celluloid, if such an opportunity should again present itself . . .

May 26

I have not been away on vacation in ten years. My sally abroad (twenty-three lectures in a foreign language) only added to my fatigue. Then right into *Three Songs of Lenin* without a break. Under very trying circumstances, with no time off. And still I could continue to work if the film's release were not being held up. If only someone would smile and say "thank you." If they'd bawl me out. Or praise me. If only they'd either encourage me or beat me with sticks.

But I've spent the last three months in the studio corridors. In constant (today or tomorrow) anticipation. Under continual tension. The torture of *uncertainty.* The impossibility of answering questions. Anonymous phone calls. And gossip. Suffocating mountains of gossip. Even trifles such as not being invited to the opening of Cinema House or Mezhrabpomfilm's refusing to give my photograph to the photo gallery of Cinema House—these serve as springboards for the wildest, most revolting fabrications.

It's hardly surprising that I'm dying to get away from this. The torture of waiting has so upset my nervous system that I can hardly talk now. I must be released from this "leave of absence for creative purposes" in the corridor. Sent out for repairs. Where there's air, sunshine, water.

Three Songs of Lenin had to be made "from scratch." And with our "bare hands." "From scratch"—there was no foundation of creative film stock (montage material), since I had not previously worked at Mezhrabpomfilm. "With our bare hands"—there was no well-equipped and specially trained cameraman who could, without retraining, immediately join in our work.

Some comrades regard the footage left from the shooting of *Three Songs* as either outtakes or retakes that should be handed over to a general film archive.

This is a mistake. These are neither outtakes nor retakes.

They are my creative stock for future films.

They are a guarantee of better quality and lower cost in future works.

Poetical work of excellence can be completed on time only if one has a large supply of poetic stock.

This is essential under the kino-eye system.

Work on *Three Songs of Lenin* lasted through almost all of 1933. During that time our group accomplished the following:

1. A group member (my assistant), Comrade Svilova, by tirelessly sifting and studying archival footage in Moscow, Tiflis, Kiev, Baku, and other cities, accomplished what we had been unable to accomplish during the nine years following Lenin's death. During these nine years, only one new film document of Lenin was discovered (in America). While in 1933 for the tenth anniversary of Lenin's death we were able to report that Comrade Svilova had located ten new film-documents:

- Lenin bent over a notebook, thinking with a pencil in his hands (original negative, 2.5 m.);
- Lenin writing (original negative, 2.2 m.);
- Lenin conversing with a paper in his hands (original negative, 3.25 m.);
- Lenin in medium shot, jotting something down in a notebook (original negative, 9 m.);
- Lenin beside Elizarov's coffin (original negative, 2 m.);
- Lenin walking behind the coffin of Elizarov (original negative, 2 m.);
- Lenin hurrying past a window on the way to a session of the Comintern congress (original negative, 3 m.);
- Lenin speaking fervently in Red Square, with Spassky Tower in background (original negative, 61 frames);
- A new shot of Lenin in the Kremlin courtyard, walking swiftly, conversing, laughing (positive, 5.2 m.).

These film-documents were submitted by Comrade Svilova to the Lenin Institute. Portions of them were printed in *Three Songs of Lenin;* they will also be edited together [and appear] as a separate release.

2. We had tried to transfer Lenin's voice to film in Leningrad back in 1931. The results were not very satisfactory. Our work was considerably more successful in 1933 when the sound man Shtro managed not only to preserve the quality of the recording but actually to obtain a better result than that of a phonograph record. We are thus able to hear Lenin speaking on film, addressing the soldiers of the Red Army.

Lenin's voice, like the film-documents of the living Lenin, is available in a separate issue.

3. Folk songs about Lenin were recorded in Azerbaijan, Turkmenistan, and Uzbekistan. Songs about Lenin, "the friend and deliverer of all the enslaved," are sung in all corners of the globe, from Europe and America to Africa and beyond the Arctic Circle. These songs are anonymous, but they are transmitted orally from *yurt* to *yurt,* from *kishlak* to *kishlak,* from *aul* to *aul,* from village to village. We included songs of the Soviet East in the film. Some songs are on the sound track, some are expressed in the images, still others are reflected in the subtitles.

November 9

The radio has just transmitted telegrams received from America on the extraordinary success of *Three Songs of Lenin* in the United States. The most important newspapers are publishing rave reviews.

Two hours ago, however, the director of the Mezhrabpom movie theater told me that he was angered by the behavior of the Moscow film distributors. It's not enough that they have refused us the Art Theater on the Arbat. It's not enough that they would not book the film at the Shock-Worker (which serves a mass of viewers on the other side of the Moscow River). Starting today, the only large theater assigned us, the Central, is no longer showing *Three Songs.*

Some foreigners went to the Mezhrabpom theater with an interpreter and complained in my presence that they had spent the whole day searching throughout the city for *Three Songs of Lenin,* had barely managed to find it, and begged to be allowed to buy tickets. But there were no tickets; they had all been sold. The director could do nothing for them.

He then turned to me again. "You should protest. This is unheard of. It's not just that the Central isn't showing the film. It's that the public is getting the impression that the film has been withdrawn. Faith in the film is being undermined."

aul. *Aul* is the word for *village* used by the mountain dwellers of the Caucasus, or the Crimean Tatars. It is also a term used by the Turkish nomads of Central Asia—trans.

I bought *Evening Moscow.* A notice invites the public to see "the great film of our time," according to Jean-Richard Bloch, at the Central in Pushkin Square. They've also printed André Malraux's comment on *Three Songs of Lenin* as an immense victory for Soviet cinema.

The public goes to the Central to see the "great film" and doesn't find it. It turns out to have been withdrawn from the screen.

Why?

Is it because viewers are walking out in the middle, can't follow the film?

Nothing of the kind. The public watches *Three Songs* with the utmost attention; sighs, exclamations, laughter can be heard. The viewers applaud almost every shot.

Is it because the theater's empty and incurring big losses?

Nothing of the kind. The film has withstood the toughest test. It was released during the week before a holiday that causes a tremendous reduction in attendance each year. The film passed this test with flying colors. In spite of the preholiday commitments of both factory and office workers, in spite of all the meetings, evening parties, concerts, etc., the film was screened during this period at the Central with higher attendance records than in all previous years.

I recalled the Proletarian Division going through the streets of Moscow to band music with banners unfurled, carrying signs: "We're going to *Three Songs of Lenin.*"

And I found it terrifying to think that a petty tyrant of a bureaucrat could withdraw the film out of personal taste or some other reason, and in so doing, spit with impunity in the face of all Soviet public opinion.

What do *Pravda,* the Comintern, the Writers' Congress matter to him? What does he care for the opinions of scholars, artists, and political figures? He has his own little "taste," his own little "reasons," his own hypocritical little ideas . . .

Evening Moscow. *Vechernaia Moskva* is a major Soviet evening newspaper—trans.

Jean-Richard Bloch. Jean-Richard Bloch (1884–1947), French writer, essayist, and member of the French Communist Party, played a leading role in establishing relations between Western and Soviet writers during the Popular Front of the 1930s. Bloch participated in the large, broadly based congresses that were held in both Moscow and Paris and organized under the banner of international solidarity against the spread of fascism.

On Mayakovsky

Mayakovsky is a kino-eye. He sees that which the eye does not see.

I loved Mayakovsky immediately, unhesitatingly. Beginning with the first book I read. It was called *Simple as Mooing.* I knew it by heart. I defended him against verbal abuse as best I could. Explained him. I had not yet met Mayakovsky personally. When I saw the poet for the first time in the Polytechnical Museum, I was not disappointed. He was just as I'd imagined him. Mayakovsky noticed me in a group of excited young men. Evidently I was looking at him with enamored eyes. He came up to us. "We're looking forward to your next book," I said. "Get your friends together," Mayakovsky answered, "and demand that they publish it soon."

My meetings with Mayakovsky were always brief. In the street, at a club, at a train station, a movie theater. He called me not Vertov, but Dziga. I liked that. "Well, Dziga, how's kino-eye doing?" he once asked me. That was in passing, at a train station somewhere. Our trains met. "Kino-eye is learning," I answered. I thought a moment and said it differently: "Kino-eye is a beacon [*mayak*] against the background of international film production's clichés." And when Mayakovsky shook my hand in parting (our trains were going in different directions), I added, stammering: "Not a beacon, but a Mayakovsky. Kino-eye is a Mayakovsky against the background of international film production's clichés." "A Mayakovsky?" The poet looked inquiringly at me. In answer I recited:

> Where the people's dock-tailed eye stops short,
> at the head of hungry hordes,
> wearing the crown of thorns of revolution
> 1916 approaches.

"You saw what the ordinary eye did not see. You saw how 'from the West red snow is falling in the juicy flakes of human flesh.' And the sad eyes of horses. And a mama, 'white, white as the brocade on a coffin.' And a violin which 'wore itself to pieces, entreating, and

Where the people's dock-tailed eye . . . A quotation from Mayakovsky's poem "The Cloud in Trousers"—trans.
the sad eyes of horses. This is probably a reference to a well-known short poem by Mayakovsky, "Good Treatment of Horses"—trans.
brocade. The Russian word for brocade is *glazet,* whose sound evokes the word for "eye" (*glaz*) used several times by Vertov in this context—trans.

suddenly began howling like a child.' You are a kino-eye. You've seen 'that which travels across mountains of time, which no one sees.' And right now you're

> . . . in the new,
> future way of life,
> multiplied
> by electricity
> and communism."

The last time I met Mayakovsky was in Leningrad. In the lobby of the Hotel Europa.

In a gloomy voice Mayakovsky asked an employee: "Will there be a cabaret tonight?" He noticed me and said: "We should have a leisurely talk. A serious talk. Couldn't we arrange a 'full-length' creative talk?"

I waited for Mayakovsky in my hotel room. I took the elevator up and thought:

> Life is beautiful
> and
> amazing.
> We'll grow
> to be a hundred
> without old age.
> Grow
> year after year
> in our vivacity.

I felt that I'd found the key to documentary sound filming, that there was "no gold more heavenly than ours," that "the wasp's bullet shall not sting" us, that "our weapon, our songs, our gold is voices ringing."

I paced up and down my room, waiting for Mayakovsky; I was happy about our meeting.

I wanted to tell him of my attempts to create a poetic cinema, how montage phrases rhyme.

I waited for Mayakovsky until midnight.

I don't know what happened to him. But he didn't come.

And a couple of weeks later he was no more.

a violin. This is a reference to a celebrated short poem by Mayakovsky, "A Violin and a Little Nervously"—trans.

More on Mayakovsky

My love for Mayakovsky's work did not in any way conflict with my attitude toward folk creation.

I never considered Mayakovsky unintelligible or unpopular. One must distinguish between popularity and trying to be popular.

Lenin, in his note "On the journal *Freedom,*" talks quite well of this:

> The popular writer leads the reader to deep reflection, to depth in study, by proceeding from the simplest common knowledge through the use of simple arguments or well-chosen examples, pointing to chief conclusions to be drawn from those data, spurring the thinking reader on to ever further questioning. The popular writer does not assume a reader who does not think or who does not want or know how to think: on the contrary he assumes the serious desire of the undeveloped reader to use his head, and he helps him in this serious and difficult work, he guides him in his first steps and teaches him to proceed further on his own. The vulgar writer assumes a reader who does not think and is incapable of thinking. He does not spur him on to the first rudiments of serious science but serves up the conclusions of a certain teaching "ready-made" in a deformed, oversimplified form, salted with jokes and witty sayings, so that the reader doesn't even have to chew; he has only to swallow this mush.

Mayakovsky is intelligible to everyone who wants to think. He does not assume a totally unthinking reader. He does not try for popularity at all, but he is popular.

> Stupefied with rapture,
> I would give
> my life
> for a single
> breath of his . . .

says Mayakovsky about Lenin.

folk creation. There is no exact equivalent for the Russian expression *narodnoe tvorchestvo,* which implies more than folk art. It is the creation of a *narod* (usually an ethnic unit) and refers to popular or folk art in the Marxist sense—trans.

We would give everything:
Our carts, and life, and children,
Just to bring him back—

says a folk song about Lenin.

The unity of form and content—that is what strikes one in folk art, and that's what strikes one in Mayakovsky as well.

I work in the poetic documentary film. That's why both the songs of the people and Mayakovsky's poetry are very near and familiar to me. The fact that a great deal of attention is now being paid to Mayakovsky as well as to folk creation tells me I've chosen the right course in my field of film poetry. Actually, *Three Songs of Lenin* was only a first significant attempt in that direction. But our party's central organ confirms this: "Despite the great difficulty of the conception, the attempt has succeeded. A truly remarkable picture, a picture of great force, infecting the viewer-listener with deep feeling." In an unsigned editorial article *Pravda* calls *Three Songs* "the song of the whole country."

We know from letters and comments that the whole country, from Vladivostok to Leningrad, expresses, through the voice of the mass of viewers, confirmation of *Pravda*'s view. The reception the film got this time, not from ten thousand, but from millions of viewers, has shown that I stand on the threshold of the right, clearly indicated path.

This is not the path of the "curly Mitreikas and clever Kudreikas" of whom Mayakovsky speaks. Nor the path of those whose verse reaches the viewer "like an arrow in the cupid-lyred chase." Nor of those whose verse "reaches like the light of dead stars." It is a path that is far from easy.

It is the path of which Mayakovsky spoke: "For every gram you mine, you labor a year." It's the path of those whose verse

. . . through labor
will break through mountains of years

"curly Mitreikas and clever Kudreikas". These quotations are from Mayakovsky's *At the Top of My Voice*, in which he satirizes two young poets, Mitreikin and Kudreiko. (The play on words is different in Russian.) —trans.

"For every gram you mine . . . " This quotation is also from Mayakovsky's *At the Top of My Voice*—trans.

" . . . through labor will break . . . " From Mayakovsky's *At the Top of My Voice*—trans.

and appear
ponderous,
visible,
like an aqueduct,
built by the slaves of Rome,
which has come down to us.

In my coming work I shall achieve a significantly greater unity of form and content than I managed to do in *Three Songs of Lenin.* And unity of form and content is a guarantee of success.

Overcoming mountains of prejudice, within his lifetime, Mayakovsky victoriously made his way into the pages of books, pamphlets, journals, into all the major newspapers. He failed, however, in one area. He could not make his way into the pages of the screen. He could not overcome the official bureaucracy of cinema. His scenarios are either rejected or included in a theme-plan, but they remain unproduced. Or they are shamelessly disfigured in the process of production. "They shifted me," said Mayakovsky,

> from editor to editor; the editors invented principles which do not exist in cinema, different every day, and they clearly believed only in their own abilities as scriptwriters. I consider that my qualifications with regard to the artistic aspect of scriptwriting allow me to insist on the necessity for carrying out my script "principles" in motion pictures as well. An attitude of this sort on the editors' part hardly aids in the campaign that is being waged to attract qualified literary forces to cinema.

The greatest poet of our time thus expended immense energy, time, and strength trying for the opportunity to appear on the movie screen "at the top of [his] voice," and he never realized his idea. Mediocre bureaucrats stuck to their own "principles." But Mayakovsky left cinema once and for all.

Several years have now passed since Mayakovsky's death. In every area of our life tremendous changes have taken place. And only the script departments continue as before to defend their hackneyed principles against the incursion of poetic filmmakers. The will to produce poetic film, and particularly poetic *documentary,* still runs up against a wall of perplexity and indifference. It generates panic. Spreads fear.

You're considered a man bent on his own destruction. Or worse—one who might destroy others as well.

V. Katanyan relates:

> He [Mayakovsky] crossed the entire stadium, striding over the barriers, from one stand to the other. He pulled out all his identity papers and press cards for the policemen who stopped him: "I'm a writer, a newspaperman, I've got to see everything. . . . " And the police let him through.

We film poets, film writers, film reporters now have to show our own management that a pass enabling us to get in everywhere is indispensable for making a poetic documentary film on a large scale; that one can't shoot a Stakhanovite conference without a pass to that conference, that one can't film a collective farm congress without being able to attend it, that one can't film a Komsomol congress if one's not there. Shooting without being able to shoot, editing without being able to edit, making a sight-sound, a visible and audible film without having the opportunity yourself to see and hear—that's the surest way to cut yourself off from reality to vain, "closet" efforts, to frantic (inevitably formalistic) attempts to find a way out of the administrative impasse . . .

If an artist's so hungry to create that he can't endure the tortures of waiting, of idleness; if he lowers his eyes and agrees to produce a film under clearly hopeless conditions—he makes a mistake.

I made that mistake when I gave in, submitted to management's demands and began to edit *Enthusiasm* even though I knew full well that all the human documents were ruined due to technical reasons. Every time you have to make concessions to the management, every time you have to make a compromise, every time you hope to break through an administrative impasse by a superhuman creative

Stakhanovite conference. Aleksei Stakhanov (1906–1977) was a mine worker in the Donbas who led a campaign for higher production in 1935. The name was then applied to Soviet workers in all sectors of industry who, during the 30s and 40s, surpassed production quotas, usually through rejection of old technical norms and through innovation and implementation of new technology—ed.

effort, you face the danger of formalism, formalism that has been forced and imposed upon you, despite your creative ideas.

Unlike literature, the cinema does not preserve poetic films (and poetic documentary in particular) in the author's original version. The test of time is not applied to these films. Even *Three Songs of Lenin* did not escape the common fate. By now we are already unable to fulfill Comrade Kerzhentsev's request to be shown a full-fledged copy of the film in the author's version. The struggle against the destruction of author's copies, of author's "manuscripts" has not, so far, produced any results.

We who work in poetic documentary film are dying for work. We're terribly hungry to create. We must make every effort to show our heads of studios, our managers, that the good author, the good director is not he who submits unconditionally to outmoded, hackneyed principles of film production. We must use the example of Mayakovsky to show that even a very great poet can be shut out of film production by these hackneyed principles.

Administrative, technical, and other such compromises, the agreement of a director to just any work—all this should not be acclaimed but, on the contrary, placed under suspicion. Either that director is completely indifferent to the final result of his work or he's so starved for work that he's given up completely, just to get his hands on a movie camera.

Right now I myself am incredibly hungry. To create, of course. Food passes by, surrounds me. If I depended only on pen and paper, I'd write day and night, write and write and write. But I must write with a camera. Not on paper, but on film. My work depends on a whole series of administrative and technical factors.

I must obtain my rights at my place of work. And if I don't manage to get anything from a given management, a given administration, I still won't give in. After all, we all remember what Mayakovsky said in an analogous situation: "Administrations pass, art remains."

I'm firm with respect to the basic line of my work, and flexible,

Comrade Kerzhentsev. Platon M. Kerzhentsev (1881–1940), Soviet political figure, diplomat, and historian, served as a member of the Agit-Prop Department of the Central Committee and of the committee in charge of broadcasting. He later became chairman of the State Committee on the Arts. He advocated strongly orienting cinema, under the control of the Ministry of Education, toward the broad education of the communist masses.

yielding about the details. Perhaps one should fight, unashamedly, for every detail, like Mayakovsky? Mayakovsky gives a poem to a newspaper. He asks: "How much will you pay?" They tell him: "Forty-five kopecks a line." "But what do you pay others?" "Everyone gets forty-five kopecks." "Then pay me forty-six kopecks a line." He categorically demands respect for his verse. If only a kopeck's worth of respect more than for the usual type of poem.

Obviously, it's not a question of being unable to do without high wages. It's a question of the attitude towards one.

Lenin said you must know what you're writing or talking about.

The art of talking about what you have not seen, what you don't know is a special one that some people unfortunately possess. I fortunately do not possess this talent. One can't build a discussion on conjectures. I have no reason to doubt that the film *Prometheus* is infected with formalism, but that's precisely why it would be essential to see it.

I managed (to a considerable extent) to make *Three Songs of Lenin* accessible and intelligible to millions of viewers. But not by sacrificing film-language. Not by sacrificing the techniques I'd found earlier.

The problem lies in not separating form from content. The problem is one of unity of form and content. Of not permitting oneself to confuse the viewer by showing him a trick or technique not generated by the content and uncalled for by necessity.

And there's no need even to set your heel "on the throat of your own song." In 1933, I decided, in thinking about Lenin, to turn to the sources of folk art. And as the future was to show (recall Gorky's speech at the Writers' Congress), I was not mistaken. The objections to this approach of mine were wrong. I was not mistaken; I foresaw things correctly.

I want to pursue this direction further.

Prometheus. A film made in 1923 by Ivan Kavaleridze. Its release was forbidden because it was considered fallacious.

Gorky's speech. Vertov seems to be referring to the speech Gorky delivered at the Writers' Congress in Moscow in 1934. Speaking before twenty-five thousand participants in the Hall of the House of Unions, Gorky, surrounded by the massive floral displays from the State Cooperative Farms and by representatives of European literature, opened a congress dedicated to establishing literature as a popular and militant agent of a socialist peace—ed.

On My Illness

I began preliminary work on *Three Songs of Lenin* while under fierce persecution from the film department of RAPP [Russian Association of Proletarian Writers, 1923–1932].

They hoped, through administrative measures, to force me to give up documentary film. The shooting of the film itself was done in Central Asia under abnormal conditions, in the midst of typhus, with no means of transport and irregular pay. Sometimes we wouldn't eat for three days at a time. Sometimes we repaired watches for the local people in order to earn money for a meager dinner. We went about covered from head to foot with napthaline, our irritated skins unable to breathe, smeared with stinking, caustic liquids, fighting off attacks of lice. Our nerves were always on edge, and we controlled them by willpower. We did not want to give up. We had decided to fight to the finish.

The editing and mixing took place in an atmosphere of incredible tension. We didn't sleep for weeks at a time. We did our utmost to have the film ready for showing at the Bolshoi Theater on the tenth anniversary of Comrade Lenin's death. The refusal to show the film in the Bolshoi Theater on that day, despite the fact that it was ready, was the first severe blow to my nervous system.

There began a struggle for the film that ended in a splendid victory. I paid a high price for this victory. It was not just a matter of the film. A broader question was at issue: the survival of the cause to which I'd dedicated my entire life.

All this was accompanied by a series of humiliations, insults, by pointed disregard, mockery, mosquito bites from a number of petty but dangerous and unprincipled people. I had to control myself, control my nerves, endure everything internally, while appearing cool and composed.

As now established by Professor Speransky's laboratory tests, "not only damage to the trigeminal nerve but a number of other nervous traumas as well have resulted in a dystrophic process within various tissues and tracts."

My illness was the result of a series of blows to my nervous system. Its history is one of "inconveniences," humiliations, and nervous shocks involved in my refusal to quit work on the documentary poetic film. By the time the struggle for *Three Songs of Lenin* was over, the illness was externally expressed in the loss of several sound, healthy teeth due to nerves.

The termination of the illness coincided with the calming of my nervous system after the conclusive demonstration of the universal victory of *Three Songs,* and especially after the recognition accorded me by the party and the government on the fifteenth anniversary of Soviet cinema.

Professor Speransky's report further states that "with a second blow to any part of the nervous system, given continued irritation of the corresponding elements, however slight, predisposition of the tissues to dystrophy will become manifest."

Until RAPP was liquidated, the blows were frontal. *Proletarian Cinema,* the official organ of cinematography, simply announced, "Either transfer to the acted film, or your mama and papa are going to suffer." Either you give up documentary film, or we will crush you by administrative measures.

Now, since the victory march of *Three Songs of Lenin,* since I have been awarded the Order of the Red Star, the blows are dealt more subtly.

You wish to continue working on the poetic documentary? Go right ahead. You have our general permission. We cannot, however, give you equal consideration in competition with other directors. You are going to have to compete on terms that are not to your advantage. They will get the best working and living conditions: apartments, cars, official trips abroad, expensive gifts, the highest wages, etc. You get the finger—doubly. You can sit in your damp hole beneath the water tank and above the sobering station for drunks. You can stand in line for the toilet, for the kitchen burner, the sink, the streetcar, and the bath. With no elevator, you can climb up to the sixth floor ten times a day. Work amid the kitchen fumes, beneath the leaking ceiling, against the drone of the water pumps, and the shouts of drunkards. You will have neither peace nor quiet. And expect neither attention nor love from us.

They say you depend on the people you've trained? Well, their faith in you will be undermined. That of your cameraman, whose interests you will be unable to defend. As for your closest comrade-in-arms and co-worker, Comrade Svilova, your skills and interests will not protect her.

Comrade Svilova is the daughter of a working man who died at the front in the Civil War. She has twenty-five years of work in cinema and several hundred films under various directors to her credit. She can claim among her achievements the creation, through many

Svilova, Vertov, and unknown third person

years of effort, of a film heritage of Lenin. On the fifteenth anniversary of Soviet cinema, when all her students and friends were rewarded, Comrade Svilova was used as an example, punished with conspicuous disregard, and received not even a certificate. Only a serious offense could justify her lack of recognition. Yet Comrade Svilova's only crime is her modesty!

"They don't like you!" says one of our film executives in reply to my bewildered questions.

The renewed dystrophic symptoms in my mouth are only the beginning of a complex intranervine deterioration. This deterioration must be halted, but how?

First of all, its causes must be eliminated. It's not enough to eliminate the nervous condition's external signs, as I do by willpower. The blockade proposed by Professor Speransky will not suffice. Nor will the usual therapeutic measures: change of climate, rest, change of diet, sea bathing, hydropathy. What's needed (and this is most essential) is to eliminate the source of all these shocks, that is, the abnormal attitude which the above-mentioned comrade explains and sums up in the phrase: "They don't like you."

Who doesn't like me then?

The party and the government? No, the party and government have given me a high-ranking award.

The press? No. The press—from *Pravda* to the newspapers of the Arctic Circle—have responded very favorably to me.

The public? No. The public, through representatives—the prominent authors, workers' collectives, artists, etc.—have made much of my film work.

Who is it, then, that does not like me?

I am a living man. To be liked is absolutely essential to me. So are care and attention. It is essential that promises given me be kept. Only then will the remedies recommended by Professor Speransky be of help.

"Not artistic"—therefore unprincipled hackwork.

"Not artistic"—therefore a narrow utilitarian approach.

"Not artistic"—therefore "the way open to bootlickers."

Does anyone think Kopalin, Svilova, Yerofeyev, Setkina, Kaufman, Belyakov, Stepanova, and Raizman are satisfied with what they're doing?

Kopalin gets an "A+" for his work but won't show it to me. Apparently he himself is not satisfied.

Kaufman's in the Ukraine shooting a script, doing senseless, useless work. He suffers. He's dissatisfied.

Svilova, the most enthusiastic of enthusiasts, flouted on the fifteenth anniversary of Soviet cinema, works from morn till late at night at Potylikha, never sure of tomorrow, never knowing whether her work will be in vain.

Yerofeyev, who has made several valuable films, just can't get under way, can't adjust to a narrow system.

Surensky, the cameraman, who got his training on *Three Songs of Lenin*, is a photographer somewhere.

"Not artistic". The word understood to be following this phrase is either *cinematography* or *picture* since the adjective *artistic* has the feminine form—trans.

Shtro, the soundman, the *Three Songs* enthusiast, writes desperate letters—he's dying to do creative work.

Leontovich, Raizman, Oshurkov? . . .

Dozens of people whom I know personally, people hungry to do creative work do not fit into the existing newsreel system.

There are cadres. Remarkable cadres. But they're not being used.

Everyone eats his fill. No one goes hungry. But the hunger and thirst for creative work is torture for many.

They are being cut off from the path to creativity by the slogan "We're not artistic cinema."

Shortly after returning to newsreel I became convinced that most people working there are laboring selflessly. It's therefore all the more essential that all their energy be channeled in a creative direction.

I believe that the active core of our colleagues favor a principled approach to artistic truth and not unprincipled hackwork.

They favor the flowering of all types of newsreel, not the Procrustean bed of a single type: telegraphic film reports and the latest news.

Not just journalism, but essays, epics, songs, and individual works that will have the whole world talking.

Of course, to build the Palace of the Soviets you have one set of terms, deadlines, and standards. And, to pitch a tent, you need another. You can't lump them together.

One set for the monumental epic.

Another for the telegraphic film reports.

We have nothing against rifles, but we're not against high caliber weapons either. Both are needed for victory.

We're for the victory of honest enthusiasts over the pushy, over tricksters, hustlers, and toadies.

We're for the victory of creative innovation over narrow-minded remakes.

We want continual preparedness for battle, not panicky rush work.

Only in this way shall we win.

I thought of a film about a young woman of our country.

Was I right to choose this theme? I think so. In selecting this theme our group anticipated a recently published speech by Kosarev that dealt with the question of the education of our young people and singled out the problem of work for young women.

The main characters. We selected several young women as objects of observation. Their choice was dictated by life itself. A single observation of their behavior is not enough, however. It's essential that the most interesting and exceptional aspect of these people's behavior be recorded on film. And here, from the very beginning, we ran into a huge obstacle, one which, for a while, seemed insurmountable.

It turned out that we had no way of shooting in sync wherever we chose to do so, since the equipment available at Mezhrabpomfilm depended completely on the presence of an electrical network. It was technically impossible to film people in the countryside, in the fields, in a natural environment; it was impossible to observe their behavior. I immediately designated this as our chief obstacle and focused my reports on the problem of constructing portable equipment that would permit shooting in sync anywhere, at any time. Much time has passed, but the business has proceeded no further. Still, we are going to solve this problem.

Shtro, the soundman, one of the best workers in our group, began studying this problem soon after the release of *Three Songs of Lenin*. He therefore took a leave of absence without pay from Mezhrabpomfilm and began working on a film that was slowly being shot by a different organization, so that he got a chance to experiment. He is now sufficiently familiar with the possibilities of all existing sound cameras to draw some definite and encouraging conclusions.

What are the technical conditions required to shoot a film that is interesting and of high quality?

First, the shooting should be instantaneous, that is, occur simultaneously with an event, with the action of a subject under observation.

Second, it should be noiseless to avoid attracting the attention of the subject being filmed and should leave no background noise on the film.

Third, it should be able to go on anywhere (in a peasant's hut, a field, an airport, a desert, etc.).

Fourth, both cameras, silent and sound, should be interconnected so that one does not impede the other, so that shooting starts without preparation and signals, so that the equipment is ever ready and requires no special marks to be synchronous.

Fifth, the sound should be of a quality sufficient to meet the demands made on it.

Sixth, the sound installation should be compact, without bulky generators, and should not depend on the presence of electrical wiring.

Seventh, the possibility of mishaps should be eliminated since we're filming scenes and people's actions that can't be repeated.

Eighth, the actions of cameraman and soundman should be maximally coordinated and fused, simultaneous—which can be best achieved by combining sound and silent recordings in one single, unified piece of equipment . . .

The speech which I was unable, for reasons of ill health, to deliver at the conference of creative workers can be briefly summed up as follows:

I share the opinion of Comrade Pudovkin, that new cadres are best trained during the film production process. I cited examples drawn from my personal experience: Comrade Setkina who went from splicing to directing, Comrade Kaufman who worked as producer and became a cameraman and director, Comrade Svilova who went from splicing to become the best editor in the USSR.

I went on to show that cadres can be trained in this way only within solidly united groups working together from picture to picture. That the artificial dispersion of such groups, the transferring of workers from one group to another group or other work prevents us from correctly organizing the training of young workers. Such is the case of Comrades Surensky and Shtro who ought to continue their studies not just during the filming but during the preparatory period as well.

You have to get to know each individual to bring out his best aspects, to become familiar with his biography and experience, to maintain relations with him, not in the sense of returning his greeting, but of removing obstacles in the way of his creative development.

The individual should not feel alone and isolated. A friendly word cheers one up, gives one strength and confidence. That friendly word, plus occasional real support are especially essential when we find ourselves up against the wall in production-administration, or in everyday life . . .

A comrade (Yerofeyev), speaking at the recent conference, said that Vertov "has a woman on his hands." That elicited laughter and exclamations: "A blonde?" "Brunette?" and so forth.

There's nothing funny about it.

It's a rather sad tale.

The *Girls of Two Worlds* were a blonde, a brunette, and a chestnut-haired woman too.

Foreign footage. The project was canned.

Maria Demchenko

and the system of agreements.

The Eclair camera will be here tomorrow.

The closer the deadline, the closer *Lullaby* moves to the film archive.

Sukhumi.

Only above the sea is the sky clear blue. Higher up it's covered with clouds all around, but after a while the sun's rays peek through the clouds, the rifts between them grow wider, and we are off to the Botanical Garden to do some test shooting. Khodzhera, her girl friend, and a librarian are with us. I have my "briefcase"—a small tin reflector folded in half and with a briefcase handle.

Beneath a cactus, on a low rock, a fragile blonde is gazing into the camera lens; there's no way of hiding from her, and the reflector gets in the way—it's impossible to divert her attention. She asks what she should do; "Nothing," we say, but she can't understand how one can do nothing in front of the camera. She turns toward me with a smile, but on hearing the sound of the camera, turns around and stares straight into the lens. Behind her head the graffiti scratched on the cactus leaves proclaim that Valya and Misha were here on such and such day in such and such year, and she turns around to see what's written, afraid that the graffiti may appear on the screen, but in that instant the camera catches her, she blows on her powder puff with displeasure, powders her nose, and we catch her once again with the lens

1936

February 29

In a speech to a plenary session of the Central Committee of Workers in the Arts, Comrade Kerzhentsev advised Shostakovich,

Maria Demchenko. Maria Demchenko (1912–) was a worker engaged in sugar beet production and was one of the most prominent shock-workers in the Stakhanovite movement—ed.

the composer, to "travel through the Soviet Union collecting the songs created and preserved by the people." He would thus make contact with the very rich stream of folk art and find that base "on which he might develop creatively."

At the Writers' Congress Gorky spoke of turning to folk art.

My experiment in this area was done in 1933 when I began work on *Three Songs of Lenin.* Except for the collecting of *chastushki* in which I was absorbed after my grade school years, I was a novice in this field. At that time almost no one collected songs. And my attempt as a film director to acquaint myself with the work of anonymous poets caused surprise and sometimes pity (at that time few people anticipated that folk art would soon become the center of our attention).

I came to know the songs of Nargorny-Karabakh. Listened to the little songs of Turkish children. Travelled all over Uzbekistan and Turkmenistan. Listened to folksingers. In Ashkhabad, in Samarkand, in Bukhara, I searched for songs of Lenin. At the same time I heard other songs. Translations were a real problem. I did some on the spot. Some I found later, already translated. Some of the songs were recorded on tape. From other songs I took only the text. In some cases Shtro, the soundman, and I recorded only the sound.

Contact with authentic folk documents had a great influence on me. That which had once moved me to collect chastushki, stirred within me once again. First of all these were song-documents. As everyone knows, I've always been keenly interested in the documentary weapon. Secondly, these songs, for all their outward simplicity, were powerful, graphic, astonishingly sincere. And their most important feature was *the unity of form and content,* that is, precisely what we writers, composers, filmmakers have not yet been able to achieve.

August 26

It's time to get to work. Each minute brings me nearer to the end.

I awoke with this thought, and still, like everyone else, went to the seashore. I regret every minute snatched from being by the shore.

chastushki. Short, rhymed folk verses that are usually four lines long and generally humorous and topical—trans.
Nargorny-Karabakh. An autonomous region of the Azerbaijan Republic—ed.

But I must get to work. I must draw up a plan. My thoughts are in Spain where the combat against the fascists is going on. My thoughts are still in Ethiopia. My thoughts are still with the canceled film, *About Woman.* I must get to work. Must begin again from the beginning. Must concentrate on one thing.

The behavior of the individual. Under conditions here in our country. Under the "right to work," "right to leisure," "right to education." Starting from the day of birth. The first steps.

In school. In a Young Pioneer camp. Exam. Childhood, adolescence, youth. Love. Marriage. A new birth.

These observations on film will be intelligible if a method of comparisons, of contrasts is used. With what should they be compared? With the behavior of the individual under conditions prevailing in capitalist countries.

September 6

High productivity through a series of administrative measures. Methods for organizing work are unlike those of the acted film.

High productivity without loss of quality. It's not a matter of producing defective products in bulk. The documentary film commanded respect while it had not settled on quantity irrespective of quality. Hacks, imitators, untalented plagiarists, hustlers, have blackened the reputation of the documentary film.

High productivity. How to achieve it? Not through moralizing sermons. Experience. Organization. Technique. Example. Invention. Stubborn labor. Not by "taboos." "However it turns out." No, not that way!

> A thief in the role of auditor.
> "Duty"—the bank auditor;
> "Profession"—hardened thief.
>
> (from an article about a thief in *Pravda* no. 262, September 22, 1936)

If kinopravda is truth shown by kino-eye, then a shot of the auditor would be in accord with kino-eye only if his mask were to be discarded and if behind the mask of auditor could be seen the *thief.*

The only way to tear off the auditor's mask is to secretly observe him, through hidden filming, that is, an invisible camera, supersensitive film and lenses with a large aperture ratio, film for night and evening observation; in addition, a noiseless camera (sight plus sound) in continual readiness, with instantaneous release, simultaneous with what's seen.

This is from the newsreel of actual occurrences. It's not in the theater but in life that the thief acts the auditor in order to rob a bank.

Or an opportunist acts the loving fiancé in order to seduce and then rob his betrothed. And the schemer acts the fool, the better to dupe his victim. And the prostitute poses as a young girl with a bow in her hair to fool a ninny. And the hypocrite, flatterer, bureaucrat, twaddler, spy, bigot, Pollyanna, blackmailer, double-dealer, time-server, hides his thoughts, plays a given role, removing his mask only when no one can see or hear. To show them unmasked—what a difficult but gratifying task!

And this is all when the individual plays a role in life. If you take a professional actor, acting in the theater, filming him *à la* kino-eye here means showing the synchrony or asynchrony of actor and man, the concurrence or dysfunction of word and thought, etc. I remember an actor, when films were still silent, who, while expiring from wounds before the camera-eye, while expressing suffering in his entire body and face, at the same time told some anecdote that made everyone laugh—obviously proud of his ability to act without emotion. If a sound camera were to record the convulsions of the wounded man, then to our amazement, we'd hear instead of moans, something diametrically opposed to what we'd see with our eyes: double entendres, jokes, mockery . . .

Apparently the actor had had to die so often before the camera, that it required no mental effort to die once more as usual. His mind was free to make jokes. His capacity for dissociation horrified me at the time.

According to kino-eye, to show Ivanov playing Petrov means showing him as a person in real life and as an actor on the stage—not passing off his stage acting as his behavior in life and vice versa. Complete clarity. Before you, you have not Petrov but Ivanov playing Petrov.

If an artificial apple and a real one are filmed so that you can't tell them apart, that shows not skill but the lack of it.

A real apple must be filmed so that any imitation would be impossible. You can bite and eat a real apple but not an artificial one. A good cameraman should make this visible.

I'm a film writer. A film poet. I write not on paper but on film.

Like any writer, I must have a creative stockpile. Recorded observations. Rough drafts. But not on paper; on film.

Like any writer, I do not work on one thing alone. Short novellas, essays, verses are written at the same time as long epic poems. Many great writers have "copied" their protagonists from people who actually existed. The portrait of Anna Karenina was modelled on one of Pushkin's daughters. I intended to write the story of Maria Demchenko on film, using Maria Demchenko. The difference is that I can't write on film after the events have occurred. I can write only as they happen. I can't record a Komsomol congress on film after it's over. I can't film a parade of athletes if I'm not present at their celebration. And, unlike certain correspondents, I can't write up an account of an event, a performance, a carnival several days before the event has taken place.

I don't ask that a cameraman be at the scene of a fire two hours before the fire has broken out. But I can't allow someone to leave a week after that fire to film it. I got permission from management to film a collective farm convention, to film Demchenko, etc., once there was nothing left to film. This was called "an agreement with management."

Right now I'm working on themes concerning women. This is not just a single topic. These are a number of films, short and long. Films about the schoolgirl, the girl in nursery school, mother and child, about abortion, the creative work of young women, the status of our young women and those abroad, about leisure and labor, the baby's first steps, first words, about the young girl, about women in youth, maturity, old age . . .

I shall write about specific individuals who are alive and active. The selection of these individuals can be agreed upon. I shall film human behavior from diapers to old age. All this is possible only within the framework of a continual process of information, shooting, and editing. A continual process of stockpiling the author's documents. A continual process of observation with camera in hand.

We must set up a creative atelier, a laboratory where one could work under special conditions, where creative ideas and organizational forms would not be mutually destructive.

In this case—a steady growth in the quantity and quality of the films released, and, at the same time, a decrease in the unit cost of film.

October 13

The lion's roar in *The Circus* is [produced by] an oxhide thong, resined and drawn taut, in a barrel with a pigskin bottom. If you slide your hand in a suede glove along the thong, the barrel roars like a lion.

Roaring barrels, wax apples, glycerine tears—all these are proper for acting.

But in an investigation? Man's behavior, not on stage, but in everyday life, under natural living conditions? If the tears and grief are real?

Is this, then, forbidden fruit? Banned from film? Not provided for in the script?

We must have a laboratory, or else it will all come to naught.

Lullaby

Lullaby is the author's fourth song based on folk material. The first three songs were devoted to Lenin. The fourth is the first song of a cycle devoted to the Free Woman to whom unemployment is unknown, threatened by neither violence nor hunger, neither torture nor the executioner's axe, the woman without fear for her children's fate, their present and their future; to the woman for whom all doors to education, to creative and joyful labor are open.

To sing this song without spreading one's self too thin or losing one's self in all the possible themes of woman (i.e., of half of humanity), one had, first of all, to keep work strictly within the limits of the set theme; second, to study and take stock of the author's previously accumulated store of film documents; third, to thoroughly study the possibilities of the archives of the Soviet Union Newsreel; fourth, to become acquainted with the folk documents on the theme; fifth, to attempt what I simply couldn't manage to do with *Three Songs of Lenin*—that is, to state in words the contents of a documentary film in sight and sound.

All five conditions have been met as far as possible during this preparatory phase. Naturally this doesn't mean that these labors won't continue during film production. The author's proper attitude to his work requires that he continue work on all five points right up to the day he delivers the film.

The Circus. A film comedy made in 1936 by Grigori Alexandrov, a former collaborator of Eisenstein's.

With respect to point five: a verbal account of the film.

I have already stated that I was unable to produce a verbal description of *Three Songs of Lenin*—our first film to be rooted in images of folk origin. Neither before nor after completion of the film. We tried to write poems and short stories, dry accounts, travel sketches, dramatic episodes; we made schemata and diagrams and so forth—but none of these helped one to see, hear, and feel this film before it was edited and screened.

This was work of a special sort, so different in construction from the ordinary films that a many-sided verbal account of it was nearly impossible to give. Even the subsequent detailed description of every single frame, both sound and silent (after completion of the film), could not give us any real idea of this picture.

If I had my way, I'd write such films not with words, but directly with image and sound. Just as an artist works, not with words, but with pencil and oils. Just as a composer writes a sonata, not with words, but directly with notes or sounds. I could do so, however, only with a special organization of the production process aimed at films of this special type. This would be possible only in the creative laboratory of which I've frequently written and spoken.

Apparently I must work much more before I am trusted to the point of being permitted to submit a report on the results of my creative experiments, not in words, but in shots. For the author of these lines, the conditions of a Michurin or a Tsytsin laboratory, are so far unattainable even in miniature, even in a mere molecule. Once again, therefore, I've made every effort—within the limits of the possibilities available to me and of my own abilities—to set forth my new song in words.

Without limiting myself in this case to synopses of themes (the right to education, the right to work, the right to create, the right to rest, the right to a happy motherhood, to a happy childhood, adolescence, youth, and old age). Nor limiting myself to schematic surveys of Soviet women in various areas of human endeavor (a collective farm woman, a blue-collar working woman, a woman engineer, a female pilot, or professor, and so on).

an artist works. In Russian, one speaks of writing a picture (*pishet kartinu*)—trans.

Tsytsin. A botanist and horticulturalist, Nikolai V. Tsytsin (1898-) was a member of the Academy of Sciences and a follower of Michurin. He was known for his breeding of wheat hybrids—ed.

The usual surveys—which one could do in an evening or two, plus an introduction, plus a conclusion—will not help anyone to understand or feel the author's new creative idea. I therefore directed my efforts entirely toward finding a way of explaining this song so that film management might hear the heartbeat of this film as yet unborn.

I hit upon the idea of assembling a composition of folk images which, while conveying an idea of the film's content through the only means currently available to me—*words*—would, at the same time, convey the aroma, the breath, and in part, the rhythm of the film to be.

This hitherto unsolvable problem (the problem of a verbal account of an as yet unmade poetic documentary film) seems to have been partially solved this time.

But then it's hardest for the author himself to judge.

There's no reason to think that a serious and honest approach to the documentary representation of life, to a picture done not on canvas but on the screen, means that one can act more lightly. I'm speaking not of the picture that copies some stereotyped pattern but of that which is the creative transformation of nature. Of that particular kind of work in which connecting links cannot be constructed and introduced into facts but must be extracted from them and, once found, tested, as far as possible, experimentally.

Lullaby, although composed of folk documents, is not at the same time a "Procrustean bed" for the film of that title. The film will be based on facts—those collected earlier as well as those gathered during the film's production. The film will pass through a whole series of stages, through various compositional drafts, deriving its connecting links from the facts obtained, not imposing them on those facts. This course is difficult, but inescapable. The very complex organism of a completed film develops through differentiation from individual cells—the shots of the montage footage. This is not a matter of a crude, mechanical permutation of shots. It means bringing out all the riches of this movement, proceeding not from abstractions you've made up but from concrete facts. It means uniting all the facts obtained on a given theme into a single harmonious whole.

The law of the conversion of quantity into quality and its corollary, the law of the interpenetration of opposites, that of the negation of negation—these laws are derived from nature and from history.

They are not imposed on nature and history as the "laws of thought."

The system of organizing newsreel footage was not our invention; it was derived from the nature and history of the newsreel film.

The very same laws of dialectics that were not invented but "extracted from the history of nature and of human society" are at work.

November 11

Today, from morning on I looked at the Spanish releases on the screen. I then tried to get into the editing room that had supposedly been given to me. It turned out that the room was occupied. What's more, the person in charge of the editing room announced that it contained secret footage and I should not be there at all. I spent today, November 11, like November 10 and all the other days of this month, in search of a place to work. In the evening I tried to work at home without the footage, from memory. But not even the cotton stuffed in my ears could save me from the surrounding noise.

Lucky Edison. He was half-deaf.

November 12

I'm trying to make use of a day off. There aren't many people at the studio. I've installed myself in the general editing room. But there's no Spanish footage. They took it for a screening yesterday and, according to the superintendent, have not returned it. I'll wait until two. The footage isn't here and apparently won't be.

I remember how angry Comrade Shumyatsky got when, owing to some administrative obstacle, Eisenstein lost twenty or thirty minutes. He spoke of wasting creative capital on trifles, of "the crime against the most precious material—the artist, the master."

Why is Comrade Shumyatsky silent about the crime against me, which is measured not in mere minutes, but in the weeks, months, and even years of creativity stolen from me? Or can't a crime

Comrade Shumyatsky. During the 1930s and 1940s, Boris Shumyatsky (1886–?) was administrator of the Soviet film industry. His appointment was made with a view toward centralizing and integrating the industry within the more general industrial program of the Five-Year Plan—ed.

against a master, not of the acted, but of the poetic documentary film be considered a crime? . . . Until Comrade Shumyatsky declares loud and clear that he considers my work useful, not harmful; until he says that I am entitled to equal rights and opportunities, as well as responsibilities, like other directors, I will continue to be deprived of the minimum conditions for producing films and living a creative existence.

November 13

Late tonight, when the radios and other domestic noises had grown quiet, I at last managed to focus my attention on my ideas about the Spanish footage. I concluded once again that I must immediately begin work on a monumental film on the events in Spain. I could guarantee its success, if they would trust me to do it as I am capable, know how, and would love to do it. The very thought of such work generates intense creative excitement in me.

As for the overhasty shorts commissioned by the export department, I must in all honesty admit that I can't produce any interesting ideas for them. For these, what's most important is the speed of execution, the promptness of telegrams, and not the monumental strength of the image. I passed that stage long ago and no longer consider myself a specialist in that form.

The impossibility of correctly organizing the editing process under standardized conditions is a huge obstacle to our work.

The impossibility of preserving, from one film to another, an author's stock of film-documents, with no right to renew that stock, no author's archive, and no permanent quarters—all this reduces the work of editing to individual, convulsive spurts, to the forming of a secret creative stockpile , to the destruction of what's already been done, to the necessity to "begin from the beginning" dozens of times and to start work anew.

The laboratory that we've organized solves all these problems by converting from a system of individual editing onslaughts to a continuous editing process, by converting from the preservation of individual montage fragments to an author's film archive.

The next very serious obstacle has been the impossibility of developing, training, and preserving the people we need under the conditions of a standardized system.

At the conclusion of a film, people are usually assigned elsewhere, and each time we've had to begin anew the work of preparing special cadres.

Under laboratory conditions, the cameraman, soundman, director, assistant, reporter, and production man would develop continually from one work to the next, grow continually, accelerating rather than retarding the release of the creative product.

Similar obstacles have stood in the way of our gathering information, as in all other areas of organization; together these obstacles form a huge, blank wall of stereotypes, resistant to living ideas and against which all our attempts to break through into films on human behavior have shattered.

The wall of the apparatus (not that of film but of bureaucracy) stands between our decision to shift from epics on the construction of industry and agriculture to a knowledge of man through his movement, growth, and behavior and the realization of that decision.

To alter this situation, in which we are vainly wasting our forces and in which all our enterprise and creative projects are mercilessly, automatically, and stupidly destroyed by the standardized forms of production prescribed for us, we have decided to form a creative laboratory.

Our laboratory shall produce films of a special type, not under stereotypical organizational conditions, but under special conditions proper to this type of film.

The first special feature of the creative laboratory will be that it will rely upon people selected by the director from the number of enthusiasts who know and care for this difficult undertaking, not on workers who happen to be assigned.

Its second special feature will be that in shooting it will rely not on "air," not on resolutions and promises, but on a concrete, tangible filming base, specially suited to our kind of work.

Its third special feature will be that for its editing it will rely not on individual montage fragments left over from some other film but on a continually active editing base with (a) an author's film archive, (b) an editing/operation room.

Its fourth special feature will be that for research it will rely not on chance, fragmentary information (from one call to the next) but on a system of continuous observation.

Its fifth special feature will be that in its organization it will rely on constant preparedness in technique and organization, to go out and film at any moment, not in haste, precipitously, upon the sounding of the alarm.

The sixth special feature of the creative laboratory will be that it will simultaneously develop several themes interrelated in terms of creation and organization, as it lovingly cultivates films in its nursery.

The seventh special feature of the creative laboratory will be that it will gradually increase the number and improve the quality of films, not by increasing the number of work crews, nor by increasing budgets, but by continually improving the work of information, organization, shooting, and editing through the efforts of a single group.

The eighth special feature of the creative laboratory will be its salutary effect on the cinematic output of other groups and other film studios, not through moralizing sermons, but by way of living examples and high-level models of cinematic creation.

The ninth special feature of the creative laboratory will be that it will not know directorial waste; the continuity of production process involving several themes means that we can successfully use a shot that did not fit into one theme in a subsequent theme.

And finally, the tenth special feature of the creative laboratory will be the almost total absence of the usual work stoppages. Given a continual readiness to film and the technical possibility of filming anywhere, at any time, under any conditions, a situation could very rarely arise in which one could not immediately replace a shooting schedule that for some reason had been broken off with another (if not on the same theme, then on another, being shot parallel).

The laboratory is needed as—

- a transition from the position "everything's impossible" to the position "everything's possible" (the "impossible" is only a problem in need of this or that in order to be solved);
- a transition from a system of continual agreements to one of continual actions.

We are confident that our experimental garden–laboratory will flourish. We're certain that we shall offer our country beautiful fruits from this garden, if only we are given the chance to grow our films in the way we know and understand, under the special conditions proper to precisely this type of film.

We're not afraid of any creative difficulties.

We love them; we delight in overcoming them.

Plan for the laboratory:

1. *The Director's Office.* A place for deliberation. A place for paperwork. A place for rough drafts, a place for writing, filming, and editing, for plans and outlines. A place for receiving visitors. A place for screenings and for checking results of individual operations on a small screen. A place for consultation with co-workers. A place for reading essential materials and studying them, pencil and scissors in hand. A place for resting after operational work and during night work. A place for breaks between operations. A place of seclusion for concentrating during difficult operational moments. A place for conceptions and crucial decisions.

2. *The Operations Room.* The place for editing operations. The place for confronting the results of separate research and filming operations. The place for initial sorting of footage immediately after filming and after the negative has been developed. The place for the second sorting of footage after the positive has been printed. The place for the third sorting of footage after themes have been designated. The place for the fourth sorting of footage (both sound and silent) within the framework of the next theme. The rough cutting of the film. Corrections and transpositions. The final check of all shots individually and of all combinations of shots, the combination of image with music, with word and intertitle. A check on tempo, rhythm. A footage count. The definitive editing.

3. *The Research and Administration Office.* The eyes and ears of the laboratory. The place of preliminary reconnaissance. The observation station. Contact by telephone, mail, and in person with people and phenomena under observation. The organization of observation posts. The preparation of research material for the director. The carrying out of research and administrative assignments. Administrative work on the filming operation. Responsibility for the means of transport, for the readiness to film at any moment.

4. *Director's Film Archive.* The place where the stock-

> pile of [documentary] footage shot by the director is kept. The place from which footage pertaining to the creative operation at hand is delivered to the operations room. The director's notebook. His rough drafts, individual shots, sketches, and other bits awaiting their turn. An editing base of special significance, increasing from picture to picture and enabling (if the size of the creative stockpile increases sufficiently) the author-director to gradually shorten the time period between the release dates of particular works.
> 5. *A Mobile Filming Unit.* "A little house on wheels." A specially equipped bus with trailer, which will technically facilitate filming at any time, in any place, under any conditions.

My proposal for the organization of a creative laboratory was impelled by the need to break away, once and for all, from the recent position of our group at Mezhrabpomfilm. Briefly, our position was this:

After finishing *Three Songs,* our group decided to turn from work on the poetic film in survey format to films on *man's behavior.* Contrary to our expectations, we met not with welcome and support but with the administration's opposition. Opposition not in words but in deeds. With prohibition not in words but in deeds. Allotted a sum of money, while forbidden each item of that sum. In practice the management's actions contradicted their decisions. Deed contradicted word. Outward agreement was in reality refusal. What the right hand signed, the left crossed out. Plus and minus. That is, zero. And, as everyone knows, "any number multiplied by zero equals zero."

All our proposals for rationalizing the labor process and our creative proposals have, when multiplied by zero, inevitably yielded the result of zero.

To film man's behavior adequately outside the studio, under natural conditions, we should concentrate within our laboratory all our long shooting experience, all our discoveries and inventions that have been dispersed en route by the compulsory and improper organization of work.

Everything done thus far by an incompetent administration for the development of our filming work should be regarded not as help but as a systematic disarmament, as the destruction of the results of the work done by our group of inventors.

The creative laboratory will put an end to the destruction of what we have sown; it will help to lay out a creative nursery, a creative garden.

1937

January 17

Is it possible that I too am acting out a role? The role of seeker after film-truth? Do I truly seek truth? Perhaps this too is a mask, which I myself don't realize?

Hardly. I like people. Not everyone, but those who speak the truth. That's why I love little children. I am drawn to such people.

That's why I love folk art. Truth is our object. All our techniques, methods, genres, and so forth are means. The ways and creation are various, but the end must be the same: truth.

Living conditions, working conditions, means of transportation, conservation of documents, the request for a particular camera, for film stock—these are means. Who needs films that do not attempt to reveal the truth? If you cannot make a film that contains truth, then make none at all. No need for such pictures. All means for truth's sake. Demand these possibilities and means. In this situation, an unassuming attitude is dangerous and inappropriate.

Truth is not pleasing to everyone. You speak an unpleasant truth; they smile and conceal their malice.

Hatred of the pleasant falsehood. Few possess it.

When critics write, they generally tend to present our means as the end. They then attack the means, thinking they attack the end. The inability to distinguish the means from the end—that's the trouble with our film critics.

You stand in line for the baths and wonder how it is that other directors contrive not to stand in line?

This must be some special talent: getting an apartment with a bath, the use of a car, the necessary equipment for shooting, etc.

Modesty and an unassuming manner are nice of course. But you notice how other comrades who are better off begin to look down upon you—a pedestrian.

"The pedestrian is no companion for the equestrian."

The neighbors who share our apartment (there are a great many) are beginning to treat us slightingly. And even suspiciously. They had been counting on getting my room after I received an award. They'd read in the papers that award-winners receive apartments and other things. There must be something wrong if I'm still in this room. Their neighbors change slowly, too slowly. They still prefer not to peep out from behind their masks. And their masks are poor ones. They'd be better off without them.

The worst truth is still the truth.

February 12

My heart. No one knew where it was. And then it couldn't bear the strain. Here it is. Aching. Nights spent with eyes wide open. My heart. Here it is. Rattling. And yet I'm cheerful, you know. Only that cheerfulness is under lock and key. Am I happy? Yes. Not through my own happiness. Through everyone else's happiness. I am the exception that confirms the rule.

My heart. Where from? Where to? It doesn't want to remain in my body. It begs to be torn out. It wants to leave. It's very ill. But I feel no envy. Killed it. Happy when other are happy. My turn will come. "Ye shall sow, but not reap." My turn will come. To sow! Sow! Sow!

Heart! Rest. Slow down. Don't tear away. Be calm. Happiness will come. Work will come. Joy will come. If only there weren't this fatigue. If only the heart endures . . .

The fact that in reworking *Girls of Two Worlds* into a totally different composition (*Lullaby*) I managed to save over three hundred lines out of two thousand should be regarded as an achievement and not a failure. For the chief merit of the new song, the new construction, is that despite the radical revision of the film's theme and construction, the best images of the first, unrealized song were not destroyed. Preserving these images of folk art instead of substituting abstract fictions—this was my goal and in this lay the entire difficulty in reorganizing my conception. I consider it not a shortcoming, but a great victory on my part that the addition of more than two hundred new lines plus a new composition enabled me to

"The pedestrian is no companion for the equestrian." A Russian proverb roughly equivalent in meaning to "oil and water don't mix" but carrying a stronger implication of class distinction—trans.

express my creative concept without completely destroying all the previously discovered footage. Had it been possible to save not three hundred but five or six hundred lines, I would certainly have done so. It takes people not a few years but decades and centuries to create certain images. To imagine that in three months of research of archival and other footage I could casually "compose" other images instead (and to what purpose, really?) would be an unforgivable error. I did not set out to do this, nor should I have done so.

I do not work for money. This must be understood. If I worked for the money, I would not be earning, on the average, less than any other director. Less, perhaps, than a number of the women who do our film splicing. My films are my children. No one can suffer more, be more concerned over the health and fate of her child than its mother.

By now, at this stage of my cinematic studies, I no longer edit films according to parts, titles, or episodes. I edit the entire film all at once: that is, I let all the pieces at my disposal interact with each other all at once.

All shots are constantly shifted, until the very end of the editing process, which involves an extremely abbreviated recapitulation of all previous stages, an entire history of its development, from the primitive construction of the old Pathé Newsreel to extremely sophisticated contemporary montage constructions.

New supervisors have always been confused and upset because in my work the "scaffolding" is removed only at the last minute (there's no other way). What if the film shouldn't come off, shouldn't turn out?

The more experienced executives, who are familiar with my work, are not alarmed. They know at this final stage Svilova and I have so familiarized ourselves with the footage, with all its nuances and possibilities, that we make all the essential improvements and changes literally in a few hours.

There's no point, therefore, in rejecting more advanced production and in returning to more primitive methods for the sake of a premature, tangible effect. Not the effects, but the work's final result must be ensured.

"The authentic, law-oriented artist strives for artistic truth; the unprincipled one, who blindly follows his own impulse, for the appearance of truth; the first brings art to its loftiest stage, the second to its lowest." (Thus spoke Goethe.)

Sunlight falls on my neighbors in the apartment building across the street. While we live in its reflected light. A slender young woman stands before a full-length mirror, wholly unaware that I'm watching her from a window across the way. She has taken off her robe and, turning about and fixing her hair, admires herself. She is bathed in light, her eyes blinded, as if by the bright lights of a stage, and she cannot see the audience, but everyone can see her. Of this she is unaware. Shading her eyes with her hands, she continues to look in her mirror.

So, moments of such intimacy in people's lives can be observed sometimes without special devices or complications. And even without special arranged experiments . . .

I remember the wife of the watchman who drowned in a well. I remember the widower who wept for two days when his wife died. Then on the third day he brought a girl in off the street, locked the door, turned on all the lights and stared at the naked girl for a long time, never touching her. I remember the girl's bewilderment, then her forwardness and attempts to arouse him, and the man's face and eyes—distant, blank, as if the girl's body were out of focus, refracted in a prism, as though he were seeing many bodies swimming before his eyes. . . . It was all very strange. The girl waited another minute, then dressed quietly and cautiously. She tiptoed out the door. I saw her leave by the street entrance below, glance up at his lighted window. . . . In the morning when I left for work, through the window I saw him still sitting in the same position.

I remember a husband and wife in a horse cab on Petrovka. She was chattering away as he smiled and stroked her hand. Suddenly the man turned pale, gasped for air. Not noticing, she went on laughing and talking. He grabbed her hand. The carriage stopped; a crowd gathered. She screamed, entreated, calling him by tender names, embraced him, whispered in his ear, kissed him, but the man was dead.

I remember many such incidents, inaccessible to the camera if scripted beforehand.

April 15

At the "front" on *Sergo Ordzhonikidze.*

No changes. The negative was edited at Potylikha. We do not know when it will be released.

At the "front" on *Lullaby.*

Very little time left. Situation confused. Undercurrents of some sort. The "rear" is not covered. I don't know what to do.

At the "front" of the experimental laboratory project. They're stalling. Shtro writes sad letters from Kiev. Surensky's leaving to do photography.

At the "front" on Soviet Union Newsreel.

A policy of quantity. Of mediocre work. Technically poor. No room for creative innovation. Production level all right, but always mere repetition of what has already been done. Not a single step forward. The fight for quality is not encouraged. Rushed work rather than an organized production process. Directors are depersonalized. The cameramen are well paid and passive. Protest is feeble.

A laboratory is essential. We must provide models. Shake up people's minds. Break their habits. Stir them out of lethargy, open the way to innovation. Then we will not recognize these same people.

If you're weak, incapable of superhuman effort, you'll drift unfeeling with the tide, copying models created by others.

This must not be. We must change the conditions for producing creative work so that each newsreel worker can contribute something of his own that's new, fresh, or discovered anew. . . .

December 20

The screen release of *Lullaby* was very strange. Limited to the preholiday period, for five days (in Moscow), and not in the center of

Sergo Ordzhonikidze. Grigori Konstantinovich (Sergo) Ordzhonikidze (1886–1937), a Georgian like Stalin, served as Commissar of Heavy Industry in the USSR. He was instrumental in the success of Stalin's campaign against Trotsky and the Left Opposition during the period from 1923 to 1927. Nominally subordinate to Molotov's Sovnarkom, Ordzhonikidze's Commissariat enjoyed considerable autonomy during the first half of the 1930s, and its sphere of influence broadened to encompass science and higher education. His death in 1937 from heart disease was attended by rumors of assassination—ed.

town. I wrote a letter to Shumyatsky about this but have received no answer.

Almost no one managed to see the picture. Everyone thought it would come out during the holidays. The posters carried no indication where or when the film would be shown. Except for *Kinogazeta* and *Evening Moscow,* the newspapers did not get a chance to discuss it.

There are a lot of other strange things that remain to be explained. The future will show what's involved here. . . .

But for the moment things are fine.

Very fine.

I'm done at last with standing in line for the lavatory, for the sink, for the bath, etc.

I've moved to a new two-room apartment. It's as though I hadn't lived till now. The contrast even makes me feel a kind of weakness. There's no telephone yet and the water, bath, etc., aren't yet working. But I no longer hear quarreling from the kitchen; I can put the teakettle on the gas when I please, and the ceiling's not dripping.

And this is so good, so soothing that it seems like a fairy tale.

Does one need very much?—perhaps I'll even recover if things go on like this. . . .

1938

A creative project remains a project if we're denied the conditions for its realization.

The sole desire to realize a project does not suffice. You must clearly visualize that under certain conditions a project can be fully realized; under others only partially, and distortedly; and under still others not at all.

Can one say that this author's idea can be realized by just any one? Just any director, manager, cameraman, assistant, etc.? No, you cannot.

Can one claim that this project can be realized with just any lighting and camera equipment, under any administrative and technical conditions, for just any deadline, using any means of transport, just any film stock? . . . You cannot make this claim, either.

You must organize victory, not wait for it to come of itself, by some miracle.

The only way to realize a nonstandard creative project lies in organizing nonstandard conditions and requirements for the writing, filming, editing—the entire creative, administrative, and technical process.

Given our insistence on the uncompromising realization of a creative project, given our hatred of the falsity and pseudotruth that hacks and hustlers attempt to substitute for multicolored truth, given our attempt to present the images born of folk art instead of premature illustrations for slogans and titles, and given our aversion to clichés—we cannot agree to those conditions that paralyze any tendency to diverge from a universal, depersonalized system of prescriptions concocted in an office, unadaptable to exceptional cases.

People, first and foremost.

They must be carefully and attentively cultivated, from one film to the next, gradually, during the work process.

The lack of a permanent group, of a group continually cultivated by the author and director, eliminates all possibility of proper growth for the poetic film.

You can't begin again every time, after each film—appointing new people, who are, for the most part, uninterested and completely unversed in the making of poetic films. We need people united in that purpose by a single dream, a single conception, a single persistence. Clarity, unity, and community of purpose can exist only within a group united by the struggle with difficulties and obstacles, united by common success and failure, victories and defeats; it is not to be found within a group of people who have come together by chance, on assignment because they happen to have been free at that particular moment.

And then come technical and administrative conditions, a foundation for creative work.

Not random conditions created for the given moment, not camera and lighting equipment that happen to turn up just then, not standard conditions for other purposes, but precisely that camera, equipment, or device, those conditions that do not hinder but facilitate the solution of the task at hand.

Not standard deadlines, or those that happen to be still in force, but that precise minimum of time required for the uncompromising realization of not just any film but precisely *our* film.

And finally, not one thousand or two thousand rubles, but the minimum required for the realization of not just any film but precisely *our* film.

September 4

A plan of action—that is what we need. Instead, people in separate departments rummage about in my scenario project, pondering for weeks over what to add to a sentence, drowning in petty details, totally uncertain, afraid of who knows what; neither prohibiting nor authorizing, dragging on and on and on. . . .

Meanwhile everything disappears—the sun, the events, the necessary people, the author's enthusiasm, the interest of those around him, and the technical possibilities. Then, one fine day, there's a sudden panic. Faster, faster . . . you've got to do the impossible; we're for art, but not at the price of an extended deadline; we must fulfill the plan, etc.

Who will restore to me the hundred days lost in getting agreement and confirmation?

September 7

Battle techniques that are forbidden. I've forbidden them to myself.

1. Untruth in the interest of truth.
2. Counting on the stupidity of others to increase chances for success.
3. Substituting the appearance of truth for truth itself.

How is one to contend with bureaucratic response, with instructions that do not represent decisions, but the postponement of decision? With an endless "tomorrow"?

How is one to explain intolerance of talent and tolerance of mediocrity?

How is one to distinguish cowardice from caution, truth from semblance, acting from nonacting, a pose from authentic emotion, fact from fiction?

Prohibition or permission—these you can understand. But what is one to do with "not prohibiting but not permitting either," with pigeonholing and shelving, with unending delay and sluggishness?

A creative project can be either destroyed or shelved for years, for one's whole lifetime.

What means will do to save it? Can one adapt any methods, the usual, disgusting methods, the despicable and humiliating, shameful methods to which wheeler-dealers and hustlers resort at every step?

Can one fight for a principled cause using unprincipled methods?

I apparently cannot.

As long as hatred of those methods has the upper hand.

As long as we seek truth through truth.

In a documentary script you cannot write in advance that "Ivanov drowned while swimming." Who knows if he will drown, or even swim?

He will live, smile, and play chess, despite the script's indication that he "went swimming and drowned."

In documentary films on human behavior you cannot make use of the usual production techniques and schemata. The plan of action here is different, as set forth in the proposal for a creative laboratory.

You cannot describe a house on fire until the actual event takes place. Perhaps there will be no fire.

Either you'll have to deny the description as a fiction, or burn the house in accordance with the script. Then, however, it will no longer be a newsreel, but the ordinary acted film with sets and actors.

The full development of the newsreel-documentary has been quite out of the question all these past years.

The most powerful weapon used in combatting newsreel-documentary films has been *failure to issue them,* their smothering by distribution.

This made all work on the newsreel-documentary pointless, and their makers were reduced to hopelessness and despair.

Is it possible—

1. To give the newsreel-documentary film rights and opportunities equal to those for films of the usual kind (keeping in mind the special features of the newsreel)?

It's possible.

2. To raise again the issue of the "Leninist ratio" for movie theater programs?

It's possible.

3. To win back the viewer's trust in these films, not by pursuing quantity, but by adapting the position: "Better less, but better"?

It's possible.

4. To make the distribution circuits sign agreements with us, stipulating the promotion of newsreel-documentary films?

It's possible.

5. To make the wage system for newsreel-documentary film workers directly proportionate to the quality and quantity of labor expended, thus replacing payment on a meaningless formal basis (number of reels)?

It's possible.

6. To reorder the system of studio work so that special and current newsreels would not halt the production of artistic documentary films?

It's possible.

1939

I'm making magazines for export. I go about indignant, saying unpleasant things to all my superiors. But I can't keep quiet.

All our work is being done for nothing. Using duplicate negatives of the lowest quality. The sixth issue of *The USSR On Screen* is being finished, while the first, from January, has not yet been printed or sent out. The factories are not printing; they scrap the duplicate negatives—and they're right to do so. You can't send footage abroad that's technically worthless.

But nothing helps. Issue after issue is being edited. Composers are choosing music. The spoken narration is being written. The sound mixing goes on, etc. And it's all for nothing, since it will be scrapped for bad workmanship.

You protest, get indignant. Your superiors look askance and think: "The man's a nervous type; his standards are excessively high; we've got to get rid of him if things are to be calm and quiet. He refuses to recognize our brilliant results. He calls it clichés, hackwork, tinkering. Well, we'll soon be rid of him now. . . ."

That's just great! A terrible earache (a complication from the flu). You suffer and can't think. Lie in bed. Wait for the doctor, but a phone call from the manager notifies you in advance that as of March 25 you're being transferred to Mostekhfilm [Moscow Studio of Technical Films].

But what about Svilova? After all she's the last member of our working group who has not yet been taken from me.

March 28

At the battlefront of *Three Heroines*. For some reason, about ten worker-specialists saw the film. The result is always the same—delight with the picture and indignation at the delay in its release. Vertov is criticized for not fighting, not complaining, not having it out with the upper echelons.

But Vertov's been hypnotized. Action equals counteraction. Construction equals destruction.

Which is better: to win a struggle, having used up one's remaining strength and quit the ranks temporarily, or to find and take on new work and construct—without, it's true, any assurance that the new work won't also be destroyed with a single wave of a hand? . . .

You cannot construct an unacted film according to some "ideal plan," removed from life, some script, written in an armchair, that makes no use of productive forces, instruments of production, the ability to employ specific conditions of a specified time and place.

An organic, natural bent for observation. For the graphic, poetic organization of these observations.

Good for Troitskaya! She refused to submit to a "scenario." She said: "I'm not going to do anything for you, film me as I am."

Kiselev, the director, complains that he can't do anything with her. I think just the opposite: What luck that the girl refuses to pose! How I'd like to film her!

A meeting of the creative section. A conference. Heiman gave a report. He began on a high level, then under the pressure of comments, got smaller, pettier, lower. Many of the speakers, starting with Katzman, jumped on him. Each spoke from his own personal, parochial point of view. Almost everyone thought it necessary to mention Vertov. I had to speak out, especially in answer to Karmazinsky who announced that from the very day he'd entered newsreel he'd fought against Vertov, although one should borrow everything valuable in Vertov's work.

You need steel nerves and ironclad health. Then one could still repeat the struggle, as for *Three Songs*. But already with *Lullaby* I no longer had the strength. The trouble made for me with *Ordzhonikidze*, the picture's endless remakes, drained me still further. *Three Heroines* was the final blow. And all because of formalities and bureaucratic prejudices.

"The most terrible enemy of progress is prejudice—it impedes and blocks the path of development." (Stanislavsky)

August 6

He doesn't have many things left.

No envy. No spite. No calm. No scenario. No cigarettes.

A breeze from the window. Feels good after the day's heat. Someone's whistling outside. It distracts me from my thoughts. And Pauline says, "It's a good thing I'm leaving." The elevator comes up. Liza says, "They must have arrived." Above the tree outside the window shine ordinary stars and the red ones of the Kremlin. Tomorrow they're chopping the tree down—to build a garage for those who know how to live well.

Why doesn't he have a car or summer cottage? Why, on a day off, does he have to drag himself with such difficulty and discomfort to the waterside to return in even greater discomfort? Wait hours for the chance to cling to the running board or squeeze into a jumble of sweating bodies?

But maybe it's good—not to live apart, not to build a pool at *one's private* summer cottage, not to pave *one's private* terrace with a mosaic of semiprecious stones? I'd just like to see how everything looks among those who do know how to live. "In your building on

Liza. Elizaveta Svilova, Vertov's wife and collaborator.

Polyanka," joked Giber, "you're the poorest relative. You have to know how to live! . . ." But I'm not envious.

All will go well.

August 7

If there were a book entitled *Vertov's System* or *Vertov's Work,* then, after a change of managements, it would be possible to quickly acquaint the new management with myself; the manager would know how to make the best use of me. Failing this, the result is that the "shoemaker makes pies" and the "pastry chef makes shoes." I'm transferred, senselessly, to completely inappropriate positions and to jobs that are alien to my creative temperament.

Any student of Pavlov's, any scientist or writer, generally has the right *to engage in observation,* but I have not. I am told that everything must be indicated in a scenario, that a scenario—is the primary thing.

However, what I consider primary is matter, nature, documentary material accumulated on film. One proceeds from film observations to their graphic organization. But one is forced to submit to the reverse order, the standard order for producing the usual actors' film: from the scenario (of the bookish, closet variety) to nature, with the obligation of forcing nature to meet the "scenario's" requirements.

All this for fear of the exception, of experiment, fear of disturbing one's peace and comfort, fear of intense light or dark, from the desire to "let me live in peace."

August 14

Creative labor—that is the sweetest relaxation. Senseless idleness and waiting—that is the most agonizing labor, the most destructive of the human organism.

The script is still not approved and returned to me. But I can't stand it any longer. I sense more and more clearly that I've been deliberately deceived. I'm absolutely not where I belong. Mostekhfilm is not for me.

I wrote a request to the manager. I'm asking for an unpaid leave. I'll write a scenario and a request. If I can't work with a camera, I'll work with the pen.

I've grown so nervous that I can't take the streetcar. Every contact in the car, in the crush, causes nervous tremors. I hold myself together by autohypnosis.

In all the other arts one has the right to "compose from nature." Why do I not have that same right? Standing idle would be impossible then: I would depend not on the acceptance procedure for the scenario but on myself.

August 30

The method of Mikhail Mikhailovich Prishvin seems to come closest to my own. Like myself, he feels that "it's possible to come with pencil or brush in hand, as painters do, and also to investigate nature in your own way, obtaining not the reasons for phenomena but their images." He says that "only painting has, in its own way, been the systematic study of nature from ancient times and has, in an artistic sense, made the same discoveries as science" (*The Foxhunt*).

I come not with a brush, but with a camera, an instrument more perfect, and I want to penetrate nature for an artistic purpose, to discover images, obtaining precious truth not on paper, but on film—through observation and experiment. This is the union of newsreel, science, and art. This is a path of discovery that will later find proof and explanation. This is the path of joy and excitement that leads the traveller into a world without masks. The path of truth, not semblance. A magnificent path, but a difficult one. Labor such as this brings real joy. The more difficult, the more joyful. And without real joy there is no true creation.

Shall I one day succeed in explaining and proving my right to such a path? . . .

He's a hunter. A hunter of film-shots. Shots of truth. Film-truth.

He does not shut himself up in an office. He leaves the cage of his room. Paints from nature. Observes. Experiments. Takes his bearings in strange surroundings. Makes instant decisions. Camouflages, making use of natural resources. And at the vital moment, fires accurately. A film-sniper. Calmness, bravery, coolness, initia-

Mikhail Mikhailovich Prishvin. Prishvin (1873-1954) was a popular Russian and Soviet painter of scenes from nature within the conventions of pictorial realism—trans.

tive, self-control. No clerical or other procedures. Simultaneous decision and implementation.

He's a scout. An observer. A marksman. A pathfinder. An explorer.

But he's a poet as well. He penetrates life for artistic purposes. He synthesizes his observations into original works of art. He makes artistic discoveries. Pours precious grains of genuine truth into songs of truth, epics of truth, into a symphony of objective reality.

But this is no longer so.

For several years now he has not hunted, explored, fired a weapon.

When he takes aim and is ready to release the trigger, he's told: "Hold fire!" They demand his official authorization. He takes steps to obtain an authorization and sometimes gets one. But meanwhile the bird flies away, the animal runs off. The authorization is of no further use to him.

Sometimes he tracks a subject for study, observation, and graphic investigation for weeks and months on end. But he's told: give us a scenario, gives us the result of your future observations in advance, in the form of a literary and directorial description of each future shot:

The result is an impossibility:

- if you have the results of observations in advance, then there's no need to make those observations;
- if you have in advance the result of an experiment not yet conducted, then there's no need to conduct the experiment. (You can stage it, but that's already quite another branch of cinema.)
- if the composition of a chemical compound, a formula, is known in advance, that is, if what you're looking for has already been found, then why look for what's already found, why discover what's already been discovered, why? . . .

The fact is that a plan of action is not a description of events that have already taken place, nor a battle plan, an observation plan, a description of observations that have already occurred. There are two sides to every battle. The enemy does not follow your plan. He has his own. You must act, taking into account the enemy's behavior.

October 18

I've been at Detfilm [Children's Film] for more than a month. During that time I have submitted many proposals. Written several requests. But no decision about what I should start work on has yet been made by the management. Saakov, the assistant manager of the artistic script section, promises to issue his proposal on behalf of the management. Until now, proposals have come from me alone—there have been no counterproposals. I'm making every effort to begin work, but so far I've met with extreme caution.

I have no real chance of making a personal choice. If I could only start shooting soon. Soon, soon, so my taut nerves don't snap, so I don't lose my mind.

"You have to know how to peddle your wares," Yutkevich says, reproachfully.

October 24

Usually it's like this: a director chooses one of the scenarios offered by a studio.

With me it's the reverse.

I make one proposal after another. While the studio still proposes nothing. It's as if I'm on stage, while the management and script department are in the auditorium.

I run my legs off, proposing one thing then another.

And the audience watches and listens. And remains silent.

And I feel as if I'm way at the bottom. Facing the first step of a long, steep staircase. My violin lies at the very top, on the landing. I move the bow . . . on air. I ask to be allowed to get my violin. I climb onto the first step. But the person in charge of the step pushes me aside and asks: "Where are you going?"

I point to my bow and explain that my violin's up there. "But what do you plan to play on the violin? Tell us, describe it to us. We'll discuss it; we'll correct it; we'll add to it; we'll coordinate it with the other steps; we'll reject or confirm it."

I say that I'm a composer. And I write not with words, but with sounds.

Then they ask me not to worry.

And take away the bow.

You want to make a film to a script.

But you're told:

"Well, who can write the script for you?"

You want to make a film without a script.

But you're told:

"This has no plan. A film absolutely must be made according to a script."

You want to make films about real people.

You're told:

"I'm firmly convinced that real people cannot be filmed in documentary fashion; we can't allow that."

Then you make a poetic film of the panorama or song variety.

You're told:

"All this is fine, but there are no real people."

In despair you decide to make an acted film, with an actor, like everyone else does.

But then you're told:

"We can't have you do that. You have a name and a creative identity. Our studio can't risk it. We've got to keep you the way your reputation in cinema demands."

Where, I ask, is the way out of this impasse? . . .

He tossed and turned in bed until morning. And, as always, awoke with a firm decision. He wanted to dress, run to the studio, leave that very day on an expedition with a cameraman, or sit down with a script writer and set forth his ideas—o.k., he'll write according to all the rules, if only they'll give him his violin as soon as possible. After all, if things go on like this, he'll forget how to play.

And, as always, on the way to the studio he's already seized with doubt, not of his ability, but of organization. And he climbs the factory stairs, enters the administrator's office, enthusiastically begins to propose a topic . . . and gets neither "yes" nor "no" for an answer. And accompanied by the distrustful smile of the official "cautious in all things," he drags himself through the streets, cursing himself for his inability to get along; his inability to offer his labor, to be cunning, and to maneuver; his inability to obtain a creative job through any means, as any ordinary film hack knows how to do.

December 25

But, still, how am I to obtain work? . . . Saakov accepted one of my proposals. He said: "We'll use it. There's something here I like. But don't disturb me for a couple of days. I'm going to be busy submitting films. It's the end of the year right now. And don't write me any more proposals and requests—we've had enough."

But I can't. I keep writing and tearing them up. Sometimes I don't tear them up. And it's all for nothing. I'm only a director, after all, and they have to give me a scenario.

I end up thinking day and night. But I can't make a decision. Why can't I? Because the decision doesn't depend on me. "You'll do what we tell you," says Saakov.

But he doesn't tell me.

Lenin said that you have to write about what you know well. I proposed: Let me make a film for you about Bialystok, my hometown. "No," said Saakov, "we're thinking about assigning you a sketch on the Carpathians"—that is, a region I know nothing about.

I could make a much deeper and more interesting report on the place where I was born and grew up. But Saakov threatens: "You'll do what you're told, or you won't work in cinema at all." I didn't refuse, but he's already giving me a preventive scare.

Everything is slowly becoming clear. Saakov said: "The studio can't risk it. You can do a sketch for an anthology but not for a full-length film."

In other words, everything I did till now I did in vain?

Before people used to direct solo, now it's different.

For one violin there are a hundred conductors.

1940

I love bathing and swimming; I do not bathe or swim.

I love the woods, sunlight, fresh air; I hang about the city, amidst gasoline fumes and soot.

Ever since childhood I've loved dogs; I have no dog. And for a number of reasons nothing comes of this business.

I'm keen on volleyball, tennis, gymnastics, riding bicycles and horses. I don't play, don't ride, don't do gymnastics, and I'm generally thinking about something else, a single gigantic, unsuccessful conception.

And I seem never to have time, to be very busy, to be on the brink of solution, to need only to focus my attention on a single mathematical point to break through any and all obstacles, intrigues, and mine fields. . . .

February 4

Can one die from hunger that's not physical but the hunger to create?

Yes, one can.

You'll die and later the critics, in analyzing the deceased's film legacy, will establish that "the form of Vertov's poetry was naturally conditioned by the content of his work."

February 7

It's one thing to play well on an excellent violin. Having the knowledge and ability to obtain that violin is quite another thing.

It's one thing to produce a film well. The ability to obtain that production is quite another thing.

Frequently, it's not the most talented artist, but the most energetic talker and the cleverest dealer who prevails.

Even the most talented, creative worker may not succeed if he doesn't know how to "get on in life."

If you decide that "the end justifies the means," then you can find a way out of the situation without too much difficulty. But you know you keep hoping to get by without making that decision. . . .

Ilyin's having a rough time with the scenario of *Tale of a Giant*. It lacks the necessary lightness. You don't feel smiles and laughter in what's written. The fairy-tale adventures haven't come off as yet.

Here's the plan: to use all cinematic possibilities to carry through the exposition of the educational footage to completion. Then, proceeding from the footage, to compose the text of a light fairy tale.

February 12

I don't isolate myself, but I am isolated. I'm not invited anywhere. I haven't received an invitation to the conference on the historical film. I'm not included in Kiselev's film *Our Cinema* (for the twentieth anni-

Ilyin. The pseudonym of Ilya Yakovlevich Marshak (1895–1953), a well-known author of stories for children.

versary). They didn't publish an article of mine that was commissioned. Apparently there's no display at the exhibit—they didn't ask me for photographs or film frames. My silence is taken to mean "I'm silent," rather than "I'm being silenced."

But I don't need anything—if I could just work.

June 17

We've managed to make the script of *Tale of a Giant* innovative in every respect. New creative problems require new creative methods, new methods of organization, a new approach to montage, to sound, etc. We're counting on invading new areas of cinema.

We're counting on creating a synthetic work—not with a "topical" but with a lasting significance. It's a serious wager.

Can this film be defeated in production? Yes, it can. It can be defeated if we attempt to squeeze the production process of an innovative work into the framework of the usual, standardized methods. If we approach the realization of this scenario bureaucratically. If in this extraordinary instance we cling to the dead letter of a given column, of a given set of directions. If we look upon the procedure established in existing directions as dogma.

Defeat will be certain if, while creating an innovative work, we dogmatically insist upon ordinary, conservative methods. A bureaucratic approach would mean the death of our film. Only by rejecting pedantry can we bring our film to successful completion.

"Whoever sees and wishes to see form alone is a petty artist." But "He who sacrifices form, is not an artist at all." (Romain Rolland, *Beethoven*)

"If we, Russian observers, compare ourselves with the Japanese, we perceive far fewer nuances in their faces than do their fellow countrymen. That is because we are not familiar with the Japanese, we have not become accustomed to distinguishing among them, with that power of attention one has for those related to ourselves. . . .

"Still more striking is our limited ability to distinguish when we pass from man to the world of animals and plants: there all rooks are black, all sparrows grey. . . ." (Prishvin, *The Cranes' Homeland*)

The Artistic Council met only on September 28. Razumny, Kuleshov, Protazanov, Shelenkov, Donskoy, Maryamov, Frolov, Saakov, the authors, and their group were present.

Maryamov said not a word. Ilyin spoke first and protested that work has been stalled since September 3, that no one is providing any clear instructions, that discussion and decision making continue to be put off.

Then Donskoy, the director, said that there was no reason to get upset, that Detfilm welcomed the arrival of Ilyin and other children's writers in cinema. That the film is remarkable, the only one of its kind, but very complex technically and in terms of production. He'd read the scenario again and would talk about it personally with Vertov.

Razumny, the director, said that although he's a veteran, he's not such a conservative. He thinks (on the basis of the highest artistic consideration) that our picture should be made into a cartoon.

Shelenkov, the cameraman, questioned the technical possibility

Artistic Council. The Council, responsible to Ivan Bolshakov, the administrative functionary of the Soviet film industry, counted among its members some of the nation's most distinguished directors. These included Protazanov, Donskoy, and Kuleshov.

Yakov Protazanov (1881–1945), a pioneer of the industry, began his career with a series of film dramas made before the Revolution. These included adaptations of works by Andreyev and Pushkin. *Father Sergius,* an adaptation of a text by Tolstoy, was, in fact, the last major production to be made under the tsarist regime. Protazanov emigrated to Paris in 1917 and remained at work there until 1923, when he accepted an invitation to return to the USSR where he was active as a director until his death. His first film following his return was *Aelita* (1924), a political science-fiction narrative with sets designed by Alexandra Exter, the constructivist artist. His other, more celebrated films include *The Forty-First* (1927) and *The White Eagle* (1928).

Lev Kuleshov (1899–1970) is generally considered one of the most important founding figures of the postrevolutionary cinema. He began as a cameraman for the Red Army (1918–1919), organized an experimental film laboratory (1921–1922), and taught in the first state film school, gathering about him a group of enterprising young artists who were to make their careers as actors and/or directors. These included Vsevold Pudovkin, Alexandra Kokhlova, Boris Barnett, Valeri Inkizhinov. Kuleshov's early experiments and pedagogic exercises in editing technique laid the basis for the theory and practice of montage, so central to the development of Soviet cinema in the postrevolutionary era. His best-known films include *The Extraordinary Adventures of Mr. West in the Land of the Bolsheviks* (1924), *The Death Ray* (1925), *By the Law* (1926), and *The Great Consoler* (1940).

Mark Donskoy (1901–1981) is best known in the West for his cinematic trilogy on the life of Maxim Gorky, adapted from the writer's own accounts of his early life and released between 1938 and 1940. *Thomas Gordeev* (1959) is another cinematic adaptation of a text by the same author—ed.

of realizing the scenario. In addition he was disturbed by the difference between the writer's and the director's versions. He began reading the literary one there, at the meeting (it later turned out that he was reading an old, unapproved version).

Kuleshov, the director, said that science is something splendid and therefore there's no reason to make a poetic film. It should be made into a technical film. He couldn't offer any advice, and no one could since first one must listen to a technical report, look at some experimental stills, etc. In short, he too declined to talk to the point.

Protazanov, the director, said that he hadn't read the scenario at all.

Then Frolov, the director, who'd been absent during Vertov's and Ilyin's remarks, summed up: so . . . first technical experiments and a conference, then an artistic conference. It would be good to hear the opinions of those who can and wish to offer advice.

With that the meeting closed.

When the destruction of something created occurs parallel to that creation, though you've worked much more, it turns out that you've achieved nothing. This time destruction seems to have been postponed. Still, attempts in that direction remain possible.

Neither Yutkevich nor Frolov has the slightest doubts about the success of the venture. Both signed a very favorable recommendation. And they don't anticipate any objections from the committee.

Is it possible that unlike what has usually happened to me in recent years, no one will turn up this time to destroy all my labor with the flourish of a pen? . . .

1941

January 8

They say Yutkevich has not left. He's at the committee, together with Frolov. They're discussing the plan for 1941. Romm is there

Romm. Mikhail Romm (1901–1971) made his debut with a highly praised adaptation of Maupassant's *Boule de Suif* (1934). He later specialized in cinematic biographies of Lenin. His *Nine Days of a Year* (1961), a portrayal of life among Soviet intellectuals, was characterized by the relative psychological subtlety and sense of nuance introduced into cinema during the years of the post-Stalin thaw—ed.

too. Apparently the fate of our film is being decided as well. In the Central Committee they haven't yet read the shorthand reports of the Artistic Council.

At the end of the workday I saw Frolov. I asked how things were going. "O.k.," he said, "keep working." "But what about the scenario?" "Bolshakov wants to read it. They'll give it to him today." Frolov didn't add anything else. I looked into his face—you could see he had doubts about the outcome.

In the evening I met Frolov again at Cinema House. "Well," I asked him, "perhaps I should still inform the Central Committee of the Komsomols?" "It'd be good," Frolov said, "if they phoned Bolshakov from there." And then he added, "Attempts are being made to transfer the scenario to Techfilm."

Thus, the worst solution is offered: the conversion of an artistic, poetic film into an educational-technical one. The annihilation of all the incredible work that Ilyin, myself, and the entire group have done.

Destruction is once again carried out parallel to creation. Once again we're left empty-handed. Another year lost. One more smashed hope. One more confirmation that nothing experimental can get through.

I must either renounce all personality or end my cinematic existence. And just when, for the first time, I have been getting support from other directors. Just when, for the first time, it turned out I wasn't alone. One needs nerves of steel. A steely persistence.

There are other ways of doing things. But I'm not capable of them. I'm just not a "businessman." And I won't kneel at my opponents' feet either.

We're proposing something new on the artistic level. Something new on the level of technique. And something new on the level of organization.

Thus, everything that clings to what is old will oppose it.

"The dead man seizes the living."

January 9

The shorthand reports have not yet arrived. I'm waiting. Thinking.

Bolshakov. Ivan Bolshakov was appointed head of the Soviet film industry in June 1929. His position was consolidated by the conversion of his department to a Ministry of Cinema in 1950. He presided over the delicate transition from the cinema of the war to the cinema of peace. The Artistic Council was responsible to Bolshakov—ed.

What prompted Bliokh to give a negative report to Romm? And what prompted Romm to back out, to try to get rid of the scenario?

Bliokh might have various reasons. Not his attitude to the scenario, but to me: ". . . Vertov is rearing his head again, and I'm stuck doing editorial work. Nothing doing. Let him wait a bit longer." After all, it was no accident that he prohibited the showing of *Lullaby.* A few correspondents saw it, and that's enough for him. . . .

Envy?

Can anyone really envy my sufferings?

Various thoughts run through my mind. There's only one thing I can't believe. I can't believe that they really don't feel the power of the conception of this new work.

Romm says: "It's almost unfeasible technically. Who knows whether it'll turn out?" As if he doesn't know that a film which says something new has to be difficult. And that's good. Just so you don't hide from the difficulties.

Strange. Very strange!

Vertov's signature—more Vertov than Ilyin. Well what of that?

Depersonalize? Drive a wedge between Vertov and Ilyin? Wipe out resistance one way or another?

Ilyin is educational; Vertov, poetic.

The educational is for Techfilm. For poetry—there's no such central committee.

And in general, things are a lot smoother without innovation.

Who needs additional worries?!

January 10

Today Ilyin went to see Mikhailov at the Central Committee of the

Bliokh. Yakov M. Bliokh (1895-1957) had served as production manager for Eisenstein's *Battleship Potemkin.* In 1928 he produced *Shanghai Document,* which was well received. His career advanced somewhat slowly. He produced a documentary sound film, *Kirov,* in 1934, and in 1935, on the occasion of the fifteenth anniversary of the founding of the Soviet cinema, he received, together with Vertov, the Order of the Red Star—ed.

Mikhailov. Vertov appears to be referring to Nikolai Aleksandrovich Mikhailov (1906-), originally a journalist, at one time editor of *Komsomolskaia pravda,* and a member of the Communist Party since 1930. From 1938 to 1952 he was the First Secretary of the Central Committee of the Komsomols. He also held the post of First Secretary of the Moscow Committee of the Communist Party and several ambassadorial posts—ed.

Komsomols. He gave him the Artistic Council's transcript (I got a copy at two in the morning). Mikhailov and Bolshakov had a telephone conversation yesterday. Bolshakov said that at the beginning of the week (i.e., the 13th, 14th, 15th) they'll decide what they'll do. From Frolov we learned that the dispute between the factory and the administration continued today as well. Each side stuck to its opinion. It's been handed over to Bolshakov to decide. I talked on the phone with Yutkevich. He's leaving for Barvikha in a half hour. He advised me to give the transcript of the Artistic Council to Bolshakov (he hasn't read it yet). He said: "You're not alone now. The whole collective is behind you. The case will be won. I'm sure that everything will be settled by my return."

The coincidence of his vote of confidence with his departure from Moscow is a stroke of bad luck.

January 13

The educational must not be opposed to the poetic. Entertainment must not be opposed to edification. It's a question of interpenetration. The enrichment of poetry through science and of science through poetry. Not dispassionate information, but the music of science. The poetry of reality. An emotional approach to the cognitive and a cognitive interest in the emotional. Research that uses the methods of the artist rather than just purely scientific methods.

Sooner or later this path shall be opened.

February 1

Ilyin, Rykachev, Ushakov, and I are in the waiting room. It's ten to twelve.

At twelve sharp Romanov arrives, greets us, and disappears in Bolshakov's office. Thirty minutes of tense excitement. They don't call us in. Someone mutters to himself: "Like people on trial."

Romanov comes out. We rush up to him. "Bolshakov said that he likes the literary scenario, but not the shooting script. The sea, birds, butterflies . . . Techfilm does that very well. You [i.e., we] won't

Rykachev and Ushakov. Rykachev and Ushakov were Detfilm executives and specialists in the production of children's films. Vertov joined their staff in 1939—ed.

improve on it. In short, Bolshakov will see Ilyin and Vertov at five this evening and make his corrections. Then we'll decide."

The time until five drags on in slow motion. We're in the waiting room at a quarter to five. Rykachev and Ushakov, the enthusiasts, are already waiting for us. We wait. It's already five. Five-fifteen. Five-thirty. It's getting on to six. Golovkin passes us.

"What?!" he exclaims in amazement, "you've been here since twelve? Still waiting?!"

"No," I answer reassuringly, "we went home."

The secretary looks at the clock. She sees how upset we are. "Everything is going to be all right," she reassures us.

Finally the secretary says, "You may go in."

We enter and sit down.

"What do you have to say?" utters Bolshakov.

"We want to know your opinion, your decision."

The conversation went on for about an hour and a half.

All in all we didn't reach an agreement on anything.

To my question whether he would support our "many-sided proposal," Bolshakov replied that he could support the experimental work with an aeronautic camera—it could be used for *The History of Aviation* and other films—but he wouldn't back *Tale of a Giant,* since it wasn't urgent.

"But what about the whole year we've lost? All this wasted effort? The cost? Energy? Nerves? Hopes? Innovations? They'll all be lost?"

"And my work," said Ilya Yakovlevich, "is to go down the drain? That is not the way we do things in literature!"

Bolshakov:

"Well, not all the books you people write are printed."

He went on to say that in conversation with Romanov he convinced him that it was not necessary to produce this film right now.

The poetry of science. The poetry of space. The poetry of unknown numbers. The poetry of immensities. The poetry of masses numbering millions. The poetry of happiness. The poetry of sorrow. The poetry of dreams. The poetry of friendship. The poetry of love. The poetry of universal brotherhood. The poetry of the universe. The poetry of labor. The poetry of nature.

Whitman:

> O for my song to be simple as the voices of animals,
> swift and
> balanced as the dropping of raindrops . . .
> All this, O sea, I'd give away joyfully, if you'd give me the
> motion of your wave, a single splash, or if you'd
> breathe into
> my verse a single salty breath, and leave in it this scent.

February 7

A few days have passed since it was all over with *Tale of a Giant.* Very strong reaction in my system. I felt a sudden, terrible exhaustion. I can't sleep. I try to keep my spirits up, but several years spent without rest are having their effect. My backbone feels broken. And I can stand up straight only with difficulty. Everything's in a fog. Right at the entrance to Detfilm I suddenly stopped and for a while I couldn't move from the pain; it felt as though a sword had gone through beneath my left shoulder blade.

February 13

What can one do to stop thinking? Apparently I'm so tired that I no longer understand anything that's happening. I haven't even the energy to take an interest in my opponents' plans, I'm afraid to look behind the scenes. . . .

How can I explain to them the necessity of treatment and rest? Can those who've rested understand those who haven't?

I could say, "In recent years I've worked a great deal without a single day of rest and I've been in a continual state of nervous tension. A tenth of my work was given to work proposals, requests,

Whitman. Vertov is apparently quoting a very free translation of the following lines from Whitman's *Song of Joys:*

> O for the voice of animals—O for the swiftness and
> balance of fishes!
> O for the dropping of raindrops in a song!
> For the sunshine and motion of waves in a song!

The style of the intertitles used in Vertov's films of the 1920s shows the influence of Whitman's work. Confirmation of this observation was received in conversation with Mikhail Kaufman in 1976—trans. and ed.

libretti, completed scenarios, administrative plans, the directorial and technical working out of my most recent project (*Tale of a Giant*). Almost half of this work was connected with training and instilling my experience in the heads of those under my command. The remaining half of my labor was unfortunately spent on providing evidence, on attempts to explain and defend my creative conceptions from destruction, on attempts to defend and preserve even the smallest working group behind me.

"And now, when I've got to begin plowing again, to begin sowing, cultivating the new garden, the new flowers and fruits, it now turns out that my physical strength has been undermined. That I can, through an effort of will, continue for at most a few days. But my head and heart can no longer endure it. My nervous system has succumbed to the procedures of approval followed by cancellation, of agreement followed by cancellation, to the sharp changes of temperature—from boiling point to absolute zero, from rapture to sudden indifference, from embraces to blows, from kisses to sessions on the grill, from battle day and night to agonized waiting, from fusion with a group to utter isolation.

"I need at least a month in a good sanitorium to restore my physical capabilities and start new, uninterrupted work. Strictly speaking, it would seem the management might have suggested this, without my reminding them. Not merely from normal humanitarian considerations, but from those of production foresight. . . ."

If you write frankly like that, they take offense. They'll offer some sort of pat phrase, a slogan. I know slogans myself. Slogans won't help you here. You've got to think things out—and think hard. Just skimming the surface won't achieve anything. "You yourself are responsible" answers the person busy with many affairs, on two phones at once, "you must be deviating from the norm, you've got off the track, you're fantasizing, causing inconveniences, inventing! . . ."

February 20

Arranged to meet Ilyin at twelve. Went to him by bus. I have the luck to get a window seat. Next to me is a stout woman. Those who are passing and squeezing toward the exit keep bumping into her. She moves away from them and keeps pressing me closer to the window. "Pardon me," she says, "we take up a lot of room together in our fur coats."

I mumble something in reply. I didn't sleep the night before. Everything is slightly foggy. I half close my eyes. Near the Hotel Moscow there's a smell of burning in the bus. The repugnant smell of burning rubber. It turns out that the galoshes of a young woman passenger up front are smoking. Her neighbor becomes indignant: "Isn't it possible to insulate a red-hot pipe?! (To the driver) Tell me, which is your terminal?" Driver: "What business is it of yours?" An argument flares up. But the passenger has to get off. When he's already outside he walks around the bus to write down its number. The conductor grumbles: "Just imagine, what whims . . . if you know how to behave, you don't put your galoshes near a pipe. 'Insulate?!' What'll they think of next!"

I get out near Gruzinskaya Station to buy cigarettes. The salesman doesn't have matches. I approach one on another corner. "Matches, please." The salesman: "Can't you see I'm busy? I'm counting my stock." "You mean even street stands close for inventory?" "And why not? Can't you come back later?—what behavior!" (And he gave me a haughty look and continued to count his match boxes.)

I walk on and think: What a strange meaning the conductor and the salesman attach to the phrase "proper behavior." One thinks that it means being able to stand in a bus in such a way that your galoshes don't smoke, and for the other, it means not buying matches if you're not buying cigarettes. You encounter this in cinema as well, in a different form.

March 13

Make a film only when not a single phrase of "cheap sentiment" remains in the scenario. Dialogue can remain, but not elaborate [dialogue], rather, restrained, warm, sincere. No loud neckties, diamond necklaces, no verbal pyrotechnics, no lofty affectation. But the most essential thing is when your own Word—irrepeatable, fresh, newly uttered, unfaded—is born.

March 18

Some are incompetent to deal with me. When they become competent either they or I will no longer be here.

Others are literal minded. They cling to the letter as to an anchor of safety. You can tear them away from the letter only when you've torn away their hands as well. Meanwhile, it's impossible to form a new word, without touching the letters. But if you can form a new word without touching a single letter, then go right ahead.

You must be strong, concentrate all your energy in order to move immovable mountains. And if you don't have the strength, then step back and gather it. Talent is not the problem, but knowing how to arrange the use of your abilities is. You've got to become a businesslike organizer, a self-administrator. Or team up with another person who's a strong organizer. Rely on him and then give free rein to your flights of invention.

A fulcrum. A fulcrum.

March 22

The joy of truth, but not of apparent truth. The joy of seeing in depth, through makeup, through acting, through a role, through a mask. To see weeping through laughter, through pomposity—paltriness, through bravery—cowardice, through politeness—hatred, through a mask of contemptuous indifference—the concealed passion of love. The joy of doing away with "appearance," of reading thoughts, and not words.

March 24

I've begun to immerse myself in aviation literature (for a film on the history of aviation). Appalled by the quantity of material that cries out to be put in the film. I envy simple topics, limited in time and space, in which a hero can be characterized in a few vivid episodes. A more thankful labor, easier and more intelligible, more pleasing to the higher echelons, critics, and for theater distribution.

What's needed, once again, is not an episode, but the episode of episodes. Not a hero, but the hero of heroes; not a document, but the document of documents; not an epic, but the epic of epics. No

film on the history of aviation. After completing work on the script *Tale of a Giant,* Vertov and Ilyin worked together for several months on a script dealing with the history of aviation. The first draft was entitled *Man in Flight.* It remained incomplete since the topic was considered inessential for production after the Soviet Union's entry into the Second World War.

one understands the real difficulty of this problem of problems. No one has any real regard for this work of works. They look down on it and look up to the ordinary, unchallenging, completely run-of-the-mill film.

Why? Because they're competent enough to perceive ordinary difficulties and incompetent when the difficulties transcend the limits of the knowledge at their command.

Work on the aviation film has come to a halt. Ilyin's distracted by other things. His attention is not focused. It's unlikely that something interesting can be done in that state. True, he does switch quickly from one project to another. He does so energetically. But he doesn't have the opportunity to penetrate into the very heart of the subject, where the question is solved in micron weights.

In order to break through from the usual to the unusual, the utmost concentration is essential.

April 1

What conditions will guarantee success?

(1) The whole rather than part. (2) Everything except the boring. (3) Real people, not those wrapped up in cotton wool. (4) Not some shashlik, but an organic construction in which the episodes are not pinned down like incoming and outgoing correspondence in a binder but merge into a living organism. (5) Better less, but better. (6) No audible prompter. (7) No foisting things on the viewer. (8) Learning from nature. (9) Within the limits of technical possibilities. (10) Within realistic time schedules. (11) Not predigested, but not difficult to take in either. (12) Most important: everything your own. A fresh idea, fresh construction, fresh language, and not the depersonalized illustration of slogans.

April 4

I went to Ilyin's. Ilya Yakovlevich said he'd found an interesting key to the scenario. From his very first words I realized that he was talking about a "time lever." I was delighted. In other words—the same as one of my solutions. This version begins like this: He and she (a pilot and a navigator) receive orders to make a test flight in a new plane. They take off. On the instrument panel they discover an unknown instrument. It's the "time instrument." They make a journey in time. They travel beyond today and speed off into the future.

It ends with a return to the shot with which the journey began.

June 26

There's been no time to write. On the 22nd everything changed drastically. War. Svilova and I responded with immediate action. We drew up a request and a plan for a film based on the words of "Poliushka-pole." This song is, as it were, a starting point for the development of a theme. Just as *Lullaby* and *Three Songs* were developed and worked out symphonically from simple melodies. Yutkevich agreed to it, Frolov agreed. They were supposed to present it to the committee. Then, the following day (apparently after agreements of some sort), the film was changed. Frolov notified me that our request was being put aside for the time being. But there was something else: *The Man with a Movie Camera*, *Newsreel Reporter,* that is, my continual theme (temporarily reviled under RAPP).

I joyfully agreed.

I've got to get in touch with Bolshakov about this matter.

July 15

On Yutkevich's advice I wrote a sketch about a film correspondent in which the capital is shown as changed, on the alert, ready to meet the enemy. He maintained that for the time being I couldn't use battle episodes, everything had to be shown indirectly. Such was the directive. "Do it and I'll approve it in fifteen minutes."

I withdrew my scenario outline with a battle episode and wrote a new one, in the direction indicated by Yutkevich. Yesterday I met Bolshakov, and to his question: "Have you got a scenario?" I answered, "Yes." And I showed him the new scenario outline. Bolshakov glanced through it and said: "No. We need battle episodes. What's happening in Moscow, in the houses, etc., will be interesting as historical material. Right now we need battle footage."

Complete contradiction of Yutkevich's point of view.

"Poliushka-pole". This song, known in English as "Field, My Field," is one of the most popular Soviet Red Army songs and serves as a sort of theme song for the army—trans.

"Whose scenario?" Bolshakov asked with annoyance. "You're writing yourself?" I answered: "I can't wait forever for a scenario from Bolshintsov. So far he hasn't given me anything." Bolshakov (continuing the whole time in a dissatisfied tone): "Will you go to the front?" "Certainly." "You won't refuse?" "I'll go. Where? What needs to be done?" "You're a cameraman?" "No, a director." "But I thought you were a cameraman as well. We're organizing a film-train or film-automobile. . . . Perhaps you'd go to the newsreel section, to see Vasilchenko?" "It's a question of the scenario, of the work on a film, of making full use of my abilities—and not of the particular department." Bolshakov picks up the phone, speaks with Vasilchenko. "Go see Vasilchenko," he says, turning toward me. "He's here now, at the committee."

With Vasilchenko.

Vasilchenko: "You've probably heard that I've been wanting to see you in newsreel for a long time? We had some big anniversary films and I wanted to assign you one of them."

Vertov: "And right now . . . what do you have?"

Vasilchenko: "Right now we've got current event magazines. There are shorts."

Vertov: " Have the shorts already been distributed among the directors?"

Vasilchenko: "Yes, they're all given out. We don't have any more scheduled. At present we're concentrating entirely on *Soiuzkino-zhurnal* ["Soviet Film Magazine"].

Vertov: "Can I make a film out of footage from the front?"

Vasilchenko: "Right now there's still not enough footage. It's too early. Later we'll use it for a full-length film."

Bolshintsov. Manuel V. Bolshintsov (1902–1954), essayist and scriptwriter, was coauthor, together with Vladimir Portnov and Friedrich Ermler, of *Peasants* (1935), produced by Lenfilm and directed by Ermler. This film was a powerful and unsparing portrayal of the Russian peasantry in the period of collectivization. He next collaborated with Ermler and Mikhail Bleiman on *The Great Citizen* (1938–39), a major production in two parts, whose point of departure was the murder of Kirov and which presented the official view of the events that precipitated the Moscow trials of 1936. From 1940 to 1943, Bolshintsov was Chairman of the Editorial Committee on Scenarios for film production and later became Senior Editor of the Central Studio of Documentary Films. During the war he also supervised the activities of the Front Line Kino Groups—ed.
Vasilchenko. The administrative head of newsreel and documentary films during the Second World War—ed.

Vertov: "Can I count on it?"

Vasilchenko: "We'll think it over, consider what to assign and to whom. I can't promise in advance. There's *The USSR on Screen*—the man working on it is very poor. It's being made from footage already used in the magazines. Can I assign it to you?"

Vertov: "Well, that may not be in my line. Or rather, it amounts to editing and not directorial work."

Vasilchenko: (picks up the phone) "Wait a minute, I just . . ."

Vertov: "Just what?"

Vasilchenko (into the mouthpiece): "Ivan Grigorevich, I'm thinking about making *The USSR on Screen* a higher-level production. I've got Vertov here. He should be assigned. . . ."

Vertov (smiling painfully): "Comrade Vasilchenko, you've got to act reasonably . . ."

Vasilchenko: (into the mouthpiece) "O.k."

Vertov: "It's hard to see any need for using a pilot as a cavalryman or a foot soldier on . . ."

That was the end of it.

Work. Then evacuation. Then work once again.

September 26

It's crucial that people know that I don't go in search of inventions in the area of "pure form." Quite the contrary. I look for the theme and those productional conditions that free me from complexities and from those filming and editing techniques that are forced on me.

Let me clarify this through an example: using a pole, a man vaults over an abyss. This can be simply a stunt if there's a bridge. But it's necessary, essential if there's no other way of crossing.

Let's suppose I have to film a documentary person in a documentary situation. But first of all it happens that I have to shoot in a tiny room in whch the bulky lighting equipment does not fit. Second, the person can't take strong artificial light; third, the equipment is being used, and I can't have it until the day after I need it. In a case like that it's simply impossible to realize your conception, much as you'd like to. You must resort to a substitute or to a course of action that is, of sheer necessity, complex—one that later, on the screen, will be found lacking in simplicity, overcomplicated. A suspicion of formalism will arise.

At the present stage of our production and technical possibilities, not every theme or human action can be recorded as the director and author might wish—far from it.

Documentary cinema is not yet a cross-country vehicle. These are still the first rails and the first locomotive.

I've spent my whole life building the locomotive, but I have not been able to obtain a broad railway network. . . .

1942

On the film: *To You, Front!* (*There Once Was a Woman Named Saule*). A *sound* film, not a sound track added to a silent film.

A synthetic film, not sound plus image. It can't be shown one-sidedly—in images or in sound alone. The images, in this case, are only one facet of a many-faceted work.

The content is expressed simultaneously in the music,

A volumetric, crystalline form.

Not an amorphous compound accompanied by narration.

The organic fusion of all the components.

We insist on direct sound recording.

You don't see an opera or a play with your ears stuffed with cotton. In this case the image is inseparable from the sound. For future sound recordings, that is, for the music, words, replies, dialogues, monologues, etc., no less creative labor is expended than on images. Everyone understands that a radio-film must be heard, a silent film must be seen. But not everyone understands that an audiovisual film is not the mechanical combination of a radio-film and a silent film, but the uniting of both so that independent existence of image or sound line is eliminated.

The result is a third composition that is neither in the sound nor the image but that exists only in the continual interaction of sound recording and image.

To You, Front! is an artistic organism and not a simple sum of shots. It obeys the higher laws of a single, integral organism, and accomplishes this not by mechanically lumping together individual

cross-country vehicle. The Russian word *vezdekhod* means a vehicle that will "go everywhere," in the manner of a jeep—trans.

shots, but "through development, complication, modification: through the tension and succession of opposing phases; through the emergence of new qualities of the subject matter."

It's not in footage length nor in the quantity of narration (as is often the case with the usual informational film) that it differs from *Soiuzkinozhurnal.* It makes a qualitative "leap" in a certain phase of material complexity. And its inner processes already flow according to different, more complex laws. It destroys that which is ossified, shatters the stereotype (including new "irritants"). And it calls for special attention, boldness.

That is how I want to see this film.

To view Vertov through glasses that date from *The Man with a Movie Camera* involves a huge, unjustified lie.

My principled opponents came to understand that long ago, and they removed those glasses after *Three Songs of Lenin.*

My unprincipled opponents brandish those antiquated glasses and continue to impose them on everyone they can find, including film production management.

This hampers, greatly hampers, the real use of Vertov "at the top of his voice" in production. . . .

Generalization as a "bird's-eye" view of life, seizing the largest possible range of phenomena. The artist should be able to show forth all the beauty and uniqueness of individuality—while at the same time disclosing the general, characteristic features of a people, of an era, of life that lie within.

A misunderstanding of the aims of dramatic composition frequently drives our authors to subject the phenomena of life to an artificial construction, to force, through strength of habit, living and complex images into "convenient" schemata.

But the sum total of exclamation marks written into the schema will not give it more life.

Does it ever occur to anyone that Vertov, in recent years, has not by any means been making films of a general panoramic nature of his own free will? That all his proposals for film portrait galleries, his

"At the top of my voice." An obvious allusion to Mayakovsky's poem, *At the Top of My Voice*—trans.

requests to make films on individuals, etc., have been unjustly rejected? That everything involving a limitation of place and a lengthening of time—for deeper and more economic portrayal—was unjustly rejected since it appeared as a violation of the established order, of the inviolable image of Vertov as the master of the vast compendium?

"You can't hatch the same egg twice," said Vertov, quoting Prutkov. But he's forced to hatch that same egg three and four times. And to insure his compliance, means of inducement are found. . . .

If day after day, hour after hour, you impress someone with the idea that he's mad, that person will finally go crazy. By forcing, day after day, hour after hour, year after year on myself and those around me the suspicion that I'm suffering from the leprosy of formalism, they place me in the hopeless situation of complete isolation. Who will offer his hand to a leper? Who will agree to work with him? Who will trust him with a real production, intended for healthy people?

They say I have "a taste for frogs" and that this is clear proof of a formalistically refined cuisine. It never enters anyone's head that a man can grow so famished that he's ready to fall upon a cat, a dog, to cook even a crow.

Meanwhile I really prefer simple, healthy food, a realistic, concrete, clear topic whose dramatic resolution is not fabricated, but written by life itself.

In the latest "simplified" version of *To You, Front!* the role of Saule and especially the role of Jamilya have been greatly attenuated. I did this without particularly wanting to, purely because I thought it necessary to protect the film and present a united front. I therefore made every single correction demanded of me, regardless of how I felt about doing so.

Let's suppose you once made a major film of poetic generalization that had a resonance throughout the entire world. Does that

Prutkov. Kozma Prutkov, the joint pseudonym of Alexei Konstantinovich Tolstoy (1817-1875) and two of his cousins, the Zhemchuzhnikovs, used for various humorous, satirical, and nonsense verse on which they collaborated for approximately a decade between 1853 and 1863—trans.

mean all other lines of development must be closed to you? That you're already doomed to do nothing but make poetic generalizations your whole life long? That on your brow, as on an elephant's cage, will be written "buffalo." That no one, looking at that sign, will dare not to believe his eyes? That the elephant labeled "buffalo" will be forced to behave like a buffalo to the end of its days . . . ?

They'll praise and condemn you through permanently affixed eyeglasses. And only an honest and courageous manager can shatter those glasses. For it's a question not of talent, but of the management of talent.

An artist should do what stirs him deeply, what is interesting and proper to him.

But after all, "even an oyster has enemies." An original artist, all the more so. That originality, in and of itself, gives rise to protest on the part of those who lack originality. The staid dislike you because you're not staid; the unprincipled, because you're not unprincipled; the terribly businesslike and mercenary, because you're not sufficiently mercenary and businesslike. There's no use even talking about the untalented, who pounce on everyone who doesn't strive always to preserve the same dull grey tone. They try to stop an artist the way you stop a clock, by grabbing hold of the pendulum.

Such people still exist. They have not yet died out. And they'll tell any director: "The clock's outdated. Broken. It should be scrapped."

Unwittingly, Kozma Prutkov comes to mind:

"A clock or watch that's not running isn't always broken, sometimes it has simply stopped and a kind passerby won't fail to nudge the clock's pendulum or wind the wristwatch."

1943

I'm very upset because *To You, Front!* was taken without its last reel to be shown to the Field Army. It was precisely that reel, after all, which had the greatest success during the last screening and firmly persuaded those present of the film's usefulness.

How could this happen?

After three on Saturday afternoon Comrade Katzman told me I'd have to wait until Monday when apparently there was to be an answer from the upper echelons regarding the film.

On the same day, at about seven in the evening, the unbelievable occurred. The woman doing the editing who was, along with myself, unexpectedly summoned, hastily cut off the last part of the film, decapitated it.

The haste was explained by the fact that Comrade Undasynov was taking the film to the front at nine that evening. And by the fact that Comrade Bolshakov telephoned to ask whether his latest remarks had been taken into account.

The main part, the brain of the film, has been removed. Only the body's been left, the head is cut off. . . .

August 14, Alma-Ata

I still lead the same strange life. I'm making various film magazines, defense sketches in the newsreel section. I shot one major film about Kazakhstan during the Great Patriotic War (*To You, Front!*). But most of my projects have not been realized because of a lack of understanding and the opposition from middlemen. There is a Kazakh saying which goes: "The top bends down on a tree heavy with fruit. . . . " Many of my projects overripened, fell. No one gathered them up. They rotted. Other project-fruits were picked and used while still green. But I have no powerful friends, that is, no fulcrum.

No one wants to be bold. They're afraid of losing their heads. I don't begrudge mine. But the middlemen maintain a different point of view. While the envious and the businessmen resist secretly but stubbornly. They carefully disguise and conceal their evil doing. Unfortunately, "the spot on a piebald cow is outside, an evil man's spot is hidden within."

All that's required of a director in the local newsreel section is to fulfill the plan; there's no question of quality. Everything is considered usable. Standards are impossibly low. Nothing is considered for rejection. "To a blind chicken, everything's seed." Quiet, submissive directors who agree to everything are preferred. Living conditions are beneath criticism. Not for everyone, but for those like myself.

the Great Patriotic War. The phrase employed in the USSR to designate the Second World War—ed.

Edison racked his brains over the invention of the electric light. Some untroubled, placid people pointed to kerosene, gas, already existing light sources. After nine thousand attempts that had produced nothing, he still continued his experiments. He didn't bother with the invention of the already invented.

I'm not being pushed on ahead, but backward, to models of the long-forgotten past.

Make a film? But there are none in the studio's program. And even if there were, it would be a sound film shot without a sound camera (the camera's been given to another studio), without a soundman (he's leaving to work in Tashkent), without administrative staff (they've been assigned elsewhere), without assistants (they've gone). In a word, without a group. Without a work collective. A director is a manager, of course, but in film production one can't limit oneself to managing all alone.

I've got to get to Moscow as soon as possible. It's a long way, the five thousand kilometers to film management, to a technical base, to home. There, at least, managers are entitled to make decisions. It might be easier to get them to take risks. Otherwise it's dreary. Sad. And "Sadness is a sea: you drown and perish; risk is a boat: you sit in it and row across." Right now the main thing is to maintain one's bearings: "A bewildered duck dives tail-first."

The main thing is to make yourself understood. But how difficult it is to explain one's ideas. . . . "However marvelous an idea may be, it pales when passing the lips." Maybe that's one of the reasons my ideas are not carried out. The management is gradually getting the wrong impression of me.

Kazakh folk wisdom says that "a man must be judged by his plans, not by what becomes of them." But in life that's not so. No one's interested in the fact that between the plan and the realization of your goal there's a huge course filled with dangers, obstacles, and opposition. That a plan which is not powerfully and promptly backed reaches the finish line covered with wounds and bloodless.

What's most precious is filtered out by the sanctioning channels. As a rule, what's filtered out is that which is new, unusual, that is to say, that part of a plan which is dearest to the author. A great deal is destroyed by the lack of administrative and technical conveniences. The more striking and original the plan, the more exposed it is to the dangers of distortion and alteration during the process of production and approval.

By nature I'm shy. I always have a shamefaced look. I usually express my inner convictions in an unsure voice. That frightens those in charge. Damn mannerism! But I have more than enough confidence in my creative abilities.

"Give me a fulcrum and I'll overturn the whole world." I could repeat that after the ancient sage. But that's just it—I don't have a fulcrum.

What might Tsiolkovsky, the inventor, have done, had he been given a fulcrum earlier? That's what you live for. You keep hoping that any moment now it'll appear. Just so it's not too late. A laboratory for creative work. The firm support of someone who has the right of decision and can give orders. Then you could make up for all you've missed.

Gorky says somewhere: "Man should be friend to man." Maybe now, when there's no reason to envy me, now when, under existing conditions, I have no opportunity to express myself, they will let me raise my head? Or perhaps not. Some hint crudely: "It's not the dog's fault if his chain is short."

No, this just shouldn't be. Even Benvenuto Cellini—who used every means, including the sword, to eliminate all obstacles to his own well-being as a creator, obstacles, that is, to constant creative work—was accused of not wanting to work. He speaks of that in his book. Times are different now. But people change more slowly than systems. Those who shrink at nothing act more quickly. They're more efficient, cruder, dirtier, and more decisive. "While the wise man thinks, the decisive man acts."

They're not ones to waste their time on a diary entry that no one reads. . . .

I read over what I wrote and saw that my pen lacked modesty. If you're going to use folk sayings, then you should not forget one other aphorism: "If you are mighty, be modest." Not always, however. Another bit of folk wisdom advises: "Before a proud man raise your head to the skies; before a modest one, bow."

That's what we'll do. I'll be modest with the modest.

And one other thing is needed: unity.

Unity not with the acquisitive [*priobretately*], but the inventors [*izobretately*]. Not with schemers, but with honest people. This must be attained.

Without unity, there's no life.

Tsiolkovsky. Konstantin E. Tsiolkovsky (1857–1935), Russian scientist, specialist in the theory of interplanetary travel.

August 15, Alma-Ata

Don't believe those who say I'm lazy. I'm ready for any work—the most difficult, as long as it's creative, useful, necessary. "A stone that's needed is no burden."

And don't believe those, either, who say: "Give him something left over from the unused topics. He'll edit anything together. Pay no attention to what he wants, knows, and loves."

A director has to love his work, for "beauty is in the eye of the beholder." All the attention, strength, and power of the director must be focused on a single, big, beloved work, not dispersed in various trivial tasks. You can throw yourself headlong into any subject.

Unless you study the question in advance, entering fully into the subject, you will end in defeat.

You must tame the subject, break it in; "an untamed horse will throw you instantly." You've got to dig deep into the material of the topic, not limit yourself to a surface acquaintance. You've got to make maximum use of all possible information, techniques, and administrative resources, otherwise the film will remain unfinished, incomplete; its essential riches will slip away. "When you strike gold, dig up to your waist."

Put no trust in those who boast only of good material, of good offscreen narration, of splendid photography, or the advantageous topic. Both as writer and director, you have to find the best possible solutions to a problem. Exotic footage that is smart and attractive can sometimes be shown practically raw and passed off as a finished, effective film. A film of this sort is an optical illusion. It does not hit the right target. To such an artist, the people's response is "Let's not talk about the silver on your gun, let's talk about how accurately it hits the target."

Someone else may have a "tongue sharper than a razor." Actually, he's not a director, but an orator. He acts as a salesman for an interesting topic and obtains it with his tongue. With that same tongue, he obtains a good crew. With his tongue he defends the footage shot by the crew. With his tongue, he defends the work of editor and soundman. With that same tongue he obtains a favorable attitude toward his film. His role in creating the film ends there. The film, however, might have been ten times better had it been given to a real director and not to a professional talker.

Try being modest with such a person. He pinched your topic from you. He looks down on you triumphantly, as though you're a nobody. His boasting is like the raving of a madman. His film is more hackneyed than a footstool. He talks to you in a smug, preaching way: "You're too original. Your time is past. Upon whom can you rely? You're too complicated for us."

But not just this self-enamored fool. Many people don't realize that this complicated path of mine finally leads to extreme simplicity, to the same complex simplicity as that in the smile or pulse of a baby. Flick a switch and a city is flooded with light. Flick a switch and electric trains whisk past. The complex becomes simple. But a complex path led to the first electric light bulb.

Film-truth is a still more complex task.

But when the goal has been reached, the liars and hypocrites will fare badly. Their masks will be torn off. No one will be able to hide from the all-seeing, unmasking eye. Words will not serve as cover for thoughts, and schemers will be unable to hide their schemes. People will have to talk frankly, like children. It will be very difficult to pass yourself off as something other than what you are.

August 22, Alma-Ata

I read in some book—I don't remember which—that feelings do not keep like preserves. They either develop or die. The same can be said of creative projects. They rot if you keep them too long. They blossom if you have the chance to realize them.

Until now, Akhmedov, the studio manager, a man who understood only quantitative fulfillment (in so many units) of the program, stood at the entrance to the room for "The Realization of Projects." The quality of a project was measured by bookkeeping standards: economy of expense, minimum technical and administrative requirements, minimum time for realization. Nothing else was taken into consideration. Any deviation from stereotypical conditions of production met with opposition. "We can't handle it!" "There's no need to complicate things!" "Come back down to earth!" and so on. The project itself also remained unintelligible to the director since, like a little schoolchild, he thought only in terms of the whole numbers and the simplest of arithmetical operations. He had no idea of the existence of even simple fractions. And he'd always imagine an artist's conception in his own confused, bizarre way. To put it figuratively, he felt that in order to measure the distance from Alma-Ata to Moscow, one absolutely had to do it in yards, which means a great waste of time and energy. He also felt there was no other, simpler way possible, that people were trying to pull the wool over his eyes. He considered directors to be subordinate beings, whose "secrets" he had long ago seen through. He felt himself to be completely versed in the business of cinema since when he shouted at directors, they kept quiet.

Such complacency in an ignoramus is an obstacle, not only to the education and further development of the superior himself, but to the people with creativity who are placed under him.

They've already transferred him to another job, but he keeps trying to manage at his old position by patronizing his successor, and since his pretended departure he's been doing even more preposterous things than during his official "reign."

I know of a case, for example, in which after assigning a documentary film about a live hero to a director, Akhmedov forbade the director to meet with him and went off, himself, to shoot with the cameramen. After having destroyed the author's project in this way and annihilated all the director's preliminary work, he strutted about during the shooting, acting like a self-proclaimed director. His absurd complacency, his unrestrained boasting, knew no limits.

Sensible people were inclined to view this last trick of his before leaving the studio not as malicious childishness, nor as an attack of imbecility, but as primitive careerist calculation. To reap a prize for his previous "fruitful" activity, to focus all attention on himself, to consign the directors to oblivion.

In any case, a fact remains a fact. No psychiatrist was called in. Evil triumphed. Muscles proved more powerful than brain. The five thousand kilometers separating him from top cinematic management proved a sufficiently safe distance for the petty "little tsar," who stubbornly delayed his resignation.

Part of his program involves the mockery of people with an intellectual bent. He doesn't suspect the melodic richness of a symphony since he feels only its rhythm. He has no notion of all the labor and complexity involved in artistic composition since he grasps only the schema, the bare verbal message.

He despises everything he does not understand, since he feels his experience (overseeing the production of local film-journals) has exhausted all of cinema's creative possibilities.

The smugness of the ignoramus totally deprives him (and those like him) of all opportunity to understand anything.

1944

March 26

After my illness, my mood changed. Action that was once vigorous, decisive, and swift is gradually slowing down and giving way to mistrustful, cold "counteraction."

The thrusts from those around me are small and still cautious. They're checking—has he recovered? Are the attacks of nerves continuing? It sometimes looks as though some are disappointed by my recovery. You catch certain glances in your direction: spiteful, sympathetic, contemptuous, hopeful . . . but mostly indifferent: "What can anyone get out of him?" they're thinking. "Working with him won't get you a prize. You can see right off he's an honest fool." Christie says: "You won't get anywhere with a nature like yours." He seems truly sorry for me. Others shrug helplessly, "We'd be glad to, but there are 'no vacancies.'" The front-line topics are all taken. The "rear" ones—would they get approval? "And you're fed up with that stuff by now, aren't you? . . . " I asked Agapov. He says he'll try to help. But only six were slated, while seven are already in production. That means I can count on minus one full-length film. Meanwhile, they're giving a short to Svilova and myself together. A commission. One reel. But with a set number of units, as for a full-length film. A significant portion of it is made of archive material. But without any right to reuse shots that have been previously issued. That is, using the remains of material that's been picked over repeatedly. You conclude that the best material was selected first, then good material, then that of average quality. We get what's left.

Apparently we'll have to order footage from outlying studios. Shoot as much as we can of the footage that we'll still need. But the writer (Vladimir Solovyov) wavered for several days, then abandoned the solution to the problem. One reel. But lots of work. As much as for a full-length film. "And then," he said, "nothing'll come of it unless we use shots that have already been used." Can't manage to get fresh footage. He's afraid his work will go for nothing.

The order for a crew was also submitted for signing more than a week ago. One moment there's no cameraman, then it's not clear what's happening with someone from administration, then they can't make up their minds to release an assistant.

Not much to tempt one. On order. A short. Will it reach the screen? Will it make a profit? Etc. No one's hot for action. The director's not besieged with volunteers. Only Svilova and I are besieging the department and management. We determined in advance not to refuse anything, so there would be no talk of our fussiness. And, more important, to work and not agonize in a waiting line.

Of course I'd be better off writing a book if there are no signs of a subject for a full-length film that's really needed, and consequently, feasible and able to find backing. At the very least a testament would remain . . . but that too is unattainable.

Liza [Svilova] and I have produced many directors: students, imitators, and simple followers. But how businesslike, calculating, submissive, honored . . . they all are.

While we are not to this day officially acknowledged, honored. . . . We take on the most thankless task: we sow and we do not reap. Our creative offspring might show more sensitivity and gratitude. They might demand that their dad and mom be allowed to continue their path "into the unknown."

The reason why Liza and I are wasting away is that the efficiency factor of our activity could be multiplied by ten.

There was deep injustice concealed beneath the way Vertov, the director, was treated recently, in handing him the ultimatum: either Sisyphean toil or the accusation of idleness.

Everyone knew about it, sympathized, some protested, but in the end they shrugged helplessly:

"You're a master of a special kind. You'll find a way out. No one else could find a way out of this predicament. But *you* can. You can contain the uncontainable. Measure the immeasurable."

And Vertov, controlling himself, set to work, preferring the most arduous labor to an accusation of idleness. Descend, and you will find nothing. Ascend, and you may still find an answer. . . .

One thing, only, remained hard to understand. Why was it Vertov in particular who'd been cut off from valuable subjects, valuable footage, from everything creatively interesting and impressive? The last problem in whose solution I participated, consisted of the following: there was no footage on the subject on hand. Newly received footage was divided between the principal "front" pictures and the

Descend . . . ascend . . . This phrase rhymes in the original and recalls the formulaic directions addressed to the hero in the traditional Russian fairy tale, as he sets off on a quest or an adventure—trans.

magazines. Edit a film—short, but covering the whole Soviet Union—on our young people's fulfillment of their pledge for the Komsomols' twenty-fifth anniversary.

It would take days on end to tell how the writers avoided doing the script, how I had to solve that problem myself; how and with what difficulties shot after shot was sought out from the most distant sources; how the subject's size was changed twice while under way; how complex the questions of the narrator's text and the music were; how artistically and technically complicated it was to combine so many and such diverse pieces of footage into a single whole; what devilish bridges and abysses were crossed in order to arrive at what was the only possible composition under the circumstances. . . . This film simply cannot be compared with any other work in which success is determined by interesting footage and an eventful theme. We were dealing with a thousandfold increase in the amount of work and pressure placed on the group. It could not have been otherwise. There was no other way to get out of the deadlock.

Similarly, it's completely unthinkable to speak of the director's creative personality and aspirations in connection with the present work. It was a question of finding the only possible solution (within the limits of the given assignment), and not of upholding one documentary genre or another. Whatever the genre chosen, we had to solve the unsolvable; and this was accomplished in a manner that was unique under the circumstances. No one, at any rate, was able to propose a better method during the film's production.

Nothing is more terrible for a man than to see his creative work misunderstood and destroyed. Particularly arduous, self-sacrificing labor. That is crippling to a creative person. There's no reason for any of it. The film will benefit the viewer even in its present form. This can already be determined, if only from the reaction of our lab assistants and women editors, who grasped the film not theoretically, but spontaneously. It can also be determined from the impression made on members of the Komsomols' Central Committee by a showing of the first version.

Is *The Pledge of Youth* a [propaganda] poster? No label of any sort is really necessary. The film's exposition is rhythmically harmonious. It does not look like a pile of raw, unworked footage. Its exposition has the form of narrative, and only in rare, individual spots does it turn into an appeal (in accordance with one of the requirements).

This time, Vertov, accused of being intractable, was the most submissive of all. From first to last, he did everything that was demanded of him. Perhaps one may admit, only this once, that Vertov did everything humanly possible to carry through an assignment which didn't correspond to his creative aims and with which he was not in agreement. And he solved it in the only way possible, within the limitations of the footage provided.

In this case, independent formal objectives were out of the question. But neither could we limit ourselves to the simplest sequential splicing of pieces. We had to resort to a superior way of organizing the documentary footage, one of organic interaction between shots, one in which shots enrich each other, combining their efforts to form a collective body. You can't help it; the art of writing in film-shots has developed along a particular path. It differs from what, during cinema's early stage of development, was called "montage." The human organism differs from that of the jellyfish.

This is by no means formalism. It's something entirely different. It's a legitimate development that must not be, ought not to be, avoided. At this point, the very content will not permit a more primitive organization of the material. It would be unfair and improper to seek out form for form's sake in the present exposition. Man's brain is incomparably more complex than that of the butterfly.

Life is continually evolving. The art of writing in film-shots may not be a lofty one, but it too can't stand still for long.

I do not go looking for formal inventions. On the contrary. I look for that theme and those production conditions that may free me most from complex methods, from forced solutions and intricacies.

I think I've already offered the example of how, when stairs are available, climbing out the window and down the water pipe would be an unwarranted stunt. It's a different story if there are no stairs. Then you'd have to use the pipe; I'd always prefer the stairs.

Creatively, I'm stronger than many think. In terms of administrative business ability, I'm behind many others. But the important thing, just the same, is the correct choice of a subject. After all, while I was still entitled to make choices and decisions, I met with no defeats (in the sense of films being rejected). I look for a subject with minimal dependence on clumsy lighting equipment which isn't on time. A subject that's needed and that can be shot at the given time of year. I try to get this subject, regardless of whether it's full-length or one reel. I'm limiting my efforts to making a series of films of living people during the Great Patriotic War. In recent years I've presented about a hundred proposals aimed in that direction. Most of them were not even favored with a reply. Although in reality they seem like only small subjects. It's just that you can't detail them in advance, since they involve observations made during the process of shooting. You can't predetermine them. . . .

I must know whether or not I'm mistaken in my desire to leave the past, the trodden path, and to try to penetrate into that which has not yet been done, say in the area of the "living documented person": a family, a brigade, a small collective that can be observed, given average technical opportunities. If this is a mistake, I want to know why. If it is not, then can't I be helped in this direction?

The choice of this kind of hero is difficult, but when it's finally made (as, for example, in the case of Pokryshkin), I'm suddenly forgotten. After all, isn't a deep desire 80 percent of success? Am I mistaken in my further wish to engage in observation over a long period of time, that with which I began my work in cinema and from which I was, against my own will, diverted into the making of broad surveys? Is the observation of the reconstruction of, say, Novorossisk, or of a shipyard, or even of a sunken ship unworthy of an artist's brush? I proposed, for example, "the rehabilitation of a man"—the return to active life of a wounded veteran. No one has explained to me why this is not valid. Did I draw up my request badly, or is it just not needed?

When I was told several months ago that I could make *Germany,* I immediately agreed, and I valued the proposal. I can understand an assignment like this. Its difficulties don't scare me. And I won't have to persuade and entreat the authors. And there'll definitely be enough footage. And advice and attentiveness from the management. In this case the difficulty is an embarrassment of riches, not scarcity. Two quite different matters.

Another example is *Liberated France.* The film is done in the Vertov manner. Yutkevich himself confirms that. One could quibble with some of the techniques. Still the film concludes with the liberation of Paris, moves in time, has a natural beginning and end. The dramatic construction absorbs all the strong techniques so they don't scare people off.

September 12

On September 8 I wrote two versions of a scenario for *Little Anya.* About a guerilla-student. I saw her. Suitable for filming. At the studio the film section seems to be giving approval.

It's odd that they haven't phoned me yet. Can something else have come up again? The "gallery of [film] portraits" will be put off again . . . searching around again? And starting all over. . . .

September 16

I spoke with Bolshintsov. He said that the proposal for a portrait of *Little Anya* met with a hostile reception. That short stories like this, about people, are the business of acting studios. They do them better. You've got to make documentary films specific to documentary cinema and not encroach on the artistic studios' sphere of activity. Nothing new!

That's how it's always been. . . .

The objections were always the same:

"You, Vertov, are violating the documentary rules you yourself established. You're becoming less documentary than any of your followers. We, the administrative management, are more orthodox with respect to the documentary than you."

Indeed. . . . Why, actually, do I break the rules I've expounded and make proposals that perplex and create doubts?

In the first place, these rules do not remain immutable. And the concept of documentary cinema does not stand still.

Second, my proposals violate not the nature of the documentary, but the standard notion of it.

Third, it's precisely up to me, who once established a series of rules, to hoist myself to a higher stage of development. To widen my sphere of activity. To break free of rules, to break their chain, if it's too short.

Fourth, man differs from the ape in that the ape remained confined to the tree, while man broke the rules and laws: he crawled down from the tree, took a club into his hands, left the forest, went into the steppe. . . . Had man not broken the rules, he would have continued to live in the tree. His development would have been hindered by the observance of rules. He would have remained an ape.

There can be no development without breaking the rules. When we forget that, we find ourselves in a blind alley.

Nevertheless, my situation is unenviable. I'm still learning. Many others are not learning, but teaching. They already know everything. And they firmly adhere to everything that is "correct" and "established."

They regard me with caution. How, for example, is one to explain the fact that the film about Pokryshkin was not assigned to me, but to someone else? . . .

It turns out that for twenty years Vertov worked to obtain the right to make a documentary film about a "living person," and finally he did obtain it—not for himself, but for another director who'd never even given it a thought. At the moment of victory they switched the victor at the finish line. A bystander opened his mouth and swallowed the long-awaited subject. The first to celebrate the wedding night was not the groom, but a guest.

Is there no one who understands that?!

September 17

Repetition is the one thing impossible on earth. If I do not record on film what I see at this moment (when I see it), then you can be certain I'll never record it. I diagnose and record at the same time. Not afterwards, not before, but only at the precise moment. A second later there will be something different. Better or worse, but different. It will not be exactly what I need, but something else. That's particularly true of human behavior. You can write a script in advance about the behavior of someone, if you know what's going to happen to him in the near future. But it will be so schematic and approximate that it will not really give you any idea what you will get on the screen. A person is revealed at rare moments that must be caught and recorded at the same time. Otherwise you would do better to film an actor. At least you'd have good acting. In documentary cinema there can be no question of "precise" preliminary coordination. If you "coordinate" a pistol shot, you'll always miss. I've never seen anything repeat itself. What has been lost has been lost forever.

Thoughts must be transmitted from the screen directly, without translation into words. Or else words must be synchronous with the thoughts and not interfere with one's grasp of them. In *Three Songs* and *Lullaby* both are present. The viewer reads the thoughts, catches them before they assume the shape of words. It's a living communication with the screen, a transmission from brain to brain. Each person grabs that which corresponds to his capabilities and knowledge. Each penetrates into the sphere of ideas, the germ of which stirs in his own consciousness. Some are hindered by force of habit; they grasp ideas only through words. Some are solely interested in words and show no interest in thoughts on the screen. My experiments have been very well received in countries where Russian is not spoken. Why did I stop speaking in public? Wasn't it that I'd noticed that my words, but not my thoughts, were grasped? . . . I express thoughts poorly in words, while good public speakers express their thoughts splendidly. But their thoughts almost always remain the prisoners of the splendid words.

A spoken text in a film helps one to understand what's happening on the screen. But a film made so that it did not require a narrator's explanations would be superior.

Three Songs of Lenin did not require a narrator. If you did add one, the screen would speak through words. Thoughts on the screen would not strike the viewer's brain directly. The narrator would be a translator, and the film would not be understood in the same way, it would take the direction of a radio monologue in words. All the richness of the film would go into the accompaniment. The diversity of perception would be stifled and channeled within a verbal flow. The author of the text would bind his thoughts into sentences. The narrator, remaining invisible, would speak those sentences. The viewer would become a listener. And, in taking in these sentences, would retranslate them into thoughts. . . .

This may be unavoidable, given the absence of film material taken from life itself, given scraps of footage that have somehow to be tied together. But it's senseless when life speaks from the screen without an assistant, without anyone giving orders, without a tutor who insists on explaining how and what the viewer should see, hear, and understand.

September 26

. . . The artist's vocation is to depict the world as he sees it. Life can teach you to see in a new way, but you must not paint what your artist's eye has not seen, you must not look at the world through your neighbor's eyes. The truth is not always easy, but works of art created by an honest hand live on; they will awaken ideas and passions, while everything engendered by fashion, by cold calculation, dies quickly, and people turn their backs on the mercenary artist and pass by his faded creations. And if you were my pupil, I'd tell you: "Better to err than to lie."

[from the play, *An Officer of the Navy*]

October 1

"Don't write any more requests," Bolshintsov says. "The question's settled. You'll make *Soviet Art*. Just let me finish the rush jobs by the end of the quarter and I'll fix everything."

But I still find it hard to wait. If I had the right to act, I would not wait a second. . . .

October 3

Just got back from unloading firewood (from a barge onto the shore). Tore off all the buttons on my coat and got all dirty. That's the way it goes.

Every day I remind Bolshintsov's secretary and the film department about speeding up the procedure for starting work. Went to see Durov, read all sorts of literature. Permission to begin work keeps being delayed and delayed. . . .

October 4

A complete surprise. Bolshintsov says he wants to make a film, *Lenin*.

A paradox? On the one hand, caution and mistrust, fear of giving me a film on even a small topic. On the other—an offer of immense proportions to make a film on a topic that encompasses everything we live by.

What's going on?

Durov. Vertov is probably referring to either Vladimir Grigorevich or to Yuri Vladimirovich Durov, members of a celebrated family of Russian and Soviet circus animal trainers—trans.

The same old thing. Once again it's all "facade."

Everyone knows there's almost no documentary footage of Lenin made during his life. The individual bits remaining have been used over and over again. And what's more, most of those have been taken out of circulation.

Three Songs of Lenin is a heroic feat of labor, the only correct solution to the problem of making a film-document of Lenin without (almost without) his image. Am I, the author of *Three Songs* supposed to reinvent what I've already done? To endure the battle again—one against all? It's inevitable, after all: no matter what I do, everyone's against it. . . .

A film of this sort can be made in a simple, intelligible manner only when there's full-fledged footage. Without it, something new must again be invented for the same subject. How can you make a film about Lenin without the essential documentary footage? That already implies showing him indirectly and is more complex than is allowed in our newsreel. "Stringing together" film-shots doesn't arouse anyone's doubts. But their superior organization often generates unfounded suspicions of deliberately complex form. Form that's complex by necessity is considered a "fallacious" directorial method. And no justification will help.

If the issue of a big, very challenging subject were raised seriously, in depth, and with full responsibility, that would be fine. But in actual fact, this is not the way it happens. When we were making a film about young people, the studio management wanted to limit it to a short. They did nothing to find a solution, to obtain the essential footage, and so forth. It all resembled evasion and sleight of hand. We were supposed to organize the remains of film-subjects and film-journals into something that would look like a solution to the problem. Complete disregard for the golden rule that "no bird can fly without support from the air." Flight is impossible without a point of leverage. And the leverage in a documentary film is the film-documents. If they're missing, all that's left is pure virtuosity in a void, that is to say, an interesting exercise perhaps, but not a film of flesh and blood.

Right now this is all being repeated. Behind the high-flown proposal—the film *Lenin*—lurks the usual untruth. Some organization apparently included a film of this sort among its current work for the anniversary of Lenin's death. They handed the assignment over to the newsreel studio. On the one hand, the studio's been thinking how to splice something or other together from God knows what, without interrupting the war jobs, the periodicals, the films already planned. And then, on the other hand, they're wondering how not to evade the assignment, how to cover up the absence of documents on Lenin through the acoustical power of the savior-narrator, that is, with the usual "appearance" of a film on the assigned subject. . . .

Nothing is likely to come of it.

As was to be expected, the idea of a *Lenin* film has already been discarded.

I reminded Bolshintsov that I was ready to make *Soviet Art.* But Bolshintsov withdrew that proposal as well. Somebody pressured him. "In the meantime, make *News of the Day.*"

I have to switch once more. Pack away my ideas and plans for the first proposal. Concentrate on the new one.

It's unhealthy to switch so suddenly.

October 11

Make observations? Or draw conclusions from others' observations? Both are possible. But in recent years real cinematic observation has been absent from newsreel footage. There are only quickly staged shots done in imitation of newsreel. However that seems to create problems only for those few who believe in drawing conclusions from observation and experiment (rather than from newspapers and books).

I'm not drawn to argument for the sake of argument. I very much dislike the sort of scholastic proof in which the process of proof itself is the main interest. I avoid argument for its own sake. As a researcher I wanted only to observe, to gather facts, and after working on them, draw my own independent conclusions. "The fusion of science with newsreel," as one of the basic kino-eye slogans went.

It's odd that our film managers tend to praise the director who does not think for himself (he who copies ready-made rules and regulations) and look askance at the author-director with his own aspirations, ideas, desires.

They ought to treat the *desire* on the part of a creative worker more seriously and attentively. Desire is not a whim or caprice.

"Desire is a great thing: for work follows desire and is almost always accompanied by success." (Louis Pasteur)

Work of this sort is joy.

Work without desire is quite another thing. Such work is misery. Especially if you realize that the work's useless, in vain. Nothing is more gruelling or painful than work of that kind. Sisyphean labor is torture.

Work that you desire can't be gruelling no matter how immense or difficult it may be. Work that is desired is the best relaxation. For me, at any rate. It's like Columbus sailing to America. Like an inventor approaching his discovery. Like a lover overcoming all obstacles between him and his beloved.

With a goal he desires, a man no longer needs prompting or encouragement.

When raw (even though somewhat interesting) footage is labeled "film," don't believe it.

It's not the man who digs a tunnel through a mountain who is slow, but he who ambles through the already finished tunnel.

If it took the author a year, and the copyist a week; it's the copyist whc's slow and not the author.

A man's efficiency factor is inversely proportionate to his garrulousness.

What's good is not what's really good, but that which is *profitable* to consider as such.

Imitation is the sincerest form of flattery.

Not a film, but a filing cabinet.

November 11

Well-wisher: You said your name's Vertov. Are you related to Dziga Vertov? You mean, you don't know him? Too bad. No, he's not dead yet. He's living in Moscow right now. . . . His tragedy is that he doesn't grow older. His creative children never liked that. They felt that the inheritance should be distributed more quickly. Children differ, you know. Some have no objection at all to speeding up the receipt of an inheritance and are even inclined to shorten their father's life. There are various ways of doing this. You must know about it—if only from literature. You don't believe it? You doubt it?

Then how can you explain the fact that Vertov is invariably passed over when they hand out production assignments, scripts, etc.? I'm no expert, but I am observant and know a thing or two from my friends in cinema. They're not so daring as to fight for Vertov. But their consciences bother them. And sometimes a blush of shame steals over their faces. They say someone has to profit from Vertov's victory and success; he himself isn't holding up the works. . . . Too bad you don't know him personally. He lives all cooped up. But there is still time perhaps to try to save him. . . .

1945

"Mayakovsky's boldness," writes Aseyev in his pamphlet on Mayakovsky, "had become absolutely 'embarrassing.' That mouth had to be stopped somehow. And—it sounds like a stupid, bad joke, but it wasn't a joke, it was very serious—they tried to have the poet declared insane. A secret consultation of medical psychiatrists was held in a building to which Mayakovsky was summoned under some pretext."

That was before the Revolution, under the old regime.

But Mayakovsky complained later as well, in addressing a portrait of Lenin:

—You grow tired.
Of defending yourself and
biting back.
Many
have got out of hand
Without you.
Many many
bastards of all kinds
Are walking
On and about
Our earth.

[from "A Conversation with Comrade Lenin"]

Aseyev. Nikolai N. Aseyev (1889–1963), poet, member of Moscow futurist group, and a friend of Tretyakov's and of Mayakovsky's, was a founding member of *LEF* and of *Novy LEF* (1928)—ed.

"Mayakovsky," writes Aseyev, "was very concerned. He tore away the sticky web of slander, mockery, jeers, cowardice which his enemies had woven around him. He thought that these were general relics of the past of which the republic had to be cleansed. They were, however, means specially devised against him, to irritate, to subvert his creative principles, to sap his energy with constant injections of the venom of ill will, of contemptuous mockery, to sabotage all his activity.

". . . At a moment of physical weakness, the great poet lost his equilibrium. He seemed to see no way out of the circle of hostility and dislike surrounding him. If only he had seen how much love and friendly sympathy surrounded him; if only he had known how time would crush his enemies!

"On April 14, 1930, at 10:15, in his office in the Lubyanskaya Passage, he killed himself with a revolver shot." (N. Aseyev, *Mayakovsky*, Young Guard, 1943)

More than once on meeting me, Mayakovsky would cheerfully say: "Chin up, Dziga, our side will win!"

And then he'd shake my hand firmly. That's the way it was when we met somewhere at a little train station in the Donbas. That's how it was in Leningrad in the lobby of the Hotel Europa shortly before his death.

And suddenly he couldn't take it any more.

Now "all one hundred volumes" of his "party books," his rich legacy, fight for him.

It's lucky he wasn't a film director. You can't preserve a film in manuscript. There are no author's copies. The distributed prints are mutilated, and what is unpublished is either stolen or dies in obscurity in one of its stages: conception, libretto, scenario plan, the single print of a film. *Lullaby* was forcibly butchered during editing and given little coverage in the press. Undervalued, unpreserved, it is destroyed. *Ordzhonikidze* was destroyed by cuts and transpositions. *Three Heroines* exists somewhere in a single "invisible" print. *A Day Throughout the World* has remained only in requests and a newspaper interview. *A Day of Our Nation* was made instead, but not by me. *Girls of Two Worlds* has remained unrealized. *When You Go Off to Fight*—the project remained unrealized because of its poetic form (they demanded that it be transposed into prose). *Tale of a Giant* has remained a scenario and shooting script. Later, a short *Song of a Giant* was produced in Kazakhstan, but not by me.

Man in Flight was put aside due to the start of the war. The film *Blood for Blood,* made under aerial bombing attacks and completed on October 16, 1941, was preserved in a single print but has now been destroyed by cuts used for the film *The Ukraine.*

All the rest is in the form of requests, scenarios—sometimes read and sometimes unread, even at the first level.

A piano is not a sofa, but you can sleep on it. However, that's not making full use of the piano. A treadle sewing machine can be used as a dinner table. That's also not full usage.

You can fan yourself with a horse's tail. But isn't it better to use a horse as a horse?

It's a question of the efficiency factor.

It's a question of the full-fledged, rather than the auxiliary use of Vertov in cinema. Right now only the little toe of his left foot is being used, the "appearance" of use is created.

Does no one understand this?

If you use kettledrums as a stool to sit on, if you sleep on a piano as on a bed, if you use a violin as a tennis racket and a flute to beat carpets—is that making the maximal use of these instruments?

It would be equally senseless to use Shostakovich, the composer, as a copyist; to have used Repin, the painter, as a bootblack; Mayakovsky, the poet, as a [tram] conductor.

And even if that use were more in keeping with one's specialty, nonetheless, it would be unfitting, absurd, senseless to make, let's say, Prokofiev, the composer, play the piano with only one finger. . . .

People are referring to the film *Farrebique,* directed by Georges Rouquier. But in the first place, Yutkevich writes that it shows the influence of Vertov. Second, Georges Rouquier is one of the documentary-film enthusiasts whose circles Vertov started organizing back in the twenties.

Remember—

The Theory of Relativity. It came to us as an imported film. But nearly a year before, Dziga Vertov had proposed making such a film.

Farrebique. *Farrebique* (1947), directed by Georges Rouquier, was a film about French peasant life with protagonists who were nonprofessional natives of the region of Aveyron. The film was planned as part of a series of four films whose subject was to have been the gradual urbanization and erosion of the peasantry, of their economy, and of their culture—ed.

Paris qui Dort of René Clair. It came as an imported film. We threw our caps in the air, but nearly two years before, Dziga Vertov proposed making an analogous film with material on Moscow. He drew up a request and a plan for the film.

Berlin: Symphony of a Great City by Walter Ruttmann. It was widely shown on our screens, though it was only an imitation of Vertov who was under attack.

We don't preserve the models of documentary cinema we've created. We wait to receive a letter from some research institute in Uruguay requesting the films of Dziga Vertov for preservation.

Our task is to defend our offspring to the last. We are the founders of documentary cinematography, and we must not cede our first place to anyone.

Do not judge by bare results. A particular defeat can be more valuable than a cheap success.

Appreciate those who invent, not those who acquire.

Remember the first steam engine, the first train, the first airplane.

Distinguish between the carving out of an underground tunnel, and a pleasant ride taken in a subway car.

Resist easy profit. Let those who sow reap the fruits of their labors. Encourage the art of the bold gardeners, not that of the fruit pickers.

1953

People ask me, "What do you think—who's more important in documentary cinema, the director or the cameraman?"

I feel like answering this question the way children do when they're asked whom they like better, "Papa or Mama?"

The children reply:

"Both!"

Because that's not the point.

It very often happens that the success of a film is determined not by the quality of the director's work, but by the topicality of its subject and eventful footage. The desire to see anything connected with a major event is so great that it's enough for a director to splice together chronologically the pieces a cameraman has shot, and he is assured of our thanks. In this case the director acts, so to speak, as the salesman for the interesting documents sent to him. And his role, in comparison to that of the cameraman, is small. His ability consists in obtaining the subject and the footage and in obtaining, as well, the right to represent that subject and footage from the management. This argues for the business sense of the director rather than for his creative talent.

But it can happen the other way around as well. Material that others are bored with, unimpressive in itself. Heterogeneous, and at first glance, impossible to put together. Not topical or eventful. No one's eager to see this material. The subject is a complex one, covering a whole series of issues, not restricted to a single place or time. In this case only the director's great effort of will, the power of his creative idea, his self-sacrifice in solving the task, only the most difficult experiments in the treatment and crossing of individual bits of footage will assure success for the film. It requires lots of minor inventions, persistent thought and parallel action, a hundred times more work than in the preceding example. In this situation you can't hide behind the material or the subject. You must provide a unique combination of the cells of a cinematic body, a way of grouping them that will resurrect the lifeless shots, direct them toward a single goal, unite them through a single idea, make unassimilable material assimilable. In this case the role of the director, particularly of the author-director, is huge and cannot be compared, in terms of the labor it demands, with work of the usual sort.

The difference between the volume of work in the two instances is no less than that between a steamboat ride and the steamboat's invention. If we start judging a director's work only by its results on the screen, we will eventually make errors, encourage the tendency toward easy, profitable work, toward disputes that have nothing to do with creativity but with something quite different; it will lead to activity, not on the level of art, but on that of business, grabbing (one way or another)for the right to represent profitable subjects and footage.

As Kapitza has put it, "It turns out that he who's plucked the

Kapitza. Peter Leonidovich Kapitza (1894–?), preeminent Soviet physicist, worked with Sir Ernest Rutherford at Trinity College, Cambridge from 1921 to 1934. Recalled to the Soviet Union, he directed the Institute of Theoretical Physics until he was removed in 1946, due to his unwillingness to participate in the Soviet program of nuclear development. He was reinstated in 1954, following the death of Stalin, and received the Nobel Prize in physics in 1978—ed.

Kinoglaz

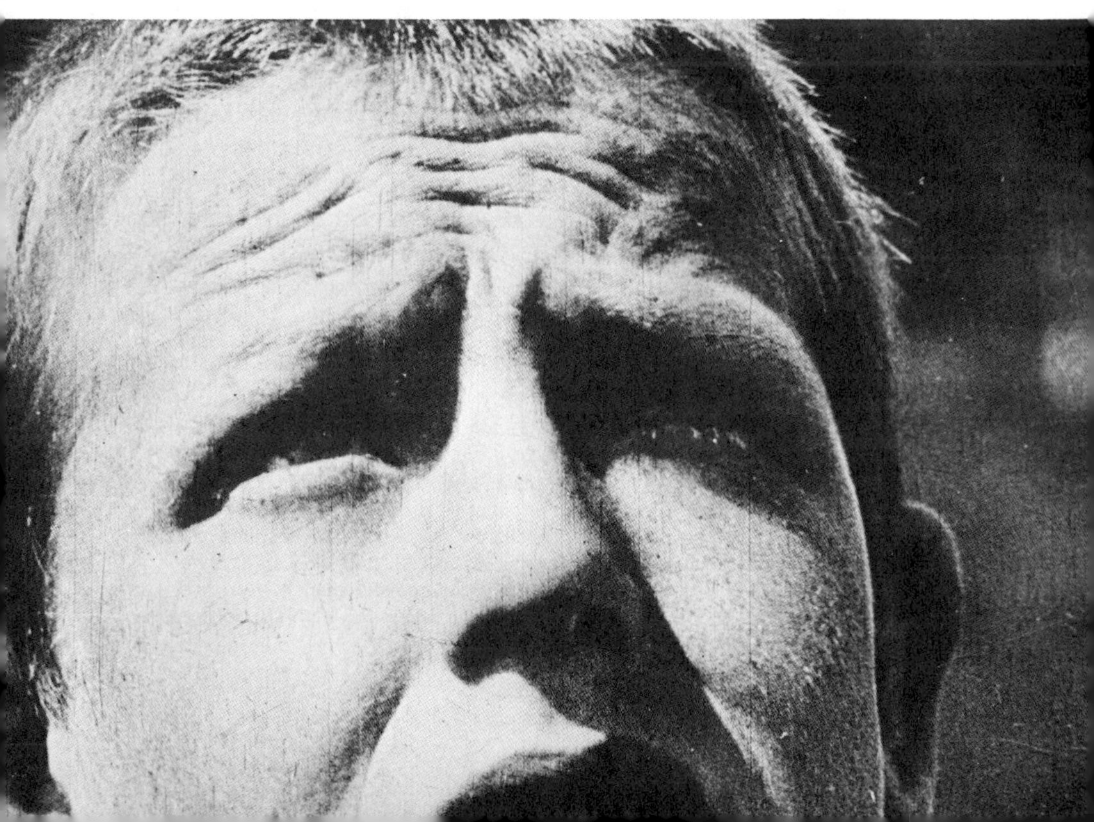

Kinoglaz

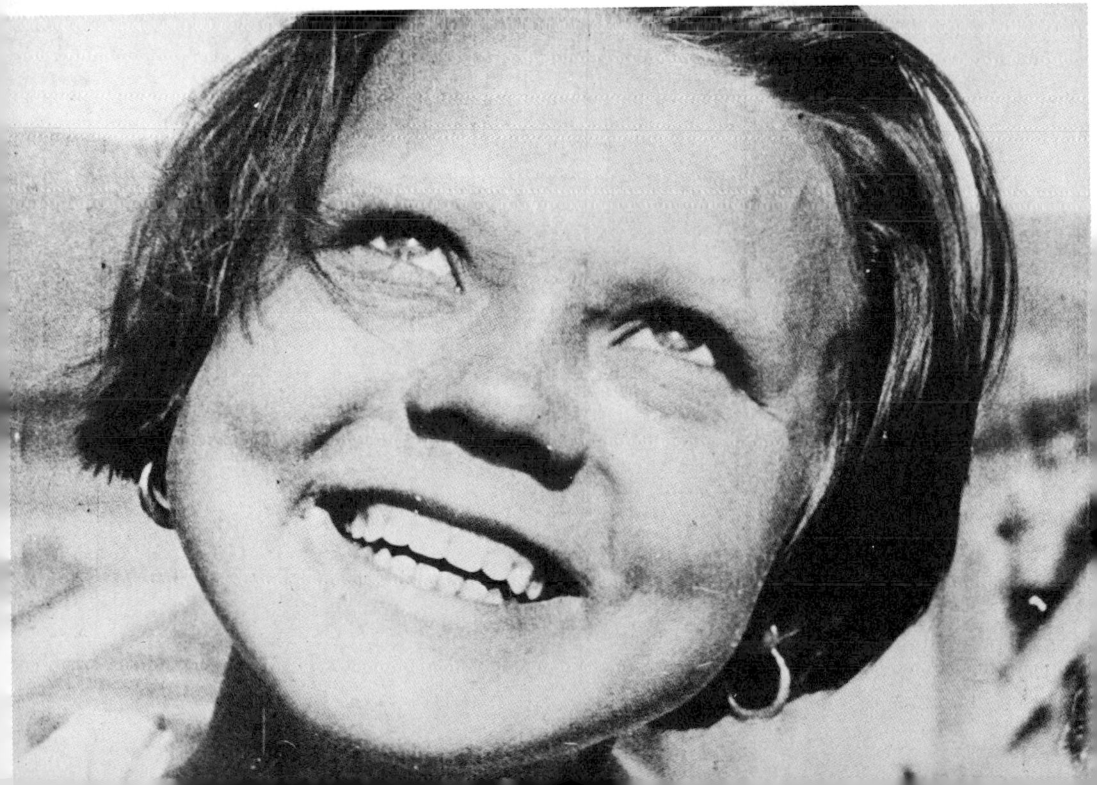

apple has done the major work, while in reality, he who planted the apple tree made the apple." This must not be.

On Editing

It's clear that editing is not an end in itself. It's important, however, to distinguish editing in the usual sense of the word from another phenomenon that resembles editing but is considerably broader and deeper than that concept.

If the task before me is to acquaint the viewer with film-documents that must be placed in a certain order (usually chronological) before they can be shown and to clarify them in a narrator's text—then that's one task.

The task before you is quite another when the subject is complex and uneventful, and you have, at your disposal, only individual, disparate little shots, with no more interconnection than the letters of the alphabet. With the letters you must form words; with the words, sentences; with the sentences, an article, an essay, an epic, etc. Actually, this is no longer editing, but film writing.

Let's combine letters to form the word *peasant* or *path* or *horse.* As a result, we have, "Winter. A triumphant peasant make the first path through the snow on his sledge."

This is the art of writing in film-shots. The complex art of film writing, which differs from the most elementary, sequential splicing of footage no less than the human organism differs from that of a jellyfish or larva.

Here we confront the organization of documentary footage in a superior form. Shots enter into organic interaction; they enrich one another, combine their efforts, form a collective body, thereby releasing surplus energy.

Life has already known considerable development from cosmic dust to the nebula, from the nebula to man.

We have no intention of reverting to the time when only primitively united formations existed in nature. We strive on, surmounting the obstacles others are ever ready to place before us.

Some Creative Projects, Proposals

Draft of a Scenario Intended to be Filmed During a Journey by the Agit-Train, The Soviet Caucasus

Boris Ogarev, a young director, working in Moscow, is without news of the fate of his family—his father, his mother, and brother—whom he has not seen since before the Revolution in Grozny, his hometown.

Ogarev closely follows newspaper announcements about the advance of the Red Army toward the Caucasus.

While looking at a map, he confides his feelings to a girl whom he knows, Nadya Morozova, who works as a saleswoman on an agit-train of the All-Russian Central Executive Committee.

The Red Army is on the offensive.

There is panic amongst the Whites in the cities under evacuation. Soldiers disobey their officers. Pillage, violence, executions.

The work of an underground organization of communists from Grozny, which is located at the rear of the Whites. Issuing an underground leaflet. Agitators. One of the most courageous workers is "Red Misha." Contact with a Green organization hiding out in the mountains.

A path in the mountains. Misha goes to negotiate with the Greens. The work at Green headquarters. Misha proposes uniting in the struggle against the Whites.

Green organization. The Greens were peasant detachments of deserters during the Civil War of 1919–20. So named because they hid out in forests, they generally fought the Whites by attacking at their rear. Occasionally they also fought the Reds—trans.

With the approach of the Reds, the underground communists grow bolder. Sorties led by Misha. Workers' reprisal against a factory owner. Misha and others are arrested as the instigators.

Moscow. Morozova shows Boris Ogarev the train in which she is to leave. Boris buys a paper at the station. While taking the money out of his wallet, he chances upon a photograph. He shows it to Morozova: "You know, that's my brother."

The photograph shows the face of "Red Misha"—energetic and looking straight ahead.

Green headquarters learn of Misha's arrest. The jailers are bribed. Escape. Misha hides amongst the Greens.

The Red troops approach Grozny. Misha prepares a decisive action by the workers.

A meeting of the underground communists at Misha's apartment. Misha's mother and father. A spy informs on them.

The second arrest of Misha and most of the communists.

The death sentence. A summary execution before retreat. An officer leads Misha aside, shoots him in the head with his revolver. Misha falls to the ground. He pretends to be dead (the bullet has only grazed his temple).

At night he crawls out from under the corpses, and sets off in the direction from which he hears cannonade.

At Red headquarters, Misha explains how to approach the city most easily.

Ogarev reads a newspaper announcement about the capture of Grozny. He ponders. Morozova arrives with news: "Our train's going to the Caucasus." Ogarev decides to leave with it.

The train en route. Ogarev at work (he heads the film section). Nadya has taken an interest in Boris.

The agitational work of the train comes to a stop at the city of N. The train has to stop there because the track is in disrepair.

N's station is in terrible sanitary condition. The courtyard of the station and the adjacent square and tracks are piled with refuse. There's dirt everywhere.

At a meeting of the train workers, Ogarev proposes that they use the free day to wipe out the breeding ground for infection. Morozova supports him. The workers arm themselves with shovels and brooms; they work cheerfully, intently. By evening the station is clean.

Return to the train. Nadya and Boris clasp hands firmly. Their friendship is growing stronger every day.

Work at the liberated Grozny's oil fields (show the fast pace of the work, people working with thorough confidence in the utility and necessity of their labor). Repair of a pipeline. Loading oil. Express freight trains.

Commissar Mikhail Ogarev [Misha] provides an example of tireless labor. Pale, ever serious, he's on his feet all day, turning up here and there; everywhere helping with advice or personal example. Legends of various sorts circulate about him. All that's known for certain is that his mother and father were brutally killed by the Whites not long before their retreat.

At the oil fields the arrival of an agit-train from the capital is announced. The commissar proposes that they greet The Soviet Caucasus by increasing their efforts. His proposal is adopted by the workers.

The arrival of the agitators. Boris Ogarev with a photographer. Filming the operations at the oil fields. Mikhail Ogarev explains things to his co-workers who've arrived from the capital.

The meeting of the two brothers. "You've grown so much older! . . . Where are mother and father? . . ."

A painful silence. Misha takes a magazine out from an inner pocket and gives it to his brother. There, on the first page is a list of victims of the White Guard.

A rally at the factory. A speech by an agitator from the train.

A worker goes up to the brothers, followed by several more. "Comrade Commissar, they're asking for you."

The speaker's platform. The Commissar, with his collar open and hand raised, is there.

Apotheosis: the poetry of labor and movement.

"By our persistent, joyful labor we shall avenge the old world's murder of our mothers, sisters, brothers, and fathers for our own benefit."

Oil-field workers at their posts.

Mending the pipeline.

Repairing a railway bridge.

Fixing railroad tracks.

"Every barrel of oil we obtain for ourselves is a slap in the enemy's face."

Oil tanks pass by in an endless chain.

Oil barges.

Close-up: the working of an internal-combustion engine.

A peasant greases a wheel axle with oil.

A railway worker-greaser.

Trains leaving to get oil.

"With millions of hands wielding the hammer of labor, we confidently forge our happiness on earth."

A worker hammering.

A peasant at his plow.

A bricklayer.

An engineer in his locomotive.

A miner at work.

Saws at a lumbermill, frantically sawing wet black logs.

Moving train wheels.

The movement of a locomotive axle.

The locomotive (hurtling toward the camera).

Racing rails.

The swift movement of cars, motorcycles, streetcars in the center of a big city.

A hammer rhythmically striking red-hot iron.

The smoking stacks of factories and plants stretching to the very horizon, as far as the eye can see. Along the screen, through the factories and plants, brightly lit, with hammers and shovels, come Commissar Misha Ogarev, Nadya,. and Boris, one after another, with a firm, demolishing stride, followed by workers—as powerful as though made of steel.

The Adventures of Delegates en route to Moscow for a Congress of the Comintern

Two foreign communists set off, through the Far East, for a congress of the Comintern in Moscow. They have very important secret documents with them. Because they're in a great hurry, they've been given a special train.

At the secret headquarters of a counterrevolutionary organization, two spies, one of them a pilot, are given orders to follow the foreigners. They both take off in a plane, in pursuit of the train.

The train has reached tremendous speed going downhill. The airplane catches up with it. It descends. One of the spies jumps out onto the roof of the train. The shadowing begins.

A famine-stricken province. An ambulance plane distributes packages, gives medical assistance, takes letters.

Suddenly the pilot receives an order to bring the communist delegates to Moscow immediately.

At N. station. The delegates transfer to the ambulance plane and fly off.

The spy is in despair.

The plane with the second spy lands at the station, takes the first spy. They fly off after the delegates.

Shadowing in the air. The ambulance plane makes an emergency landing (minor damage). The passengers spend the night in a field. The spies attack. The delegates are killed and thrown into water.

The documents are stolen. The spies change into the delegates' suits and continue their flight.

A chance witness, a peasant boy, informs the district Soviet about what's happened.

The Kremlin. Preparations for the congress are in progress.

Khodynka. The delegates arrive in their planes.

The Comintern receives a telegram announcing the death of the delegates.

Khodynka. A detachment of Soviet planes flies to meet the foreign plane. A chase. Trick effects. A skirmish in the air. Leaps from plane to plane.

The documents are retrieved.

Outline for the Scenario of *The Eleventh Year*

Eight miles from the city, cars leave the coke furnaces, rise into the air, and head for the Makeyev Metalworks where they're emptied straight into a blast furnace.

The Eleventh Year

You are in the Donbas. You are in mining country. You go up into the buildings overlooking the mines. You descend, with the miners, beneath the earth. You leave the elevator cage. Horse-drawn wagons with their drivers are running along a drift. You descend into the lower galleries. You make your way on all fours to the coal face. Miners crawl along, holding lamps in their teeth. Cutting by hand and with machine. A scraper rakes the coal out into a car.

You return to the earth's surface with a car loaded with coal.

The car leaves the cage. Now, on the bridge, it has overturned and dumped its coal. Elsewhere coal is being emptied straight into train cars.

You are at an iron mine. Cars head for the quarry. Ore is extracted. The cars load up. They ascend to the earth's surface. They're emptied into train cars. The train cars filled with ore leave for the factories.

You ride around the blast furnace section on a locomotive. You watch a car filled with ore rise toward a blast furnace and empty its load above it.

You spend several days amidst ore and coal, fire and iron, cars and cranes, blast furnaces and blowers, intently observing workers' faces, the work of machines. You try to fathom the tremendous significance of this work for the proletarian state.

Whether it's "pig" going by you or a crane snatching the "pig" out of the furnace and cautiously carrying it to a machine, you never forget that that "pig" and that crane are doing battle on the socialist front.

You visit the factory committee, the party cell, the worker's dwelling, and you see before you not the slaves of capital, but proud warriors of the peaceful construction of socialism, the soldier-builders of the proletarian nation.

You leave the factories of Dnepropetrovsk and travel down the Dnepr River. First by steamer, then by motorboat. Then by *dub* to Kichkas.

You make stops along the way. You see the rapids: "Kaidats," "Adder's Jaws," "The Insatiable."

You just can't believe it's possible to control this raging element, to stop squandering the rapids' furious energy, to harness and use the water's unbridled force.

But thousands of construction workers are already flocking to the banks of the Dnepr. The digging has begun. Workers' settlements are springing up. Railroad tracks are being laid. Bricks and cement are being brought in. The best engineers are directing the preliminary work.

Through the will of the workers and peasants who are implementing their own planned economy, an immense dam—the largest construction project in Europe—will be built here. The water will rise thirty-seven meters over the rapids and, submerging them, will make possible the complete navigation of the Dnepr.

It's hard to imagine that these villages, located near the Dnepr, and Kichkas, a well-built German colony, and this high bridge on whose span a train is passing, will be inundated.

dub. Literally "oak," the *dub* is a boat made of oak planks or carved from the trunk of an oak tree and is used on the Dnepr and Bug rivers—trans.

Ships, loaded with grain, wood, sugar, will pass downstream, over the former rapids.

Oil, metal products, salt, and imported goods will head upstream, inland.

A vast quantity of water will fall from a height of 150 feet. Its colossal energy will be channeled to the turbines of a hydroelectric station.

Two hundred sixty thousand, later 485,000, kilowatts will pass through cables to factories, villages, cities—

to light village streets, peasant huts, schools, village reading-rooms;

to set separators, mills, winnowing machines, threshers in motion;

to provide cheap energy for places that require artificial irrigation;

to raise crop yields, to create a highly productive agricultural center; to set machines, factories, plants in motion; to turn flywheels;

to run hammers, cranes, lifts;

to generate new factories, plants, new machinery;

to open up the broadest future prospects for the development of the productive forces of the Ukraine and the entire Soviet Union.

Based on massive cooperation by the population,

on that of the masses of workers and peasants filled with enthusiasm for building,

our country is undergoing electrification,

growing toward a bright socialist future.

And today,

on the tenth anniversary of the great October Revolution, the proletariat of England, France, Germany, Poland, America, the oppressed peoples of India, Egypt, Australia, all those workers who still live beneath the yoke of capital

greet our country as the seat of socialism, as the world's only country of *Soviets*,

the country of liberated labor.

Together with the workers of Kharkov, Kiev, Ekaterinoslav,

together with the workers of the Donbas and the Dnepr,

together with the proletarians of Moscow and Leningrad,

together with the workers and peasants of the entire Soviet Union,

the whole world of the oppressed and the hungry

celebrates our great holiday.

The Man with a Movie Camera

(A VISUAL SYMPHONY)

The Man with a Movie Camera constitutes an experiment in the cinematic transmission of visual phenomena without the aid of intertitles (a film with no intertitles), script (a film with no script), theater (a film with neither actors nor sets).

Kino-eye's new experimental work aims to create a truly international film-language, *absolute writing in film*, and the complete separation of cinema from theater and literature.

Like *The Eleventh Year*, *The Man with a Movie Camera* is, on the other hand, closely connected to the radio-eye period, which kinoks define as a new and higher stage in the development of nonacted film.

I

You find yourself in a small but extraordinary land where all human experiences, behavior, and even natural phenomena are strictly controlled and occur at precisely determined times.

At your command and whenever you wish, rain may fall, a thunderstorm or tempest arise.

If you like, the downpour will stop. The puddles will immediately dry up. The sun will shine forth. Perhaps even two or three suns.

If you wish, day will turn into night. The sun into the moon. Stars will appear. Winter will replace summer. Snowflakes will whirl. A pond will freeze. Frost patterns will cover the windows.

You can, if you choose, sink or save ships at sea. Cause fires and earthquakes. Make wars and revolutions. Human tears and laughter obey your command. Passion and jealousy. Love and hatred.

According to your strict schedule, people fight and embrace. Marry and divorce. Are born and die. Die and come to life. Die again and again come to life. Or kiss endlessly in front of the camera until the director is satisfied.

We are at a film studio where a man with a megaphone and script directs the life of a fake land.

The Man with a Movie Camera

II

And this is no palace, merely a facade of painted plywood and veneer.

And those are not ships at sea, but toys in a tub. Not rain, but a shower. Not snow, but feathers. Not the moon, but a set.

None of this is life, but play. Play rain and snow. Make-believe palaces and cooperatives. Villages and towns. Pretend love and death. Pretend counts and bandits. Pretend tax collector and Civil War.

Playing at "revolution." Make-believe "abroad."

Playing at "the new life" and "the construction of socialism."

III

High above this little fake world with its mercury lamps and electric suns, high in the real sky burns a real sun over real life. The film-factory is a miniature island in the stormy sea of life.

The Man with a Movie Camera

IV

Streets and streetcars intersect. And buildings and buses. Legs and smiling faces. Hands and mouths. Shoulders and eyes.

Steering wheels and tires turn. Carousels and organ-grinders' hands. Seamstresses' hands and a lottery wheel. The hands of women winding skeins and cyclists' shoes.

Men and women meet. Birth and death. Divorce and marriage. Slaps and handshakes. Spies and poets. Judges and defendants. Agitators and their audience. Peasants and workers. Worker-students and foreign delegates.

A whirlpool of contacts, blows, embraces, games, accidents, athletics, dances, taxes, sights, thefts, incoming and outgoing papers set off against all sorts of seething human labor.

How is the ordinary, naked eye to make sense of this visual chaos of fleeting life?

V

A little man, armed with a movie camera, leaves the little fake world of the film-factory and heads for life. Life tosses him to and fro like a straw. He's like a frail canoe on a stormy sea. He's continually swamped by the furious city traffic. The rushing, hurrying human crowd surges 'round him at every turn.

Wherever he appears, curious crowds immediately surround his camera with an impenetrable wall; they stare into the lens, feel and open the cases with film cans. Obstacles and surprises at every turn.

Unlike the film-factory where the camera is almost stationary, where the whole of "life" is aimed at the camera's lens in a strictly

Mikhail Kaufman

determined order of shots and scenes, life here does not wait for the film director or obey his instructions. Thousands, millions of people go about their business. Spring follows winter. Summer follows spring. Thunderstorms, rain, tempests, snow do not obey any script. Fires, weddings, funerals, anniversaries—all occur in their own time; they cannot be changed to fit a calendar invented by the author of the film.

The man with the camera must give up his usual immobility. He must exert his powers of observation, quickness, and agility to the utmost in order to keep pace with life's fleeting phenomena.

VI

The first steps of the man with the movie camera end in failure. He is not upset. He persists and learns to keep pace with life. He gains more experience. He becomes accustomed to the situation, assumes the defensive, begins to employ a whole series of special techniques (candid camera; sudden, surprise filming; distraction of the subject; etc.). He tries to shoot unnoticed, to shoot so that his own work does not hinder that of others.

VII

The man with the movie camera marches apace with life. To the bank and the club. The beer hall and the clinic. The Soviet and the housing council. The cooperative and the school. The demonstration and the party-cell meeting. The man with the movie camera manages to go everywhere.

He is present at military parades, at congresses. He penetrates workers' flats. He stands watch at a savings bank, visits a dispensary and train stations. He surveys harbors and airports. He travels—switching within a week from automobile to the roof of a train, from train to plane, plane to glider, glider to submarine, submarine to cruiser, cruiser to hydroplane, and so on.

VIII

Life's chaos gradually becomes clear as he observes and shoots. Nothing is accidental. Everything is explicable and governed by law. Every peasant with his seeder, every worker at his lathe,

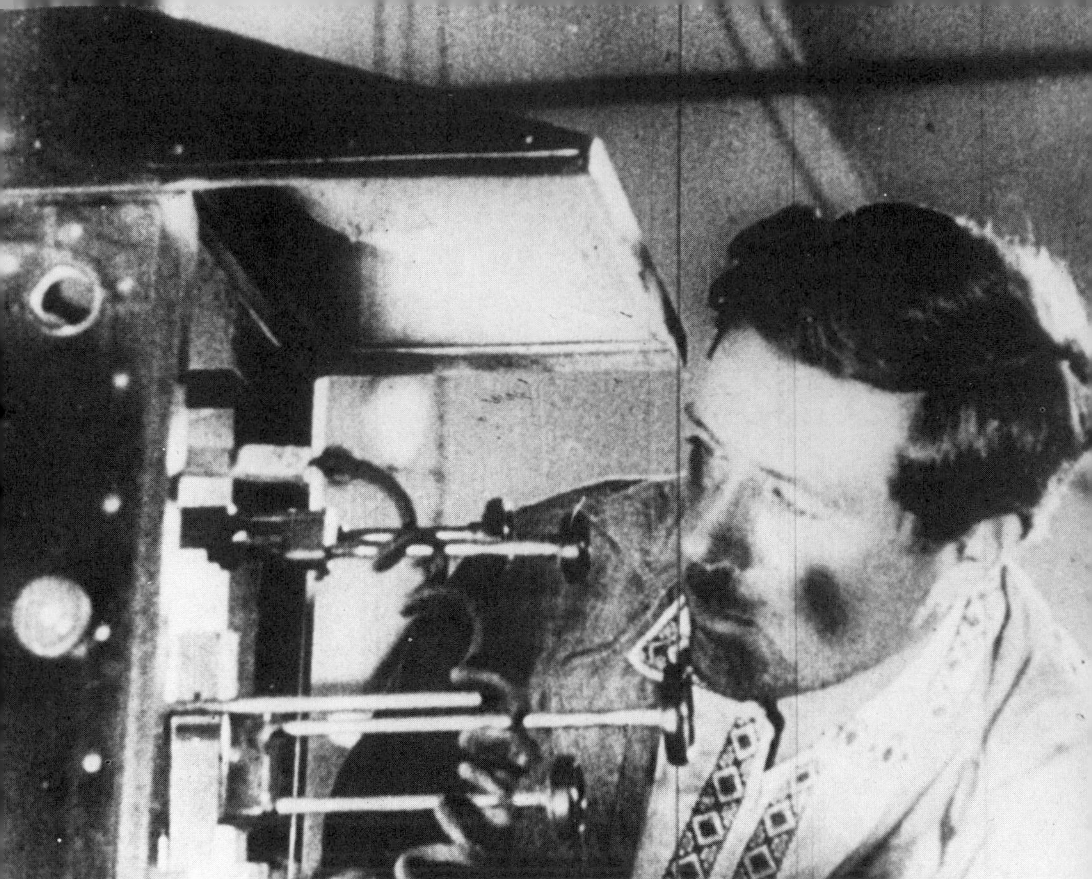

The Man with a Movie Camera

every worker-student at his books, every engineer at his drafting table, every Young Pioneer speaking at a meeting in a club—each is engaged in the same great necessary labor.

All this—the factory rebuilt, and the lathe improved by a worker, the new public dining hall, and the newly opened village day-care center, the exam passed with honors, the new road or highway, the streetcar, the locomotive repaired on schedule—all these have their meaning—all are victories, great and small, in the struggle of the new with the old, the struggle of revolution with counterrevolution, the struggle of the cooperative against the private entrepreneur, of the club against the beer hall, of athletics against debauchery, dispensary against disease. All this is a position won in the struggle for the Land of the Soviets, the struggle against a lack of faith in socialist construction.

The camera is present at the great battle between two worlds:

The Man with a Movie Camera

that of the capitalists, profiteers, factory bosses, and landlords and that of workers, peasants, and colonial slaves.

The camera is present at the decisive battle between the one and only Land of the Soviets and all the bourgeois nations of the world.

Visual Apotheosis

Life. The film studio. And the movie camera at its socialist post.

Note: A small, secondary production theme—the film's passage from camera through laboratory and editing room to screen—will be included, by montage, in the film's beginning, middle, and end.

Sound March

(*FROM THE FILM* SYMPHONY OF THE DONBAS)

I

A clock is ticking.

Quietly at first. Gradually louder. Louder still. Unbearably loud (almost like the blows of a hammer). Gradually softer, to a neutral, clearly audible level. Like a heart beating, only considerably stronger.

Footsteps approaching, climbing a staircase. They pass. The sound dies away. A clock is ticking. Again approaching footsteps. They come close. Stop. The clock ticks, like the beating of a heart.

The first sound of a tolling church bell. The reverberation dies out, giving way to the ticking of a clock. The second stroke of a church bell. The reverberation dies out, giving way once more to the ticking of a clock. The third stroke of a church bell, gradually expanding into a feast-day carillon.

Fragments of the church service (the better known motifs) are commingled with the sound of the bells. The chimes, mingled with the motifs from the service, cannot maintain solemnity for long. A note of irony appears. The solemnity is continually undercut. The religious motifs seem to dance about.

For a moment or two the sounds disappear, replaced by the ticking of a clock, then once again waves of sounds quickly begin to rise. A long, powerful factory whistle bursts in to meet and intercept them. After the first whistle, a second, then a third, sunder the music and the tolling. As if frightened, the sounds slow down and come to a halt. Freeze. The church bell tinkles a last two times. All is quiet.

II

The ticking of a clock, like the beating of a heart.

A signal for action—a long, piercing whistle.

Then a second whistle and a third.

Against the background of drawn-out whistles, a procession of Pioneer drums, Komsomol motifs, and workers' bands develops.

The strong, triumphant blast of a whistle which then gradually dies away. One long, resonating note remains, like the humming of a motor.

III

A single humming sound. The breathing of a factory is heard in the distance.

The sounds of a joyful military march (a brass band) draw nearer.

The band is close by. For a moment the sounds are restrained for a shrill trumpet signal (Charge! Forward!). The same march

Enthusiasm

played faster, but more quietly—so that the background noise of the nearby factory can be heard. Still faster, more excitedly, quietly, then suddenly—the comic squeal of a cross tumbling to the ground. The band emits a cry of delight. A whistle. A cross tumbles once again with a comic squeal. The band applauds enthusiastically. A whistle. A bell falls with a comically simpering sound effect and on hitting the ground emits a death moan (or rather, it has the attitude of a "death moan," evoking not pity, but grins).

Enthusiastic cries of "HURRAH" (from the band) punctuate this rapid, ironic etude. The victorious band's "hurrah" turns into a Komsomol march, then into general merriment and a dance of youth.

Somewhere a clock is ticking. A clock?

Enthusiasm

IV

The ticking of a clock, like the beating of a heart. The wireless starts transmitting. We begin to hear the factory's heart—the power station. The pulse of the power station is performed in turn by various groups of instruments. For quite some time we hear this electric pulse beneath the earth and in the mines, at the blast furnaces, and throughout the factory's other sections. The electrical pulse beat is intensified by the combined working of all the percussion groups, plus other instruments, after which it begins to grow fainter; now it is already heard far off in the distance. The wireless is transmitting a message. A fanfare's cry, repeated three times, cuts in sharply against the background of growing audible alarm. A momentary lull so that the wireless is heard; after which a general review of factory noises, by groups, begins: (1) the underground scraper machines and coal cutters, (2) the drilling machines, (3) the steam hammers, (4) the tractors, (5) the thunderous crash of the rollers, (6) the shrill sounds of steel, (7) the hissing and rumbling, (8) the explosions, (9) the raging sea of fire.

Gradually joining these are groups of (1) signals (factory whistles, cries of shunting engines, banging against cast-iron and copper plates, sirens, etc.), (2) the greeting and calling wind instruments, (3) the light drumroll, (4) kettledrums and clashing cymbals, (5) propellers, (6) deafening radio cries, (7) socialist trains speeding furiously off into the future.

Amid the waves of enthusiastic sound the ear catches the tune of "The Internationale," greatly accelerated and amplified.

A flood of sound to a piano playing "The Internationale" distinctly; a swelling of sound to the Kremlin clock, chiming "The Internationale"; once again a flood of sound to the pianist. While, at that very moment—the stroke of midnight.

The pianist rises, closes the piano lid (a thump) tight, not in utter silence, but against the sound of the wireless that has reemerged. . . .

Symphony of the Donbas (*Enthusiasm*)

I

A church with crosses, chimes, double-headed eagles, the tsar's monogram and crown, with anathema pronounced against the Revolution, the pope, a religious crusade, drunkenness, brawling, women weeping, idlers, unconsciousness, broken heads, and the moaning of the wounded, with "God Save the Tsar," old women in a state of addiction, religious icons kissed, ladies in coats of Persian lamb, crawling on their knees, and other such *shades of the past.*

Transformed (not gradually, but in a revolutionary leap, with an explosion of crowns, crosses, icons, etc., with the shades of the past executed by the hurricane blaze of socialist factories)

into a club for factory youth with red stars, a revolutionary banner, with Pioneers, Komsomols, a radio fan listening to the march, "The Final Sunday," a girl Komsomol sculpting a bust of Lenin, a parade, *the Five-Year Plan for the construction of socialism.*

II

On the one hand—the Five-Year Plan for the construction of socialism.

On the other—the Donbas with a glaring work stoppage: cars arrested in midair, blast furnaces needing coke, coke furnaces needing coal, mines needing coal hewers, engineers, machines.

Enthusiasm

The result: *a revolutionary alert.*

A Donbas worker speaks at a large rally: "The country's threatened with a coal shortage." To the accompaniment of a wireless alert, the sound screen hurls out the words: "[Work] Stoppage! Stoppage! Stoppage!" The entire hall rises in response to the Donbas worker's appeal "to pay our coal debt to the nation" with a mighty "Internationale." The sounds of "The Internationale" carry from the hall to accompany Komsomol detachments of volunteers leaving for the Donbas front.

At the Donbas the secretary of a party cell, greeting the first convoys of volunteers on arrival, exhorts them to overcome obstacles; the shock-workers of both sexes solemnly promise to produce. The newly arrived Komsomols are taught mining. The shock-workers, the enthusiasts commence the attack.

Coal comes out of the earth. Coal for factories. Coal for locomotives. Coal for coke furnaces.

Coal has arrived. The conveyors and sorting machines have started up. The aerial chains of coal-filled carts have begun to move. The blast furnaces are operating at full speed. *Metal has arrived.* The rolling and open-hearth steel sections are competing with each other. Rolled steel, open-hearth, rolled, open-hearth, rolled, open-hearth—*in a single creative thrust toward socialism.*

"For the cause (a many-voiced echo) of *socialism* (many-voiced echo) . . . Hur-r-r-ra-a-ah!" . . . (montage).

III

Trains loaded with coal and metal leave the Donbas. They are met by convoys with grain. A team of collective farmers declares itself a shock brigade and challenges another brigade to socialist competition. The collective farm workers go singing into the battle for grain. Parades with music and song.

When these greetings and slogans, the military band music, the sounds of parades, speeches, and revolutionary songs *enter* the factory, *take root in* the sounds of machines, the cries of workers, the sounds of competing shops, and when, in their turn, the sounds

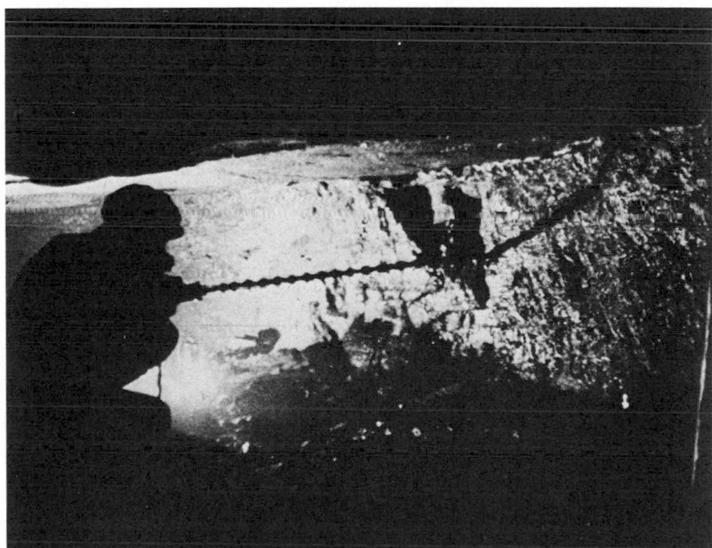

The Man with a Movie Camera

of the All-Union Stokehold arrive at the square, enter the streets, accompanying the socialist parades with their machine music—all the work of liquidating the Donbas work stoppage turns into a gigantic communist Sabbath, a gigantic "day of industrialization," into a red-starred, red-bannered campaign.

Wireless messages run past in the glow of the blast furnaces. Socialist whistles rush off, hooting, into the future. The night is continually shot through with fireworks of blinding steel sparks. Bessemer sun after sun rises. The sounds of the machine tools merge with that of "The Internationale."

And special machines compute the enthusiasm of the Donbas workers, converting it into figures.

She and *An Evening of Miniatures*

I hereby submit a request to make a film, *She.*

The film follows the train of thought of a composer writing a symphony, *She.* The composer's thought (and with it, the film) moves from woman under capitalism to woman under socialism and dwells on concrete, present-day examples. The film concludes with Marusya B., awarded the Order of Lenin for her taming of the Dnepr.

Together with *She,* I'm submitting a request for *An Evening of Miniatures* to be shot alongside the first film. It includes the following sketches and feuilletons:

1. "Shades of the Past"
2. "Hands"
3. "At Dawn"
4. "A scene at the registrar's office" [for births, deaths marriages, and divorces]
5. "A scene in court"
6. "Song without words"

I ask that these subjects and titles be reserved for me.

I will be able to make them more specific during a leave of absence following completion of the film on Lenin.

A Young Woman Composer

The theme of Woman is vast.

In the past I've devoted individual *Kinokalendar*s and *Kinopravdas* to this theme. In *Three Songs of Lenin* I also strongly emphasized this theme. It's clear to me that I'll have frequent occasion to return to it in the future as well.

I'm presently limiting my aim to the creative work of a young woman composer who's preparing her first big symphonic piece for International Women's Day on March 8.

Given the lack of film-documents (especially foreign ones), it looks as though I'll have to use, in addition to my own personal remembrances and notebook entries, press material, partly domestic and partly from abroad; vivid, graphic quotations; sentences from conversations with women on collective farms; snatches of songs; etc.

It's as if we are participating in the creative process of the young woman composer's work. We follow her thoughts.

The thoughts turn into visible images.

Into poetic images.

Into musical ones.

Into pictures, now into sounds, now into notes, now words.

A Day Throughout the World

A film on a theme from Gorky. Based on an article with the same title by Mikhail Koltsov.

I talked with management about this theme immediately after the article appeared. I proposed making this film for the twentieth anniversary of the October Revolution. I announced this in the press. Got Koltsov's approval.

The delay on the film about young women of two worlds makes this theme, previously on reserve, the order of the day. It can go into production immediately. First of all because we don't have to write a script right away. Koltsov's article suffices for the first stage of work—selecting the documentary material. As follows from Comrade Koltsov's article and words, the script in this instance can be composed after the selection of material. It merely sums up the "day throughout the world." Second, this theme does not require the immediate use of an Eclair. A selection of footage will be made in foreign film archives. All our technical and administrative difficulties thus fall by the wayside. In this instance, success and victory will depend to some extent on my brain, my diligence—in comparison to the situation with the film about the young women in which I must depend, not on myself, but on an administrative and technical base. This work with footage may prove to be the situation we're aiming for: 90 percent creative work and 10 percent stalling, instead of the existing inverse ratio. Third, the selection of footage for this theme will allow us to take what we need for the film on young women of two worlds simultaneously with the survey of the capitalist world. We save both themes at once. Fourth, bringing out an antifascist survey of the capitalist world for the twentieth anniversary of the October Revolution is the direct duty and task of Mezhrabpomfilm.

Experience and simple calculation suggest that this task is excessive for the ordinary acted film. With veterans of documentary film in our organization such as Comrade Svilova and your humble servant, it would be utterly stupid to let an opportunity of this kind slip by. Especially, since we are literally starving to create. You have only to let us loose. If only we could get our teeth into the material. Then you'd see what artists doomed by the impasse of production to such a long and agonizing fast, are capable of.

The selection of footage.

Footage for the film, *A Day Throughout the World,* is to be selected on the basis of Comrade Koltsov's article and on the results of an analogous experiment already made in the newspaper chronicle. The selection can begin at once and should be made by the film's director. It's a matter not of mechanical but of creative selection made with extreme foresight. This is work no less intense than shooting. Work that should enable us to arrange shots taken by capitalist firms in a combination to be directed against capitalism. Work that wrests the weapon from the enemy's hands and turns that same weapon against him. I cannot entrust this work to anyone else. No one can carry it through but the film's author.

The same holds true for the selection of shots for the film on woman under capitalism. It's not a matter of choosing shots of workers' demonstrations, jobless women, colonial slave women, etc. It's a matter of selecting precisely those shots that will, through the foresight of the author-artist, form a graphic work of art when combined with the Soviet footage. This work cannot be regarded as auxiliary; it is basic, decisive work.

Altogether, for both films we will select approximately thirty-five thousand feet of footage. If we pay for all the footage, it will cost between three and four thousand rubles. If, as is customary, they exchange 50 percent of the foreign footage for the corresponding amount from our film archive, it will cost about two thousand rubles. If we manage to exchange all their footage for footage from our film archives or specially shot footage for the total amount, then we'd need currency only for my journey.

On compromise solutions:

Back in 1922 Comrade Lenin pointed out the need to produce newsreels "on the life of the peoples of all lands." He also cited examples: England's colonial policy in India, the work of the League of Nations, people starving in Berlin, etc. Have these directions of Comrade Lenin's lost their urgency today?

A vague compromise solution, trying to hide, cushioned from everything happening in the capitalist world surrounding us—none of this can lead to any good.

When we've completed one of my film proposals, we'll be dragged out from under the cushions and asked: How is it that you, an organization producing films on international themes, thought it possible to limit yourselves in your only documentary film to praising things here, without comparing them to the reality of capitalist countries? Where are the criteria for distinguishing good from bad? No excuse, no references to the difficulties encountered will help us. We'll be told, quite rightly: difficulties exist to be overcome. Victory never comes of itself.

"The rainbow appears over the earth only after a powerful storm and terrible flashes of lightning. . . . "

Note: Comrade Koltsov has agreed to act as consultant on *A Day Throughout the World.*

The Girl at the Piano

(DRAFT FOR A SCENARIO)

The author (D. Vertov) proposes a special kind of film to be made under this tentative title. Musical and poetic, and at the same time instructive. An epic of science fiction, without using a magician or talisman.

The author recalls how as a young child the enthusiasm he shared with friends of his own age gradually shifted from fairy tales with magicians to those of nature itself: to the astonishing phenomena on the earth, beneath it, and in the sky.

The author recalls how he and friends his age were seized with an interest in educational fantasy and especially in the phenomena of cosmology and astronomy. He fired questions at adults. Why do pedestrians slip and fall on frozen sidewalks? And why do they stop falling if you sprinkle sand on the ground? Why does a locomotive revolve its wheels in place, without moving forward? Why did a glass fall quickly, not slowly, to the floor? Because if it were to fall slowly, it wouldn't break. We children were amazed at everything and could find the fantastic in the most ordinary things. Then we became accustomed to the situation, resigned ourselves to "you'll find out when you grow up," and stopped asking. Our fantasies (we often fantasized to music) were, for the most part, based on a lack of educational data and either died or got sidetracked. That must not happen to Soviet children.

We must feed their fantasies.

After all, art and knowledge intermingle in their daydreams.

We are not going to hamper that; it's a very good thing.

I'd like to make a series of films with precisely this combination of music and poetry, on the one hand, and education plus fantasy, on the other.

The following draft for a proposed science-fiction epic is the first step in that direction.

Should my project be approved, I could start working out specifics immediately.

So . . . *The Girl at the Piano.*

A girl is playing the piano.
    The starry night
        stares at her
            through the open terrace windows.
The moon shines bright upon her hands.
The moon shines bright upon the keyboard.
And it seems to her that it is not sounds
    but the rays of wondrous distant worlds,
        the rays of twinkling stars
            that ring out beneath her fingers.

She loves music.
But she also loves astronomy.
It is a science with such poetic allure!
But she must not get distracted.
Closer to earth.
Closer to earth.
A train rushes by.
A train rushes by through the night.
She's sleeping in a comfortable compartment.
A book clutched in her hands.
She fell asleep while reading.
And it's as though she'd made an arrangement with the paper.
She's travelling to an area where a search is being made for a meteorite that has recently fallen.
It's night.
The train rushes along.
The girl sleeps in her compartment.
A conductor enters.
Wakes her up.
Hands her an urgent telegram.

In which the editors inform her of strange happenings in the area where the meteor fell. They are especially evident in a youth camp over which the meteor passed when hitting earth. She's instructed to transfer at M. station to a plane in order to reach the place indicated by morning.

And in the plane
she flies over a mountain range
and lands
near the camp.
It's morning.
Tropical vegetation.
The children are exercising.
She draws nearer.
She sees nothing unusual.
She looks around very intently.
The instructor is demonstrating the last exercise.
Suddenly sounds of some sort arise from all sides.
The instructor's legs are creeping in different directions.
The children's legs are creeping every which way.
It's so slippery!
Lying flat, the instructor and the children slide about in all

directions on the green playing field.

It's impossible to hold on to a bush or a blade of grass.

Everything's as slippery as quicksilver.

She sees smaller objects creeping along, drawn to larger ones. And she starts to realize that the friction coefficient has neared zero. That the attraction to the center of the earth has grown equal to the resistance of the earth's surface. And now, as a result, nothing can prevent the normally unnoticeable, mutual attraction of bodies.

Absorbed in her observations, she finds herself in the field of action of the unknown force.

And she's now already on her back, sliding off a hillock.
smiling at an automobile that has suddenly slid
with its wheels still,
smiling at a train on an embankment rushing furiously on,
while not advancing an inch.

"So that's how essential friction turns out to be!
And only counterdemonstration allows us to fully understand it."
So she thinks to herself.
as she continues to slide along the grass.
"But after all, I'm only dreaming."
And she rubs her eyes.
The strange music dies away.
There's no one on the playing field.
The exercises have long been over.
She lies in a hammock
thinking of the meteorite.
Maybe it's not a meteorite at all?!
Maybe it's a specially constructed interplanetary spaceship?
And all that's just happened
is the result of experiments by scientists from outer space?
But no.
She's dreamed it.

You know she so loves music, scientific experiment, and daydreams!

She spends the whole day wandering about the camp in the hope of glimpsing something else fantastic.

But the day passes as usual.
It's now perfectly clear
that her imagination ran away with her this morning.
Tired

and a little disappointed
she sits down on a bench near the volleyball court.
She leans back against a tree,
and when she's made herself comfortable, she half closes her eyes.
And immediately the music starts up.
Her body feels strangely light.
She sits, barely touching the bench.
Any minute now she could take off into the air.
She jumps to her feet.
She wants to take a step.
But something's pulling her upward.
And instead of a step,
she unwittingly takes a little leap.
But she's not the only one to whom this is happening.
She sees that a volleyball player at the net, who's jumped up to try to reach and stop the ball, has flown over the net himself and landed smoothly in his opponent's territory.
She wants to test that sensation;
she jumps up,
flies higher than a tree,
and settles gently, like a bird, on a small branch.
And the branch does not break beneath her weight.
Something has happened to her body's weight.
"My weight's reduced to one-sixth of itself," she reasons to herself.
"This could occur on a significantly smaller planet, say on the moon.
But nothing around me has changed.
That means only gravity has changed."
And indeed,
on the tennis court,
on the basketball court,
in the gymnastic complex,
as far as her eyes can see,
strange things are happening:
None of the players are running,
but smoothly flying about.
Each step by a runner on the track
seems a gigantic fifteen- or twenty-foot one.

Gymnasts,
    literally holding on to their ropes or poles with two fingers,
        climb to the very top without the least effort.
The children, playing around, break all world records in
    discus, throwing and grenade hurling.
She watches
    a ball go flying from the soccer field to the other side of
        a tall building,
            and without stopping, go on,
                to land beyond a nearby grove.
She imagines the goalie's astonishment,
    who never before,
        in kicking a ball,
            had had such a result.
But now a second ball comes flying.
This time out of the volleyball court.
The ball's flying straight toward her.
She screws up her eyes.
That doesn't help, of course.
The ball hits the girl.
She gently falls down from the branch.
She descends slowly.
Now she's already touching the bench.
She starts.
Opens wide her astonished eyes.
The music stops at once.
The weight returns to her body.
How solid the bench is!
How rough the tree feels against her!
The ball lies at her feet.
She picks it up
and throws it to the players.
The ball flies normally.
The earth's gravity has returned.
Could it be that the scientists from outer space have
    concluded their experiment in their ship?!
If only she hasn't dreamed all this once again,
    since she sat down to rest and closed her eyes.
In any event,
    on the following day,

when the children were resting outdoors after lunch,
during the "quiet hour,"
the music started up again,
and, at the same time, even stranger things began to happen.

A children's magazine,
which slipped out of the hands of a sleeping boy,
did not fall, but just hung there in the air.

Several children, still clutching their blankets, pushed off from their mattresses while sleeping, escaped from their cots, and rose without waking into the air.

"If it weren't for the tree branches that have held back the flying children, they'd rise higher and higher," our girl thought.

"These scientists from outer space must have read our Tsiolkovsky. They're conducting an experiment in the complete absence of gravity. Like him, they assume that water, air, and all of our usual surroundings remain in place. The only thing absent in the present theoretical instance is gravity."

She watches
the teenagers, now awake, float among the trees,
learning how to move in an atmosphere devoid of gravity.
Some flit from bush to bush,
using their arms as brakes.
Others float higher,
from branch to branch, from tree to tree.
Still others are already doing group exercises,
helping one another and joining hands.
And here's our girl.
How lightly she has pushed off from the summer house
from which she had been observing the scene.
She has pushed off carefully, parallel to the earth,
like a swimmer in a pool.
She knows
that if she pushes off upward without meeting any obstacle,
she could break away from the planet completely
and leave it behind forever.
Hmm . . . what about trying it anyhow?
How sweet the forbidden fruit!
She's always loved the unknown.
With a strong spring, she pushes off from the planet,

rises higher and higher
and who knows how it all might have ended,
if the earth's gravity had not suddenly and sharply
asserted itself
and put an end to all that music?
And in fact the music did cease at once.
And, our girl has dropped like a stone.
The earth is rushing up with threatening speed.
Death is inevitable.
But the girl's smiling.
As usual, she's foreseen it all.
"A delayed jump," she remarks
and opens
a parachute that has mysteriously materialized.
There's a jolt.
She jumps up on her bed.
The book has dropped from her hands.

But, of course. She's in the train compartment. And the train is rushing along through the starry night.

Still not quite awake, she picks up the fallen book.
She leafs through it, looking for the chapter in which
Tsiolkovsky writes about what happens when gravity is absent.

And she seems to be standing before a movie screen
and a classroom filled with students.
And the students regard her
as their teacher.
They're obviously waiting for her to start talking.

And she seems to summon up the courage and talks, telling the students:

"What we have seen on the screen
is only my dream, evoked by a scientist's musings.
But they are useful musings.
They help us to fathom things,
to which, from force of habit, we pay no attention,
that we consider obvious.
In the early years of childhood,
we shower adults with endless "Why?"s.

Then we get used to unintelligible answers. To the lack of answers. To half answers. We get used to invariable repetition. We cease to go to the roots of things. And, after adjusting to our surroundings, we stop asking, "Why?"

Meanwhile even a law such as that of universal gravity has not yet been given a fully satisfactory explanation. This law is confirmed by all observation, experimentation, calculation. But we accept it without yet being able to explain it, as we should, completely. In an attempt to more *thoroughly* understand it, together with the usual study of the law of gravity, we explore several fantastic assumptions. "Let's imagine," says Tsiolkovsky, the scientist, "that by some miracle, the earth's gravity has vanished. Let us describe what will occur then." "Man," says Tsiolkovsky, "has grown so accustomed to his surroundings that there could be no more appropriate way of describing what happens when gravity is absent. . . .

"We've grown used to a stone's falling down a well, a weight's pressing against the floor, a man's falling when he stumbles, etc., etc.

"However, as we saw today on the screen, with a change in the force of attraction, this very ordinary, self-evident phenomenon (falling) cannot occur. What will occur will seem fantastic to us.

"But that which seems fantastic on earth is fully possible on some other planet. For example, on a tiny planet of a hundred or so feet, gravity would not be noticeable. You could disregard the actual gravity of such a planet. There are many such tiny planets. But even on a significantly larger planet with a surface of six thousand miles, a man's weight would merely equal a bit less than a pound.

"A jump from the surface of that planet would lift you eight hundred to one thousand feet.

"With a powerful leap from the first, small planet you'd leave it forever."

The new teacher talks about the sun,

where a man would be crushed by his own weight.

About Jupiter,

where, because of his weight, a man could barely drag himself along.

She talks about the gravitational pull on Mars and on the moon.

(Recall what took place on the volleyball court.)

She replies to questions from the fascinated students with vivid examples.

And imperceptibly, she joins the class, in leading their talk away from the film-fantasy, to the conclusions of popular science.

The bell signals the end of the lesson,
but the excited students ask for still more
"science-magic."

"In the Soviet Union," says the teacher, "the flight of the imagination is neither eccentric nor an object of ridicule."

She takes a decanter of water from the table
and lifts it high above her head.
"Watch closely, I'm releasing my grasp."
(The decanter falls calmly to the table and doesn't break.)
"Watch, I'm taking out the stopper."
(The water in the decanter immediately starts to boil.)
She pours the water into a glass.
(The water flows very slowly.)
She puts the stopper on the decanter.

(The boiling stops in the decanter. But the water in the glass continues to ripple, then grows calm and turns to ice.)

"What kind of tricks are these?" the teacher asks. "Well, think it over, use your imagination."

"You're on the moon,"
the class answers in a chorus.

With the help of someone's sketching, a lunar landscape appears behind the teacher . . .

She smiles.
and, continuing to smile,
closes her eyes very, very slowly.
The music starts up.
And austere,
sharply outlined,
black-and-white landscapes,
craters,
mountains,
valleys—
all the fantastic surface of the moon—
float off into the depths,
carrying off our smiling, dreamy girl.
And it seems to her
that music,
science,
poetry
have woven into a single,

joyous dancing circle.
And not sounds,
but the rays of twinkling stars,
the rays of wondrous distant worlds
ring out beneath
her fingers.
Growing more distant,
the moon above the piano
gradually takes on the appearance of
a gigantic cup,
then of a large plate,
then the usual appearance of the moon in the starry sky.
It's night on earth.
The terrace windows are open.
The universe
with its starry eyes
watches over
the girl,
dreaming at the piano.

Letter from a Woman Tractor Driver

(A FILM-SONG)

I hereby submit as my fourth proposal a film to be made to the words of a song by Vinnikov:

Dear friend. The wheat is ripening;
the flood-meadows' bloom is fading;
you're off to the border these days
to smash the enemy with your fierce tank.

It feels good to be among the wide-open spaces of the
collective farm—
each ear of grain is long and heavy;
but the fields don't stand untended,
though you went with your friends to the front.

Your tractor does not stand idle;

it's ready; it's at full speed;
and I drive, as you taught me,
boldly to the harvesting.

And towards evening I imagine that,
as a star blazes up beyond the forest,
you my darling, my happy tractor driver,
are coming to meet me as always.

In the storm of battle, behind clouds of smoke,
you crush all our foes into dust
and fight for us there, sweetheart.
In your place, I work in the fields.

On the harvest fronts I will
battle for the well-being of our country,
just as you, defeating the enemy in your tank,
fight on the field of war.

The leader of a tank subunit, camouflaged in a forest, gets this letter from his sweetheart.

During a lull in action, he opens the letter.

A photograph of a smiling young woman with light-brown hair falls out of the envelope. She's at work on a tractor.

The photograph is passed round.

The commander is proud of his sweetheart and readily agrees to read the letter to his comrades.

The song is heard as the letter is read.

We see the wide-open spaces of collective farm fields.

Pictures of a bustling harvest.

And amidst it all—young women patriots, steering the ships of the steppes.

And here's our young woman, familiar to us through her picture.

She skillfully drives her machine.

She's fighting for grain, for the harvest.

She must gather every last ear of grain.

The fields of the collective farm also represent a front.

She has taken over her sweetheart's job.

And along with her—her women friends.

We see them—in many different montage shots, within the rhythm of the song—storming the thick grain.

Waves ripple across the field.

Like a sea, millions of ripe ears of rye, wheat, oats, barley rustle, now bend to earth, now spring up.

The song carries us further and further away.

Women at threshing machines,

the enthusiasts at work on livestock farms,

women gathering scrap iron,

driving heavy trucks,

driving trains, steamboats,

young women at machines

go into action.

The theme of women replacing their husbands, of sisters replacing their brothers, of daughters replacing their fathers, of young women taking over their sweethearts' posts, focuses once more on the image of our young woman, in the words of her letter to her sweetheart.

The soldiers listen with bated breath to the letter-song of the young patriot.

An alarm signal stops him from reading the letter through.

Everyone takes up his combat post.

An order from the commander—and the tanks have rushed off where they were directed.

"Full speed ahead!"

And, reaching top speed, crushing bushes and smashing trees, the tanks hurry to cut off the enemy's path.

All of our various mechanized weaponry join visually in the song, made thunderous with the sounds of war.

And in the *battle*—

unfolding with lightning speed, general, synthetic (done with montage),

in the symphonic interaction of previously shot and recently obtained combat shots—

the song's final couplet takes on a new quality:

she is on the harvest front

and

he is on the battlefront.

To You, Front!

A woman is carrying a baby wrapped in a blanket in her arms, and lifting a corner of the blanket, she whispers to the baby:

"You have your papa's eyes. And as soon as papa comes home . . ."

Adolph Hitler's face appears on the screen.

The panorama of a factory, out of focus, is dimly visible behind Hitler.

"The Russian winter has halted our offensive. But spring follows winter. When the trees begin to bloom, we'll launch hundreds of fresh divisions, newly armed, against the Land of the Soviets! We will crush the weary Reds and their exhausted reserves."

Spring. In the mountains the almond trees' flowering branches, still bare of leaves, stand out in their whiteness. The apricot is starting to blossom. Spring is coming, the rivers are flooding, the steppe is blooming.

The *akyn,* Nupreis, leads the singing. The music of the *dombra* is heard.

High mountains, glaciers. At the top of a glacier stands a pyramid of ice. There are twenty-eight names on the pyramid. And the first one is Klochkov.

A voice can be heard, singing of the Panfilov heroes.

Soviet citizens have climbed the nameless mountain and named it "The Twenty-Eight," in memory of the heroes who halted the enemy near Moscow. From its summit you can see the whole country.

On the right are the Altai mountains; on the left is the Caspian Sea. The Tien Shan crown the monument, while there in the north, forests rustle. And all this is one sector behind a mighty front.

We travel along the glacier. A stream flows from beneath the ice. Ever swelling, it thunders louder and louder.

Birds fly over the mountains.

A map of Kazakhstan, shot from above, appears for a second on the screen—as though seen through gaps in the clouds.

Northern Kazakhstan, shot from above.

The wind stirs the trees, lifts the wheat, whips the water of the lakes.

akyn. A folksinger or bard in Kazakhstan and Kirghizia, who improvises verses to the accompaniment of the *dombra*—trans.

dombra. A two-stringed instrument used in Kazakhstan—ed.

Panfilov heroes. Soldiers in an infantry division under the command of General Panfilov during the Great Patriotic War. In October 1941, this division defended the approach to Moscow against the Nazis. Because ammunition was in short supply, they bound hand grenades to their bodies and hurled themselves directly under the German tanks—ed.

The voice sings.

"There's no better wheat in the world than the wheat of the land irrigated by the rivers Tobol and Ishim."

The voice sings of the guards at the rear. Those who have set records in working the land pass by to the accompaniment of the song. The song names them.

The wheat is replaced by a sea of millet. The tufts of the millet resemble the plumes of a great army.

The voice sings on, praising the send-off of Bersyev who turned in the biggest millet harvest.

"He who creates a hundred seeds from one does not fear the enemy. He who grows three ears of grain where only one had grown before is growing victory."

Semidesert. Huge flocks of sheep pass by.

Lambs run after their mothers. Some sheep have two, some three, and some even four lambs.

The lambs frolic.

The voice sings.

"They do not fear you, Hitler. But you should fear them. Once in his childhood songs the Cossack dreamed of a single mother's bearing two or three lambs, but Zavodsky, the academician and guardsman of the rear, in battle against you, increased the sheep's fertility—not in song or dream, but out in the field."

Old shepherds tend their sheep. An old man carries a lamb on his shoulders. The song names him and says that this man will defeat you, Hitler.

The lambs frolic. A stallion gallops about the steppe. He runs through feather-grass, along the steppe where scattered clumps of grass yield to barren earth. The stallion runs. The landscape swiftly changes.

A lasso flies past. The stallion is caught. The lasso's taut like a *dombra* string. A Cossack woman holds onto the other end of the lasso and gallops after the horse she's trying to tame.

The voice sings.

"A horse is a man's wings. Cossack horses are strong and swift."

The horse gallops. The woman is directing it somewhere.

A field. Posts can be seen in the field.

The woman goads her own mount on. She barely catches up with the stallion when she lets the lasso sag, hurls its loop about a post, brakes the lasso. The stallion falls, snorting.

Several women rush upon him, saddle and bridle him.

The horsewoman leaps into the saddle. The stallion jumps, rears.

The horizon sways. The horse jumps and tries to throw its rider. And suddenly it gallops off into the distance.

A quiet song is heard. It tells of a woman who's breaking in a horse for the Red Army. Try to overtake her. Try to defeat her. And think again whether you can defeat her husband.

The horse gallops. And suddenly it has slowed down. It's tamed. Foam drips from its bit. The tamed horse passes.

On either side of a road people are hoeing beets.

A vast beet field is being hoed.

After the swift gallop, all of this work seems majestically slow.

A pile of beetroots. A woman and a Cossack stand beside it.

The horsewoman shouts:

"Maria Demchenko, Utembygerov—greetings!"

Utembygerov is working with his brigade, fertilizing the beets, sprinkling the field with phosphates.

The voice sings.

"Ukrainians, brothers to the Cossack people, have taught the Cossacks to plant beets. The Karatau have given their phosphates and fertilizers to the fields."

A field. In the field stand piles of beetroots. Suddenly they change into sugar loaves.

The voice sings.

"When our soldiers pass through the enemy's lines, where stood a throng, now stands a desert. When we pass through a desert, where a desert was, a crop now springs."

A huge field, white with baskets of cotton. Women are gathering the cotton. A brigade of Cossack, Ukrainian, Belorussian, Russian, and Uzbek women.

The whole field is singing, in different languages, repeating the song of Nupreis in chorus.

"There, where a desert stood, where the tortoise burrowed into sand—a harvest now grows."

The field of cotton gives way to a rice field.

Rice plants bending over water. The crop is mirrored in the calm water.

Stepping softly with their shaggy legs, camels pass through the steppe, carrying heavy bales of cotton. The camel chain moves on;

a boy driver is singing. He sings the tune of Nupreis's song, repeating it in his own way: Kazakhstan has arisen—from the taiga to the Tien Shan. From the Altai to the Caspian. A camel stretches his long neck, nibbles at the bale, and steals cotton from himself.

The boy stops his song short and says to the camel:

"What are you doing? You're eating gunpowder, you know. You'd better listen to what I'm singing."

The boy repeats his song:

"From the taiga to the Tien Shan, from the Altai to the Caspian, Kazakhstan has arisen."

In the distance a railway station can be seen.

A Minute of the World

A panorama of the world—recorded during one of the gravest and most difficult minutes in world history—passes before us.

This minute, imprinted on film and creatively organized into a film composition, shows the great in the small: the world from the perspective of a single minute on a certain day in a certain year of a certain era.

A minute is brief, but in sixty seconds, values that were centuries in the making can be destroyed. One minute of Hitler is a minute of death, of destruction, evil. A minute of arson, of pogroms, violence, torture, a minute of hangings, executions, torment, gas-chamber buses [*dushegubki*], of child murder, of burning alive, a minute of lies, of provocation, of enslavement, of burying alive. A minute of annihilation of all that is civilized, progressive, free. A death sentence on Life.

Our minute is a minute of Creation, a minute of Reconstruction, a minute of Creative Work, a minute of the defense of Life, a minute of struggle for liberation from savage cannibal hordes, a minute of the affirmation of Life. The minute of the restored mine shaft, of the factory risen from ashes, of the resurrected mine, village, poultry farm, city. The minute of the Liberated Earth. The minute of those rescued from the enemy's prison, from slavery, from destruction, from death.

The artist's minute. The poet's minute. The composer's minute. The minute of the guerilla—the people's avenger. The sharpshooter's minute. The antitank rifleman's minute. The aviator's minute. The minute of the battery, battalion, army.

The allies' minute. America's minute. The minute of England, of Italy. The minute of the second front.

Moscow reports that in one minute an important announcement will be broadcast. A minute of tense expectation. We use this minute to show how many joys, fears, dramas, births, deaths, acts of heroism at work and at war, how many events, big and small, have taken place in these brief sixty seconds. The little minute turns into the Minute of the World, into an instantaneous survey of the world, into a mighty document meant not only for contemporaries, but for future generations as well.

A minute elapses so that Moscow can transmit an important announcement. It's the High Command's proclamation of the Great Victory.

Moscow salutes the Red Army.

Moscow is saluted by the world.

Gallery of Film Portraits

I would like to make a series of short films about living people of our own time.

I propose the "Gallery of Film Portraits" as the most immediate project.

And eventually this would mean an All-Union album of film-portraits of people in the Land of the Soviets during the days of the Great Patriotic War.

Supporting this proposal are the examples cited in my article "About Love for the Living Person" as well as the circumstances that, when I made films of this sort, however laconic, they were always equally well received by all categories of viewer.

A return to this aspect of my activities—temporarily impeded—seems timely to me.

In the present case I should not combine, as hitherto, the duties of scenarist, text writer, and director but should focus my attention on direction. The writer-portraitist or sketch writer is thus assured of my fervent, unpaid participation.

Little Anya

(A FILM PORTRAIT)

It was a sunny autumn.

We were sitting on a bench in a park.

To our right towered the Kremlin.

Before us was the Moscow River.

The girl was in military uniform. The medals on her chest shone austerely. Her curly, blond hair showed beneath her beret. Her eyes were turned, calmly and somewhat pensively, to the river. When a cutter would pass swiftly by, creating a wave, her face always brightened. And a pleasant smile spread from her blue eyes to her half-open lips.

The moment was right for the conversation I'd been anticipating. And I said in a low voice:

"You promised to tell me more about yourself. Why the nickname 'Canary'? What are the medals for, and where are you from?"

"Canary," smiled the girl, "was a temporary nickname. They called me that when I worked as a radio operator. No one calls me that any more."

She was silent for a while. Then, looking straight ahead, she began her story.

Her name is Anya. She finished grade school in Briansk. That was just before the start of the Great Patriotic War. She didn't want to hurt her mother who had no one but her, after all. But the Germans were drawing nearer. She couldn't stand idle. She went to the recruiting office and asked to be sent off to war.

At the office she was told: "You're too young, too small. Go home, little girl."

She turned seventeen. She was very short. She seemed an utter child. And all her efforts were in vain. They would not accept her for war duty.

The Germans drew still nearer. She went off to dig trenches. And then she got what she wanted, after all. She wanted to be a radio operator, a scout, and a parachutist. The commander said to her: "You won't be afraid?"

Her answer was "No," and it didn't matter that she was small. She knew what she wanted. She felt strength within herself. She wasn't scared of anything.

She completed her military training course well. And now she was in a plane, flying toward the Germans' rear lines. She was supposed to jump on receiving a prearranged ground signal. But the signal didn't come, and they had to go back.

Then they flew again, and again had to go back. This happened several times. Finally, one night in April the jump took place. She leapt from the plane and pulled the parachute ring in time; from lower down, she saw some trees rushing up towards her. She landed in a forest. She was hanging on a pine, a very tall one. She got out her knife and cut through the shroud lines. But for some reason the branch she was holding onto broke. And the girl fell down.

She hit the ground hard and lost consciousness. When she came to, she couldn't move. Her whole body ached, especially her right arm.

Snow all around. Night. Cold. But fatigue took over, and the girl fell asleep.

In the morning she saw the sky above her and the parachute on top of the highest tree. She thought: "The Germans will see it. I've got to take the parachute down." But she couldn't move. Her arm must be broken. She couldn't see any blood. Her legs were completely frozen. She tried to get up and simply couldn't.

She herself doesn't recall how long she lay there. But with her left hand she took out a photo of her mother. She looked at her and said:

"I'm going to live. I'm going to live a long time."

No sooner had she said that than she saw Germans running by. And there seemed to be a lot of them. Some were turning off to the right, others moving to the left. Someone was shouting. A command rang out. Were they looking for her? Perhaps they'd already seen the parachute? No, they passed by. Once more Anya attempted to crawl off somewhere. She even closed her eyes from the pain.

Suddenly she heard a voice over her:

"Stand up! Hand over your weapon!"

A real partisan with a rifle in his hand was bending over her.

Anya said that she was a Russian, from Moscow. But her documents were German; they had been necessary for her assignment. She was taken to headquarters. Everything was straightened out there. Then they managed to establish radio contact with Moscow. Her right arm didn't work. The transmitter was beside her bed. And she learned to use her left hand. A partisan doctor healed her. He'd made his way to the partisans from an encirclement. Little by little she learned how. And the Moscow correspondent said everything was going well.

Once she radioed information so precise that our pilots managed to destroy a huge enemy airport. All the German planes were wiped out. Not one managed to take off.

And when she got well, she began to work better. She followed the detachment everywhere on her "little humped-back horse."

That's what the partisans called her intelligent horse. How could she ever forget her "little humped-back horse"?! He understood so well that Anya was small that he bent down to make it easier for her to get into the saddle.

She was quite astounded to receive her first medal. "They're lifting my morale," she thought. "Encouraging me. Can it be that they remember little Anya there on the great wide earth?"

Eighteen months in Belorussia and the Ukraine. With the partisans on her little horse. They fought together and sang together. (She sings a melody, then the words.)

"Many have died, many survive. . . . How often have we broken out of an encirclement. . . . How often have we said goodbye, thinking it was forever. . . . "

And now that they've called her to Moscow to go to college, now that she's found her mother, escaped by some miracle, from German slavery, she still sees before her, she remembers daily, almost all her friends from the front.

At this moment, Anya turns toward me. But when she sees the notebook in my hand, she is suddenly silent and embarrassed and has to hurry. She has to make it to the stadium too, you see. She's got a five-hundred motor race today.

And she has lots to do at the Institute. You see, she's the women's organizer and the monitor of her dorm.

And the most important thing . . . tomorrow there's an English exam. She's got to review everything from the very beginning.

And indeed there is an exam.

And on the exam little Anya readily answers the questions in English.

It's her last exam. And Anya's dying to go home to her mother. The gifts for her are all purchased. Anya's things are packed. And our brief acquaintance ends on the platform of the train station.

Just before the train leaves, Anya confides a secret: "I keep a diary all the time. It's a diary for my daughter. I'm going to get married. And I'll definitely have a daughter. So I write in my diary, 'My dear daughter, learning things is so interesting in high school and with partisans and in English class. The more you learn, the better you understand that one must fight for happiness; it doesn't come all by itself. And a happy life is really possible if you understand happiness as the happiness of creation, as creative work that is free and open to everyone. . . .' "

The train whistle ended her sentence. The train started off, and I followed it with my eyes.

On my way home, I thought: why not do a portrait of this person on film? Inventing nothing, just as she's described here. This person's documentary. Just right for the screen, in both appearance and content. As I know from experience, that does not often happen in documentary cinema.

Publishing History

From Articles, Public Addresses

WE: Variant of a Manifesto. Reprinted from the journal *Kinofot* [''Film-photo''] no. 1, 1922. The first appearance in print of the program of the kinok-documentalist group formed by Vertov in 1919. As Vertov testifies, the original conception for the manifesto goes back to 1919. In the article ''From Kino-Eye to Radio-Eye'' he writes: ''Moscow. The end of 1919. An unheated room. A small vent-window with a broken pane. Next to the window a table. On the table, a glass of yesterday's undrunk tea that has turned to ice. Near the glass is a manuscript. We read: 'Manifesto on the Disarmament of Theatrical Cinematography.' One of the variants of this manifesto, entitled 'WE,' was later (1922) published in the magazine *Kinofot* (Moscow).''

The Fifth Issue of *Kinopravda*. Reprinted from the journal *Teatral'naia Moskva* [''Theatrical Moscow''] no. 50, 1922.

Kinoks: A Revolution. Reprinted from the journal *LEF* no. 3, 1923. Portions of a projected book by Vertov. The article is one of the more important theoretical statements made by the director during the mid-1920s. While in part developing the theses of the manifesto ''WE,'' it sums up the creative experience that Vertov received while working on the magazines *Kinonedelia* [''Film-week''] and *Kinopravda* [''Film-truth''] and on his first short films, *The Anniversary of the Revolution*, *The Battle of Tsaritsyn*, and *The Trial of Mironov*. Vertov also summarizes his theoretical observations from those years on the specific nature of cinema.

On the Organization of a Film Experiment Station. Draft of a report to the management of Goskino. Dated March 5, 1923. This document develops the main idea of the article "He and I" (1922): the need for regulating the system for producing newsreels, the right to experiment. [Appeared in print for the first time in the 1966 Soviet edition.]

Advertising Films. Theses for an article. Dated March 18, 1923. [Appeared in print for the first time in the Soviet edition of 1966.]

On the Significance of Newsreel. An abridged shorthand report of a talk by Vertov at a public debate held at Proletkino ["Proletarian Cinema"] on April 20, 1923. [Appeared in print for the first time in the 1966 Soviet edition.]

***Kinopravda* [1923].** Reprinted from the journal *Kinofot* ["Film-photo"] no. 6, 1923.

On the Film Known as *Kinoglaz*. Draft of a report to the management of Goskino. Dated 1923. [Appeared in print for the first time in the 1966 Soviet edition.] In essence this document represents a request to make *Kinoglaz,* the film that Vertov made in 1924. A list of dramatis personae is attached to the report. The director includes a cameraman, a postman, a bourgeois, a plainclothesman, a student, a woman fish dealer, a milkwoman, a Pioneer group, a fire brigade, first-aid attendant, a cyclist, a [horse]cab driver, a speculator, a Chinese magician, a junkman, a lady with a dog. The scenes of action listed include a Pioneer camp, a train, a steamer, a home for invalids, a flophouse, a cemetery, a bakery, a field, a village, a worker's room, a maternity hospital, an airport, a sports field, a bath, a prison, etc. The first list is entitled "instead of actors"; the second, "instead of a studio."

On the Significance of Nonacted Cinema. An abridged shorthand report of a talk by Vertov at a public debate held at ARRK [Association of Workers in Revolutionary Cinematography] on September 26, 1926. [Appeared in print for the first time in the 1966 Soviet edition.]

***Kinoglaz* (A Newsreel in Six Parts).** Reprinted from the newspaper *Pravda,* July 19, 1924. In the article, Vertov sets forth in detail the creative conception of the film *Kinoglaz* and mentions that his plans are not limited to shooting a single film. Like Eisenstein's cycle of films, linked by the general title "To the Dictatorship" (*Strike* was the first and only picture to appear), Vertov's conception of "an offensive of movie cameras" was broad and included many plans. But, like Eisenstein, he managed to shoot only one film of the projected series.

The Birth of Kino-Eye. Theses for an article. Dated 1924. [Appeared in print for the first time in the 1966 Soviet edition.]

On *Kinopravda.* An abridged shorthand report of a speech by Vertov at a conference of the kinoks on June 9, 1924. [Appeared in print for the first time in the 1966 Soviet edition.] The speech clearly characterizes Vertov's attitude toward so-called intermediate trends in cinematography (according to the kinoks, the films of Eisenstein were included in this category). Calling works of this type "acted films in newsreel trousers," "surrogates," etc., Vertov mistakenly saw in them a danger for the Soviet documentary. The triumphant success of *The Battleship Potemkin,* which followed soon after, refuted these views. New material pertaining to the history of the [film] journal *Kinopravda* is also contained in this speech.

Artistic Drama and Kino-Eye. An abridged shorthand report of a talk by Vertov at a public debate "Art and Everyday Life" on July 15, 1924. [Appeared in print for the first time in the 1966 Soviet edition.]

The Essence of Kino-Eye. Reprinted from the newspaper *Kino,* February 3, 1925. Slightly abridged.

To the Kinoks of the South. Vertov's reply to the letter of some film fans concerning the prospects for developing a movement of kino-eye circles. Dated March 1925. Abridged. [Appeared in print for the first time in the 1966 Soviet edition.]

***Kinopravda* and *Radiopravda* (By way of proposal).** Reprinted from the newspaper *Pravda,* July 16, 1925.

The Same Thing from Different Angles. Theses for an article. Dated July 15, 1926. [Appeared in print for the first time in the 1966 Soviet edition.]

The Factory of Facts (By way of proposal). Reprinted from the newspaper *Pravda,* July 24, 1926.

Kino-Eye. Reprinted from the collection *Na putiakh iskusstva* [''On the Paths of Art''] (Moscow: Proletkul't, 1926). Slightly abridged.

On *The Eleventh Year.* An abridged shorthand report of a talk by Vertov at a discussion of the film at the ARRK [Association of Workers in Revolutionary Cinematography] on February 16, 1928. [Appeared in print for the first time in the 1966 Soviet edition.]

The Man with a Movie Camera. Theses for an article. Dated 1928. [Appeared in print for the first time in the 1966 Soviet edition.]

From Kino-eye to Radio-eye (From the kinoks' primer). Theses for an article. Dated February 19, 1929. [Appeared in print for the first time in the 1966 Soviet edition.]

From the History of the Kinoks. An abridged shorthand report of a talk by Vertov on February 21, 1929. [Appeared in print for the first time in the 1966 Soviet edition.]

Letter from Berlin. Dated July 8, 1929. Written by Vertov during the period of his official journey to Germany and other countries. Abridged. [Appeared in print for the first time in the 1966 Soviet edition.]

Replies to Questions (To the editors of the newspaper *Kinofront* [''Film-front'']). Dated April 25, 1930. Abridged. [Appeared in print for the first time in the 1966 Soviet edition.]

Let's Discuss Ukrainfilm's First Sound Film: *Symphony of the Donbas* (The author on his film). Reprinted from the newspaper *Sovetskoe iskusstvo* [''Soviet Art''], February 27, 1931. Slightly abridged.

First Steps. Reprinted from the newspaper *Kino,* April 16, 1931.

How We Made Our Film About Lenin. Reprinted from the newspaper *Izvestiia,* May 24, 1934.

Without Words. Reprinted from the newspaper *Rotfilm,* August 14, 1934.

I Wish to Share My Experience. Variant of an article written in connection with the fifteenth anniversary of Soviet cinema. Dated 1934. [Appeared in print for the first time in the 1966 Soviet edition.]

***Three Songs of Lenin* and Kino-eye.** An abridged shorthand report of Vertov's talk at a discussion of the film *Three Songs of Lenin* at ARRK [Association of Workers in Revolutionary Cinematography] on October 27, 1934. [Appeared in print for the first time in the 1966 Soviet edition.]

***Kinopravda* [1934].** Reprinted from the journal *Sovetskoe kino* ["Soviet Cinema"] nos. 11–12, 1934. Abridged.

My Latest Experiment. Reprinted from *Literaturnaia gazeta* ["Literary Newspaper"], April 18, 1935. Abridged.

On the Organization of a Creative Laboratory. Theses for an article. Dated October 2, 1936. [Appeared in print for the first time in the 1966 Soviet edition.]

The Truth About the Heroic Struggle. Reprinted from the newspaper *Kino,* November 7, 1936.

In Defense of Newsreel. Theses for a talk by Vertov at the celebration of the twentieth anniversary of Soviet cinema. Dated 1939. [Appeared in print for the first time in the 1966 Soviet edition.]

About Love for the Living Person. The article was published posthumously. Reprinted from the journal *Iskusstvo kino* ["The Art of Cinema"] no. 6, 1958.

From Notebooks, Diaries

Dziga Vertov kept a diary during almost the entire mature period of his creative life. Notes starting in 1924 and ending in 1953 have been preserved in his archive. With the exception of individual fragments (for example, his remarks about V. Mayakovsky) all of this material—which is of tremendous importance in clarifying the development of documentary cinema and the artist's theoretical views and personal fate—was published [in the 1966 Soviet edition] for the first time.

Some Creative Projects, Proposals

Draft of a Scenario Intended to be Filmed During a Journey by the Agit-train, The Soviet Caucasus. Dated 1920. [Appeared in print for the first time in the 1966 Soviet edition.] The scenario is of interest as one of Vertov's plans at the beginning of the twenties for producing acted films (*Automobile*, *Incident in a Department Store*, *The 30,000 Chervontsi,* etc.). As can be seen from the published [film] proposal, the director intended to present a dynamic montage of documentary shots and titles to accompany the commissar's speech at the finale of the picture. The clear, lightly felt musical rhythm of these shots is one of the characteristic features of the poetic style of Vertov the documentarian. The scenario was never filmed.

The Adventures of Delegates en route to Moscow for a Congress of the Comintern. Scenario plan. Dated May 5, 1923. [Appeared in print for the first time in the 1966 Soviet edition.] One's attention is drawn by the close external resemblance of this conception to the genre of the "red detective" popular in the twenties. However the essential difference is that Vertov does not take the events he describes at all "seriously." He intended (as in the scenario, *Incident in a Department Store*) to interpret them in a grotesque, parodistic-ironic manner on the screen. After finishing his account of the adventures of the delegates, the director makes a very significant comment: "To be filmed as a satire on the detective [film]." For its day such an artistic solution was an innovation. The scenario was never filmed.

Outline for the Scenario of *The Eleventh Year.* Dated

1927. [Appeared in print for the first time in the 1966 Soviet edition.] The working out of the *Eleventh* in the scenario provides a graphic example of how carefully the director approached the exploration and poetic comprehension of the material from life that he made the basis of his film. Vertov makes the following comment—pointing to the compositional solution of his conception—on the scenario:

> All parts of the film-object are linked by the movie camera's journey (rather than by the journey of a delegation, as first proposed). This journey is subdivided into the following basic stages/chapters:
>
> 1. journey to the iron mines, coal mines, and factories;
> 2. journey to the Dneprostroi [State Dnepr Construction Project];
> 3. electrical prospects (factory, village, cooperative);
> 4. anniversary of October, or the great broadcast exchange of messages between liberated and oppressed peoples.

***The Man with a Movie Camera* (A visual symphony).** The author's [film] proposal. Dated March 19, 1928. [Appeared in print for the first time in the 1966 Soviet edition.]

Sound March (From the film *Symphony of the Donbas*). Variant plan for the sound track of the film. Dated December 31, 1929. [Appeared in print for the first time in the 1966 Soviet edition.] The world's first detailed sound score for a poetic documentary film, clarifying Vertov's original conception of the picture. The director's conception of the sound track for *Symphony* is astonishing in its artistic integrity and in the sharpness of the depiction of the battle between two opposing themes: church (the bells tolling, the divine service) and factory (whistles, industrial noises, "The Internationale"). One's attention is drawn toward Vertov's strongly underscored hyperbole and his sharpness in resolving these themes into sounds.

***Symphony of the Donbas* (*Enthusiasm*).** The author's libretto for the film. Dated 1930. [Appeared in print for the first time in the 1966 Soviet edition.]

She* and *An Evening of Miniatures. Proposals for films, addressed by Vertov to the management of Mezhrabpomfilm. Dated March 25, 1933. [Appeared in print for the first time in the 1966 Soviet edition.]

A Young Woman Composer. Proposal for a film. Dated 1936. [Appeared in print for the first time in the 1966 Soviet edition.]

A Day Throughout the World. Proposal for a film, addressed to the management of Mezhrabpomfilm. Dated April 30, 1936. [Appeared in print for the first time in the 1966 Soviet edition.]

***The Girl at the Piano* (Draft for a scenario).** Dated October 1939. Reprinted from the collection *Voprosy kinodramaturgii* [''Questions of Film-dramaturgy''] no. 4, 1962.

Letter from a Woman Tractor Driver (A film-song). [Film] proposal. Dated July 15, 1941. Published here for the first time. The proposal was submitted to the management of the *Soiuzdetfilm* [''State Children's Film''] accompanied by the following letter from Vertov:

> From the very first day of the start of hostilities I fervidly switched from working on finishing *A History of Aviation* to defense themes. My first proposal for a defense film-song was, as far as I know, the first proposal handed in by anyone.
>
> I didn't passively greet the failure of the Committee's scenario studio to produce on time the short stories ordered for me. To make up for what had been lost, I wrote two film shorts myself.
>
> In enclosing my fourth creative proposal, I declare:
>
> a. that it is completely in accord with my abilities as a director of poetic films;
>
> b. that in its plan for production this film relies on actually existing film footage;
>
> c. that the filming of the two episodes with characters won't present any special difficulties;
>
> d. that the creation of this film-song can be begun immediately, since the work begins with—and is guaranteed through—the selection of film footage.

To You, Front! The author's original variant libretto for the film of the same name. Dated 1942. [Appeared in print for the first time in the 1966 Soviet edition.]

A Minute of the World. Proposal for a film. Dated February 4, 1944. [Appeared in print for the first time in the 1966 Soviet edition.]

Gallery of Film Portraits. A proposal. Dated August 25, 1944. Reprinted from the journal *Iskusstvo kino* ["The Art of Cinema"] no. 4, 1957.

***Little Anya* (A film portrait).** Dated September 8, 1944. Reprinted from the journal *Iskusstvo kino* ["The Art of Cinema"] no. 4, 1957.

Filmography

Kinonedelia. Weekly newsreels. Forty-three installments. Produced by the Film Committee of the People's Commissariat of Public Education (Moscow). June 1, 1918 through December 24, 1919. Written and directed by Dziga Vertov.

The Anniversary of the Revolution. Historical chronicle. Twelve reels. Produced by the Film Committee of the People's Commissariat of Public Education (Moscow). 1919. Directed by Dziga Vertov.

The Battle of Tsaritsyn. Three reels. Produced by the Revolutionary Military Council and the Film Committee of the People's Commissariat of Public Education (Moscow). 1919. Written and directed by Dziga Vertov.

The Mironov Case. One reel. Produced by the Revolutionary Military Council and the Film Committee of the People's Commissariat of Public Education (Moscow). 1919. Written and directed by Dziga Vertov.

The Disinterment of Serge Radoneski. Film-reportage. Two reels. Produced by the Film Committee of the People's Commissariat of Public Education (Moscow). 1921. Written and directed by Dziga Vertov.

The Propaganda Train of the Russian Central Executive Committee. Travelogue. One reel. Produced by the Russian Central Executive Committee and the Film Committee of the

People's Commissariat of Public Education (Moscow). 1921. Written and directed by Dziga Vertov.

A History of the Civil War. Historical chronicle. Thirteen reels. Produced by the Photo-Film Division (Moscow). 1922. Written and directed by Dziga Vertov.

The Trial of the Socialist Revolutionaries. Three reels. Produced by the Photo-Film Division (Moscow). 1922. Written and directed by Dziga Vertov.

***Kinokalendar* (State Film-Calendar).** Daily and weekly (flash) newsreels. Fifty-five issues. Produced by Goskino (Kultkino). July 21, 1923 through May 5, 1925. Written and directed by Dziga Vertov. Includes "Lenin Film-Calendar."

Kinopravda. Film-newspaper. Twenty-three issues. Produced by Goskino (Moscow). June 5, 1922 through 1925. Shooting plan, intertitles, and direction by Dziga Vertov. All installments of the *Kinopravda* appeared under this title, with the exception of the eight listed below.

> *Yesterday, Today, Tomorrow* (*Kinopravda* no. 13). Film-poem, dedicated to the October ceremonies. Three reels. 1923.
>
> *Autumn Pravda* (*Kinopravda* no. 16). Lyrical landscape newsreels. Three reels. 1923.
>
> *Black Sea—Sea of Ice—Moscow* (*Kinopravda* no. 19). Camera trip from Moscow to Sea of Ice. One reel. 1924.
>
> *Pioneers' Pravda* (*Kinopravda* no. 20). One reel. 1925. Cameraman: Mikhail Kaufman.
>
> *Leninist Kinopravda* (*Kinopravda* no. 21). Film-poem on Lenin. Three reels. 1924. Cameramen: G. Guiber, A. Levitski, A. Lemberg, N. Novitski, M. Kaufman, E. Tisse, et al.
>
> *Lenin Lives in the Peasant's Heart* (*Kinopravda* no. 22). Film-narrative. Two reels. March 13, 1925. Cameramen: M. Kaufman, A. Lemberg, I. Belyakov.

Radio-Kinopravda (*Kinopravda* no. 23). One reel. 1925. Cameramen: M. Kaufman, I. Belyakov, E. Bouchkin.

Give Us Air. Special issue. One reel. Produced by Goskino (Moscow). 1924. Written and directed by Dziga Vertov. Cameraman: Mikhail Kaufman.

Kinoglaz. (Life Unrehearsed). First series. Six reels. Produced by Goskino (Moscow). 1924. Written and directed by Dziga Vertov. Cameraman: Mikhail Kaufman.

Forward, Soviet! (The Moscow Soviet: Past, Present, and Future). Newsreels. Seven reels. Produced by Goskino (Kultkino) (Moscow). 1926. Written and directed by Dziga Vertov. Cameraman: I. Belyakov. Film scout: Kopalin. Assistant to the director: Elizaveta Svilova.

***One Sixth of the World* (Gostorg's Import-Export. *Kino-Eye's Travels through the USSR*).** Film-poem. Six reels. Produced by Goskino (Kultkino) and Sovkino (Moscow). 1926. Written and directed by Dziga Vertov. Assistant director and chief cameraman: Mikhail Kaufman. Cameramen: I. Belyakov, S. Benderski, P. Sotov, N. Constantinov, A. Lemberg, N. Strukov, I. Tolchan. Film-scouts: A. Kagarlitski, I. Kopalin, B. Kudinov.

The Eleventh Year. Newsreels. Six reels. Produced by the Ukrainian Film and Photography Administration (VUFKU) (Kiev). 1928. Written and directed by Dziga Vertov. Cameraman: Mikhail Kaufman. Assistant to the director: Elizaveta Svilova.

The Man with a Movie Camera. Film-feuilleton. Six reels. Produced by the Ukrainian Film and Photography Administration (VUFKU) (Kiev). 1929. Written and directed by Dziga Vertov. Chief cameraman: Mikhail Kaufman. Assistant to the director: Elizaveta Svilova.

Symphony of the Donbas (Enthusiasm). Documentary sound film. Six reels. Produced by Ukrainfilm. 1930. Written and directed by Dziga Vertov. Cameraman: B. Zeitlin. Sound engineer: P. Shtro. Assistant to the director: Elizaveta Svilova.

Three Songs of Lenin. Documentary sound film. Six reels. Produced by Mezhrabpomfilm. 1934. Written and directed by Dziga Vertov. Cameramen: D. Sourenski, M. Magidson, B. Monastyrsky. Sound engineer: P. Shtro. Score by I. Shaporin. Assistant to the director: Elizaveta Svilova

Lullaby. Documentary sound film. Seven reels. Produced by Soiuzkinokhronika. 1937. Written and directed by Dziga Vertov. Co-director: Elizaveta Svilova. Soiuzkinokhronika cameramen. Score by D. and D. Pokrass. Sound engineer: I. Renkov. Lyrics by V. Lebedev-Kumach.

In Memory of Sergo Ordzhonikidze. Special issue. Two reels. Produced by Soiuzkinokhronika. 1937. Editor: Dziga Vertov. Co-director: Elizaveta Svilova.

Sergo Ordzhonikidze. Documentary sound film. Five reels. Produced by Soiuzkinokhronika. 1937. Directed by Dziga Vertov, I. Bliokh, E. Svilova, V. Dobronitsky, Soloviev, Abjibeliachvili. Score by I. Dunayevsky. Sound engineers: I. Renkov, S. Semenov. Musical arrangements by D. Blok. Lyrics by Lebedev-Kumach.

Hail the Soviet Heroines! Special issue. One reel. Produced by Soiuzkinokhronika. 1938. Written and directed by Dziga Vertov. Co-director: Elizaveta Svilova. Soiuzkinokhronika cameramen.

Three Heroines. Documentary sound film. Seven reels. Produced by Soiuzkinokhronika. 1938. Script by Dziga Vertov and Elizaveta Svilova. Directed by Dziga Vertov. Chief-cameraman: S. Semenov, with staff of Moscow, Khabarovsk and Novosibirsk newsreel studios. Train views: M. Troyanovsky. Score by D. and D. Pokrass. Sound engineers: A. Kampovski, Fomine, Korotkevitch. Lyrics by Lebedev-Kumach. Assistant to the director: S. Semov.

In the High Zone. Film-reportage shot on the front of the Great Patriotic War (Film-Newspaper no. 87). Produced by the Central Newsreel Studio. 1941. Directed by Dziga Vertov. Cameramen: T. Bunimovitch, P. Kassatkin.

Blood for Blood, Death for Death (The Misdeeds of the

***Fascist Invaders in the USSR*).** One reel. Produced by the Central Newsreel Studio. 1941. Filmed by cameramen serving at the front. Directed by Dziga Vertov.

Newsreel Cameraman in the Line of Fire. Film-reportages shot on the fronts of the Great Patriotic War. (Film-Newspaper no. 77). Written and directed by Dziga Vertov. Co-director: Elizaveta Svilova. Aerial sequences by N. Vikhirev.

To You, Front! (Kazakhstan for the Front). Documentary sound film. Five reels. Produced by the Alma-Ata Film Studio. 1942. Written and directed by Dziga Vertov. Co-director: Elizaveta Svilova. Chief cameraman: B. Pumpiansky. Score by G. Popov, V. Velikanov. Sound engineer: K. Bakk. Lyrics by V. Lougovskoy.

In the Mountains of Ala-Tau. Documentary sound film. Two reels. Produced by trhe Alma-Ata Studio. 1944. Written and directed by Dziga Vertov. Cameraman: B. Pumpiansky. Co-director: Elizaveta Svilova.

The Oath of Youth. Three reels. Produced by the Central Documentary Film Studio. 1944. Directed by Dziga Vertov, Elizaveta Svilova. Cameramen: I. Belyakov, G. Amirov, B. Borkovsky, B. Dementiev, S. Semenov, V. Kossitsyn, E. Stankevitch.

Daily News. Film-newspaper. Produced by Central Documentary Film Studio, 1944 through 1954. As issue numbers suggest, Vertov's involvement was occasional.

- 1944: no. 18.
- 1945: nos. 4, 8, 12, 15, 20.
- 1946: nos. 2, 8, 18, 24, 34, 52, 67, 71.
- 1947: nos. 6, 13, 21, 30, 37, 48, 51, 65, 71.
- 1948: nos. 8, 19, 23, 29, 34, 39, 44, 50.
- 1949: nos. 19, 27, 43, 45, 51, 55.
- 1950: nos. 7, 58.
- 1951: nos. 15, 33, 43, 54.
- 1952: nos. 9, 15, 31, 43, 54.
- 1953: nos. 18, 27, 35, 55.
- 1954: nos. 31, 46, 60.

Index

In addition to last names, first names and the initial of the patronymic are included wherever possible. Unfortunately, in many cases they remain unavailable.

Designer:	Randall Goodall
Compositor:	TriStar Graphics
Printer:	Vail-Ballou Press
Binder:	Vail-Ballou Press
Text:	Autologic Helvetica Light
Display:	Autologic Helvetica Bold